## DATE DUE

D1240421

# FIRST AMENDMENT LAW

## IN A NUTSHELL

### FOURTH EDITION

By

**JEROME A. BARRON**
Harold H. Greene Professor of Law
The George Washington University Law School

**C. THOMAS DIENES**
Lyle T. Alverson Professor of Law
The George Washington University Law School

**THOMSON**
★ ™
**WEST**

*Nutshell Series, In a Nutshell*, the Nutshell Logo and West Group are trademarks registered in the U.S. Patent and Trademark Office.

COPYRIGHT © 1993 WEST PUBLISHING CO.

© West, a Thomson business, 2000, 2004

© 2008 Thomson/West

> 610 Opperman Drive
> St. Paul, MN 55123
> 1–800–313–9378

Printed in the United States of America

**ISBN:** 978–0–314–17736–0

J.A.B. for the memory of Professor
Arthur Selwyn Miller.

C.T.D. for his wife Peggy and daughter Kim.

_____

And to Justice William J. Brennan, Jr., for his
enduring contribution to the free speech which
the people of this country continue to enjoy.

\*

# PREFACE TO THE FOURTH EDITION

In this edition, we retain almost all of the features which characterized the three previous editions. This Nutshell begins with the philosophical foundations of First Amendment law. Furthermore, when we discuss the various topics which comprise First Amendment law we make reference to, and are influenced by, the law review literature. Our intended readership remains law students and instructors in First Amendment law, constitutional law, communications law, internet law and related fields. But we also know that practicing lawyers have found this book useful and we have tried to meet their needs as well.

In this edition, we have kept the basic organizational structure of its predecessors. The book is divided into four parts. Part One on Background and Methodology deals with the history and theory of the First Amendment. This part is theoretical in that it considers the various rival rationales for First Amendment protection. At the same time, Part One is practical since it considers the tests the courts use to resolve the First Amendment issues with which they must deal, *i.e.*, standards of review, categorization, and balancing. Part Two deals with Content Based Regulation and Low Value Speech. Here a range of problems such as commercial speech, obscene speech, indecent speech and child pornography are considered. Part Three on General Approaches deals with the issues that involve the public forum doctrine, freedom of association, government-sponsored environments and the myriad issues arising under freedom of the press. Part Four on Freedom of Religion addresses Establishment Clause and Free Exercise Clause issues as well as the "play in the joints" between them.

In 1993, when the first edition of this book was published, we noted the emergence of First Amendment law as a core two or three credit course in the J.D. curriculum. Previously, First Amendment issues had simply been part of the constitutional law course. Now, fifteen years later, the First Amendment law course is an established feature of the American law school curriculum. At the same time, the focus of the Supreme Court on First Amendment issues has, if anything increased. In the light of these developments, we believe the need for book such as this is greater today than when we wrote the first edition.

Therefore, we have tried to write a clear and concise guide to the vast First Amendment case law that has by now been generated by the Supreme Court. With that objective in mind and recognizing that electoral law is itself now a separate course, we have eliminated the electoral process as a separate chapter in this book. Instead, we now just cover those electoral cases which seem to be of particular First Amendment concern to the current Supreme Court. We have put these cases into a trim and final section of the freedom of association chapter. By so doing, we will have sufficient space to continue to set forth not just the holdings of the cases but their larger significance as well. We will also be able to continue to highlight some of the concurring and dissenting opinions of the Justices. We believe this will give the reader a feel for the debate, conflict and changing trends which are often the hallmarks of important Supreme Court First Amendment cases. This is especially important with the advent of the Roberts Court.

This edition of *First Amendment Law in A Nutshell* features some of the changing trends. An example of both a changing trend and conflict on the Court is found in our discussion of *Garcetti v. Ceballos* (2006) where in a 5-4 opinion the Court, per Justice Kennedy, continued to move away from applying *Pickering*-type balancing to public employee speech. First Amendment protection was denied to the speech of government employees when such speech was undertaken in line of duty. If the rule were otherwise, the judiciary would have a "new, permanent and intrusive" oversight role with respect to the exercise of discretion on the part of government managers. Other Justices prefer a *Pickering*-type balancing test to the categorical approach taken by the majority in *Garcetti*.

Another continuing trend which is covered is the increasing protection given to commercial speech even when government has found such speech to be sufficiently harmful to merit regulation  Similarly, the erosion of *Tinker v. Des Moines Independent School District* (1969) was illustrated by the Court's decision in *Morse v. Frederick* (2007). There a high school student with leave to watch the Olympic Torch Relay in Juneau Alaska had unfurled a banner bearing the phrase "BONG HiTS 4 JESUS." Rejecting a First Amendment challenge, the Court upheld the school principal's suspension of the student on the ground that the banner could be interpreted as supporting illegal drug use. Unlike the armbands in *Tinker*, the banner in *Morse* was not political. Moreover, the threat of illegal drug use was far more serious than the minimal intrusion involved in *Tinker*.

*Garcetti* and *Morse* illustrate the Court's particular focus on special First Amendment environments. Another special environment, of course, is the Internet. To what extent should it receive First Amendment protection? This edition discusses the Court's effort in *United States v. Williams* (2008) to deal with a federal statute prohibiting the marketing and pandering of virtual child pornography even though direct federal regulation of virtual child pornography had failed on First Amendment grounds in *Ashcroft v. Free Speech Coalition* (2002).

Finally, the religion chapters chronicle the continuing struggle between separationists and accomodationists in the area of freedom of religion. In this connection, the two Ten Commandments cases are given appropriate and detailed attention. One, *McCreary County v. ACLU* (2005), involves a victory for the separationists and the other, *Van Orden v. Perry* (2005) involves a victory for the accomodationists. A fascinating aspect of the two cases was that Justice Breyer was in the majority in both cases.

In summary, in this volume as in previous ones, we have tried to reflect the full scope of the Supreme Court's First Amendment case law. Our aim has been to summarize and analyze this case law fairly, impartially and concisely. We have tried to describe not only the First Amendment law positions which have prevailed but those which have not. We have learned from past editions that the winds of doctrine can sometimes take a change of course. Finally, it is our hope that you, our readers, enjoy reading this book as much as we have in preparing it.

JEROME A. BARRON

C. THOMAS DENES

Washington, D.C.
July 2008

*

# OUTLINE

---

# PART TWO.   CONTENT–BASED REGULATION AND LOW–VALUE SPEECH

## PART THREE.   GENERAL APPROACHES

# TABLE OF CASES

**References are to Pages**

XVII

## TABLE OF CASES

# TABLE OF CASES

## TABLE OF CASES

# TABLE OF CASES

# TABLE OF CASES

\*

# FIRST
# AMENDMENT
# LAW

## IN A NUTSHELL

### FOURTH EDITION

\*

# PART ONE
# BACKGROUND AND METHODOLOGY

---

## CHAPTER I
## TEXT, HISTORY AND THEORY

A literalist reading the First Amendment would conclude that only Congress is subject to its prohibitions. The common law of sedition, judicial injunctions, and executive enforcement actions would lie outside its compass. While neither the Supreme Court nor commentators have been especially concerned with the textual fact that Congress is the only specific addressee of the First Amendment, it is clear today that the First Amendment guarantee extends to all federal governmental action. Thus, in the famous Pentagon Papers case, in which the Department of Justice unsuccessfully sought injunctive relief to prevent publication by leading newspapers of classified material involving the Vietnam War, the First Amendment was applied as a limit against federal judicial and executive action. *New York Times Co. v. United States*, 403 U.S. 713 (1971).

A literal reading would also suggest that the states are not bound by the guarantees of freedom of expression. While Madison proposed a restriction on such state action as part of the Bill of Rights, this was not adopted. Furthermore, *Barron v. Baltimore*, 32 U.S. 243 (1833) held that the Bill of Rights applied only against the federal government. But in *Gitlow v. New York*, 268 U.S. 652 (1925) the Supreme Court simply assumed that freedom of speech and the press "are among the fundamental personal rights and 'liberties' protected by the due process clause of the Fourteenth Amendment from impairment by the States." Subsequently, all the guarantees of the First Amendment have been held to be binding on the states. While there have been some suggestions that the guarantees of free expression under the Fourteenth Amendment have less force and sweep less broadly against the states than the explicit protections provided by the First Amendment, this view has not prevailed. See *Roth v. United States*, 354 U.S. 476 (1957). The mantle of protection afforded freedom of expression against state action by the Fourteenth Amendment has been treated as equivalent to that applicable to federal action under the First Amendment.

But what is the scope of the constitutional protection afforded freedom of expression? Justice Black, a consummate textualist, argued that the First Amendment is framed in absolute terms and that the First Congress did all of the balancing of interests required when they framed the Amendment. But notwithstanding this inspiring tribute to an absolute First Amendment, it doesn't take a course in constitutional law to realize that government in fact imposes a myriad of restraints on speech and press—obscenity and libel law, prohibitions on perjury, blackmail, commercial fraud, and on solicitations and incitement to illegal conduct. As Justice Holmes said in *Schenck v. United States*, 249 U.S. 47 (1919), "[t]he most stringent protection of free speech would not protect a man in falsely shouting fire in a theatre and causing a panic."

How are the absolutist words of the First Amendment and the fire metaphor of Justice Holmes to be reconciled? Consider again the First Amendment text. The constitutional guarantee protects against an "abridging" of the "freedom of speech." Not every restriction on speech necessarily constitutes an "abridging" of the right. Nor does the phrase "the freedom of speech or of the press" necessarily mean that all variants of the spoken or the written word are protected. Of course, even this more modest approach to the language of the First Amendment presents its own analytical problems. What constitutes an "abridgment"? What communication should be subsumed under the phrase, "the freedom of speech or of the press"? One approach to these problems of interpretation would be to consider the original intent of the Amendment's Framers. What was the scope of protection envisioned by those who wrote, defended and enacted the First Amendment?

Under the common law, freedom of the press clearly encompassed freedom from governmental restraints prior to publication. It was the system of crown licensing against which John Milton so eloquently protested in *Areopagitica* (1644). As Blackstone explained: "The liberty of the press [consists] in laying no *previous* restraints upon publications, and not in freedom from censure for criminal matter when published." 4 Blackstone, *Commentaries* (1769). But the elimination of licensing in England in 1694 did not mean that the publisher operated free of governmental restraint. Publishers could still be prosecuted for constructive treason for imagining or encompassing the death of the King. Even more important, they could be punished for the crime of seditious libel, an amorphous open-ended offense extending to almost any criticism of government. It was this common law system that was transported into colonial America. The question is did it survive the adoption of the First Amendment?

The historian Leonard Levy argued in his controversial *Legacy of Suppression* (1960) that the Framers simply adopted the common law understanding that freedom of the press means the absence of prior restraint and not much else. (This same view had been adopted by Justice Holmes writing for the Court in *Patterson v. Colorado*, 205 U.S. 454 (1907).) But a quarter century later, Levy revised his views and acknowledged that "freedom of the press merely began with its immunity from previous restraints." Levy, *Emergence of a Free Press* (1985). Nevertheless, Levy continued to insist that the Framers had a narrow view of freedom of speech and press, that they did not intend to abolish the common law of seditious libel, "and that the First Amendment was as much an expression of federalism as of libertarianism." In short, the First Amendment was conceived of as a limit on congressional legislative power and not as a platform for the construction of a system of free expression. For Levy, it was only the battle over the Alien and Sedition laws in 1798 that produced a broader libertarian conception of freedom of expression.

A great First Amendment scholar of an earlier generation, Zechariah Chafee, contended that "the First Amendment was intended to wipe out the common law of sedition, and make further prosecutions for criticism of the government without any incitement to law-breaking, forever impossible in the United States of America." 2 Chafee, *Free Speech in the United States* (1941). For Chafee, and indeed for most of the modern academy, the First Amendment initiated the dawn of a new relationship between the governors and the governed. It is the people who possess absolute sovereignty; the rulers are the agents and servants of the people. A society which permits punishment for seditious libel is simply incompatible with the new regime set up by the First Amendment.

One of the great paradoxes of First Amendment history is that many of those who participated in the enactment of the First Amendment also participated in the enactment of the Alien and Sedition laws. Did late eighteenth century America believe that these laws were consistent with the First Amendment? The Supreme Court of that time did not have an opportunity to pass on this question because the laws were repealed. In 1964, Justice Brennan, writing for the Court, put the matter to rest: "[A]lthough the Sedition Act was never tested in this Court, the attack upon its validity has carried the day in the court of history." *New York Times v. Sullivan*, 376 U.S. 254 (1964).

But neither the language nor the history of the First Amendment has had as profound an influence on the development of First Amendment law as the values and the functions served by the freedom of expression. Two general theoretical approaches to First Amendment interpretation have emerged. The first is the instrumental, utilitarian or consequentialist approach; the second is the intrinsic or nonconsequentialist approach. In the utilitarian approach, the First Amendment is valued in terms of the benefits it provides to the society it serves, such as the search for truth, the process of self-government, and as a structural safety valve for discontent. The second or intrinsic/non-consequentialist approach sees free expression as an end in itself, stressing the value of free expression to the speaker. The two perspectives are reflected in the observation of Justice Brandeis that "those who won our independence ... valued liberty both as an end and as a means." *Whitney v. California*, 274 U.S. 357 (1927).

## A. THE MARKETPLACE OF IDEAS MODEL

The instrumental approach to the First Amendment which has won the most favor with the courts has been the marketplace of ideas theory. While tracing its lineage to the writings of John Milton and John Stuart Mill, it was given its classical American expression in the judicial writings of Justice Holmes: "But when men have realized that time has upset many fighting faiths, they may come to believe even more than they believe the very foundations of their own conduct that the ultimate good desired is better reached by free trade in ideas—that the best test of truth is the power of the thought to get itself accepted in the competition of the market, and that truth is the only ground upon which their wishes safely can be carried out." *Abrams v. United States*, 250 U.S. 616 (1919) (Holmes, J., dissenting). In his classic essay *On Liberty* (1859), John Stuart Mill provided a rationale for protecting the marketplace of ideas against censorship which still endures: "If the opinion is right, [humanity is] deprived of the opportunity of exchanging error for truth; if wrong, they lose, what is almost as great a benefit, the clearer perception and livelier impression of truth, produced by its collision with error."

Critics of the marketplace model challenge the premises of the theory as well as whether a marketplace of ideas comports with contemporary reality or indeed ever existed. They challenge the assumption that a marketplace of ideas will produce truth.

They question whether the receptors of communication are the rational decision-makers the model necessarily posits. Successful appeals to our emotions and our basic instincts, the ability of opinion-makers—and demagogues—to condition behavior, our natural tendencies to conformity and habit, all challenge reliance on unfettered dialogue as a response and a remedy for harmful ideas. Robert Post, *Reconciling Theory and Doctrine in First Amendment Jurisprudence*, 88 Cal. L. Rev. 2353 (2000), argues that the truth-seeking function of the marketplace of ideas requires more than that speech is involved. "It requires an important set of shared social practices, the capacity to listen and engage in self-evaluation, as well as a commitment to the conventions of reason, which in turn entail aspirations towards objectivity, disinterest, civility and mutual respect."

Critics question the assumption of the marketplace advocates that there is an objective category of truth or that truth is necessarily the highest value at stake in the battle of ideas. Indeed, from the perspective of democratic theory, it may be argued that it is the idea valued by the majority, sound or unsound, false or true, which is the paramount value. Further, it can be questioned whether the marketplace of ideas theory overvalues cognitive speech, inviting repression of speech that does not contribute to the competition in ideas. Then there are those "failure of the marketplace" theorists who attack the marketplace of ideas theory not so much because they challenge its premises but because they believe it no longer exists, if it ever did. These critics point out that the marketplace is controlled by dominant media and that entry to the media is far from free. They contend that the dominant media control not only entry but content, excluding participation by the citizenry at large. Finally, critics ask, even if we were to assume that truth or the wise policy will ultimately emerge, can society always afford the delay? For example, apartheid or genocide may be challenged by speech and, perhaps, in the end will be seen to be wrong and unjust. But, in the interim, many victims will have suffered and died.

## B. THE SELF–GOVERNMENT MODEL—CIVIC REPUBLICANISM AND CIVIC VIRTUE REVIVED

One approach to free speech theory emphasizes the value of freedom of expression to self-government in a democratic society: "Implied here is the notion of civic virtue—the duty to participate in politics, the importance of deliberation, and the notion that the end of the state is not neutrality but active assistance in providing conditions of freedom which in turn are the 'secret of happiness.' " Lahav, *Holmes and Brandeis: Libertarian and Republican Justifications for Free Speech*, 4 J.L. & Pol. 451 (1987). Justice Brandeis in *Whitney* expressed this idea with memorable terseness: "Political discussion is a political duty."

Self-government as a rationalizing principle for freedom of expression was influentially developed by the political philosopher Alexander Meiklejohn. He argued that the principle of freedom of speech "is a deduction from the basic American agreement that public issues shall be decided by universal suffrage." Meiklejohn, *Free Speech and Its Relation to Self-Government* (1948). In the American polity, political sovereignty resides with the people. If they are to perform their self-governing function, they must be free both to criticize their government and to receive information concerning its workings. In *New York Times v. Sullivan*, Justice Brennan characterized this right of the people to criticize government without fear of reprisal as "the central meaning of the First Amendment."

Professor Cass Sunstein similarly argues that free speech disputes "should be resolved with reference to the Madisonian claim that the First Amendment is associated above all with democratic self-government." Sunstein, *Democracy and the Problem of Free Speech* (1993). He is critical of the marketplace of ideas theory, built on the model of a deregulated economic marketplace. It is speech that furthers "democratic deliberation" that is the focus of the free speech guarantee. Thus Sunstein accepts that government has a "reasonably broad power" to regulate speech not furthering this objective, including commercial speech, libelous speech, scientific speech with potential military applications, speech invading privacy, certain forms of pornography and hate speech. He is tolerant of government regulation of campaign financing and laws designed to promote public access to the media.

Professor Vincent Blasi has provided a provocative critique of the self-government thesis. In an age of mass society, mass media, and big government with resultant voter alienation, he questions whether the individual citizen has the time, interest or capacity to perform the role of individual decision-maker. In short, he doubts whether today's citizen is up to the tasks demanded by the idea of civic virtue. He argues, therefore, that big media are the appropriate and worthy adversaries of big government. In this countervailing power theory, Professor Blasi argues that the media are the surrogates for the public. Blasi, *The Checking Value in First Amendment Theory*, 1977 Am. B. Found. Res. J. 521. The implication of this theory is that the self-government model is no longer realistic or descriptive of the workings of our democracy.

There are problems with the self-government thesis. Meiklejohn argued that it was not critical that everyone should speak—only that everything worth saying should be heard. Meiklejohn argued for protection only for public speech: "Private speech, or private interest in speech, on the other hand, has no claim whatever to the protection of the First Amendment." Meiklejohn sharply distinguished between public or political speech which is absolutely protected, and private speech which is given the more limited protection of the due process clause. The paradox of Meiklejohn's First Amendment theory is that, although it is intensely absolutist, it is also unusually narrow.

While Meiklejohn originally narrowly confined the category of public speech to speech bearing directly or indirectly on issues with which voters have to deal, he was later to recant. He recognized, belatedly, that speech about education, philosophy, the social sciences, literature and the arts also contributes to the capacity to engage in meaningful self-government. Similarly, Judge Robert Bork who once argued for full protection only for political speech [Bork, *Neutral Principles and Some First Amendment Problems*, 47 Ind. L.J. 1 (1971)], and not for other categories of speech, reconsidered and provided a new enlarged version of political speech. This definitional problem is also present in Professor Sunstein's version of the self-government thesis. Government is given "reasonably broad power" to regulate speech which does not further democratic deliberation. But the calculus for determining what speech is in and what is out remains unclear. Apart from problems of definition, consider the adequacy of the self-government model as an explanation for the values served by free expression. Is literature, a poem, or a song sung by a "rapper" constitutionally protected speech only if it ultimately contributes to political democracy? Or are they protected because they contribute to the development of the human personality? Is the First Amendment a right of the public to information—-a collective right—-or a right of the individual? See *Symposium, Access to the Media—-1967 to 2007 and Beyond; A Symposi-*

*um Honoring Jerome A. Barron's Path–Breaking Article*, 76 Geo. Wash. L. Rev. 101 (2007).

## C. THE LIBERTY MODEL— SELF–FULFILLMENT AND AUTONOMY

Freedom of speech is valued as an end in itself as well as a means. It is part of the liberty of the person. Professor Edwin Baker has observed: "The liberty theory justifies protection because of the way the protected conduct fosters individual self-realization and self-determination without improperly interfering with the legitimate claim of others." Baker, *Scope of the First Amendment Freedom of Speech*, 25 U.C.L.A. L. Rev. 964 (1978). Professor David Strauss has argued for a persuasion principle prohibiting government, except in extraordinary circumstances, from suppressing speech on grounds that "the speech will persuade those who hear it to do something of which the government disapproves." Strauss, *Persuasion, Autonomy, and Freedom of Expression*, 91 Colum. L. Rev. 334 (1991). He grounds this principle on the idea of the autonomy of the individual and her right to make choices free from coercion.

Critics of the liberty model contend that, if it is to be the justification for freedom of speech, it is entitled to no greater judicial protection than any other form of self-expressive conduct. For example, a pianist engages in self-expression, develops her talents, and enhances her personality by her work.

But we do not give the pianist's activity a form of heightened protection under the Constitution. She simply enjoys the usual protection the Due Process Clause provides from unreasonable regulation. Judge Robert Bork, for example, argues that the liberty model does not distinguish speech from any other human activity: "[One] cannot on neutral grounds choose to protect speech [using this rationale] more than [one] protects any other claimed freedom." Bork, 47 Ind. L.J. at 25. In short, what makes freedom of speech so special if self-fulfillment or autonomy is to be its rationalizing principle?

## D. ADDITIONAL THEORIES OF FREE EXPRESSION

The marketplace, self-government and liberty models are the most commonly used justifications for the special protection afforded freedom of expression. But they are hardly the only justifications for that special protection. While some commentators have sought to argue for the primacy of one or the other of the three justifications, the "preferred position" of freedom of speech can be viewed as resting on a composite of all these theories and other theories as well.

*The Safety–Valve Theory.* One of the lesser-used rationales is the safety-valve theory of the First Amendment. Justice Brandeis in *Whitney* captured the essence of this approach when he warned "that it is hazardous to discourage thought, hope and imagination; that fear breeds repression; that repression breeds hate; that hate menaces stable government; that the path of safety lies in the opportunity to discuss freely supposed grievances and proposed remedies.''

*The Tolerance Theory.* Dean Lee Bollinger has argued that the special value of freedom of speech lies in its ability to promote and teach tolerance. In this view, in the hurly-burly of a heterogeneous society, adherence to the free speech value is itself a bulwark for strengthening tolerance; it emphasizes self-restraint as the appropriate response even to the ideas we hate. Thus, if the Nazis march though a predominantly Jewish suburb of Chicago, the proper response is not prohibition of the march but self-restraint while it takes place. Through the exercise of tolerance, we learn how to participate in a conflict-based society and, indeed, we are better prepared thereby for all our social encounters. Freedom of speech is "concerned with nothing less than helping to shape the intellectual character of the society." Bollinger, *The Tolerant Society: Freedom of Speech and Extremist Speech in America* (1986).

Vincent Blasi, in "Free Speech and Good Character: From Milton to Brandeis to the Present," in *Eternally Vigilant* 61 (Bollinger and Stone, eds., 2002), develops this theme of good character: "[A] culture that prizes and protects expressive liberty nurtures in its members certain character traits such as inquisitiveness, distrust of authority, willingness to take initiative, and the courage to confront evil. Such character traits are valuable, so the argument goes, not for their intrinsic virtue but for their instrumental contribution to collective well-being, social as well as political.''

*Economics and Public Choice.* The theories just discussed reflect relatively well-established ways of looking at the First Amendment and the values it serves. There are, however, new voices providing different perspectives on the functions of freedom of expression and the appropriate limits of governmental regulation. One such new voice has its roots in economics and in public choice theory. For example, Judge Richard Posner has employed cost-benefit analysis to explore when government can regulate expression which has the attributes of a public good. Posner, *Free Speech in an Economic Perspective*, 20 Suffolk U.L. Rev. 1 (1986); Posner, "The Speech Market and the Legacy of *Schenck*," in *Eternally Vigilant* 121 (Bollinger and Stone, eds. 2002).

Professor Daniel Farber picks up on Posner's approach to explain the usefulness of economic analysis for the resolution of free speech issues: "The crucial insight of public choice theory is that because information is a public good, it is likely to be undervalued by both the market and the political system.... Our polity responds to this undervaluation of information by providing special constitutional protection for information-related activities." Farber, *Free Speech Without Romance: Public Choice and the First Amendment*, 105 Harv.L. Rev. 554 (1991). Because the market does not naturally protect information, speech is somewhat vulnerable.

Since the market has no natural inclination to promote speech, it is necessary to provide motivations for individuals to engage in the socially useful function of providing information. Government must not set obstacles to that process; it is the responsibility of government not to over-regulate speech or suppress it. See Farber, *Expressive Commerce in Cyberspace: Public Goods, Network Effects and Free Speech*, 16 Ga. St. U. L. Rev. 789 (2000) ('' '[I]n an economy in which core activity is informational,' distinguishing commodities from expression becomes even more difficult.'').

## E.  CRITICS OF SPECIAL PROTECTION FOR FREE EXPRESSION

The student should not forget, however, that there are also new voices who argue that freedom of speech does not merit special protection and, indeed, may be an over-valued commodity, at least in some contexts. Richard Delgado protests the protection of racist speech. He contends that employing values like tolerance as a justification for special protection for racist expression in fact serves to further devalue those already in a subordinate place in the society as a result of discrimination and racism. Feminists like Catherine MacKinnon contend that freedom of speech over-values publications which serve to expose women to violence, rape and subordination. Such criticisms reflect the need for a continuing reexamination of the values and functions served by the First Amendment. They also suggest the need for considering how the demands of the First Amendment are to be reconciled with competing values and interests.

# CHAPTER II

# FIRST AMENDMENT METHODOLOGY

## A. CATEGORIZATION AND BALANCING

Speech can hurt. Reputations may be ruined; hatred and violence can be incited; personal privacy may be invaded; classified material can be revealed; threats can intimidate; fraud can cause economic injury; morality and good order can be upset. In short, government may well have legitimate interests in what is spoken or written in the marketplace of ideas. How can such legitimate interests of government be reconciled with the text, history and theory of the First Amendment?

One approach has been to recognize categories of speech which are either unprotected speech under the First Amendment or which enjoy something less than full First Amendment protection, *i.e.*, so-called "low value" speech. In *Chaplinsky v. New Hampshire*, 315 U.S. 568 (1942), the Court made an observation which has had profound significance: "There are certain well-defined and narrowly limited classes of speech, the prevention and punishment of which have never been thought to raise any constitutional problem. These include the lewd and obscene, the profane, the libelous, and the insulting or 'fighting words'—those which by their very utterance inflict injury or tend to incite an immediate breach of the peace. It has been well observed that such utterances are no essential part of any exposition of ideas, and are of such slight social value as a step to truth that any benefit that may be derived from them is clearly out-weighed by the social interest in order and morality." Bollinger and Stone, Dialogue, in *Eternally Vigilant* 1 (Bollinger & Stone, eds., 2002) argue that the categorical treatment of low value speech has "a salutary role in free-speech jurisprudence, [since] without this doctrine—if the Court could not allow some room for government to regulate libel, commercial advertising, threats, incitement, and obscenity—there would be irresistible pressure to dilute the overall standards of free-speech protection, even for more fundamentally important expression such as criticism of government."

While *Chaplinsky* cataloged a variety of categories of expression that did not merit First Amendment protection, more recent Supreme Court decisions have taken a more flexible—and more imprecise—approach to categorical analysis. Some categories of speech are usually treated as lying outside the domain of full First Amendment protection—obscenity, fighting words, child pornography, true threats, fraud, and illegal incitement to violence. The question then becomes a definitional one. Does the publication at issue constitute obscenity, fighting words, etc.? If so, the expression has, at least until recently, enjoyed only the protection generally available to activity affected by government regulation, *i.e.*, the reasonableness standard of the Due Process Clause. If the publication is not within one of the unprotected categories, then it must be reviewed under the appropriate First Amendment standards. Other categories of lower value speech do enjoy some constitutional protection but not necessarily as much as that which would be afforded to political speech, which is at the core of the First Amendment. Commercial speech and libelous speech, for example, were once considered outside the realm of protected expression. Now they enjoy significant but not full protection under the First Amendment. There are still other categories of speech, such as offensive or indecent speech, hate speech, and female pornography, which some contend should receive reduced or no First Amendment protection. These categories of expression, while theoretically still enjoying full First Amendment protection, are presently subjects of intense controversy.

How do the courts go about identifying categories of low value speech entitled to lesser or no First Amendment protection? At least part of the answer lies in the observation in *Chaplinsky* that low value speech does not implicate the values and functions that the First Amendment was designed to serve. For example, it has been successfully argued—the objections of Justice Black, Douglas and Brennan notwithstanding—that obscenity does not contribute to the marketplace of ideas or the governance of a democratic society. Thus, it is not part of "the freedom of speech" protected by the First Amendment. At other times, the courts have emphasized the severe harms that can result from the speech category at issue. Examples include child pornography, commercial fraud, libelous statements which are calculatedly false, illegal incitement to violence and true threats, such as cross burning with an intent to intimidate.

The factors which lead courts to identify categories of low value speech are sometimes summarized under the term definitional balancing. As was explained by Melvin Nimmer, who initially coined the term, definitional balancing involves a general calculus of the competing interests implicated by government regulation of that category of speech. The courts fashion general rules for speech within the category which governs the disposition of particular cases. Thus, in libel cases the courts have fashioned an intricate body of rules or principles reflecting the clashing values of reputation and free expression.

The alternative to categorization as a method for reconciling the legitimate interests of government with the values of the First Amendment is balancing on a case-by-case basis. This ad hoc balancing should be distinguished from the definitional balancing discussed above. In ad hoc balancing, the courts consider the competing interests implicated by the facts of the particular case. The courts are not seeking to fashion general rules for the disposition of future cases but instead to resolve the case before them. Case by case balancing comes in a variety of unpredictable forms. It can involve a strict review or a deferential review or something in between.

In some instances, the courts apply strict scrutiny involving a presumption that the government regulation at issue is invalid under the First Amendment. Government must seek to justify its regulation by demonstrating that it is employing narrowly tailored or necessary means to achieve a compelling government interest. In other cases, the courts will employ a form of balancing which, in essence, is rationality review. In such instances, the presumption is cast in favor of the government regulation and the challenger must show that the law is unreasonable. On still other occasions, the courts will employ varying standards between these extremes. While strict scrutiny and deferential review involve forms of weighted balancing which in the usual run of cases serve to indicate the outcome, these intermediate standards do not have the same measure of predictability. Indeed, these intermediate situations are usually quite fact specific.

The definitional balancing used in the process of fashioning categories of low value speech and the accompanying rules is a modern replay of the older debate between absolutists and balancers which dominated the Supreme Court's First Amendment decisions in the 1950s. While Justice Black proclaimed his faith in the absolutism of the First Amendment, he accommodated important governmental interests by distinguishing speech from action. Meiklejohn, while also proclaiming a fervent belief in the absolute protection accorded by the First Amendment, was in fact much less absolutist in practice. Under his approach, whole categories of speech—those not involving core political speech—were not protected by the First Amendment at all. Judge Bork, a self-pronounced First Amendment absolutist, limits his absolutism to core political speech as well. For example, he would not protect commercial speech or advocacy of the violent overthrow of government.

On the other side of the line from the absolutists with their emphasis on rules were the balancers such as Justices Frankfurter and Harlan, and more recently, Powell, Stevens and Breyer. In a sense, the balancers are more forthright than the absolutists since their approach calls for the competing interests involved to be placed up front and weighed in deciding the case. If the First Amendment interests in a given context merit primacy, it is because the speech interest outweighs the government interest in maintaining the particular regulation and not because of any preordained hierarchy of interests embodied in a rule. The Achilles heel of this approach, however, is that it provides no before-the-fact bright-line litmus test to identify which interests will prevail.

The balancing involved in cost-benefit analysis is criticized by Jed Rubenfeld, *The First Amendment's Purpose*, 53 Stan. L. Rev. 767 (2001), on grounds that it cannot generate categorical answers consistent with paradigm cases reflecting core First Amendment principles. He argues for "purposivism"—an absolutist approach based on an inquiry into a law's purpose which "would eliminate most cost-benefit, balancing-test rhetoric so common in today's free speech jurisprudence." Judge Richard Posner defends pragmatic cost-benefit analysis, reflecting "[c]oncern with consequences both systemic and immediate [which] implies a comparison of good and bad consequences, and therefore a 'balancing' of them." *Pragmatism v. Purposivism in First Amendment Analysis*, 54 Stan. L. Rev. 737 (2002).

The modern use of categorical analysis and case-by-case balancing involves a more sophisticated effort to reconcile the competing demands of government's interest in protecting citizens from harm and the values and functions of the First Amendment. One analytical advantage definitional balancing enjoys is that it tends to give greater protection to core First Amendment speech. Before the analytical process can be undertaken, the relevant category of expression—fully protected or low value speech—must be determined. The weakness of this approach is that the boundaries of the categories are often blurred and the assumptions which lie behind the categories often go unarticulated.

In its foray into reviewing hate speech laws, *R.A.V. v. St. Paul*, 505 U.S. 377 (1992), the Court added a new wrinkle to categorical analysis. Even if speech falls into one of the categories of "unprotected speech," the regulation may still violate the First Amendment if the law draws distinctions among subcategories of speech which cannot be justified. Judicial statements that fighting words or obscenity enjoy no First Amendment protection, reasoned Justice Scalia, are not literally true: "What they mean is that these areas of speech can, consistently with the First Amendment, be regulated because of their constitutionally proscribable content (obscenity, defamation, etc.) not that they are categories of speech entirely invisible to the Constitution, so that they may be made the vehicle for content discrimination unrelated to their distinctively proscribable content. Thus, the government may proscribe libel; but it may not make the further content discrimination of proscribing only libel critical of the government." The St. Paul hate speech law had been narrowly construed by the Minnesota courts as limited to fighting words, but only fighting words that provoke violence "on the basis of race, color, creed, religion, or gender." The law as interpreted created a new discrimination between forms of fighting words—a subcategory—based on speech content and viewpoint which the state failed to show was "reasonably necessary" to a "compelling" governmental interest.

Justice White, concurring, responded that the demand that government proscribe all of the low value speech category, or none at all, was simplistic and at odds with accepted First Amendment analysis: "It is inconsistent to hold that the government can proscribe an entire category of speech because the content of that speech is evil, but that the government may not treat a subset of that category differently without violating the First Amendment;

the content of the subject is by definition worthless and undeserving of constitutional protection."

*R.A.V.* did not hold that all forms of content-based discrimination within a proscribable area of speech is subject to strict scrutiny. When there is no threat of viewpoint discrimination, strict scrutiny does not apply. For example, the Court said that the First Amendment permits content discrimination "based on the very reasons why the particular class of speech at issue . . . is proscribable." This exemption from strict scrutiny was used in reviewing the constitutionality of Virginia's cross burning law in *Virginia v. Black*, 538 U.S. 343 (2003). The Virginia law prohibited cross burning with "an intent to intimidate a person or group of persons." In holding the law unconstitutional, the Virginia Supreme Court had relied on *R.A.V.* since the law "selectively chooses only cross burning because of its distinctive message." But the United States Supreme Court invoked *R.A.V.*'s caveat. "The First Amendment permits Virginia to outlaw cross burnings done with an intent to intimidate because burning a cross is a particularly virulent form of intimidation. Instead of prohibiting all intimidating messages, Virginia may choose to regulate this subset of intimidating messages in light of cross burning's long and pernicious history as a signal of impending violence." Cross burning is a form of intimidation "most likely to inspire fear of bodily harm." While the Virginia cross burning law was unconstitutional because it made burning the cross prima facie evidence of an intent to intimidate, the Court 6–3 established that a properly drawn cross burning statute limited to "true threats"—a category of low value speech subject to regulation—is constitutional. See Ch. IV, D.

*R.A.V.* indicates that First Amendment analysis does not necessarily end with a determination that it is low value, or even unprotected speech, that is being regulated. The student must still ask if the mode or form of regulation satisfies applicable First Amendment standards. This may involve particularized rules and standards; it may involve a form of balancing such as was used in *R.A.V.*

## B.  CONTENT–BASED v. CONTENT–NEUTRAL REGULATIONS

One of the methodological tools of pervasive importance in First Amendment law draws a distinction between content-based and content-neutral government regulation. Content-based regulation involves government regulation of expression based on what is being said—the content of the message. Content-neutral regulation involves restrictions which may burden First Amendment expression but without regard to the message being communicated. If a government regulation is determined to be content-based, it is presumptively invalid. While the Court has stated that "above all else, the First Amendment means that government has no power to restrict expression because of its message, its ideas, its subject matter or its content," *Police Dept. of Chicago v. Mosley*, 408 U.S. 92 (1972), this is an overstatement. Rather, when using content-based restrictions, government must demonstrate that the communication falls into one of the categories of low-value speech or must justify the regulation by showing that it is necessary to a compelling governmental interest.

Content-neutral regulation, on the other hand, is perceived as imposing a lesser burden on First Amendment values. Thus, the Court will employ some less stringent mode of balancing. The degree of scrutiny is likely to reflect the severity of the regulation's restriction on protected speech. In some cases, the courts use the standard fashioned in *United States v. O'Brien*, 391 U.S. 367 (1968): "A government regulation is sufficiently justified . . . if it furthers an important or substantial government interest; if the government interest is unrelated to the suppression of free expression; and if the incidental restriction of alleged First Amendment freedoms is no greater than is essential to the furtherance of that interest." Sometimes in reviewing content-neutral time, place and manner regulations of "public forums" (See Ch. 9, A), the courts require that content-neutral laws regulating the public forum be "narrowly-tailored to serve a significant government interest and leave open ample alternative channels of communications." *Perry Educ. Ass'n v. Perry Local Educators' Ass'n*, 460 U.S. 37 (1983). The Court has held that there is no difference between these standards. Under either standard, government need not use the least-restrictive means; it is sufficient if the means used are direct and effective.

Some commentators have criticized this "intermediate scrutiny" as excessively deferential in application, generally resulting in regulations being upheld. But in *City of Ladue v. Gilleo*, 512 U.S. 43 (1994), the Court did hold unconstitutional a law prohibiting homeowners from displaying signs but also providing for numerous exceptions, even assuming that it was a content-neutral law. The law prohibited too much protected expression, almost completely foreclosing a unique and important means of communication. The Court questioned whether there were adequate communication alternatives to the banned signs. But in spite of *City of Ladue v. Gilleo*, the intermediate scrutiny applied to content-neutral regulation is far less demanding than the strict scrutiny standard used for content-based regulation.

*Boos v. Barry*, 485 U.S. 312 (1988) involved both content-based and content-neutral regulation. The Court held invalid a District of Columbia ordinance prohibiting the display of signs critical of a foreign government within 500 feet of that government's embassy. Justice O'Connor set forth a number of factors which were critical to the Court's conclusion: the display clause of the ordinance involved core First Amendment political speech; it prohibited political speech on public streets and sidewalks which are traditional public fora; it was content-based. The display provision was labeled content-based since the determination of whether individuals could picket depended on whether or not their message was critical of a foreign government. It did not matter that the ordinance covered all messages critical of the foreign government regardless of the nature of the criticism, *i.e.*, it was not based on viewpoint. The critical feature was that the ordinance focused on the subject matter of the message. Such a content-based regulation could not withstand strict scrutiny analysis even if a compelling government interest was involved, *i.e.*, good relations with foreign countries. The ordinance was invalid because it was not narrowly tailored to that interest and there were less restrictive alternatives. The ordinance in *Boos* involved a second clause which allowed the police to disperse demonstrators who gathered within 500 feet of a foreign embassy. The lower court had interpreted this "congregation clause" to permit the police to disperse demonstrators only when they reasonably believed there was a threat to the peace and security of the embassy. So construed, the congregation clause was simply a content-neutral place and manner regulation. In light of the fact that the clause did not reach a substantial portion of protected activity, the congregation clause of the ordinance was not overbroad and constituted reasonable regulation.

The so-called "Son of Sam" case illustrates the presumptive invalidity of government regulation when it is based on the content of the publication. A New York law required that income earned by an accused or convicted criminal from published works describing the crimes be deposited in a victim compensation fund. Justice O'Connor, for a unanimous Court, struck down the New York law: "A statute is presumptively inconsistent with the First Amendment if it imposes a financial burden on speakers because of the content of their speech." *Simon & Schuster, Inc. v. Members of New York Crime Victims Bd.*, 502 U.S. 105 (1991). The Son of Sam law singled out income derived from expressive activity and was directed only at works having a specified content. Because of the financial disincentive to publication which the act created and its differential treatment among authors, *Simon & Schuster* applied the strictest form of review to the New York law. The state did have a compelling interest in compensating victims from the fruits of the crime, but the law was not narrowly tailored since it was significantly over-inclusive. New York's Son of Sam law applied to works on any subject so long as the work expressed the author's thoughts or recollections about the crime, however tangentially or incidentally. If the author admitted to committing the crime, it didn't matter whether the author was ever actually accused or convicted. As such, the law would reach a host of valuable publications. It would have covered *The Confessions of St. Augustine*, Henry David Thoreau's *Civil Disobedience*, or the writings of Martin Luther King, Jesse Jackson, Malcolm X or Bertrand Russell describing their encounters with the law.

In a concurring opinion in *Simon & Schuster*, Justice Kennedy indicated that he would have gone even further than the Court. Since the Son of Sam law "imposes severe restrictions on authors and publishers, using as its sole criterion the content of what is written," it was unconstitutional. Any balancing, even strict scrutiny, was unnecessary: "The regulated content has the full protection of the First Amendment and this, I submit, is itself a full and sufficient reason for holding the statute unconstitutional." At least in this context, Justice Kennedy was an absolutist.

Generally, when a law is deemed content-based and involves fully protected expression, the application of the strict scrutiny standard results in the law's invalidity as is demonstrated by both *Boos* and *Simon & Schuster.* See also *R.A.V. v. St. Paul,* 505 U.S. 377 (1992). But this is not always the case. In *Burson v. Freeman,* 504 U.S. 191 (1992), a Tennessee law which prohibited the solicitation of votes and the dissemination of campaign materials within 100 feet of a polling place was upheld. Writing for a plurality, Justice Blackmun noted that the regulation involved core political speech, that it barred speech in a quintessential public forum, and that it was a content-based regulation. Strict scrutiny was thus invoked. Nonetheless, the Court held the regulation valid even though the characteristics enumerated by Justice Blackmun were identical with the display provision held invalid in *Boos.* In this instance, the state had a compelling interest in protecting another fundamental right—"the right to cast a ballot in an election free from intimidation and fraud." Since a restricted area around polling places was necessary to preserve the fundamental right, the 100 feet provision was not "an unconstitutional compromise." In a spirited dissent, Justice Stevens, joined by Justices O'Connor, and Souter, characterized the Court's analysis as "neither exacting nor scrutiny. To borrow a mixed metaphor, the plurality's scrutiny is 'toothless'."

In a concurrence, Justice Kennedy, who had adopted an absolutist position in *Simon & Schuster*, now discovered an exception to the absolutism he expressed there. While Justice Kennedy in *Simon & Schuster* had rejected the compelling interest analysis for reviewing content-based regulation, in *Burson* the state's interest in protecting the fundamental right to vote apparently trumped the presumption against content-based regulation. Concurring in *Burson*, Justice Scalia said he viewed the Tennessee polling restriction law to be a regulation of a non-public forum where a state can validly impose content-based regulations. In a nonpublic forum, a law regulating speech need only be reasonable and viewpoint-neutral. (See Ch. IX, B).

The foregoing analysis demonstrates that the distinction between content-based and content-neutral regulation raises a host of problems. Initially, there is the question as to the wisdom of drawing such a distinction in the first place. Either form of regulation reduces the quantity of speech in the marketplace and inhibits the ability of individuals to express their ideas. Further, a content-neutral regulation may be more restrictive of speech than a content-based law. For example, a total ban of all speech from a particular area may be content-neutral, but it is a severe burden on First Amendment values.

Professor Geoffrey Stone suggests three characteristics of content-based regulation that might serve to justify the distinction. First, "content-based restrictions distort public debate in a content-differential manner." Second, content-based restrictions are subject to an increased risk that government is in fact acting because it disapproves of the particular message. While the Court has extended the presumption against content-based restrictions beyond laws that discriminate among viewpoints to laws that categorize on the basis of subject-matter, there is a continued fear that any content-based regulation hides an improper government bias against particular speech. Third, government efforts restricting speech because its communicative impact "usually rest on constitutionally disfavored justifications," (*e.g.*, paternalism or curbing offensiveness). These concerns, in Stone's view, do not arise with the same frequency in content-neutral regulation. Stone, *Content–Neutral Restrictions*, 54 U. Chi. L. Rev. 46 (1987). Content-neutral regulation arguably involves a lesser danger to First Amendment values.

Even accepting the doctrinal distinction, it is uncertain when a law will be labeled content-based or content-neutral. For example, should the presumption against the validity of content-based speech be limited to laws that discriminate on the basis of viewpoint or should it extend to laws that discriminate on the basis of the subject matter of the speech? At least at present, laws which discriminate based on the subject matter of the speech, which regulate an entire category of speech, are deemed content-based and are presumptively invalid. For example, a law prohibiting all picketing within a proscribed distance of a public school during school hours but which specifically excepts labor picketing from the ban is invalid. Such a law is a content-based regulation which could not survive strict scrutiny review. *Police Dept. of Chicago v. Mosley*, 408 U.S. 92, 408 U.S. 92 (1972). Similarly, in *Carey v. Brown*, 447 U.S. 455 (1980), a statute barring all residential picketing except for labor disputes was held unconstitutional using equal protection and freedom of speech principles. The statute was not narrowly drawn to promote privacy in the home even assuming that privacy was a more compelling governmental interest than quiet schools. The student should note that the laws involved in *Boos v. Barry*, 485 U.S. 312 (1988), *Simon & Schuster, Inc. v. Members of New York Crime Victims Bd.*, 502 U.S. 105 (1991), and *Burson v. Freeman*, 504 U.S. 191 (1992) were all treated as content-based regulations and reviewed under the strict scrutiny standard even though the regulations were not viewpoint-based.

Even taking the broader meaning of content-based regulation, how does a court determine that a law is content-based? Professor Tribe states there are two ways in which a law can be determined to be content-based: "[I]f *on its face* a governmental action is targeted at ideas or information that government seeks to suppress, or if a governmental action, neutral on its face, was *motivated* by (*i.e.*, would not have occurred but for) an intent to single out constitutionally protected speech for control or penalty." Tribe, *American Constitutional Law* (2d ed. 1988).

The case law discussed above demonstrates that when a law facially discriminates between messages it will normally be characterized as content-based. But in *City of Renton v. Playtime Theatres*, 475 U.S. 41 (1986), a law regulating the location of "adult" theaters was deemed to be a content-neutral regulation because it was directed only at the "secondary effects" of adult theaters and not the messages involved—the "adult" themes of the movies. "Secondary effects" such as crime were used to justify the law; the burden of speech was only an incidental by-product of the restriction. The critical issue is the nature of the government's justification. If the government seeks to justify the law because of some harm perceived to flow from the message, the regulation is content-based. If the law is "justified without reference to the content of the regulated speech," it is content-neutral.

This "secondary effects" doctrine of *City of Renton* has been criticized since it is susceptible to manipulation. A court which wishes to escape the consequences of a content-based regulation can simply categorize it as an indirect burden on speech involving "secondary effects." Whether this "secondary effects" doctrine will be limited to sexually indecent speech or will be applied to other laws that facially discriminate on the basis of content is uncertain. If it is so limited, the possibilities of manipulation will of course be reduced. Erwin Chemerinsky, *Content Neutrality as a Central Problem of Freedom of Speech: Problems in the Supreme Court's Application,* 74 S. Cal. L. Rev. 49 (2000), cites *Renton* as illustrative of a "major problem" with the Court's application of content-neutrality— "its willingness to find clearly content-based laws to be content neutral because they are motivated by a permissible content-neutral purpose." The *Renton* approach, he argues, confuses the designation question with whether the law is justified by a sufficient purpose. The *Renton* ordinance "was clearly content based on its very terms."

*City of Renton* was applied in *City of Los Angeles v. Alameda Books, Inc.,* 535 U.S. 425 (2002). The Court 5–4 reversed a lower court decision which granted plaintiff's motion for summary judgment and held unconstitutional an ordinance prohibiting establishment of more than one adult entertainment business in the same building. See Ch. V, C. The plurality opinion by Justice O'Connor determined that the law was a content-neutral time, place and manner regulation subject to intermediate scrutiny under *Renton*. It was reasonable for the city to infer that reducing the concentration of adult establishments would reduce crime rates. Justice Kennedy, concurring, said that calling such an ordinance content-neutral was a "legal fiction" since the law described the regulated speech by its content. Nevertheless, he argued that the use of intermediate scrutiny for a zoning law directed at secondary effects was correct. Such a law does not "automatically raise the specter of impermissible content discrimination, even if [such laws] are content-based, because they have a prima facie legitimate purpose." Justice Souter, in a portion of a dissent joined by Justices Stevens and Ginsburg, argued that while intermediate review was appropriate, there were varieties of such review with variations of justification. "Thus, the Court has recognized that this kind of regulation, though often called content-neutral, occupies a kind of limbo between full-blown, content-based restrictions and regulations that apply without any reference to the substance of what is said."

*City of Renton* does recognize that whenever government regulates because of the harm arising from the speech content—the *communicative impact* of a law—it will be labeled as content-based and will be presumptively invalid. In defending its statute proscribing flag burning, Texas cited the value of the flag as a symbol of nationhood and national unity. The Court determined that this interest was related to the message: "These concerns blossom only when a person's treatment of the flag communicates some message, and thus are related 'to the suppression of free expression.'" Since the harm the state sought to combat flowed from the speech, the law was content-based. It failed to survive strict scrutiny review. *Texas v. Johnson*, 491 U.S. 397 (1989).

The government's purpose or motive in regulating can be a key determinant of how the law will be labeled. But if regulation is facially content-neutral and government claims a content-neutral justification, should the courts probe to determine if the law is content-based? This issue has been especially important in the context of symbolic speech or expressive conduct where the regulation is ostensibly directed at conduct. The Court has often shown a reluctance to probe behind facially content-neutral laws when government offers a justification unrelated to the communication involved. Thus in *United States v. O'Brien*, 391 U.S. 367 (1968), a federal statute prohibiting the destruction of a draft card was upheld despite an argument that the law was content-based and aimed at anti-Vietnam War protests. The Court refused to probe the actual purpose of Congress in enacting the law. Rather, the law was labeled a content-neutral regulation which was reasonably designed to promote the administrative needs of the selective service system.

There are several reasons the courts are reluctant to probe purpose. First, the legislature is a collegial body having many motives. Second, a legislature confronted with a law struck down for an impermissible motive may simply re-enact it, developing a permissible justification. Finally, probing motive or purpose places courts in an uncomfortable position. Particularly in a First Amendment context, their own predilections and subjective judgments may intrude too easily into the purpose determination. The extent to which courts will be willing to probe behind a facially content-neutral law which government seeks to justify by citing harms unrelated to the speech remains uncertain. The more the court believes that there are underlying content-based motivations underlying the government regulation, the more vulnerable the regulation should be to content-based analysis. The authors believe that the Supreme Court is increasingly willing to accept content-neutral justifications for facially content-neutral laws, even when probing the purpose might yield a contrary result.

*Turner Broadcasting System, Inc. v. FCC*, 512 U.S. 622 (1994) reviewed the constitutionality of regulations requiring cable television stations to devote a portion of their channels to transmissions of local broadcast television. The Court, per Justice Kennedy, determined that these must-carry provisions "on their face, impose burdens and confer benefits without reference to the content of speech." While the regulations burdened speech by limiting the unfettered control of cable operators over the use of channels and of cable programmers by making it more difficult to secure carriage on the limited channels available and by drawing distinctions between speakers, the Court determined that the regulations were not "a subtle means of exercising a content preference." Nor was the "manifest purpose" of the regulations based on the message. Justice Kennedy stated: "Our review of the Act and its various findings persuades us that Congress' overriding objective in enacting must-carry was not to favor programming of a particular subject matter, viewpoint, or format.…" Rather the regulations were designed to preserve access to free television programming for those without cable by assuring the continued operation of broadcasters. But for four dissenting justices, the asserted interests of the government in furthering localism and diverse programming used to justify must-carry regulation "all make reference to content."

Because the laws in *Turner* were content-neutral, the Court held that the government did not have to employ the least speech-restrictive means of regulation. Such laws were seen as involving a less serious danger of censorship of ideas. Therefore "narrow tailoring" required only that the law not gratuitously burden substantially more speech than needed to implement government's legitimate interests. On remand, the district court held that substantial evidence supported Congress's judgment that the challenged must-carry regulations further the important governmental interest in preserving local broadcasting by providing for its carriage on cable systems and the Supreme Court affirmed 5–4. *Turner Broadcasting System, Inc. v. FCC*, 520 U.S. 180 (1997) (*Turner II*). See Ch. XIII, F, 1. But regulation of indecent speech on cable was held to be a "content-based restriction subject to strict scrutiny" in *United States v. Playboy Entertainment Group, Inc.*, 529 U.S. 803 (2000) (signal bleed provisions of federal Telecommunication Act held unconstitutional). Similarly, the Communication Decency Act prohibiting the knowing transmission over the internet of "indecent" or "potentially offensive" material to a minor was held to be a content-based criminal regulation of speech subject to strict scrutiny in *Reno v. American Civil Liberties Union*, 521 U.S. 844 (1997) (provision held unconstitutional). See Ch. V, C.

Abortion protests have proven a fertile ground for controversy over whether an injunction or regulation is content-based. For example, in *Hill v. Colorado*, 530 U.S. 703 (2000), the Court 6–3 upheld a statute making it unlawful for anyone, within 100 feet of a healthcare facility to "knowingly approach" within eight feet of another person without that person's consent, "for the purpose of passing a leaflet or handbill to, displaying a sign to, or engaging in oral protest, education or counseling with such other person." Justice Stevens, for the Court, found the statute to be a content-neutral time, place and manner regulation since the law was not adopted "because of disagreement with the message [the speech] conveys," and the state interests in protecting access and privacy and providing clear guidelines "are unrelated to the content of the demonstrators' speech." The fact that the regulation was limited to protest, education or counseling and did not extend to casual conversation did not make the law content-based. It applied to all protest, all counseling and to all demonstrators "whether or not the demonstration concerns abortion, and whether they oppose or support the woman who made an abortion decision." Justice Scalia, joined by Justice Thomas, dissenting, viewed this as another abortion case in which the Court abandoned constitutional principles. The law, he argued, "is obviously and undeniably content-based" since speakers wishing to communicate any message other than one of protest, education, or counseling can do so. Justice Kennedy, dissenting, also labeled the law content-based.

## C. OVERBREADTH AND VAGUENESS

A First Amendment claim is usually raised by challenging the constitutionality of the application of a law to a particular person. For example, if the state seeks to punish the seller of a Bible for obscenity, the seller would have a solid constitutional defense. Given the facts, the law is invalid *as applied*. The parameters of permissible regulation under the obscenity law would be determined through a case-by-case evolutionary process.

A First Amendment challenge can also be directed against the law itself. This is called a facial challenge—the litigant is challenging the law *on its face*. For example, if the obscenity law proscribes sexually provocative, but non-obscene, publications, the litigant will raise the specter of potential applications of the law to constitutionally protected speech. Even if the law reaches unprotected speech, the law can be challenged because it also reaches protected speech. This is the overbreadth doctrine: "[A] governmental purpose to control or prevent activities constitutionally subject to state regulation may not be achieved by means which sweep unnecessarily broadly and thereby invade the area of protected freedoms." *NAACP v. Alabama*, 357 U.S.

449 (1958). The law is not narrowly tailored to its legitimate concerns.

Furthermore, the overbreadth challenge can be made even though the law was constitutionally applied in the particular case or even though the litigant could be regulated under a constitutionally narrower law. Ordinarily a litigant is not allowed to raise the legal rights of a party not before the court because of the third-party standing doctrine. In overbreadth cases, the legal rights of those who are engaging in protected activity may be raised by those engaged in unprotected activities. This is so even though those engaging in the protected activity are not before the court. Professor Henry Monaghan argues that the overbreadth doctrine is not really an exception to the third-party standing rule. Rather the doctrine represents an application of the traditional precept that "a litigant has always had the right to be judged in accordance with a constitutionally valid rule of law." Monaghan, *Overbreadth*, 1981 Sup. Ct. Rev. 1. Under this analysis, the overbreadth challenger has standing to ask to be judged according to constitutionally valid norms even though the tightening of the law would not personally benefit him. Dorf, *Facial Challenges to State and Federal Statutes*, 47 Stan. L. Rev. 235, 242 (1994), similarly argues that litigants should be able to challenge overbroad laws since the Constitution permits only the application of constitutional rules.

Why do the courts in the case of the overbreadth doctrine depart from the usual as-applied method of analysis as well as from the third party standing rule? The overriding reason lies in the judicial concern that protected freedom of expression not be chilled by the overbroad law. Citizens may avoid constitutionally protected activity and the overbreadth will go unchallenged. Courts have also expressed concern over the danger of selective enforcement under an overbroad law, especially those involving broad grants of discretion to administrators.

Critics of the overbreadth doctrine argue that it allows courts to anticipate constitutional issues and engage in abstract, premature and speculative decision-making in defiance of ordinary justiciability principles. Since a determination that a law is overbroad does not really explain why the law is defective or what is necessary to cure it, courts can avoid their responsibility to fashion a coherent body of First Amendment law to guide legislatures and courts. The exception to ordinary standing rules allows a party engaging in unprotected conduct to claim the benefits of the First Amendment and escape punishment even though she is not really harmed by the overbreadth. Finally, the law cannot be applied even to its proper concerns until it has been given a limiting construction that eliminates the potentially unconstitutional applications.

Considerations such as these led the Court in *Broadrick v. Oklahoma*, 413 U.S. 601 (1973) to formulate the "substantial overbreadth" doctrine. This doctrine requires "that the overbreadth of a statute must not only be real but substantial as

well, judged in relation to the statute's plainly legitimate sweep." While *Broadrick* originally limited
the "substantial overbreadth" requirement to regulations of conduct, it has been extended. *New York
v. Ferber*, 458 U.S. 747 (1982); *Brockett v. Spokane
Arcades, Inc.*, 472 U.S. 491 (1985). *Broadrick* does
not really explain what is needed to render overbreadth substantial. *Members of the City Council of
the City of Los Angeles v. Taxpayers for Vincent*, 466
U.S. 789 (1984) upheld a law prohibiting the posting of signs on public property, rejecting an overbreadth challenge. The fact that a law may have
impermissible applications, the Court reasoned,
does not alone make it overbroad: "[There] must be
a realistic danger that the statute itself will significantly compromise recognized First Amendment
protection of parties not before the Court for it to
be challenged on overbreadth grounds."

*Board of Airport Comm'rs. v. Jews for Jesus, Inc.*,
482 U.S. 569 (1987) employed the overbreadth doctrine to invalidate a regulation prohibiting persons
from engaging "in First Amendment activities within the central terminal area at the Los Angeles
International Airport." The restriction arguably
reached even talking or reading or the wearing of
campaign buttons. Moreover, the regulation was not
limited to activity which would be disruptive of the
normal operations of the airport. As Justice O'Connor explained, "the resolution at issue in this case
reaches the universe of expressive activities, and, by
prohibiting all protected expression, purports to create a virtual 'First Amendment free zone [at the

airport].' " In contrast, a more narrowly drawn regulation designed to prevent solicitation at airports was upheld against First Amendment challenges, although restrictions on distribution of publications were invalidated. *International Society for Krishna Consciousness, Inc. v. Lee*, 505 U.S. 672 (1992).

The overbreadth doctrine has been used extensively in reviewing broad grants of discretion to administrators. Thus in *City of Lakewood v. Plain Dealer Publishing Co.*, 486 U.S. 750 (1988), the Court invalidated an Ohio ordinance which vested unguided discretion in the mayor to deny permits to coin-operated newspaper machines on city sidewalks: "[A] facial challenge lies whenever a licensing law gives a government official or agency substantial power to discriminate based on the content or viewpoint of speech by suppressing disfavored speech or disliked speakers." The facial challenge succeeded even though the administrator had not in fact discriminated based on content or viewpoint.

Similarly in *Forsyth County, Georgia v. Nationalist Movement*, 505 U.S. 123 (1992), a permit ordinance, allowing the county administrator to adjust permit fees up to a maximum of $1000 per day, was invalidated as overbroad. This sliding scale ordinance had no definite standards other than that it was to be adjusted "to meet the expense incident to the administration of the Ordinance and to the maintenance of public order in the matter licensed." Even though the Nationalist Movement was charged only a $100 fee, as far as the ordinance was concerned, it could as well have been $1000. The ordinance allowed the administrator to discriminate on the basis of content or viewpoint and was therefore impermissible. Justice Blackmun declared that "the Court has permitted a party to challenge an ordinance under the overbreadth doctrine in cases where every application creates an impermissible risk of suppression of ideas, such as an ordinance that delegates overly broad discretion to the decisionmaker...." The county argued that the ordinance was content-neutral because it was aimed only at the "secondary effects" of offsetting the costs of maintaining public order. Justice Blackmun responded: "It is clear, however, that, in this case, it cannot be said that the fee's justification 'has nothing to do with content.'" The costs that the administrator would consider in setting the fee would reflect those associated with the public's reaction to the speech. "Listeners' reaction to speech is not a content-neutral basis for regulation." The permit law was, therefore, held to be content-based regulation.

The overbreadth doctrine has been actively used in reviewing local regulation of charitable solicitations. In *Village of Schaumburg v. Citizens for a Better Environment*, 444 U.S. 620 (1980), the Court invalidated an ordinance prohibiting charitable soliciting unless the organization used at least 75% of receipts for "charitable purposes." The Court reasoned that the Village's interests in preventing fraud could be better served by measures that were less intrusive on free speech than a direct prohibition on solicitation. Again in *Secretary of State of Md. v. Joseph H. Munson Co.*, 467 U.S. 947 (1984), the Court invalidated a Maryland law that authorized a waiver of a 25% limitation on expenses if it prevented the charitable organization from soliciting contributions. The regulation operated on the erroneous premise that high solicitation costs are an accurate measure of fraud; the high fundraising costs could be due to protected First Amendment activity. The law was held to be substantially overbroad. See also *Riley v. National Fed. of Blind of N.C., Inc.*, 487 U.S. 781 (1988) (law prohibiting professional fundraisers from retaining "unreasonable" fee, where fees exceeding 35% were rebuttably presumed unreasonable held unconstitutional because the law was not to be "narrowly tailored" to the state's interest in preventing fraud).

But in *Illinois ex rel. Madigan v. Telemarketing Associates*, 538 U.S. 600 (2003), the Court held that "states may maintain fraud actions when fundraisers make false or misleading representations designed to deceive donors about how their donations will be used." While Telemarketing Associates had allegedly told the public that a significant amount of each dollar donated would go to the charitable purpose, only 15 cents or less was made available. Justice Ginsberg said that "fraudulent charitable solicitation is unprotected speech." In the solicitation cases discussed above, the statutes imposed prior restraints when fundraising fees exceeded a specified level; such statutes "categorically ban solicitations when fundraising costs run high." But high fundraising costs do not necessarily establish fraud. Justice Ginsburg summarized: "So long as the emphasis is on what fundraisers misleadingly convey, and not on percentage limitations on solicitors' fees *per se*, such actions need not impermissibly chill protected speech."

In *Virginia v. Hicks*, 539 U.S. 113 (2003), the Court unanimously rejected a First Amendment overbreadth challenge to a municipal public housing authority trespass policy. A low income housing development was plagued with crime and drugs. After the city conveyed streets in the development to the public housing authority, that agency adopted a policy authorizing police to notify those nonresidents unable to demonstrate "a legitimate business or social policy for being on the premises," that they must leave and not return. When Hicks returned to the development following notification, he was arrested for trespass.

The Supreme Court, per Justice Scalia, held that the trespass policy was not shown by Hicks to be "substantially overbroad judged in relation to its plainly legitimate sweep." While the housing authority allegedly followed an unwritten rule that all persons seeking to distribute flyers had to obtain the manager's permission, which created a threat that discretion would be used to prohibit distasteful or offensive speech, there was no showing that the policy was used to bar anyone involved in constitutionally protected speech. The written rules applied to all individuals who entered the development and did not single out those engaging in protected speech. The basis for arrest was not speech but the non-expressive conduct of entering in violation of the notice-barment rule. Even assuming the invalidity of the unwritten rule, Hicks had failed to show that the "trespass policy as a whole prohibits a 'substantial' amount of protected speech in relation to its many legitimate applications." Unconstitutional applications of the trespass policy could be remedied through as-applied litigation. Justice Scalia also suggested that it is rare for overbreadth challenges to succeed against regulations not specifically addressed to speech or conduct (such as picketing or demonstrating) necessarily associated with speech.

The student should be aware that overbreadth as a constitutional infirmity may appear to be a greater problem for the legislative draftsman than is the case. Courts can place a savings curative gloss on laws that would otherwise be facially overbroad. In *Osborne v. Ohio*, 495 U.S. 103 (1990), the state law appeared ripe for an overbreadth challenge since it punished showing a minor in a "state of nudity" unless the presentation was made for a bona fide scientific, educational, artistic, etc., purpose. While Osborne was appealing his conviction to the United States Supreme Court, the Ohio Supreme Court gave a narrowing construction to the law and limited its application. The United States Supreme Court responded by holding that the narrowed statute was no longer impermissibly overbroad. Further, the Court held that the narrowed statute could "be applied to conduct occurring before the construction provided such application affords fair warning to the defendant.'' The Court reasoned that Osborne would not have been surprised that his photos of nude male minors violated the law. Nevertheless, the Court did overturn the defendant's conviction since the jury had not been instructed in accord with the statute as narrowed.

Closely related to the doctrine of overbreadth is the due process prohibition against vagueness. A law is vague if persons of "common intelligence must necessarily guess as at its meaning and differ as to its application." *Connally v. General Construction Co.*, 269 U.S. 385 (1926). A law must be sufficiently precise so that those bound by it can understand the conduct which will subject them to the sanctions imposed by the law. This is a notice concern and the doctrine of vagueness is at root a due process concept. Special clarity is demanded when fundamental First Amendment rights are involved.

Both overbreadth and vagueness are concerned with the facial validity of the law. Just as the overbreadth doctrine mandates specificity and precision in legislative drafting so the doctrine of vagueness requires clarity in legislating. Just as the courts worry over the chilling effect on protected speech and the dangers of selective enforcement in overbreadth analysis so these same concerns drive the vagueness inquiry. Both doctrines reflect the belief that the legislature is capable of drafting the law more narrowly so that it is limited to conduct that is the legitimate concern of government. But the doctrines of overbreadth and vagueness are not identical. A law can be perfectly clear that it extends to both protected and unprotected speech. Such a law is overbroad but it is not vague. When a law is vague, its potential parameters cannot be easily ascertained. Therefore, it is not clear whether the law reaches protected expression. Most important, the procedural aspect of the overbreadth doctrine, creating an exception to the third party standing rule, does not apply to vagueness challenges.

Both vagueness and overbreadth problems are capable of being cured by means of judicial interpretation. Savings constructions of overbroad or vague statutes are often undertaken. It should be mentioned that important considerations of federalism influence this area. In the main, state statutes are given a "savings construction" by the highest state court, not federal courts. Similarly, federal courts are the appropriate forums to provide savings constructions to federal statutes. Even a United States Supreme Court decision that a law is overbroad establishes only that the state law as authoritatively interpreted by the state courts at the time of the Supreme Court's decision is unconstitutional. It is thus still open to a state court to place a subsequent curative, narrowing and validating construction on the law. Similarly, the state legislature can repair the infirmities of its vague or overbroad law. It should also be noted that the vagueness doctrine does not necessarily apply to nonregulatory government action, such as public subsidies for the arts.

See *National Endowment for the Arts v. Finley*, 524 U.S. 569 (1998) ("But when the Government is acting as patron rather than as sovereign, the consequences of imprecision are not constitutionally severe.").

The Court in *City of Chicago v. Morales*, 527 U.S. 41 (1999), rejected a First Amendment overbreadth challenge to Chicago's Gang Congregation Ordinance but held that the law was unconstitutionally vague. The ordinance allowed police to prevent persons reasonably believed to be gang members from loitering in public places. Justice Stevens, for the Court, concluded that the law did not violate the First Amendment overbreadth doctrine since the law did not bar conduct that was aimed at delivering a message. But the Court held that the law was facially unconstitutional for vagueness because the ordinance gave the police too much discretion and failed to give enough notice to citizens who wanted to use the streets.

In *Virginia v. Black*, 538 U.S. 343 (2003), a Supreme Court plurality concluded that a provision of Virginia's cross-burning law stating that "[a]ny such burning of a cross shall be prima facie evidence of an intent to intimidate a person or group of persons" is unconstitutional on its face. The Virginia Supreme Court had held this provision unconstitutionally overbroad. Justice Scalia says that the plurality is relying on the overbreadth doctrine, although Justice O'Connor does not do so expressly. The plurality concluded that "the prima facie provision strips away the very reason why a

State may ban cross burning with an intent to intimidate." While cross burning may mean that a person intends constitutionally proscribable intimidation (i.e., a true threat), it may mean only that a person is engaged in core political speech; cross burning can be "a statement of ideology, a symbol of group solidarity." By failing to distinguish among the different types of cross burnings, the provision chills constitutionally protected political speech and can skew jury deliberations towards conviction even where the evidence of intent to intimidate is relatively weak. "The prima facie evidence provision in this case ignores all of the contextual factors that are necessary to decide whether a particular cross burning is intended to intimidate. The First Amendment does not permit such a shortcut." Justice Scalia, joined by Justice Thomas, concluded that "[t]he notion that the set of cases identified by the plurality in which convictions might improperly be obtained is sufficiently large to render the statute *substantially* overbroad is fanciful."

## D. PRIOR RESTRAINT

Freedom of expression in Anglo–American law began with protection of freedom of the press. The vehicle for this press protection was the doctrine of prior restraint: the printed word did not have to be submitted to the King's censors before it could go forth. Even the most minimalist understanding of the First Amendment conceives it to provide a presumption against prior restraint. Thus in *Lovell v. Griffin*, 303 U.S. 444 (1938), the Supreme Court had little difficulty in striking down an ordinance prohibiting the distribution of printed materials without prior approval of the county manager.

The doctrine of prior restraint is not limited to administrative censorship despite its unhappy origins with the censorious practices of English licensors in the seventeenth century. In American constitutional law, if a law requires judicial approval before a publication can issue, or before speech or protest can occur, this too will be viewed as a prior restraint. In *Near v. Minnesota*, 283 U.S. 697 (1931), a trial court "perpetually enjoined" as a public nuisance a scurrilous publication called *The Saturday Press* pursuant to a Minnesota law authorizing such injunctions. Chief Justice Hughes declared that the "injunctive scheme was the essence of censorship." *Near* established the doctrine that there is a presumption against prior restraint: "[T]he fact that the liberty of the press may be abused by miscreant purveyors of scandal does not make any the less necessary the immunity of the press from previous restraint in dealing with official misconduct. Subsequent punishment for such abuses as may exist is the appropriate remedy, consistent with constitutional privilege."

*Near* recognizes a distinction between freedom from prior restraint and freedom from subsequent punishment. A prior restraint prevents a communication from entering the marketplace of ideas. Subsequent punishment assumes that the communication has entered the market and the question is whether the disseminator of the communication can be punished. For many, freedom from prior restraint is the more important freedom. The original rationale for the prior restraint doctrine was historical. *Near* divorces the doctrine from its unique historical justification by extending it beyond administrative licensing schemes.

What rationale other than history exists for the presumption against prior restraint? Professor Thomas I. Emerson has provided a rationale for the expanded prior restraint doctrine: "A system of prior restraint is in many ways more inhibiting than a system of punishment; it is likely to bring under government scrutiny a far wider range of expressions; it shuts off communication before it takes place; suppression by a stroke of the pen is more likely to be applied than suppression through a criminal process; the procedures do not require attention to the safeguards of the criminal process; the system allows less opportunity for public appraisal and criticism; the dynamics of the system drive toward excesses as the history of all censorship shows." Emerson, *The System of Freedom of Expression* (1970).

Should one accept the distinctions drawn by Professor Emerson? Arguably fear of subsequent punishment is itself a prior restraint. Government is seeking to deter the expression against which the law is directed. Prior restraints involve sanctions in the form of contempt orders. Contempt is a form of subsequent punishment for speech that has occurred. Indeed, it can be argued that allowing a prior judicial or administrative determination whether or not proposed expression is protected burdens expression less than punishing the speaker. Some scholars contend that the procedural ease of securing an injunction compared with the procedural hurdles characterizing subsequent punishment schemes invites greater censorship and that this difference justifies the prior restraint doctrine. As Alexander Bickel put it: "[A] criminal statute chills, prior restraint freezes." Bickel, *The Morality of Consent* (1975).

Was the *Near* Court wise in extending the prior restraint doctrine to judicial injunctions? Administrative censorship has been disfavored at least in part because there has been no prior judicial determination that the speech is unprotected. Judicial orders, on the other hand, involve a judicial determination that the speech in question should not enter the marketplace. Also, some persons argue that judges are likely to be more protective of fundamental freedoms than administrators. On the other hand, advocates of treating judicial orders as prior restraints contend that judicial orders usually carry more force and authority than administrative ones. This is especially evident in the case of the collateral bar rule, which requires that a judicial order must normally be obeyed pending appeal unless the injunction is frivolous or the issuing court lacks jurisdiction. *Walker v. Birmingham*, 388 U.S. 307 (1967) [contempt order for disobeying an *ex parte* judicial restraining order banning a civil rights march in violation of an ordinance was upheld]. Although a judicial order may constitute a violation of the First Amendment, it cannot simply be defied. Review must be sought, at least where an expedited review procedure is available.

What other government regulation besides injunctions will be labeled as prior restraint remains uncertain. A cease and desist order issued by an administrative agency barring the use of sex-designated help wanted ads in newspaper was held not to be a prior restraint. *Pittsburgh Press v. Pittsburgh Comm'n on Human Relations*, 413 U.S. 376 (1973). Protective orders issued by a court in connection with the discovery process do not constitute prior restraints. *Seattle Times Co. v. Rhinehart*, 467 U.S. 20 (1984). In both of these situations, the government regulation operates prior to the issuance of the communication. Nevertheless, the Court viewed the burden on speech in these cases to be less than in the classic prior restraint context, *i.e.*, licensing and injunctions. Similarly, *Alexander v. United States*, 509 U.S. 544 (1993) held that a RICO-imposed massive forfeiture of a sexually oriented materials business was not a prior restraint.

What is the legal effect of invoking the prior restraint doctrine? The modern doctrine is that "[a]ny system of prior restraint of expression comes to [the Court] bearing a heavy presumption against its constitutionality." *Bantam Books, Inc. v. Sullivan*, 372 U.S. 58 (1963). The government "thus carries a heavy burden of justification for the imposition of such a restraint." *Organization for a Better Austin v. Keefe*, 402 U.S. 415 (1971). But what must government show in order to meet its burden and overcome the presumption?

In *Near v. Minnesota*, Chief Justice Hughes identified three exceptional cases where prior restraints might be valid. First, there was a national security exception, *e.g.*, publishing the sailing date of a troop transport. Second, there was an obscenity exception to enforce "the primary requirements of decency." Third, the "security of the community life may be protected against incitements to acts of violence and the overthrow by force of orderly government." None of the exceptions was met under the *Near* facts. Chief Justice Hughes was not clear on whether these exceptions were illustrative of a larger principle or were simply closed-end exceptions to an otherwise absolute prohibition against prior restraint. This larger principle would involve a weighted balancing of the potential harm to the public interest against the prior restraint doctrine. The tenor of the case law supports the view that it has been the weighted balancing approach which has been dominant.

In the famous *Pentagon Papers* case, *New York Times Co. v. United States*, 403 U.S. 713 (1971), the Executive sought to secure an injunction against leading newspapers, such as the *New York Times* and the *Washington Post*, from publishing classified material concerning the Vietnam War. There was no statutory authorization for such a judicial order. In a short *per curiam* opinion, the Court held that the Executive had failed to meet the heavy burden of justification required for such a judicially imposed prior restraint. Justices Black and Douglas adopted an essentially absolutist position and indicated there were no circumstances which would authorize a court to abridge freedom of the press "in the name of equity, presidential power and national security." Justices Brennan, Stewart, White and Marshall, joining the *per curiam* order, adopted less absolutist positions. Justice Brennan adopted the *Near* approach but would allow injunctions only when the nation "is at war" and only upon "proof that government must inevitably directly and immediately cause the occurrence of an event kindred to impairing the safety of a transport already at sea." Justices Stewart and White both rejected the Executive's contention that the courts should issue an injunction on a showing of "grave and irreparable threat to the public interest." Rather, it was necessary for the Executive to establish that disclosure "will surely result in direct, immediate, and irreparable damage to our Nation or its people." Justice Marshall adopted a "rule-of-law" approach embraced by many of the justices in the majority, stressing the absence of any authorizing legislation supporting the Executive's request. It is interesting that some of the majority justices indicated that they would have authorized the issuance of the injunction if such legislation had existed even though the injunction would still have had the characteristics of a prior restraint.

Three justices—Chief Justice Burger and Justices Blackmun and Harlan—dissented. Justice Harlan in dissent reasoned that the courts, in the context of a case like the *Pentagon Papers*, should determine only that the subject matter of the injunction involved the foreign relations power and that the determination of irreparable harm to national security was made by the head of the executive department concerned. In Harlan's view, and that of the dissenters generally, it was the function of the Executive and not of the courts to balance the competing interests.

The *Pentagon Papers* case illustrates that the presumption against prior restraints can be overcome only by an overriding governmental interest such as extreme danger to national security. Nevertheless, the Court continues to allow some prior restraints. Municipal permit systems for parades and demonstrations are allowed as long as the discretion of the administrator of the system is narrowly confined. Ordinances cannot be drawn to allow content or viewpoint discrimination. *Forsyth County, Ga. v. Nationalist Movement*, 505 U.S. 123 (1992). (Content-based permit fee system vesting excessive discretion in administrator held unconstitutional. See Ch. II, C). But in *Thomas v. Chicago Park District*, 534 U.S. 316 (2002), a city park ordinance requiring a permit before conducting large-scale events, designed to reconcile competing uses, was held to be a content-neutral time, place and manner restriction. While the law provided limited discretion to the licensing authority, it contained adequate standards to guide the official's decision and render it subject to effective judicial review and therefore was constitutional.

In the obscenity context, the courts regularly allow injunctions against the exhibition or distribution of obscene publications. See *Paris Adult Theatre I v. Slaton*, 413 U.S. 49 (1973) (injunction permitted against exhibition of "adult" movies). Even film licensing has been upheld if the licensing is not excessively vague or overbroad and adequate procedural standards are satisfied. *Freedman v. Maryland*, 380 U.S. 51 (1965). Ch. V, D. The demanding procedural standards set forth in *Freedman* do not apply to permit systems which are content-neutral time, place and manner regulation of the public forum. See Ch. IX, A. *Thomas v. Chicago Park District*, 534 U.S. 316 (2002) ("Such a traditional exercise of authority does not raise the censorship concerns that prompted us to impose the extraordinary procedural safeguards on the film licensing process in *Freedman*."). Nor has the Court altogether foreclosed the possibility that gag orders and other prior restraints aimed at protecting the fair trial rights of criminal defendants may in some extraordinary circumstances be valid. Nevertheless, the Court has made it unmistakably clear that gag orders directed to the press are presumptively invalid prior restraints. *Nebraska Press Ass'n v. Stuart*, 427 U.S. 539 (1976).

As *Thomas v. Chicago Park District*, 534 U.S. 316 (2002) indicates, not all prior restraints are subject to the heavy burden of justification associated with the classic doctrine. In *Madsen v. Women's Health Center*, 512 U.S. 753 (1994), in reviewing an injunction limiting demonstrations outside an abortion clinic, the Court held that strict scrutiny does not apply to injunctions imposed without reference to speech content. Chief Justice Rehnquist, for the Court, reasoned that there was no indication that the issuance of the restraint depended on the subject matter or viewpoint of the protesters. Therefore, the content-neutral injunction imposed only an incidental burden on speech. Nevertheless, the Court did accept that there were clear differences between an injunction and general laws. The Chief Justice reasoned that the enhanced risks of censorship and administrative discrimination required a somewhat more rigorous standard than is generally applied to content-neutral time, place and manner regulations: "We must ask instead whether the challenged provisions of the injunction burden no more speech than necessary to serve a significant government interest."

Applying this standard, the Court upheld some provisions and invalidated others. For example, a 36–foot buffer zone in front of the abortion clinic to assure access was held constitutional but the same buffer on the back and sides of the clinic was held to burden more speech than necessary to serve the legitimate government interest in access. Justice Scalia, dissenting, rejected the new "intermediate-intermediate scrutiny." He argued "that a restriction upon speech imposed by injunction whether nominally content-based or nominally content-neutral is at least as deserving of strict scrutiny as a statutory, content-based restriction." In form, the injunction is classic example of prior restraint and, in effect, there is an equivalent danger of judicial viewpoint censorship.

In *Schenck v. Pro–Choice Network of Western New York*, 519 U.S. 357 (1997), the Court applied *Madsen* in reviewing a variety of restrictions on anti-abortion protesters. While a variety of restrictions designed to allow access to clinics and protect public safety and order were upheld, including fixed buffer zones, the Court struck down "floating" buffer zones (e.g., no demonstrations with fifteen feet of a person or vehicle), because they burdened more speech than necessary to satisfy the relevant governmental interests.

# PART TWO

# CONTENT–BASED REGULATION AND LOW–VALUE SPEECH

---

## CHAPTER III

## ADVOCACY OF ILLEGAL CONDUCT

First Amendment law is essentially a product of the twentieth century. More specifically, it has its origins in the World War I era, emanating from prosecutions under the federal Espionage Act which prohibited activities disruptive of the war effort. The defendants argued that the Act could not be applied to their antiwar advocacy consistent with the First Amendment. In *Schenck v. United States*, 249 U.S. 47 (1919), Justice Holmes, writing for the Court, set forth the famous clear and present danger test defining when speech can be the basis for criminal punishment: "The question in every case is whether the words used are used in such circumstances and are of such a nature as to create a clear and present danger that they will bring about the substantive evils that Congress has a right to prevent. It is a question of proximity and degree." The student should note that the focus of the danger test is on the factual context, the actual circumstances under which the speech occurs. It looks to the probable effects of the advocacy.

While the clear and present danger formulation may appear restrictive of governmental power to limit advocacy deemed subversive, in the early life of the test, the showing needed to satisfy the test was not rigorous. Schenck's conviction was affirmed, as were the Espionage Act convictions of Frohwerk and Debs, *Frohwerk v. United States*, 249 U.S. 204 (1919); *Debs v. United States*, 249 U.S. 211 (1919), in spite of the feeble character of their antiwar protests—speechmaking and pamphleteering which had little hope of persuading the public. The analysis of Holmes in each of these cases adopted what was the dominant judicial approach of the time permitting the punishment of advocacy which has a tendency to produce harm. The requirement of intent was generally satisfied by citing the speech and allowing the jury to speculate about its possible effects. As Holmes said in *Schenck*: "If the act (speaking, or circulating a paper), its tendency and the intent with which it is done are the same, we perceive no ground for saying that success alone warrants making the act a crime." This is the "bad tendency" test.

An irony of the clear and present doctrine in these formative years is that when Holmes, with whom the doctrine is most closely associated, was writing for the majority, the defendant was convicted. In *Abrams v. United States*, 250 U.S. 616 (1919), Holmes, now writing in dissent, began to develop a more-speech protective formulation of his danger test. Only an emergency that would not allow dialogue justified any exception to the sweeping protection of the First Amendment. Even opinions we loathe must be tolerated, "unless they so imminently threaten immediate interference with the lawful and pressing purposes of the law that an immediate check is required to save the country." But why wait for an emergency? It might then be too late. Holmes' response to this concern was to point to the Nation's commitment, wise or foolhardy, to the marketplace of ideas.

In *Gitlow v. New York*, 268 U.S. 652 (1925), Justice Sanford, for the Court, sought to draw a distinction limiting the occasions for invoking the danger doctrine. *Schenck* and *Abrams*, he argued, involved prosecutions under a statute directed against particular evils threatening the war effort. The judicial inquiry was directed to whether the Espionage Act could be constitutionally applied to the particular advocacy of the defendants. The legislature itself had not condemned the speech involved as harmful to the public well-being. Sanford contended that the clear and present danger test was intended by the Court to apply only to this class of case. Even in this context, Sanford argued for a highly restrictive interpretation of *Schenck* and *Abrams*. Such a statute can be constitutionally applied to the specific speech of a defendant "if [the expression's] natural tendency and probable effect was to bring about the substantive evil which the legislative body might prevent," *i.e.*, if it had a "bad tendency." Gitlow, on the other hand, was being prosecuted under an anarchy law that prohibited advocacy of the overthrow of the government by force and violence. The legislature itself had determined that such advocacy involved a danger that government could suppress. In such cases, reasoned Justice Sanford, there is only a limited judicial role: "It is sufficient that the statute itself be constitutional and that the use of the language comes within its prohibition." Justice Sanford applied a highly deferential reasonableness test. The legislature could reasonably determine that it was appropriate to "suppress the threatened danger in its incipiency." Holmes and Brandeis dissented in *Gitlow* because there was no present danger of an attempt to overthrow the government.

In *Whitney v. California*, 274 U.S. 357 (1927), a case which, like *Gitlow*, dealt with a state sedition statute proscribing advocacy, Justice Brandeis wrote a concurrence which has become one of the primary documents in the literature of the First Amendment. His concurrence, building on the Holmes dissents, provided a formulation of clear and present danger which rejected the narrower view of the doctrine taken by Justice Sanford and greatly influenced the later life of the doctrine. Justice Brandeis rejected Justice Sanford's distinction based on the nature of the statute. Indeed, Brandeis rejected the idea that the legislative determination of the existence of a danger was the critical factor. The highly deferential reasonableness approach to such a statute, which Sanford used, would make judicial review essentially meaningless. Chief Justice Burger would later adopt the same theme: "Deference to a legislative finding cannot limit judicial inquiry when First Amendment rights are at stake." *Landmark Communications, Inc. v. Virginia*, 435 U.S. 829 (1978). In *Whitney*, Brandeis argued: "Whenever the fundamental rights of free speech and assembly are alleged to have been invaded, it must remain open to a defendant to present the issue whether there actually did exist at the time a clear danger; whether the danger, if any, was imminent; and whether the evil apprehended was one so substantial as to justify the stringent restriction interposed by the legislature." Critical to understanding Brandeis's approach to the danger test is his declaration that even if the legislature has condemned specific advocacy, "[o]nly an emergency justifies repression."

While Brandeis and Holmes sought to forge a more speech protective danger test, an alternative had been offered by an influential federal district judge, Learned Hand. In a district court case interpreting the language of the Espionage Act, *Masses Publishing Co. v. Patten*, 244 F. 535 (S.D.N.Y.1917), Hand declared: "If one stops short of urging upon others that it is their duty or their interest to resist the law, it seems to me one should not be held to have attempted to cause its violation." Hand argued that a distinction must be drawn between legitimate agitation and direct incitement to violent resistance. Only the latter could be punished consistent with the First Amendment. Hand's incitement test is in fact an absolutist approach; advocacy of illegal conduct, short of incitement, is absolutely protected.

But why can incitement be constitutionally proscribed? Hand answered that such speech was not within the guarantee of freedom of speech: "Words are not only the keys of persuasion but the triggers of action, and those which have no purport but to counsel the violation of law cannot by any latitude of interpretation be a part of that public opinion which is the final source of government in a democratic state." In modern terms, language of incitement should be categorically excluded from the protections of the First Amendment. Robert Bork, for example, would later adopt an even broader absolutist approach than did Learned Hand. For Bork, speech advocating the forcible overthrow of government is not political speech within the protection of the First Amendment: "Such speech violates constitutional truths about processes and [is] not aimed at a new definition of political truth by a legislative majority." Bork, *Neutral Principles and Some First Amendment Problems*, 47 Ind. L.J. 1 (1971).

Whereas the danger test focused on the actual circumstances in which the speech occurred, Hand's test looks to the language of the speaker. If it is simple advocacy of agitation, it is protected speech; if it is incitement, it is unprotected speech. But is this distinction workable? Dissenting in *Gitlow*, Holmes had said: "Every idea is an incitement.... The only difference between the expression of an opinion and an incitement in the narrower sense is the speaker's enthusiasm for the result. Eloquence may set fire to reason." When Marc Antony delivered his Funeral Oration, was he engaged in incitement? He did not use words of incitement but the crowd was incited—a result which he intended. Should a speaker who uses language of incitement that is *ineffective* in arousing his audience still be subject to prosecution?

Whatever the merits of the *Masses* or incitement test, it did not find acceptance in the formative years of First Amendment law. Hand himself subsequently abandoned it. In the 1930s and 1940s, the Holmes–Brandeis version of the clear and present danger doctrine was increasingly used by the Supreme Court to protect advocacy of illegal conduct. The Court expressly recognized that the Holmes–Brandeis version of clear and present danger had become the authoritative formulation in *Dennis v. United States*, 341 U.S. 494 (1951)—a case which paradoxically did not in fact adhere to their formulation.

*Dennis v. United States* (1951) must be read against the virulent anti-Communism of the McCarthy era. The petitioners were 50 leaders of the American Communist Party who were convicted under the federal Smith Act of 1940, which prohibited conspiracy to advocate the overthrow of the government by force and violence. The Smith Act was a sedition law directed at speech; it was like the legislation considered in *Gitlow* and *Whitney*. While Chief Justice Vinson gave lip service in *Dennis* to the clear and present danger test, the test used was not the speech-protective formulation of the danger test fashioned by Holmes and Brandeis. Instead, Vinson adopted a formulation developed by Learned Hand in the Second Circuit opinion below: "In each case [courts] must ask whether the gravity of the 'evil' discounted by its improbability, justifies such invasion of free speech as is necessary to avoid the danger." If the potential harm is sufficiently great, such as the overthrow of the government, the speech may be suppressed even if it is highly improbable that it will bring about the harm. Even more critical, the demand for imminence is purged from the danger test by the *Dennis* formulation. In the Holmes–Brandeis formulation, "[o]nly an emergency justifies repression." But for the *Dennis* Court, confronting a "highly organized conspiracy, with rigidly disciplined members," and given "the inflammable nature of world conditions," the conspiracy itself was sufficient danger to justify suppression.

In a long concurrence, Justice Frankfurter castigated the relevance of the danger test to the problem presented in *Dennis*; it was "too inflexible for the non-Euclidean problems to be solved." He urged instead that the competing interests must be balanced. But it was the legislature, not the non-representative courts, who should do the balancing. This view was a throwback to the Sanford opinion in *Gitlow* against which Holmes had protested in dissent and it advocated a "reasonableness" approach to judicial review which Brandeis had specifically criticized in *Whitney*. When the legislature has made a determination that speech is dangerous to the public well-being, Justice Frankfurter argued that judicial review should be highly deferential. But Justice Black stated in dissent in *Dennis* that "[s]uch a doctrine waters down the First Amendment so that it amounts to little more than an admonition to Congress."

Critics of the danger test contend that *Dennis* proves the test's inadequacies. From a free expression perspective, in the crunch the doctrine did not deliver. But the doctrine's defenders ask whether any test would have done any better. They argue that the deficiency was not in the danger doctrine, but in the hysteria of the times. In short, are there circumstances when no doctrine is hardy enough to withstand the wrath of the majority?

In *Yates v. United States*, 354 U.S. 298 (1957), the Court provided a savings construction to the Smith Act which had the effect of narrowing *Dennis* and moving the danger test closer to its Holmes–Brandeis origins. Justice Harlan read the Smith Act not to reach advocacy of abstract doctrine but only the advocacy of concrete illegal action. Vinson in *Dennis* had indicated that advocacy of speech itself could be proscribed; Harlan made it clear that it was only advocacy of illegal action that could be proscribed. Indeed, Harlan labored to find in *Dennis* a recognition that mere advocacy, even when joined with intent, was too far removed from concrete action to fall within the statute. It is questionable whether Vinson intended or even understood this distinction. While *Yates* does not use the language of imminence and emergency, its stress on "advocacy of action" can be read as requiring a greater degree of immediate danger than the "gravity of the evil" test employed in *Dennis*. For some commentators, therefore, *Yates* partially restored imminence to its former significant role in the workings of the danger test. Others see *Yates* as reading the *Masses* incitement test into the clear and present danger doctrine. Harlan's focus is on the nature of the advocacy and not on the actual danger presented by the circumstances under which the speech occurred.

The possibility of wedding the incitement with the danger test suggested by *Yates* arguably came to fruition in *Brandenburg v. Ohio*, 395 U.S. 444 (1969). Brandenburg was convicted for violating an Ohio criminal syndicalism law punishing advocacy of violence as a means of achieving industrial or political reform. The law in *Brandenburg* was, like *Dennis* and *Yates*, a law directed at speech itself. Reversing *Whitney*, which had upheld a California version of the same law, the *Brandenburg* Court, in a laconic *per curiam* decision, achieved the feat of re-formulating the clear and danger doctrine without mentioning the words "clear and present danger." *Brandenburg* held the Ohio law violative of the First Amendment. The new standard forged by the Court in *Brandenburg* provides that a state cannot forbid the advocacy of illegal action "except where such advocacy is directed to inciting or producing imminent lawless action and is likely to incite or produce such action." The *Brandenburg* test focuses on the probability and imminence of the danger arising from the speech similar to the elements in the Holmes–Brandeis danger formulation. But *Brandenburg* nowhere mentions the clear and present danger test and cites as authority, not Brandeis in *Whitney*, but *Dennis* and *Yates*. Since *Dennis* and *Yates* are arguably doctrinally inconsistent, this citation could be confusing. Given the emphasis on incitement in the Brandenburg formulation, *Yates* alone, with its emphasis on advocacy of action, was the more appropriate precedent.

Commentators disagree on the proper interpretation of the *Brandenburg* standard. Some perceive it as the adoption of an incitement test focusing on the language of the speakers and, therefore, as a modern formulation of the *Masses* standard. Under this approach, regardless of the imminence of the danger actually existing, the speaker is protected so long as he does not actually use the language of incitement, *i.e.*, Marc Antony. Others see *Brandenburg* as focusing on the factual circumstances surrounding the speech and the speaker's intent. The inciting character of the language, in this approach, is only an element in assessing the danger posed by the advocacy. If the danger is imminent and serious enough, even the bland speaker is in jeopardy.

Professor Gerald Gunther, arguing for yet another interpretation, says that *Brandenburg* in fact represents a merger of the *Masses* incitement test with the Holmes–Brandeis danger test. The government must prove both (1) that the speaker sought to incite his audience and that (2) there existed an imminent danger that serious harm would result. Gunther views this interpretation of *Brandenburg* as producing "the most speech-protective standard yet evolved by the Supreme Court." Gunther, *Learned Hand and the Origins of Modern First Amendment Doctrine: Some Fragments of History*, 27 Stan. L. Rev. 719 (1975). The authors believe that the Gunther understanding of *Brandenburg* is the most authoritative, but the student should be aware of the fact that the courts oscillate among these alternative interpretations of *Brandenburg*.

A later example of the two part approach to *Brandenburg* urged by Gunther is *Hess v. Indiana*, 414 U.S. 105 (1973), where the Court overturned the conviction of an antiwar protester for disorderly conduct for using words such as "we'll take the fucking street later." In a *per curiam* opinion, the Court concluded that Hess' statements could not be interpreted as advocating any action. Further, it was not likely to produce imminent disorder since "at worst it amounted to nothing more than advocacy of illegal action at some indefinite future time." In *NAACP v. Claiborne Hardware Co.*, 458 U.S. 886 (1982), speech threatening reprisals in connection with an NAACP sponsored boycott of white merchants was held to be protected advocacy, citing *Brandenburg*. In *Claiborne*, one of the statements was made by civil rights activist Charles Evers, who said to a black audience: "If we catch

any of you going in any of them racist stores, we're
going to break your damn neck." But the Court
concluded that advocacy of force and violence alone
would not justify suppression. A speaker must be
free "to stimulate his audience with spontaneous
and emotional appeals for unity and action in a
common cause." When such appeals do not incite
the lawless action, the advocacy is protected. In
addition to *Hess* and *Claiborne Hardware*, see *Watts
v. United States*, 394 U.S. 705 (1969) [conviction for
threatening the life of the President was reversed
where the speaker was engaged in political hyperbole rather than actually threatening violence];
*Bond v. Floyd*, 385 U.S. 116 (1966) [antiwar advocacy was held, based on *Yates*, not to justify Bond's
exclusion from the Georgia legislature].

The clear and present danger test is typically
associated with problems of subversive advocacy
and street violence. The danger test, however, has
been used in a variety of factual contexts. For
example, only when out-of-court contemptuous behavior presents a clear and present danger to the
fair administration of justice may it be punished.
*Bridges v. California*, 314 U.S. 252 (1941); *Wood v.
Georgia*, 370 U.S. 375 (1962). Criminal sanctions
against a newspaper for reporting the confidential
proceedings of a state judicial disciplinary commission were overturned since the *Brandenburg* test
had not been satisfied. *Landmark Communications,
Inc. v. Virginia*, 435 U.S. 829 (1978). The danger
test has also been used to define the circumstances
under which a gag order might validly be issued

against the media to prohibit publication of material potentially interfering with a defendant's right to a fair trial. *Nebraska Press Ass'n v. Stuart*, 427 U.S. 539 (1976) [gag order held not to meet the requirements of the clear and present danger doctrine]. A loyalty oath not limited to incitement of lawless action was held unconstitutional. *Communist Party of Indiana v. Whitcomb*, 414 U.S. 441 (1974).

The diversity of the above cases illustrates the myriad paths that clear and present danger has traveled from its beginning in anti-subversive legislation. The variety of the situations in which the courts have used clear and present danger brings an element of unpredictability to identifying the occasions when the doctrine applies. Furthermore, there is some doubt as to whether its use in these new settings has accomplished anything that would not more easily be achieved by use of a strict scrutiny standard. Indeed, it may be that, at the present time, the clear and present danger is nothing more than strict scrutiny cast in more ambiguous formulaic terms.

# CHAPTER IV

# DANGEROUS AND OFFENSIVE SPEECH

## A. FIGHTING WORDS

The "fighting words" doctrine originated in *Chaplinsky v. New Hampshire*, 315 U.S. 568 (1942). Chaplinsky, a Jehovah's Witness, had been convicted for calling a city marshal a "God-damned racketeer and a damned fascist." In affirming the conviction, the New Hampshire Court had given its sweeping statute a narrowing interpretation limiting its application to fighting words. These were words which were defined as having a "direct tendency to cause acts of violence by the persons to whom, individually, the remark is addressed." The court explained that such face to face speech is inherently likely to cause a breach of the peace: "The test is what men of common intelligence would understand would be words likely to cause an average addressee to fight."

In affirming the conviction below, the United States Supreme Court in *Chaplinsky* adopted the savings construction of the New Hampshire Supreme Court as the basis for a new doctrine indicating a category of expression which constituted unprotected speech—"[words] which by their very utterance inflict injury or tend to incite an immediate breach of the peace." The imprecise line between fighting words and protected speech that is merely offensive or provocative causes some to question the value of the fighting words doctrine.

What is the rationale for the fighting words doctrine? The *Chaplinsky* Court answered by saying that such expression does not contribute to the exposition of ideas or the search for truth. Any benefit to society from such speech is outweighed by the societal interest in order and morality. Commentators have likened fighting words to verbal assaults, more akin to conduct than the communication of ideas. Fighting words exemplify what Justice Douglas meant when, concurring in *Brandenburg*, he referred to words so brigaded with action that they enjoy no First Amendment protection. For adherents of the view, championed by Professor Thomas Emerson, that the speech-action dichotomy was the appropriate dividing line between protected and unprotected expression, fighting words fell on the action side of the line. Finally, given the Court's emphasis on the likelihood of violence from such speech, fighting words could be characterized as necessarily presenting a clear and present danger.

How does the fighting words doctrine differ from the *Brandenburg* formulation of the clear and present danger test? Fighting words situations involve face to face encounters. The clear and present danger doctrine, on the other hand, usually involves incitement of crowds and/or subversive advocacy directed to the public generally. Whereas clear and present danger doctrine looks to the actual danger presented by the circumstances, the fighting words doctrine, as fashioned in *Chaplinsky*, looks to whether the speech is likely to cause the average addressee to fight. Fighting words involves an assumption about how a reasonable person would react; its focus is not on the reaction of the actual addressee. The concern of the fighting words doctrine is with the words of the speaker and not the actual danger presented by the specific factual context. In summary, the fighting words doctrine is a category of low value speech unprotected under the First Amendment.

Although the fighting words doctrine is often relied on by government in First Amendment cases to justify regulation, in fact, labeling speech as fighting words has not been a dispositive ground of decision in very many Supreme Court cases since *Chaplinsky*. Generally, the Court has found breach of the peace and disorderly conduct statutes that have been defended on a fighting words rationale to be facially overbroad. Indeed, it could be argued that overbreadth has eclipsed the fighting words doctrine. In *Gooding v. Wilson*, 405 U.S. 518 (1972), the Court ignored the abusive language directed by the defendant to police officers and focused instead on the Georgia statute as it has been construed by the state courts. Breach of the peace had been used by the Georgia courts to cover merely offensive language and so swept too broadly. *Houston v. Hill*, 482 U.S. 451 (1987) similarly invalidated an ordinance on overbreadth grounds which made it a crime to "assault, strike, or in any manner, oppose, molest, abuse or interrupt any policeman in the execution of his duty." A unanimous Supreme Court in *Houston v. Hill* labeled the law substantially overbroad on its face. Justice Brennan noted that the ordinance extended to protected speech and was not limited to fighting words.

In *R.A.V. v. City of St. Paul*, 505 U.S. 377 (1992), the Court, per Justice Scalia, delivered a fighting words opinion that four concurring Justices charged constituted a "radical revision" of First Amendment law. In an effort to save a St. Paul hate-speech ordinance, the Minnesota Supreme Court had authoritatively interpreted the ordinance as limited to fighting words as defined by *Chaplinsky*. The United States Supreme Court unanimously reversed but was bitterly divided on the rationale for its result. Justice Scalia, speaking for five Justices, held that the St. Paul ordinance, as interpreted, was facially unconstitutional because it was discriminatory on the basis of speech content and underinclusive. The St. Paul ordinance, by singling out for sanction only fighting words based on race, color, creed, religion or gender, was selective on the basis of content or viewpoint. For example, fighting words expressing hostility on the basis of political affiliation, union membership, or homosexuality were not covered. Justice Scalia said that while we have said some "categories of expression are not within the area of constitutionally protected speech," that did not mean these were "categories of speech entirely invisible to the Constitution."

While fighting words as such might be outside the First Amendment, this did not mean that fighting words could "be made the vehicles for content discrimination unrelated to their distinctively proscribable content." While agreeing that St. Paul had a compelling interest in combating discrimination, the ordinance was not a reasonably necessary means serving that interest. There were content-neutral alternatives available to St. Paul, *e.g.*, eliminate the underinclusiveness by proscribing all fighting words.

Justice White, speaking for the four concurring justices, rejected the Court's extension of First Amendment protections to speech that was admittedly in the category of fighting words, and protested the Court's distortion of the strict scrutiny standard. The consequence of Scalia's reasoning was that even if a compelling interest were shown, an ordinance like the St. Paul ordinance was still invalid since it was not narrowly tailored—not all fighting words were proscribed. For the concurring Justices, this was a distortion of strict scrutiny analysis. The logical consequence of the Scalia approach would be to reduce the sum total of speech in the marketplace since the only way to comply with the *R.A.V.* rationale would be to ban much more speech than heretofore. Scalia's response to this might be that the only speech excluded was fighting words—low-value speech categorically lacking full First Amendment protection.

The four concurring justices in *R.A.V.* argued that the ordinance, even as limited to fighting words, was facially overbroad and invalid. Justice White declared: "Although the ordinance reaches conduct that is unprotected, it also makes criminal expressive conduct that causes only hurt feelings, offense, or resentment, and is protected by the First Amendment. The ordinance is therefore fatally overbroad and invalid on its face." The concurring Justices believed that the familiar ground of substantial overbreadth would have been sufficient to deal with this case without getting into the content-neutral and underinclusiveness issues raised by Scalia. For the concurring Justices, the majority had unnecessarily reached out to attack "political correctness" when the case could have been more appropriately disposed of through traditional overbreadth analysis.

Because of the Court's preoccupation with overbreadth in fighting words cases, there has been little doctrinal development regarding what expression will constitute fighting words. While *Chaplinsky* had focused on an objective test, the cases applying the doctrine have often focused on the factual circumstances in which the expression occurs. Instead of asking whether the words used would cause an average addressee to fight, the courts have looked at whether the language was used under circumstances that would be considered personally provocative, creating an actual threat of imminent disorder. For example, in *Lewis v. New Orleans*, 415 U.S. 130 (1974) (*Lewis II*), Justice Powell, concurring, observed that it would be highly improbable that the words used would provoke a physical encounter "between the middle aged woman who spoke them and the police officer in whose presence they were uttered." Similarly, in *Cohen v. California*, 403 U.S. 15 (1971), it was deemed unlikely that any individual actually present would have been provoked to violence by the defendant's wearing the words "Fuck the Draft" on his jacket in the courthouse.

The more the courts focus on the actual factual content to discern the potential for violence, the more fighting words approximates the clear and present danger doctrine. The use of the overbreadth doctrine in fighting words cases creates increasing question as to the continued viability of the fighting words doctrine. In *R.A.V.*, Justice Scalia insists that fighting words cannot be proscribed if the law that bans them is content-based and underinclusive. Whether the cumulative effect of all these developments will finally bury the fighting words doctrine remains to be seen.

## B.  HOSTILE AUDIENCES

A speaker who uses fighting words is subject to restraint. The speaker who intentionally incites his supporters to imminent illegal conduct can be suppressed. But what if the danger from inflammatory speech arises not from those in sympathy with the speaker but from the reaction of a hostile crowd? This is the problem of the hostile audience or the heckler's veto. If a breach of the peace is threatened, who should the police arrest—the speaker or the crowd?

In *Terminiello v. City of Chicago*, 337 U.S. 1 (1949), a demagogue gave a virulent racist speech; outside the auditorium where he was speaking, a hostile crowd became agitated and violent. The police arrested the speaker, Terminiello, for disorderly conduct. The Supreme Court, 5–4, reversed the conviction because the statute under which Terminiello was convicted was interpreted, in charging the jury, to include speech which "stirs the public to anger, invites dispute [or] brings about a condition of unrest." A conviction resting on this ground was defective since freedom of speech is protected "unless shown likely to produce a clear and present danger of a serious substantive evil that rises far above public inconvenience, annoyance or unrest." In explaining this principle, Justice Douglas declared: "[A] function of free speech under our system of government is to invite dispute. It may indeed best serve its high purpose when it induces a condition of unrest, creates dissatisfaction with conditions as they are, or even stirs people to anger." *Terminiello* would suggest that there is no heckler's veto and that the danger of disorder arising from hostile crowd reaction does not justify suppressing the speaker. By analogy, in the school desegregation context, the violent response of those opposed to the assertion of the constitutional right to desegregated education will not justify denial of that right. *Cooper v. Aaron*, 358 U.S. 1 (1958). In the free speech context, only the use of fighting words or incitement to a clear and present danger should justify moving against the speaker.

Two years after *Terminiello*, the principle that the hostility of the citizenry does not justify the suspension of constitutional rights appeared to be placed in jeopardy in *Feiner v. New York*, 340 U.S. 315 (1951). At an open-air meeting, speaker Irving Feiner lambasted President Truman, the mayor of Syracuse, and the American Legion. The crowd became unruly. The police ordered the speaker to stop. When he refused, they carted him away under a disorderly conduct statute. In affirming Feiner's conviction, Chief Justice Vinson for the majority declared: "We are well aware that the ordinary murmurings and objections of a hostile audience cannot be allowed to silence a speaker, and we are also mindful of the possible danger of giving over-zealous police officials complete discretion to break up otherwise lawful public meetings." But in this case, Feiner had intentionally incited the crowd to riot. For the majority, Feiner had deliberately created a clear and present danger of public disorder. In dissent in *Feiner*, Justice Black, joined by Justice Douglas, took a very different view of the facts leading to Feiner's arrest. There was, in their view, no imminent danger of disorder. Feiner was simply a lawful public speaker refusing to obey an unlawful police command. *Feiner* makes clear that the facts in a hostile audience case are likely to be ambiguous and open to quite divergent interpretations. Logistically, it is usually going to be easier for the police to arrest the speaker than the crowd. To justify the arrest, the police are likely to be impelled to characterize the speaker as agitating the crowd to imminent violence. It becomes essential then for the courts to take a particularly demanding look at the facts.

Does *Feiner* validate the heckler's veto? Subsequent cases suggest that *Feiner* should be read narrowly and that *Terminiello* provides the more authoritative principle for governing hostile audience cases. In *Cohen v. California*, 403 U.S. 15 (1971), Justice Harlan cited *Feiner* for the proposition that the state's police power can be used to "prevent a speaker from intentionally provoking a given group to hostile reaction." In *Gregory v. City of Chicago*, 394 U.S. 111 (1969), the Court rejected a heckler's veto of a civil rights protest march to the Mayor's home led by Dick Gregory. The police ordered the marchers to leave the area when white homeowners threatened violence. The refusal of the marchers to leave led to a disorderly conduct conviction. But the Supreme Court reversed the conviction since the marchers were engaged in lawful political protest. In these circumstances, the conviction could not rest on the refusal to obey a police order to disperse.

In civil rights cases involving mass protest by demonstrators, a critical factor has been whether there is any actual danger of violence created by the protest. Generalized police fears of potential disorder cannot justify breaking up the demonstration. It is the responsibility of the police to handle the crowd. That their lot would be easier without the demonstration cannot be a justification for stopping the demonstration. *Edwards v. South Carolina*, 372 U.S. 229 (1963); *Cox v. Louisiana*, 379 U.S. 559 (1965). Citing *Terminiello* and *Gregory*, the Illinois Supreme Court rejected the efforts of the Village of Skokie, Illinois to prevent the Nazis from marching through their community, displaying the swastika. Even though Skokie had a substantial Jewish population including a large number of Holocaust survivors, the Illinois court concluded: "[I]t has become patent that a hostile audience is not a basis for restraining otherwise legal First Amendment activity." *Village of Skokie v. National Socialist Party*, 373 N.E.2d 21 (Ill.1978). In sum, the cases support the proposition that only fighting words or intentional incitement to imminent violence will justify the suppression of speech, not the reactions of a hostile crowd.

## C.  OFFENSIVE SPEECH

In *Chaplinsky v. New Hampshire*, 315 U.S. 568 (1942), the Court declared that profane and insulting words were of such slight social value as to lie outside the protection of the First Amendment. Such words "by their very utterance inflict injury." Therefore, they can be proscribed regardless of whether or not their use threatens violence or disorder. Dissenting in *Rosenfeld v. New Jersey*, 408 U.S. 901 (1972), Justice Powell characterized this category of expression as offensive speech, which he defined as "the willful use of scurrilous language calculated to offend the sensibilities of an unwilling audience." The focus then of the offensive speech category lies not in the offensiveness of the idea but on the mode of expression.

What is the argument for the view that offensive speech is a category of expression which does not merit First Amendment protection? Offensive speech, it has been urged, is more akin to conduct than to speech. Offensive speech includes epithets and insults that appear to have no central place in the marketplace of ideas. Such offensive speech could be considered a form of intentional infliction of emotional distress or a form of public nuisance. The offending expression may take the form of hate speech directed against discrete groups identifiable on the basis of race, gender, religion, nationality or sexual persuasion. The state interest in protecting these groups is reflected in the civil rights and the equal protection decisions of the courts.

Nevertheless, the courts have rejected the argument that offensive speech lacks constitutional protection or that speech which causes hurt feelings, anger or resentment can be proscribed consistent with the First Amendment. The classic statement of this view is found in Justice Harlan's opinion for the Court in *Cohen v. California*, 403 U.S. 15 (1971). A young man who wore a jacket bearing the words, "Fuck the Draft" while in a courthouse was convicted for disturbing the peace. In overturning his conviction, Justice Harlan assumed that the basis for the conviction was the offensiveness of the words on Cohen's jacket and not any conduct on his part. He questioned whether it was appropriate for the state to punish such communication absent any proof of incitement to illegal conduct. The message did not fall into any of the established categories of low value speech such as fighting words or obscenity. Neither did a captive audience rationale apply. If Cohen's jacket upset a spectator in this public place, it was easy enough for the spectator to look away. The real issue for Justice Harlan in *Cohen*, then, was whether the states "acting as guardians of public morality, may properly remove this offensive word from the public vocabulary." His answer was that the states did not have such authority consistent with the First Amendment.

Harlan emphasized the value of freedom of speech in developing a more capable citizenry and recognizing the premise of individual dignity on which our system rests. These values are served even when speech is tumultuous and offensive: "That the air may at times seem filled with verbal cacophony is, in this sense, not a sign of weakness but of strength." Particularizing this constitutional policy perspective, Justice Harlan warned that the state's concern with offensive language is "inherently boundless." Offensive speech was a camel that if left to its own devices would soon take over the tent. As he stated so memorably, "one man's vulgarity is another's lyric."

Harlan was concerned with the excessive preoccupation with cognitive values underlying the effort to suppress offensive speech. Words are selected not only for their cognitive force but for their emotional appeal: "We cannot sanction the view that the

Constitution, while solicitous of the cognitive content of individual speech, has little or no regard for that emotive function which, practically speaking, may often be the more important element of the overall message sought to be communicated." "Fuck the Draft" conveys a different message than "The Draft is Unfair" or "Resist the Draft." Finally, Justice Harlan warned that prohibiting a particular manner of speech comes perilously close to restricting the underlying idea: "[W]e cannot indulge the facile assumption that one can forbid particular words without also running a substantial risk of suppressing ideas in the process. Indeed, governments might soon seize upon the censorship of particular words as a convenient guise for banning the expression of unpopular views."

The rejection in *Cohen* of relegating offensive speech to a category of low value speech has endured. *Erznoznik v. Jacksonville*, 422 U.S. 205 (1975) struck down an ordinance prohibiting drive-in movie theaters from showing films containing nudity visible from a public street. Justice Powell, for the Court, stated: "Much that we encounter offends aesthetic, if not our political and moral, sensibilities. Nevertheless, the Constitution does not permit the government to decide which types of otherwise protected speech are sufficiently offensive to require protection for the unwilling listener or viewer." Overbreadth cases such as *Gooding v. Wilson*, 405 U.S. 518 (1972) and *Lewis v. New Orleans*, 415 U.S. 130 (1974) similarly relied on *Cohen* for the principle that the state cannot proscribe speech merely because it is vulgar and offensive. More recently, the concurring Justices in *R.A.V. v. St. Paul*, 505 U.S. 377 (1992) cited *Cohen* in grounding their determination that the hate law was over-broad on the following principle: "The mere fact that expressive activity causes hurt feelings, offense, or resentment does not render the expression unprotected." (White, J., concurring).

In short, at this time, offensive speech is fully protected speech. While there are categories of un-protected expression, the Supreme Court has been quite insistent that offensive speech is not one of them. Whether the various contemporary move-ments to enact specific laws directed at hate speech or female pornography or indecency will create ex-ceptions to this principle remains to be seen. See Ch. VIII.

## D.  TRUE THREATS

In *R.A.V.*, the Court held a St. Paul hate-speech ordinance facially unconstitutional because it dis-criminated between classes of fighting words based on speech content and was underinclusive. The city failed to satisfy strict scrutiny review because there were content-neutral alternatives available. While R.A.V. involved application of the law to cross burn-ing, the Court's facial disposition of the case avoid-ed the factual context. Still, most lower courts re-viewing statutes directed against cross burning have held them unconstitutional.

It was not very surprising then when the Virginia Supreme Court held its state law, which made it unlawful to burn a cross "with the intent of intimidating any person or group of persons," was facially unconstitutional. The state court reasoned that the Virginia cross burning statute was analytically indistinguishable from the ordinance which was held unconstitutional in *R.A.V.* since it selectively discriminated only against cross burning because of its distinctive message. The Virginia court also held that a provision of law making the burning of the cross prima facie evidence of an intent to intimidate unconstitutionally overbroad because of the enhanced probability of prosecution chills protected speech. In *Virginia v. Black*, 538 U.S. 343 (2003), the Court concluded "that while a State, consistent with the First Amendment, may ban cross burning carried out with an intent to intimidate, the provision in the Virginia statute treating any cross burning as prima facie evidence of intent to intimidate renders the statute unconstitutional in its current form." Justice O'Connor, for the Court, after reviewing the history of the KKK, began from the premise that "while a burning cross does not inevitably convey a message of intimidation, often the cross burner intends that the recipients of the message fear for their lives. And when a cross burning is used to intimidate, few if any messages are more powerful."

Justice O'Connor observed that, even when symbolic or expressive speech is involved, offensive or disagreeable speech is protected. Nevertheless, the government "may regulate categories of expression consistent with the Constitution." One such category is the "true threat," which she defined as encompassing "those statements where the speaker means to communicate a serious expression of an intent to commit an act of unlawful violence to a particular individual or group of individuals ... Intimidation in the constitutionally proscribable sense of the word is a type of true threat ...." Quoting *R.A.V.*, Justice O'Connor observed that "a prohibition on true threats 'protect[s] individuals from the fear of violence' and 'from the disruption that fear engenders,' in addition to protecting people 'from the possibility that the threatened violence will occur.'"

Some cross burnings fit within the definition of true threats. But didn't the Virginia law, by proscribing only cross burnings, discriminate on a content-basis against a particular class of true threats? Justice O'Connor, however, noted that *R.A.V* indicated that the First Amendment permits content discrimination "based on the very reasons why the particular class of speech at issue ... is proscribable." Virginia can proscribe cross burnings done with the intent to intimidate, said Justice O'Connor, "because burning a cross is a particularly virulent form of intimidation." There is a long and persuasive history that indicates cross burning can indicate impending violence. Virginia can single out forms of intimidation "most likely to inspire fear of bodily harm."

Speaking for a plurality, Justice O'Connor next argued that the prima facie evidence provision of the Virginia law was facially invalid. As the law was interpreted and applied, "the provision chills constitutionally protected political speech because of the possibility that a State will prosecute—and potentially convict—somebody engaging only in lawful political speech at the core of what the First Amendment is designed to protect." Cross burning may be intended to intimidate, but it may not. It may be intended as a statement of ideology or serve some other purpose, e.g., to express anger. The Virginia law made no effort to distinguish among the various types of cross burnings; contextual factors were ignored. "The First Amendment does not permit such a shortcut; [as interpreted, the provision] is unconstitutional on its face."

Justice Scalia, joined by Justice Thomas, dissented from that part of Justice O'Connor's opinion facially invalidating the prima facie evidence provision. While Justice Scalia argued that the plurality was holding the provision unconstitutionally overbroad, Justice O'Connor did not expressly use the overbreadth analysis (See Ch. II, C). It would be wrong, Justice Scalia argued, to hold a law overbroad just because of the possibility that individuals who engage in protected speech will be subject to arrest and prosecution; overbreadth turns on whether such persons can be convicted under the law. The plurality failed to establish that the Virginia law is substantially overbroad.

Justice Souter, joined by Justices Kennedy and Ginsburg, would have held the Virginia ban on cross burning to be an unconstitutional content–based law under *R.A.V.* They reasoned that the "virulence exception" from *R.A.V.* was inappropriate since the expressive act of cross-burning is generally associated with a particular message of white Protestant supremacy. Further, the prima facie evidence provisions impedes any effort to determine in particular cases whether there is an effort to suppress ideas; it skews jury deliberations towards convictions where evidence of intent to intimidate is weak and arguably consistent with an ideological reason for burning. Since the *R.A.V.* exception does not avoid the danger of suppressing particular views or ideas and the statute could not survive strict scrutiny, the statute, as a whole, violates the First Amendment.

Justice Thomas, dissenting, rejected imputing an expressive component to cross burning—"whatever expressive value cross burning has, the legislature simply wrote it out by banning only intimidating conduct undertaken by particular means." He concluded that "this statute prohibits only conduct, not expression." Even if the statute implicated the First Amendment, alleging an "inference of intent to intimidate" from cross burning presented no constitutional problem; it was not an irrebuttable presumption. "Considering the horrific effect cross burning has on its victims, it is also reasonable to presume intent to intimidate from the act itself."

Whether *Virginia v. Black* applies only to cross burnings or extends to other contexts, e.g., swastikas, the "Nuremburg" cases involving Internet postings allegedly threatening abortion providers, will have to be determined. Whether the ideological and intimidating aspects of cross burning can be meaningfully distinguished in applying the laws is uncertain. It is clear, however, that "true threats" now constitute a category of low value speech subject to regulation.

# CHAPTER V

# OBSCENITY AND INDECENCY

## A. OBSCENITY

In the first half of the twentieth century, a number of famous books such as Theodore Dreiser's *An American Tragedy*, D.H. Lawrence's *Lady Chatterly's Lover* and Henry Miller's *Tropic of Cancer* all fell afoul of the obscenity laws. In determining whether a work was obscene, the American courts followed the English case of *Regina v. Hicklin*, (1868) L.R. 3 Q.B. 360. The *Hicklin* test made the measuring mark of obscenity the effect of isolated excerpts within a work on particularly susceptible persons in the community. Such a test held the art and literature of the community hostage to its most susceptible and troubled members. Particular passages of an otherwise valuable work might condemn the whole. How was this possible in a society governed by the First Amendment? In *Roth v. United States*, 354 U.S. 476 (1957), the Supreme Court provided an answer in a controversial and influential opinion authored by Justice Brennan.

Justice Brennan began from a highly speech-protective premise: "All ideas having even the slightest redeeming social importance—unorthodox ideas, controversial ideas, even ideas hateful to the prevailing climate of opinion—have the full protection of the [First Amendment] guaranties, unless excludable because they encroach upon the limited area of more important interests." But obscenity did not fall within that principle since, "implicit in the history of the First Amendment is the rejection of obscenity as utterly without redeeming social importance." The result followed automatically: "We hold that obscenity is not within the area of constitutionally protected speech or press." Thus, neither the clear and present doctrine nor any other First Amendment test applies to speech determined to be obscene. The critical question thus became—what is obscenity?

In defining obscenity, Brennan limited the concept to appeals to the prurient interest in sex. He provided a new definition of obscenity to replace the *Hicklin* standard: "whether to the average person, applying contemporary community standards, the dominant theme of the material taken as a whole appeals to prurient interest." If the material meets this standard, arguably it lacks the "social importance" that would give the material First Amendment protection. Alternatively, some have argued that even if the material was prurient and otherwise satisfied the test, it still might be redeemed; it would be protected under the First Amendment if it were shown to have some social importance.

What does prurience mean? There was no occasion in *Roth* to consider the question whether the materials sold were obscene since the issue was the First Amendment validity of the federal statute barring the mailing of obscene material used in convicting Roth. The Model Penal Code defines material as prurient if it reflects "a shameful or morbid interest, in nudity, sex or excretion, and if in addition it goes substantially beyond customary limits of candor in describing or representing such matters." Arguably this definition of prurience limits obscenity to "hard core" pornography. In *Jacobellis v. Ohio*, 378 U.S. 184 (1964), Justice Stewart, concurring, tried to define hard-core pornography but gave it up, saying: "I know it when I see it." While this comment was much scoffed at, it does focus on the ambiguity of any obscenity definition, including "hard-core" pornography. But *Roth* rejected a vagueness challenge to the obscenity law.

An important element of the *Roth* test is its clear rejection of the *Hicklin* test that the appropriate measuring rod of obscenity is the most susceptible person. Brennan reshaped the test so that the measure was the average person. The result was that more material fell on the protected side of the line rather than on the obscene side of the line. But what of the harm that can be done to children who in terms of their development are emotionally and mentally immature? What of the harm that materials that would not appeal to the average person pose for the immature or disturbed adult? Chief Justice Warren, concurring in the result in *Roth*, recognized the problem: "It is manifest that the same object may have a different impact, varying according to the part of the community it reached." *Ginsberg v. New York*, 390 U.S. 629 (1968) embraced the concept of variable obscenity, which focuses on the target audience of the material and its peculiar susceptibility. *Ginsberg* upheld a New York law prohibiting distribution to minors of materials deemed to be obscene to minors. This introduced into obscenity law the phenomenon that the same material which would be non-obscene to the average adult could be obscene if marketed to high school students. See *Mishkin v. New York*, 383 U.S. 502 (1966) [materials targeted at sado-masochistic groups held to be obscene].

Chief Justice Warren's concurrence in *Roth* also recognized that in an obscenity prosecution it is a person, not the book, that is on trial. The conduct of the obscenity defendant, he reasoned, should be the focus of concern. This perspective generated another gloss on the emerging obscenity law. Suppose material was clearly not obscene but the defendant marketed the material in a salacious and pandering manner? *Ginzburg v. United States*, 383 U.S. 463 (1966) held that pandering—commercial exploitation where the "leer of the sensualist" is manifest— could render otherwise non-obscene material obscene. In *Ginzburg*, the Court relied heavily on the fact that Ginzburg tried to mail his publications from Intercourse and Blueball, Pennsylvania and ultimately mailed them from Middlesex, New Jersey. Similarly, the advertising of the materials at issue stressed their sexual candor.

The critical element in *Roth* is its premise that obscenity lacks any social importance and thus is unprotected under the First Amendment; government justification does not have to meet any heightened standard of judicial review. Is it possible to identify a category of material which is completely devoid of social importance? Professor Frederick Schauer has argued that "refusal to treat pornography as speech is grounded in the assumption that the prototypical pornographic item on closer analysis shares more of the characteristics of sexual activity than of the communicative process." Schauer, *Speech and "Speech"—Obscenity and "Obscenity": An Exercise in the Interpretation of Constitutional Language*, 67 Geo. L.J. 899 (1979). From this perspective, pornography is essentially noncognitive; it is a form of sexual experience and not part of the communication of ideas. Some would question whether it is so clear that pornography lacks a cognitive component. For example, feminist scholars contend that female pornography with its portrayal of woman as object stands for a degrading idea—the subordination of women. But even if one accepts Professor Schauer's premise that pornography is non-cognitive speech, the question remains whether the First Amendment should be limited solely to protection of ideas. If one accepts the liberty model of speech, it can be argued that even obscene material can aid in self-awareness and self-development.

In any case, the exclusion of "obscenity" from First Amendment protection makes it essential that the courts identify a test of obscenity that is sufficiently clear and narrow that it does not sweep in protected speech. Defining obscenity has become akin to squaring the circle. In the years following *Roth*, the Court struggled to more clearly define the boundaries of obscenity. In *A Book Named "John Cleland's Memoirs of a Woman of Pleasure" v. Attorney General*, 383 U.S. 413 (1966), also known as the *Fanny Hill* case, Justice Brennan, for a plurality of the Court, significantly revised the *Roth* test. Three elements now had to be satisfied to characterize a work as obscene: "(a) the dominant theme of the material taken as a whole appeals to a prurient interest in sex; (b) the material is patently offensive because it affronts contemporary community standards relating to the description or representation of sexual matters; and (c) the material is utterly without redeeming social value."

The patent offensiveness element suggests that even if material appeals to the prurient interest, it still is not obscene unless it goes substantially beyond customary levels of community tolerance. Patently offensive material constitutes an affront to contemporary community standards of decency. *Manual Enterprises, Inc. v. Day*, 370 U.S. 478 (1962). Unfortunately, *Memoirs* did not tell us what community was relevant. Was it the national community? *Jacobellis* said it was. On the other hand, an obscenity prosecution takes place in the local community where the harm occurred; shouldn't the standard of that community apply? It might also be asked—is there a national community?

But even if material is prurient and patently offensive, *Memoirs* indicates that it is still "redeemed" if it is not "utterly without redeeming

social value." Was this phrase co-extensive with
the "without redeeming social importance" concept of *Roth*? Could a book be saved by the inclusion of a quote from Aristotle amidst a collection
of pornographic pictures? For some persons, sexual
stimulation itself gives a book value. In *Miller v.
California*, 413 U.S. 15 (1973), Chief Justice Burger questioned whether the "utterly without redeeming social value" element had any meaning at
all and argued that it was essentially unprovable.
It is clear that the three-part *Memoirs* test does
protect more material than would be protected under *Roth*. But the *Memoirs* test represented the
views of only three Justices. And, in the years
following *Memoirs*, no test for obscenity was able
to capture a majority of the Court.

Beginning with *Redrup v. New York*, 386 U.S. 767
(1967), the Court began issuing *per curiam* rever-
sals of convictions indicating that at least five members of the Court, using different tests, did not
deem the material obscene and therefore, unprotected. Thirty-one cases followed the *Redrup* approach. As a consequence, the lower courts were
deprived of any guidance at all with respect to an
authoritative definition of obscenity. In 1973, the
Court finally tired of this confusion. In *Miller v.
California*, 413 U.S. 15 (1973), for the first time
since *Roth*, a majority of justices forged a common
definition of obscenity: "(a) whether 'the average
person, applying contemporary community standards' would find that the work, taken as a whole,
appeals to the prurient interest; (b) whether the

work depicts or describes, in a patently offensive way, sexual conduct specifically defined by the applicable state law; and (c) whether the work, taken as a whole, lacks serious literary, artistic, political, or scientific value."

The *Miller* test re-affirms the pruriency and patent offensiveness elements of *Roth* and its progeny. One of the novel features of *Miller* was that it stressed specificity in order to limit obscenity to hard-core pornography. Applicable state laws were required to specifically describe what would constitute patently offensive conduct. *Miller* defined such conduct to include "patently offensive representations or descriptions of ultimate sexual acts, normal or perverted, actual or simulated" and "patently offensive representations or descriptions of masturbation, excretory functions, and lewd exhibitions of the genitals."

This demand for specificity did not necessarily mean new legislation had to be enacted or that the reach of obscenity law was markedly limited. Courts in fact provided narrowing constructions of existing statutes by simply reading them to embody the *Miller* standards. *Ward v. Illinois*, 431 U.S. 767 (1977). The fact that an obscenity statute is overbroad does not necessarily render it unconstitutional if the overbreadth is curable. Thus a state statute which defined pruriency to include lust was held unconstitutional "only insofar as the word 'lust' is understood as reaching protected materials." *Brockett v. Spokane Arcades, Inc.*, 472 U.S. 491 (1985). Also, the Court has reaffirmed the principal that non-obscene materials can be made obscene by a pandering mode of distribution. *Splawn v. California*, 431 U.S. 595 (1977). In short, *Ginzburg* survived *Miller*. Similarly, the variable obscenity standard fashioned in *Ginsberg v. New York*, 390 U.S. 629 (1968) where obscenity is defined by its target audience has been reaffirmed. *Pinkus v. United States*, 436 U.S. 293 (1978).

One of the objectives of *Miller* was to limit the number of obscenity cases coming to the Court. During the reign of the national contemporary community standard doctrine of *Jacobellis v. Ohio*, 378 U.S. 184 (1964), the Court had to review the obscenity cases on an ad hoc basis since the issue of obscenity was a question of constitutional fact. *Miller* repudiated *Jacobellis* and ruled that contemporary community standards should be evaluated on the local level at least for the first two elements of the *Miller* test—pruriency and patent offensiveness. It followed that the local jury could be instructed to apply "contemporary community standards" without any further guidance. No expert testimony would be needed in order to make a finding of obscenity with respect to these two elements since it depended on local community reactions. *Paris Adult Theatre I v. Slaton*, 413 U.S. 49 (1973). In the case of a federal prosecution, the prevailing community standard becomes the area from which the jurors are drawn. *Hamling v. United States*, 418 U.S. 87 (1974). It should be noted also that children are not considered part of the community for determining contemporary community standard but sensitive persons are included. *Pinkus v. United States*, 436 U.S. 293 (1978). The specter of the same material being obscene in one locale, and protected speech in another jurisdiction, is obvious. But the *Miller* approach does not preclude independent appellate review of a jury determination of obscenity. In *Jenkins v. Georgia*, 418 U.S. 153 (1974), the Supreme Court reversed the conviction of a movie theater owner for showing the film, *Carnal Knowledge*. The Court held that the First Amendment would not allow the materials to be labeled obscene unless they "depict or describe patently offensive 'hard-core' sexual conduct."

The Age of Technology has raised a novel issue in this area: Can community standards be applied to the Internet? In *Ashcroft v. American Civil Liberties Union*, 535 U.S. 564 (2002), the question presented was: does the use by the Child Online Protection Act (COPA) of "community standards" to designate content that is harmful to minors violate the First Amendment? The Court of Appeals had held that the Supreme Court's community standards case law did not apply to the Internet and the Web because Web publishers could not control the geographic reach of those who received their communications. Justice Thomas, speaking for a majority of the Court, rejected the view that community standards could not be applied to the Internet. The Court stated its "quite limited" holding as follows: COPA's reliance on community standards did not by itself make the law "substantially overbroad" under the First Amendment. There was, however, no majority opinion on whether, when juries were asked to apply a community standards to the pruriency and patent offensiveness aspects of the *Miller* test, national or local community standards would apply. Only Justice Scalia and Chief Justice Rehnquist joined Justice Thomas in his view that community standards did not have to be "defined by reference to a precise geographic area." If juries were not instructed about "geographic specification" concerning community standards, Thomas contended, the result would be that jurors would draw on their personal knowledge of the community or area from which they came. Justice O'Connor, concurring, declared that under *Jenkins* jurors could apply a number of standards including a national one. Justice Stevens, in dissent, insisted that community standards should not be applied to the Internet. He warned that what was offensive in a "Puritan village" would under COPA become a crime if posted on the World Wide Web.

A dramatic change in *Miller* from the *Roth–Memoirs* test was the Court's repudiation of the "utterly without social value" test. Under *Miller*, even if a work has some social value it may still be labeled unprotected obscenity. How does this square with the basic principle of *Roth* that obscenity enjoys no First Amendment protection because it lacks any redeeming social importance? The answer may be that it is only "serious literary, artistic, political or scientific" values that is redemptive; it is only serious value of this kind which gives the work redeeming social importance. In short, the domain of the material that could be redeemed was considerably reduced. Unfortunately, the specificity sought by the Court in its *Miller* test was somewhat at cross purposes with the inherently subjective quality of making an assessment about "serious" value. The student should also note that the serious value element of the *Miller* test is an objective standard, *i.e.*, whether a reasonable person would find the work taken as a whole to have such serious value. *Pope v. Illinois*, 481 U.S. 497 (1987). Critics of this "objective" standard question whether it is meaningful to talk about an objective standard of artistic or literary value.

In the evolution of obscenity law in the Supreme Court, a problem that merits attention is the question of the relationship between the Court's obscenity doctrine and the privacy interests of the individual. In *Stanley v. Georgia*, 394 U.S. 557 (1969), the Court held, per Justice Marshall, that an individual could not be criminally punished for the private possession of obscene material consistent with the right of privacy: "If the First Amendment means anything, it means that a State has no business telling a man, sitting alone in his own house, what books he may read or what films he may watch." But in *Paris Adult Theatre I v. Slaton*, 413 U.S. 49 (1973), the Court made it clear that the operative words in *Stanley* were "in his own house." The constitutional protection provided the privacy interest does not extend to the showing of two "adult" movies in a commercial establishment even to consenting adults. As Chief Justice Burger stated: "The idea of a 'privacy' right and a place of public accommodation are, in this context, mutually exclusive." Commercialized obscenity implicates the public interest in the "quality of life and the total community environment, the tone of commerce in the great city centers, and, possibly, the public safety itself." No right of privacy prevents the state from reaching the suppliers of obscenity, *United States v. Reidel*, 402 U.S. 351 (1971) [conviction for mailing obscene materials upheld], or from purchasing obscene materials, *United States v. Twelve 200–Foot Reels*, 413 U.S. 123 (1973) [conviction for importing obscene materials for personal use upheld].

Are *Miller* and *Paris Adult Theatre I* an improvement over *Roth* and its progeny? Justice Brennan wrote a thoughtful dissent in *Miller* and *Paris Adult Theatre I* which provided his answer to that question. His *Paris* dissent was basically a chronicle of the objectives which had driven the *Roth-Memoirs* definitions and the conflicts within the Court which prevented consensus. Concepts such as pruriency, patent offensiveness, serious value, etc., Brennan argued, vary with the person making the judgement. They cannot provide adequate standards for distinguishing between protected and unprotected speech and cannot provide the essential guidelines for those who must administer obscenity law. Brennan recognized that *Roth* had not worked and he believed that *Miller* would not work either. What then was the proper approach? Brennan responded that he would retain a concept of obscenity only for special problems, such as protection of children or a

captive adult audience. Whatever the merits of
Brennan's dissent, the Supreme Court succeeded in
its *Miller* goal of disengaging itself from reviewing
the finding of obscenity on a case by case basis.
Defining the obscene has been largely relegated to
the lower courts.

## B.  CHILD PORNOGRAPHY

Can a state proscribe the knowing distribution of
material which portrays minors in a sexually explicit but non-obscene manner? Since such a portrayal
does not violate the *Miller* test, one might assume
that it would constitute protected expression under
the First Amendment. But where child pornography
is concerned, *Miller* does not tell the whole story. In
*New York v. Ferber*, 458 U.S. 747 (1982), the Court
unanimously upheld New York's child pornography
law and thereby fashioned a new category of unprotected speech. Justice White for the Court in *Ferber*
reasoned that the states are entitled to greater
leeway in regulating materials that encourage sexual exploitation and abuse of children. Specifically,
"[a] trier of fact need not find that the material
appeals to the prurient interest of the average person; it is not required that sexual conduct portrayed
be done so in a patently offensive manner; and the
material at issue need not be considered as a
whole."

What is the rationale for this departure from
*Miller* for visual materials that constitute child pornography? The *Ferber* Court did not stress the low

value of the speech so much as the severe harm that flowed from child abuse and the need to secure effective state regulatory power over it. Justice White identified five factors justifying the departure from *Miller*. First: "It is evident beyond the need for elaboration that a State's interest in 'safeguarding the physical and psychological well-being of a minor' is compelling." Second: "The distribution of photographs and films depicting sexual activity by juveniles is intrinsically related to the sexual abuse of children." Third: "The advertising and selling of child pornography provide an economic motive for and are thus an integral part of the production of such materials, an activity illegal throughout the Nation." Fourth: "The value of permitting live performances and photographic reproductions of children engaged in lewd sexual conduct is exceedingly modest, if not *de minimis*." Fifth: "Recognizing and classifying child pornography as a category of material outside the protection of the First Amendment is not incompatible with our earlier decisions." But Ferber had argued that the New York law was overbroad in that it would extend to material with serious, literary, artistic or scientific value. Justice White responded by stressing that the requirement for facial invalidity is "substantial overbreadth." While he acknowledged that the law might yield some arguably impermissible applications, this was only a tiny fraction of the material covered: "We consider this the paradigmatic case of a state statute whose legitimate reach dwarfs its arguably impermissible applications."

State regulation of child pornography came before the Court again in *Osborne v. Ohio*, 495 U.S. 103 (1990). The defendant had been convicted for violating a statute prohibiting the possession or viewing of any material or performance showing a minor, not one's child, in a state of nudity. The defendant was convicted on the basis of four photographs of a nude male adolescent in sexually explicit poses. Hadn't *Stanley v. Georgia*, 394 U.S. 557 (1969) held that a person could not be convicted for possessing obscene materials in his own home? Justice White's answer was "Yes" but this case involved child pornography. The interests of the state underlying child pornography laws far exceeds the interests of the state in proscribing the possession of obscene materials. The state here was not asserting a paternalistic interest in regulating an individual's thoughts but an interest in protecting the victims of child pornography. Wasn't the Ohio statute overbroad in that it proscribed nudity, which *Erznoznik* and other cases had indicated was protected expression? In this instance, the Ohio Supreme Court had supplied a narrowing savings construction limiting the statute to a prohibition on nudity "where such nudity constitutes a lewd exhibition or involves a graphic focus on the genitals." Even though the defendant had fair warning that his conduct was criminal under the statute, it was unclear whether the jury had been properly instructed and so the conviction was reversed and remanded.

The advent of the Internet and the World-wide Web has produced virtual child pornography, *i.e.,* "computer imaging" which gives the impression that children and minors are being depicted even though they are not. In *Ashcroft v. Free Speech Coalition*, 535 U.S. 234 (2002), the Court, per Justice Kennedy, held that the Child Pornography Prevention Act (CPPA) extending the federal ban on child pornography to virtual child pornography was substantially overbroad and violated freedom of speech. The issue was whether the CPPA violated the First Amendment "where it proscribes a significant universe of speech that is neither obscene under *Miller* nor child pornography under *Ferber*." The reason that virtual child pornography did not fall under *Ferber* was that actual children were not involved and, therefore, the state's interest in protecting children was not involved either. *Ferber* had as its focus the production of the work rather than the content of the work. This was because production was "intrinsically related" to the sexual abuse of children: "*Ferber's* judgment about child pornography was based upon how it was made, not on what it communicated."

The government contended that virtual child pornography served to arouse pedophiles and stimulated them to engage in illegal activity: "But the mere tendency of speech to encourage unlawful acts is not a sufficient reason for banning it." The government also argued that virtual pornography is indistinguishable from child pornography. But protected speech cannot be banned as a way to suppress unprotected speech. The overbreadth doctrine forbids government from banning unprotected speech if substantial protected speech is thereby forbidden or chilled. Finally, a provision of the CPPA that bans sexually explicit images that are advertised or distributed in a way that gives the impression that minors are engaged in sexually explicit conduct is also overbroad and an infringement on freedom of speech. The pandering rationale of *Ginzburg* does not save this provision since it bans substantial speech falling outside of that rationale. Moreover, the state provision does not require that "the context be part of an effort at 'commercial exploitation.'"

In summary, like obscenity, child pornography is a category of unprotected speech. However, the creation of ambiguous categories of unprotected expression with respect to material dealing with sex does appear to remove one of the principal justifications for the development of a concept of unprotected obscenity in First Amendment law in the first place. Obscenity was supposed to be a benchmark. Anything not obscene in the sexually-oriented materials field was protected. This is no longer the case. On the other hand, recognizing pornography as a category of unprotected expression can be justified on the ground that the harm of child abuse is what the state is seeking to suppress. Arguably this is an example of legislating because of the secondary effects of the speech. Speech is only incidentally burdened. The state is allowed to regulate because of its identified interests in protecting children. *Ashcroft v. Free Speech Coalition* indicated, the governmental interest in protecting children is critical to the unprotected status of child pornography.

After the Supreme Court decision in *Ashcroft v. Free Speech Coalition*, 535 U.S. 234 (2002), Congress enacted a new law which criminalized the pandering or solicitation of child pornography in specified circumstances. In *United States v. Williams*, 128 S.Ct. 1830 (2008) the Court, per Justice Scalia, upheld the law, 7–2. Justice Scalia described the law as prohibiting "offers to provide and requests to obtain child pornography." Instead, the focus of this law, unlike its predecessors, is not on the "underlying material" but on the "collateral speech" that brings such material into the marketing and distribution of child pornography. The law was directed at anyone who "advertises, promotes, presents or distributes" child pornography. In distinguishing *Free Speech Coalition,* Scalia identified a number of considerations. First, the law had a *scienter* requirement. Second, the law was concerned with transactions—and commercial transactions at that—but it was not limited to those. A person could distribute child pornography without expecting money in return. Third, the statements or actions of the person charged with pandering child pornography must show that he "objectively believe[s] that the material [at issue] is child pornography." Fourth, the law provides that the defendant intend that his listener really believes that the material in question is child pornography. It is irrelevant that a reasonable person might think otherwise. Fifth, the statute's definition of proscribed "sexually explicit conduct" is very similar to the definition of "sexual conduct" which was upheld against an overbreadth challenge in *New York v. Ferber*, 458 U.S. 747 (1982). Unlike the situation in *Free Speech Coalition,* the new law demands that there be a "visual depiction of an actual minor." Even though the sexual intercourse may be simulated, "it must involve actual children (unless it is obscene)." The key is that a reasonable viewer must believe that the actors are really engaging in sexually explicit conduct on camera.

The court next asked this question: Did the law criminalize a "substantial amount of protected activity?" The Court's answer was in its holding: "We hold that offers to provide or requests to obtain child pornography are categorically excluded from the First Amendment." Justice Scalia then responded to the contention in Justice Breyer's dissent that Congress had made an "end run around" the protection extended to virtual child pornography in *Free Speech Coalition* "by prohibiting proposals to transact in such images rather than prohibiting the images themselves." Justice Scalia rejected this contention. The law would only be invoked when "the speaker believes or intends the listener to believe that the subject of the proposed transaction depicts *real* children."

Finally, the Eleventh Circuit below had ruled that the vagueness doctrine constituted an alternative ground on which to base the facial invalidity of the law at issue in *Williams*. But the Court ruled that the Eleventh Circuit was in error on this point. The fact that close cases may result from a law's application is not a basis for applying the vagueness doctrine: "What renders a statute vague is not the possibility that it will sometimes be difficult to determine whether the incriminating fact it establishes has been proved; but rather the indeterminancy of precisely what that fact is." But there is no indeterminancy problem with this law. Under the law, the defendant must believe, or communicate to another the belief, that the "material [involved] is child pornography" and his statement must communicate that belief.

## C. INDECENT SPEECH

*Ferber* exploded the doctrinal boundaries established in *Miller*. The Court recognized a new category of non-obscene sexually explicit speech which is not protected by the First Amendment. The bright line between unprotected obscenity and protected speech with a sexual content had been breached. In truth, there had been earlier indications that protected expression could, in some circumstances, be regulated because of its indecent content. But *Ferber's* recognition of a category of indecent expression which could be regulated marked the first time that a majority of justices relegated a category of nonobscene indecent speech to a clearly unprotected status.

In *Young v. American Mini Theatres, Inc.*, 427 U.S. 50 (1976), the Court upheld a Detroit Anti–Skid Row ordinance prohibiting "adult" places of entertainment from being located in proximity to each other. The ordinance defined such "adult" places as those "presenting material distinguished or characterized by an emphasis on matter depicting, describing, or relating to, 'specified sexual activities,' or 'specified anatomical areas.'"

Justice Stevens, writing for a plurality, sounded a familiar theme of First Amendment jurisprudence: "Selective exclusions from a public forum may not be based on content alone, and may not be justified by reference to content alone." But for the plurality, this did not mean that the sexual content of the material could not be used as a basis for the regulation. Two considerations were critical for the Court. First, the use of content in the Detroit zoning ordinance was done "without violating the government's paramount obligation of neutrality in its regulation of protected communication." Simply, the law was not viewpoint-based; it distinguished only on the basis of subject matter. However, subject matter discrimination is usually enough to involve the presumption against content-based regulation. Second, "it is manifest that society's interest in protecting this type of expression is of a wholly different, and lesser, magnitude than the interest in untrammeled political debate. . . ." Justice Stevens reasoned that "few of us would march our sons and daughters off to war to preserve the citizen's right to see 'specified sexual activities' exhibited in the theaters of our choice." The conclusion followed that the state government could classify places of entertainment by the sexual content of the material offered. The regulation was a reasonable means for the city to preserve the quality of its neighborhoods.

*American Mini–Theatres*, however, does not reflect Supreme Court acceptance of a hierarchy of speech with indecent speech relegated to some lower value because of its content. A majority of Justices in fact rejected the plurality's acceptance of content-based regulation. Justice Stewart, speaking for four dissenters, championed the two-tier approach which distinguished between unprotected obscenity and otherwise protected expression: "The fact that the 'offensive' speech here may not address 'important' topics—'ideas of social and political significance,' in the Court's terminology, does not mean that it is less worthy of constitutional protection."

Justice Powell, who provided the crucial fifth vote for saving the ordinance, rejected the plurality's thesis "that nonobscene, erotic materials may be treated differently under First Amendment principles from other forms of *protected* expression." (emphasis added). His concurrence was based on the conclusion that the Detroit ordinance was a *content-neutral* time, place or manner regulation. First Amendment concerns, he asserted, were implicated "only incidentally and to a limited extent." Reasonableness was the appropriate standard of review for such a content-neutral regulation and the limited Detroit zoning ordinance was a reasonable place regulation. Justice Powell stressed that "adult" movies were not being banished from Detroit. Dispersal was all that was required.

When in *City of Renton v. Playtime Theatres, Inc.*, 475 U.S. 41 (1986), the Court next considered a land use regulation controlling the location of "adult" movie theaters, it was Justice Powell's content-neutral time, place and manner approach that prevailed. Chief Justice Rehnquist concluded that the "predominant concerns" of the ordinance "were with the secondary effects of adult theaters, and not with the content of adult films themselves." The Renton, Washington ordinance, which prohibited adult motion picture theaters from locating within 1000 feet of residential property, churches, parks, or schools, was designed to "prevent crime, protect the city's retail trade, maintain property values, and generally [protect] and [preserve] the quality of [the city's] neighborhoods, commercial districts, and the quality of 'urban life,' not to suppress the expression of unpopular views." Apparently the judicial concern that subject-matter discrimination might mask impermissible government viewpoint censorship was not controlling in this context. Perhaps the indecent content of the speech played some part in the Court's approach. The *City of Renton* Court held that the "content-neutral" ordinance served a substantial interest and allowed for reasonable alternative avenues of communication. In proving the harmful secondary effects that would flow absent its regulation, the city of Renton was allowed to rely on any relevant evidence. The city was not required to develop independent evidence of harm.

In *City of Los Angeles v. Alameda Books, Inc.*, 535 U.S. 425 (2002), the Court, per Justice O'Connor, clarified what was necessary to show a substantial government interest under *Renton*. A Los Angeles ordinance forbade the operation of more than one adult business in the same building. The federal court of appeals below had held that the city had failed to show that the prohibition served a substantial governmental interest. That court ruled that the city had failed to make a showing that reasonably linked multiple-use adult businesses and "negative secondary effects." The Supreme Court reversed. Any evidence which demonstrates that the ordinance at issue serves a substantial governmental interest will suffice. Thus, the city could reasonably rely on a study showing that a ban on multiple-use businesses served the substantial government interest in reducing crime even though the study was conducted prior to the present version of the ordinance. The city is not required to show that the approach taken by the ordinance is the only approach that would serve that interest. Cities seeking to justify ordinances on the basis of the secondary effects doctrine need only show that there is a reasonable relationship between the ordinance and the "secondary effects of protected speech."

If bringing clarity to the secondary effects doctrine was the objective of the Court in the *Alameda Books* case, the separate opinions appeared to be embarked on a more revisionist mission. Justice Kennedy in his concurrence opined that ordinances such as those found in *Alameda Books* and *City of Renton* were not content-neutral but content-based. Justice Souter, dissenting, said that these ordinances although categorized as content-neutral were in fact in a "kind of limbo" situated between regulations that were clearly content-based and regulations that were applicable without any reference at all to what was being said.

For many, the secondary effects doctrine has mischievous First Amendment consequences. Critics contend that the secondary effects doctrine diverts attention from the content-based character of the regulation. It facilitates the use of a standard of review appropriate for government regulation in general rather than the stricter standard of review appropriate for content regulation. Basically, First Amendment interests are subordinated by characterizing speech as being only incidentally affected. The secondary effects doctrine's emphasis on the absence of any viewpoint censorship ignores the danger that the content-based character of the law may mask impermissible censorial objectives on the part of government. The student should recall that Justice Stevens' plurality approach in *American Mini Theatres* did not deny the content-based character of the regulation, but sought to justify the relevance of the content to regulation. Neither the majority in *American Mini Theatres*, nor in *City of Renton*, however, accepts the hierarchy of speech interests that Justice Stevens urged upon the Court.

Further, the Court has limited the ability of the states to regulate nudity when used as a means of expression. In *Erznoznik v. Jacksonville*, 422 U.S. 205 (1975), the Court struck down a nuisance law preventing drive-ins from showing nudity in films when visible from the street. A zoning ordinance that barred live entertainment from a commercial zone was held unconstitutional when it was applied to nude dancing. *Schad v. Mt. Ephraim*, 452 U.S. 61 (1981). Indeed, *Schad* extended First Amendment protection to nonobscene nude dancing and reaffirmed that even a zoning ordinance dealing with indecent or offensive expression must be narrowly drawn to further substantial governmental interests. *Compare New York State Liquor Auth. v. Bellanca*, 452 U.S. 714 (1981) and *City of Newport v. Iacobucci*, 479 U.S. 92 (1986), which upheld local ordinances prohibiting nude dancing in places where liquor is served emphasizing the state's power over liquor regulation pursuant to the Twenty-first Amendment. But in *Barnes v. Glen Theatre, Inc.*, 501 U.S. 560 (1991), the Court upheld a prohibition on totally nude dancing as part of a general ban on public nudity. In *Glen Theatre*, Chief Justice Rehnquist stated "that nude dancing of the kind sought to be performed here is expressive conduct within the outer perimeters of the First Amendment though we view it as only marginally so." See Ch. X, C. Whether this portends that nudity and other forms of indecent and erotic expression will ultimately be relegated to a lower level of First Amendment protection remains unclear.

In summary, while the Court continues to give support to the principle that nudity and other indecent and erotic—but non-obscene—speech is fully protected under the First Amendment, decisions like *Glen Theatre* and *City of Renton* suggest an increasing readiness on the Court's part to accept regulation of indecent expression. Indecency is not yet an unprotected category of expression like obscenity. Nor has it been formally relegated to a category of lesser protection. But the cases discussed above suggest that the Court may be willing to create a new category of low value speech for indecency. However, one must be cautious in making this assessment since the Supreme Court in the "dial-a-porn" case, *Sable Communications, Inc. v. FCC*, 492 U.S. 115 (1989), invalidated a federal statute which totally banned indecent "dial-a-porn." The Court, per Justice White, said: "Sexual expression which is indecent but not obscene is protected by the First Amendment." Moreover, the Court applied strict scrutiny to invalidate the regulation of indecent speech in *Sable*.

Broadcasting regulation provides support for the proposition that indecency is a category of low-value speech enjoying no, or lesser, First Amendment protection. In *FCC v. Pacifica Foundation*, 438 U.S. 726 (1978), the Supreme Court upheld FCC sanctions against a broadcaster for airing indecent material. "Seven dirty words" were repeatedly used in a recording by comedian George Carlin broadcast on Pacifica radio in the afternoon. They were heard by the complainant, a father in the company of his young child. The FCC had characterized Carlin's monologue as patently offensive, though not necessarily obscene, and had justified its regulation by drawing analogies to the law of nuisance. Could the

FCC impose sanctions on a broadcaster for using nonobscene expression which was concededly protected in the print context? For a majority, Justice Stevens answered in the affirmative in a narrow opinion stressing the special context of broadcasting with its pervasive presence and its inability to exclude children from the audience. A broadcast that might be permissible at midnight was inappropriate in the middle of the afternoon when children were likely to be in the audience. *Pacifica* does not stand for the idea that indecency can be proscribed, even in broadcasting, but rather that it should be channeled to appropriate times.

But Stevens, speaking for a plurality, went further and argued that "the constitutional protection accorded to a communication containing such patently offensive sexual and excretory language need not be the same in every context." The social value of speech, he declared, varies with the circumstances. It was appropriate to consider the indecent content of the speech in the special context of broadcasting: "And of all forms of communication, it is broadcasting that has received the most limited First Amendment protection." Just as in *American Mini Theatres*, Justice Stevens contended that indecent content is relevant in assessing the validity of regulation of even protected speech. Once again in *Pacifica*, he sought to establish hierarchies of expression with indecency relegated to the lower end of the protected spectrum. As he put it, "the broadcasting of patently offensive references to excretory and sexual organs and activities [while protected] surely lie at the periphery of First Amendment concern."

Once again, however, as in *American Mini Theatres*, in this regard Justice Stevens spoke only for a plurality. Justice Powell, joined by Justice Blackmun, concurring, specifically declined to adopt a hierarchical view of First Amendment protection: "I do not subscribe to the theory that the Justices of this Court are free generally to decide on the basis of its content which speech protected by the First Amendment is most 'valuable' and hence deserving of the most protection, and which is less 'valuable' and hence deserving of less protection." For the concurring Justices, the case turned on the unique characteristics of broadcasting combined with society's interest in protecting its children from inappropriate speech and the interest of the captive adult audience from being assaulted by offensive and indecent speech in their homes.

That *Pacifica*'s emphasis on indecent speech has little relevance outside the broadcast context is indicated by the *Sable* case mentioned above. Justice White, for a unanimous Court, found the telephone context of "dial-a-porn" to be totally different than broadcasting: "There is no 'captive audience' problem here; callers will generally not be unwilling listeners.... Placing a telephone call is not the same as turning on a radio and being taken by surprise by an indecent message." In the telephone context, government had less restrictive means, short of a total ban, for protecting minors. Arguably, the principle that emerges from *Pacifica* and

*Sable* is not that indecency is a special category of low value speech subject to lesser First Amendment protection. It is rather that government has a valid interest in protecting minors and that, in the broadcasting context, that interest is stronger than it is in the telephone context or the print media context.

*Pacifica* and *Sable* dealt with regulation of indecency in broadcasting and telephony respectively. In *Denver Area Educational Telecommunications Consortium, Inc. v. FCC*, 518 U.S. 727 (1996), the Supreme Court considered First Amendment challenges to regulation of indecent expression on cable television. Three provisions of the Cable Television Consumer Protection and Competition Act of 1992, Secs. 10(a), (b) and (c) were under review.

Sec. 10(a), authorizing a cable operator to refuse to transmit indecent expression on leased access channels, was upheld by a 7–2 vote. Justice Breyer, joined by Justices Stevens, O'Connor and Souter, concluded that, rather than choose any single First Amendment standard now for the regulation of indecency on cable television—whether it be by analogy to broadcast, common carrier, or bookstore—the wiser course was simply to hold that "the Government may directly regulate speech to address extraordinary problems, where its regulations are appropriately tailored to resolve those problems without imposing an unnecessarily great restriction on speech." The dynamic nature of technological change in telecommunications made it premature to select "one analogy or one specific set of words now." Justice Breyer essentially applied a balancing approach which sought to weigh the competing First Amendment interests of the various participants affected, *i.e.*, cable operators, cable programmers, and cable viewers.

Justice Breyer found Sec. 10(a) valid on several grounds. First, Sec. 10(a) was based on the "extremely important" interest of protecting children from indecent speech, an interest that *Sable, Ginsberg* and *Ferber* had found to be compelling. Second, Sec. 10(a) had to be understood in context. In the absence of a federal law, leased access programmers would have had no access to cable channels "free of an operator's control." Third, the problem addressed by Congress here was "remarkably similar" to the problem addressed by the FCC in *Pacifica*. Cable television was as accessible to children and as uniquely pervasive, and, hence, as subject to regulation, as over-the-air broadcasting. Fourth, Sec. 10(a) did not *require* cable operators to ban indecent speech but only authorized them to do so. A look at the programming cable operators permitted on their non-leased access channels indicated that concern here might be more "theoretical than real." Justices Thomas, Scalia and Chief Justice Rehnquist, concurring, agreed that Sec. 10(a) was valid but on the basis of a quite different rationale. They contended that cable should be analogized to the print media and that the free speech right of the cable operator to editorial discretion should trump the free expression claims of programmers and viewers.

Sec. 10(b) of the 1992 Cable Act sought to limit children's exposure to indecent programming on leased access channels and required cable operators transmitting such programming to segregate it on a separate channel. The separate segregated channel would then be blocked unless the subscriber requested otherwise. Sec. 10(b) also obliged leased access programmers to notify cable operators of "patently offensive" programming 30 days before the schedule broadcast date. The Court, per Justice Breyer, struck down Sec. 10(b) by a 6–3 vote. The expense and burden caused by these restrictions would lead cable operators to ban programming they might otherwise allow. In defense of Sec. 10(b), the government argued that the "segregate and block" requirements were the least restrictive means of implementing the compelling government interests in protecting the physical and psychological well-being of children. *Pacifica* did not require that regulation of indecency on television should be subject to the strictest standard of review. Justice Breyer declared in *Denver Area* that it was not necessary to decide whether *Pacifica* required a lesser standard of review for indecent speech because Sec. 10(b) failed to meet both strict and less strict First Amendment standards of review. The "segregate and block" restrictions were neither reasonably nor narrowly tailored to protect children. The Court pointed out that the 1996 Telecommunications Act, which requires television sets in the future to be manufactured with a v-chip thus giving parents the option of blocking sexually explicit or violent programming, is tellingly less restrictive.

Sec. 10(c), authorizing the FCC to issue regulations permitting cable operators to deny the use of public access channels for programming containing indecent or obscene speech, was struck down by a 5–4 vote. Although the Court by validating Sec. 10(a) had permitted regulation of indecent speech on leased access channels, Justice Breyer, joined by Justices Stevens and Souter, distinguished leased access channels from public access channels. There had been no showing that patently offensive programming directed to children was a problem on public access channels. It therefore could not be assumed that a harm existed or that it needed to be redressed. Sec. 10(c) did pose, however, a real risk that borderline offensive programming would not be broadcast. Justice Kennedy, joined by Justice Ginsburg, protested the application of a less rigorous *Pacifica*-type standard of review. They agreed that Sec. 10(c) was invalid but they reached that result by characterizing public access channels as designated public forums to be evaluated by the strict scrutiny standard of review. Sec. 10(c) did not meet that standard since there had been no showing that it was the least restrictive alternative available for the protection of children. In summary, a majority of the Justices in *Denver Area* did not adopt the strict scrutiny test in reviewing the provisions of the 1992 Cable Act at issue. The *Denver Area* opinions show a reluctance to apply traditional First Amendment doctrine to indecency regulation of cable.

But in *United States v. Playboy Entertainment Group, Inc.*, 529 U.S. 803 (2000), the Court applied strict scrutiny review to what it deemed a content-based regulation of cable television. A cable programmer posed a First Amendment challenge to Sec. 505 of the Telecommunications Act of 1996 regulating "signal bleed." "Signal bleed" results when, because of incomplete signal scrambling or blocking, part of the image or picture still remains on the television screen. Sec. 505 required cable operators either to scramble sexually explicit channels or to limit programming on such channels to certain hours when children were less likely to be in the audience. The Court, per Justice Kennedy, held that Sec. 505 constituted a content-based regulation which failed to meet the narrowly-tailored aspect of the strict scrutiny standard of review. Sec. 504 of the 1996 Act permitted viewers who wished to do so to block sexually explicit programming. Sec. 505 limited cable operators to transmitting sexually explicit programming during the late evening "safe harbor" or to block scrambling sexually explicit channels altogether. Since Sec. 504 presented a much less restrictive alternative, Sec. 505 could not qualify as a narrowly tailored means of accomplishing the governmental objective, *i.e.* the protection of children. Justice Kennedy emphasized that Sec. 504 gave cable operators the ability to block sexually explicit channel on an individual basis: "The option to block reduces the likelihood, so concerning to the Court in *Pacifica*, that traditional First Amendment scrutiny would deprive the government of all authority to address this sort of problem." Since *Playboy Entertainment* had applied strict scrutiny to indecent speech regulation and *Pacifica* had not, did *Playboy Entertainment* trump *Pacifica*? On this point, Justice Kennedy observed that broadcast television, unlike the situation in cable television, cannot be blocked.

In *Reno v. ACLU*, 521 U.S. 844 (1997), the Supreme Court had its first encounter with the Internet. Certain provisions of the Communications Decency Act of 1996 (CDA) prohibiting transmission of indecent or patently offensive material on the Internet to persons under 18 years old were struck down. Each of the challenged provisions of the CDA used different prohibitory words. One provision applies to indecent material while the other was directed to patently offensive material. Neither term was defined. This lack of definition was bound to produce uncertainty among speakers. Such vagueness raised First Amendment concerns because of the chilling effect it had on free expression and the fact that the CDA was a criminal statute. Justice Stevens, for the Court, ruled that these content-based regulations carrying criminal sanctions must be evaluated under a strict scrutiny standard of review. The undefined terms used by the CDA work against the contention that the C.A. has been narrowly tailored to satisfy the statutory objective of protecting minors from detrimental material. The overbreadth was not diminished by the CDA's requirement of knowledge that a person must be a minor before its sanctions could go into effect. Nor did the statutory defenses of good faith and reasonable effort to avoid transmission to minors constitute the narrow tailoring necessary to cure the invalid overbreadth.

Of course, Justice Stevens observed, each communications medium raised its own unique issues, but there was no justification for less than full protection for the Internet. The deferential review applied to broadcasting was not appropriate for the Internet. Broadcasting received more limited protection than other media because warnings could not prevent the listener from being surprised by unwanted program content. Such surprise was unlikely on the Internet because one had to undertake a number of affirmative steps to access it. Unlike the case with broadcasting, a child had to have some degree of ability and sophistication to use the Internet.

The Internet, unlike broadcasting, had no history of regulation. On the contrary, the Internet had developed as an unregulated communications medium. Technological scarcity had justified the more deferential review accorded to broadcast regulations but the Internet was not a scarce medium at all. Therefore, Justice Stevens reasoned, there was no basis for reducing the degree of scrutiny which should be applied to the Internet. The Court decided to leave the Internet unregulated and concluded that the most effective way to do that was by applying the strict scrutiny standard of review. Indecent speech was, after all, still protected speech. Adults had a right to receive indecent speech if less restrictive means were available to protect children. It had not been shown that this was not the case.

Indeed, software might well be available to limit the access of children to indecent material on the Internet. Since more narrowly tailored alternatives were available, the challenged provisions of the Communications Decency Act failed to meet the strict scrutiny standard of review.

*Reno v. ACLU* involved speech-repressive legislation with respect to which the affected classes of speakers—Internet Service Providers, civil liberties groups, media organizations—were on the same side against the government. In *Reno*, the Court applied the strict scrutiny standard of review and held that the blanket restrictions on protected expression could not be justified. When conflicts arise among Internet Service Providers or between an Internet Service Provider and the general public, the Court will then be presented with a *Denver Area*-type case, a case of First Amendment interests in conflict, *i.e*, cable programmers, cable system operators, and the viewing audience all posited conflicting First Amendment claims. It may, therefore, be premature to conclude that the strict scrutiny standard of review will be applied to all future Internet regulation.

In retrospect, if we consider the Court's indecent speech decisions, it is clear that there is tension and ambiguity. While indecent speech is not a category of unprotected expression or even lesser protection, the character of the speech in the context of the particular communications medium may be critical in assessing the First Amendment validity of a regulation.

## D. FIRST AMENDMENT "DUE PROCESS"

While the Court has held that prior restraints are presumptively invalid, obscenity is a context where they have been tolerated. See *Near v. Minnesota*, 283 U.S. 697 (1931) ["the primary requirements of decency may be enforced against obscene publications" by prior restraint]. For example, even film licensing has been upheld. *Times Film Corp. v. Chicago*, 365 U.S. 43 (1961). But such a licensing scheme must not be vague or vest excessive discretion in the administrator. *Joseph Burstyn, Inc. v. Wilson*, 343 U.S. 495 (1952) [film censorship based on "sacrilegious" content held unconstitutional]. Also the licensing law must provide "procedural safeguards designed to obviate the dangers of a censorship system." *Freedman v. Maryland*, 380 U.S. 51 (1965). In *Freedman*, the Court imposed stringent procedural requirements for administrative licensing. First, the board has the burden of showing that a film is unprotected expression. Second, only a judicial proceeding will suffice to impose a valid final restraint on a film's exhibition. Third, the state, either by statute, or by authoritative judicial construction, must afford the exhibitor a procedure under which he is either issued a license or the censorship board is required to go to court to restrain the showing of the film in controversy. The *Freedman* standards reflect a clear preference for a judicial, rather than an administrative determination of obscenity. But it is unclear whether all of the standards are applicable to prior restraint schemes that do not provide for content-based censorship.

In *FW/PBS, Inc. v. City of Dallas*, 493 U.S. 215 (1990), the Court invalidated an ordinance providing for zoning, licensing and inspections of "sexually oriented businesses." The Court held that *Freedman* was violated since the licensing scheme lacked time limits and it failed to assure prompt judicial review. Speaking for a plurality, Justice O'Connor then went on to explain that it was unnecessary "that the city bear the burden of going to court to effect the denial of a license application or that it bear the burden of proof once in court." Since the applicant could not operate his business without a license, she reasoned, the applicant could take a license denial to court. Justice Brennan, joined by Justices Blackmun and Marshall, concurring, declared that it is the "transcendent value of speech that places the burden of persuasion on the state." Justice White, joined by Chief Justice Rehnquist, concurring and dissenting, analogized the Dallas ordinance to a content-neutral time, place and manner regulation, and concluded that none of the *Freedman* standards need be met. Justice Scalia, concurring and dissenting, argued that the Dallas law need not comply with First Amendment standards since the city could constitutionally have proscribed a business specializing in sexual materials rather than just licensing it—"a business devoted to the sale of highly explicit sexual material can be found to be engaged in the marketing of obscenity, even though each book or film it sells might, in isolation, be considered merely pornographic and not obscene." For Scalia, Dallas could stop such "pandering" under the authority of *Ginzburg v. United States*, 383 U.S. 463 (1966) and *American Mini Theatres'* approval of prohibitions against "concentrated pornography."

Prior restraints in the form of injunctions have also been upheld in the obscenity context. In *Paris Adult Theatre I v. Slaton*, 413 U.S. 49 (1973), the Court approved the use of injunctions against the showing of obscene films; injunctions provide "a constitutionally acceptable standard for determining what is unprotected by the First Amendment." The restraint was imposed only after a full adversarial proceeding and a judicial determination that the material was obscene. But this principle does not mean that a state can authorize judges to enjoin a theater from showing "any obscene motion picture," simply because the theater had previously shown obscene films. *Vance v. Universal Amusement Co.*, 445 U.S. 308 (1980). The state may, however, close a business as a nuisance when it is used for prostitution, even though it also sells protected adult materials. First Amendment limitations have no "relevance to a statute directed at imposing sanctions on nonexpressive activity." *Arcara v. Cloud Books, Inc.*, 478 U.S. 697 (1986).

Executive power to engage in searches and seizures in combating obscenity is also subject to First Amendment limits. Large scale civil seizure of publications must be preceded by an adversary proceeding and a judicial determination that they are obscene. *Quantity of Copies of Books v. Kansas*, 378 U.S. 205 (1964). And this is true even if the seizure is taken pursuant to state racketeering (RICO) laws. *Fort Wayne Books v. Indiana*, 489 U.S. 46 (1989). But a search and seizure of a single copy of a film for use as evidence is valid without an adversary proceeding and judicial determination of obscenity. *Heller v. New York*, 413 U.S. 483 (1973).

In summary, the mandate of due process in enforcement of valid laws, which has enhanced force when First Amendment rights are threatened, does apply to enforcement of obscenity laws. Nevertheless, prior restraint is used and often upheld. Perhaps it is the unprotected character of obscenity that produces this result. The objective is to assure a prompt judicial determination whether the materials at issue are protected speech or unprotected obscenity.

# CHAPTER VI

# DEFAMATION, PRIVACY AND MENTAL DISTRESS

## A. CONSTITUTIONALIZING LIBEL LAW

Prior to the 1960s, the First Amendment was generally considered irrelevant to libel law. In *Chaplinsky v. New Hampshire*, 315 U.S. 568 (1942), libel had been placed in that class of utterance which is "no essential part in the exposition of ideas." *Beauharnais v. Illinois*, 343 U.S. 250 (1952) upheld a group libel law since libelous utterances are not "within the area of constitutionally protected speech." At common law, the libel plaintiff had to prove only that the defendant published a defamatory statement concerning her. Fault was irrelevant; falsity was presumed; truth was an affirmative defense. Critical social commentary and criticism were protected by a limited conditional privilege. In short, state protection of personal reputation was the dominant policy value, relatively unhampered by First Amendment concerns.

In *New York Times v. Sullivan*, 376 U.S. 254 (1964), the Court reversed course, holding that "libel can claim no talismanic immunity from constitutional limitations. It must be measured by standards that satisfy the First Amendment." For the first time, the Court imposed First Amendment limitations on the ability of a public official to recover for criticism relating to his official conduct. L.B. Sullivan, the Montgomery, Alabama police commissioner, had sued the New York Times and four Black clergymen based on a full page fundraising advertisement. The ad, which never mentioned Sullivan, contained statements, some inaccurate, critical of police handling of student demonstrations in Montgomery. A jury verdict of $500,000, upheld by the Alabama Supreme Court, was unanimously overturned by the United States Supreme Court.

Justice Brennan, for the Court, relied heavily on the democratic, citizen-critic model of the First Amendment. The case was considered, he said, "against the background of a profound national commitment to the principle that debate on public issues should be uninhibited, robust, and wide-open, and that it may well include vehement, caustic and sometimes unpleasantly sharp attacks on government and public officials." The principle that falsity and defamatory content do not deprive publications concerning the official conduct of public officials of First Amendment protection, declared Justice Brennan, had been established in the debate over the Sedition Act of 1798. Although the Supreme Court had never declared the Sedition Act unconstitutional, Justice Brennan said it had been found invalid in the bar of history. This reflected "a national awareness of the central meaning of the First Amendment"—legal restraints on citizen "criticism of government and public officials [are] inconsistent with the First Amendment." Nor was this "central meaning" limited to the criminal sedition context since civil damage may be even more inhibiting on free expression—"the pall of fear and timidity imposed upon those who would give voice to public criticism is an atmosphere in which the First Amendment freedoms cannot survive." Critics of *New York Times* have questioned whether the press was as intimidated and fearful in its criticism of officials as Brennan claimed.

Dangers of press self-censorship, Brennan continued, could not be adequately met by allowing simply an affirmative defense of truth. Even though state recognition of such a defense had been considered the essential safeguard of press freedom from the time of the Zenger trial, it was now deemed insufficient to protect the citizen-critic. Would-be critics of government might still be deterred by doubts concerning their ability to prove defamatory statements are true. Instead, the Court fashioned a new constitutional privilege. The public official plaintiff suing for a libelous publication critical of his official conduct could succeed only by proving, by clear and convincing evidence, "that the statement was made with 'actual malice'—that is, with knowledge that it was false or with reckless disregard of whether it was false or [not]."

Actual malice should not be confused with common law malice necessary for punitive damages, which requires bias or ill-will. Nor is it an aggravated form of negligence. Actual malice refers to a defendant publisher's subjective awareness that his statement is false or that there is a high probability that it is false. Reckless disregard requires that the defendant have "serious doubts as to the truth of [the] publication." *St. Amant v. Thompson*, 390 U.S. 727 (1968); *Garrison v. Louisiana*, 376 U.S. 947 (1964) ["calculated falsehood" must be proven]. Since actual malice is a constitutional fact, appellate courts "must exercise independent judgement and determine whether the record established actual malice with convincing clarity." *Bose Corp. v. Consumers Union*, 466 U.S. 485 (1984). An appellate court must examine the record to determine if clear and convincing evidence exists from which a jury could find actual malice. A jury's credibility determinations are, however, reviewed under a "clearly erroneous" standard. *Harte–Hanks Commun., Inc. v. Connaughton*, 491 U.S. 657 (1989).

But why is there liability if the public official proves actual malice? Justices Black, Douglas and Goldberg, concurring, noted that actual malice, especially its "recklessness" element, is "an elusive, abstract concept, hard to prove and hard to disprove," inviting local jury bias to operate. If media self-censorship is such a critical concern, shouldn't an absolute constitutional privilege be provided? Otherwise, fear of litigation with its heavy costs and potential liability can continue to chill expression. Perhaps the conditional character of the constitutional privilege adopted by the Court in *New York Times* reflects a concern that states be allowed to protect reputation, that citizens not be deterred from seeking public office by fear of unfair criticism, that press irresponsibility be curbed. While Justice Brennan does not cite these concerns, the Court may have been implicitly balancing the competing interests and imposing a heavy burden of proof on public official plaintiffs as a precondition to liability. Perhaps Justice Brennan's opinion adopts an absolutist approach—publication made with "actual malice" is unprotected speech enjoying no First Amendment protection. In *Garrison v. Louisiana*, 376 U.S. 947 (1964) [*New York Times* standard applied to criminal libel actions], Justice Brennan cited *Chaplinsky* for the proposition that calculated falsehood has slight social value. In short, the actual malice standard would be a product of definitional, not ad hoc, balancing.

Critics of *New York Times* not only cite the important state interest in protecting the reputation of public officials and in controlling an irresponsible media, they often question Justice Brennan's premises. Does the citizen really have an overriding interest in hearing false, defamatory statements? In *Gertz v. Robert Welch, Inc.*, 418 U.S. 323 (1974), Justice Powell was to say that, while there is no such thing as a false idea, "there is no constitutional value in false statements of fact." Justice Brennan's response, echoed by Justice Powell in *Gertz*, is that we protect falsity in order to safeguard truth. Justice Brennan stated: "[E]rroneous statement is inevitable in free debate, and [it] must be protected if the freedoms of expression are to have the 'breathing space' that they 'need to survive.' " In fact, the Court would later impose the burden of proving falsity on the plaintiff in cases involving public figure plaintiffs, at least if the speech involves "matters of public concern." *Philadelphia Newspapers, Inc. v. Hepps*, 475 U.S. 767 (1986).

*New York Times* set forth an actual malice standard for a public official suing over criticism of his official conduct. The privilege was soon extended to "anything which might touch an official's fitness for office" [*Garrison v. Louisiana*, 376 U.S. 947 (1964)], including charges of criminal conduct. *Monitor Patriot Co. v. Roy*, 401 U.S. 295 (1971) [bootlegging]; *Ocala Star–Banner Co. v. Damron*, 401 U.S. 295 (1971) [perjury]. In *New York Times*, the Court made it clear that the First Amendment prohibited making "an otherwise impersonal attack on governmental operations [into] a libel of an official responsible for those operations." The evidence was constitutionally insufficient to establish that statements critical of the police libeled the police commissioner. Later, "public officials" was defined to include "those among the hierarchy of government employees who have, or appear to have, substantial responsibility for or control over the conduct of public affairs." *Rosenblatt v. Baer*, 383 U.S. 75 (1966) [*New York Times* applies to nonelected officials]. Candidates for public office also must prove actual malice. *Monitor Patriot Co.*

## B. PUBLIC FIGURES AND PUBLIC ISSUES

Commenting on *New York Times*, Professor Harry Kalven suggested that its rationale provided an invitation "to follow a dialectic progression from public official to government policy to public policy to matters in the public domain...." Kalven, The New York Times Case: *A Note On "The Central Meaning of the First Amendment*," 1964 Sup. Ct. Rev. 191. After all, expression relevant to the citizen-critic in performing her democratic duty does not stop at the conduct of the public official. In *Curtis Publ'g Co. v. Butts*, 388 U.S. 130 (1967) and *Associated Press v. Walker*, 388 U.S. 130 (1967), however, Justice Harlan observed for a plurality that the seditious libel analogy—the "central meaning of the First Amendment"—does not apply outside the public official context. But he did not urge that the states in public figure cases were therefore free of the First Amendment in framing their libel laws. Rather, the plaintiff who is a "public figure should be allowed to recover for libel if she proves highly unreasonable conduct constituting an extreme departure from the standards of investigation and reporting ordinarily adhered to by reasonable publishers." Had this gross negligence standard carried the day, the public law of libel might be markedly different today. But it did not. Chief Justice Warren concurred in the result but joined four dissenters in concluding that the actual malice standard applies to public figure cases. Religious, business and professional persons often play an influential role in our democracy; the citizen critic may have a vital interest in the activities of these public figures. Such individuals, he added, usually have ready access to the media to influence policy and to counter criticism.

The rationale of the majority of justices in *Butts–Walker* suggested that the critical factor in the availability of the *New York Times* privilege was not the status of the plaintiff as a public figure but the public interest in the subject of the libelous publication. In *Rosenbloom v. Metromedia*, 403 U.S. 29 (1971), the Court appeared to move toward this position. While the plaintiff, a "smut-peddler," was not a public figure, his activities involved a matter of public interest. Justice Brennan wrote: "The public's primary interest is in the event; the public focus is on the conduct of the participant and the content, effect and significance of the conduct...." A matter of public interest and concern does not become less so simply because a private figure is involved. But Justice Brennan wrote only for a three justice plurality. The remainder of the justices were sharply divided. When the Court spoke definitively, it was not the public interest in the subject matter that was controlling, but the status of the libel plaintiff.

## C. PUBLIC FIGURES AND PRIVATE FIGURES

The public issue approach of the *Rosenbloom* plurality was rejected in *Gertz v. Robert Welch, Inc.,*

418 U.S. 323 (1974). Gertz, a prominent civil rights attorney, sued the publisher of *American Opinion*, the outlet of the right-wing John Birch Society, for statements claiming Gertz had various communist connections. The lower court, however, had overturned the jury verdict in Gertz's favor ruling that the "actual malice" standard had to be applied when the publication concerned a public issue. In reversing 5–4, the Supreme Court held that "so long as they do not impose liability without fault, the States may define for themselves the appropriate standard of liability for a publisher or broadcaster of defamatory falsehood injurious to a private individual."

Justice Powell, writing for the Court, acknowledged the danger of media self-censorship from departing from the actual malice rule. But free speech interests had to be balanced against the competing legitimate state interests in compensating individuals for the harm they suffer from defamatory falsehood. Two factors were cited by Justice Powell as justifying a lesser degree of constitutional protection in libel actions by private figures. First, "[p]ublic officials and public figures usually enjoy significantly greater access to the channels of effective communication and hence have a more realistic opportunity to counteract false statements than private individuals normally enjoy." The private libel plaintiff's lack of means of self-help enhanced the state's interest in the balancing analysis. Justice Brennan, dissenting, argued that effective access to the media for self-help was seldom available to any libel victim regardless of status. Second, Justice Powell cited the "compelling normative consideration" that public figures voluntarily choose to run "the risk of closer public scrutiny." The private person, on the other hand, has not relinquished his interest in protecting his reputation and therefore has a "more compelling call" for judicial protection. Justice Brennan responded that membership in society makes us all public persons to some degree. Justice Powell summarized: "[P]rivate individuals are not only more vulnerable to injury than public officials and public figures, they are also more deserving of recovery." For Justice Brennan, the risk of exposure "is an essential incident of life in a society which places a primary value on freedom of speech and press." A negligent misstatement rule (which most states were to adopt after *Gertz*) provided great risk of self-censorship and inadequate protection for free speech values.

How could the danger of press self-censorship in matters relevant to self-government, but involving only a private figure, be avoided? Part of the *Gertz* Court's answer lies in its rejection of strict liability. States cannot impose liability without fault. The Court provided another safeguard: "[W]e hold that the States may not permit recovery of presumed or punitive damages, at least when liability is not based on a showing of knowledge of falsity or reckless disregard for the truth." Where the libel involves speech of public concern, even a private libel plaintiff must prove "actual injury." Justice Powell said actual damages include "impairment of reputation and standing in the community, personal humiliation, and mental anguish and suffering." This probably means that a libel plaintiff can recover for mental distress even if it is not proven to flow from reputational harm. The ambiguity of the Court's definition of actual damages invites damages for embarrassment and humiliation and presumed damages generally to be awarded under the guise of compensation. Justice White, dissenting, was critical of the Court's further restraining a state's freedom to fashion its libel law outside the public official context.

*Gertz* makes the availability of the *New York Times* privilege turn on the status of the plaintiff. But how do we distinguish a public figure from a private figure plaintiff? Justice Powell identifies two alternative bases for labeling a person a public figure. "In some instances an individual may achieve such pervasive fame or notoriety that he becomes a public figure for all purposes and in all contexts. More commonly, an individual voluntarily injects himself or is drawn into a particular public controversy and thereby becomes a public figure for a limited range of issues. In either case, such persons assume special prominence in the resolution of public questions." Generally, both the all-purpose or total public figure and the limited-purpose or "vortex" public figure have access to the media to engage in self-help and have voluntarily assumed the risk of adverse publicity. Justice Powell warned that since a "total public figure" is subject to broad media exposure, few persons should qualify. The person's name must be almost a matter of common knowledge, *e.g.*, Johnny Carson, before he is labeled a total public figure.

Defining a limited purpose or vortex public figure has been likened to nailing a jellyfish to a wall. Such a person is a public figure only for a limited range of issues and only for commentary relevant to that issue. *Time, Inc. v. Firestone*, 424 U.S. 448 (1976), rejected labeling as a public figure a wealthy socialite involved in a bizarre scandal and divorce. Vortex public figures "thrust themselves to the forefront of particular public controversies in order to influence the resolution of the issues involved." The Court held that neither element of this two part test was satisfied. There was no "public controversy" even though the divorce may have been of public interest. Nor was filing for divorce or the holding of a press conference done in a "voluntary" effort to attract public attention to influence the resolution of any public issue.

Subsequently, a scientist receiving federal funds who bore the brunt of Senator Proxmire's "Golden Fleece" award because of his research was held not to be a public figure. *Hutchinson v. Proxmire*, 443 U.S. 111 (1979). Hutchinson had not voluntarily sought the public spotlight in order to influence others regarding public issues and was not otherwise well-known. The media attention was solely a product of the libelous publication itself. The Court also has held that the refusal of a subpoenaed person to appear before a grand jury investigating espionage is not sufficient to make him a public figure. *Wolston v. Reader's Digest Ass'n*, 443 U.S. 157 (1979). While Wolston's activities may have made him newsworthy, he had not sought to thrust himself into the public spotlight to influence public debate. While the *Gertz* Court had suggested that a person might be involuntarily thrust into the vortex, the *Wolston* Court did not discuss whether the plaintiff might be an involuntary public figure.

The Court's efforts to provide guidance concerning the public figure label have not been markedly successful. Lower courts continue to struggle over the status of lesser known entertainers, criminals, corporations, and others who attract media attention. Courts often treat "public interest" and "public controversy" as synonymous. Voluntary involvement in activities that attract public attention, *e.g.*, criminal or unethical conduct, often suffices to establish the "voluntariness" element. The status of a person who was once a public figure but who has subsequently retired to anonymity remains uncertain. And yet, the availability of the *New York Times* privilege turns on just such determinations.

### D.  PUBLIC SPEECH AND PRIVATE SPEECH

*Dun & Bradstreet, Inc. v. Greenmoss Builders, Inc.*, 472 U.S. 749 (1985), involved a libel action by a construction contractor against the credit reporting agency. A confidential report provided to five subscribers falsely claimed that Greenmoss had filed for bankruptcy. The jury had awarded plaintiff presumed and punitive damages even though actual malice had not been proven. The Vermont Supreme Court, reversing a grant of a new trial, ruled that the media protections established in *Gertz* do not apply to nonmedia defendants. Adoption of such a rule would significantly limit the reach of the public law of libel. While *New York Times* and *Gertz* had involved media publications, the Court has never indicated that the constitutional privilege applies only to the media. Further, the justices have disagreed about whether the media enjoy special constitutional privileges not available to citizens generally. Generally, however, the Court has treated the Speech and Press Clauses as providing the same protection [See Ch. XIII, A, discussing the Press Clause]. When the Court granted review in *Dun & Bradstreet*, it was expected to address the issue whether the *Times* privilege applies in nonmedia cases.

Instead, the Court held that "permitting recovery of presumed and punitive damages in defamation cases absent a showing of 'actual malice' does not violate the First Amendment when the defamatory statements do not involve matters of public concern." Justice Powell, writing for a plurality, applied, as he had in *Gertz*, a balancing analysis. While speech involving "matters of public concern" was "at the heart of the First Amendment's protection," Powell reasoned that "speech on matters of purely private concern is of less First Amendment concern." The "reduced constitutional value" of private speech meant that the state interest in protecting private reputation justified abandoning the *Gertz* damage rules. Would it permit the state to abandon other media safeguards in private speech cases, *e.g*, could the state use strict liability or impose the burden of proof of falsity on the plaintiff? The plurality in *Dun & Bradstreet* did not address these issues. But the emphasis on the diminished First Amendment significance of private speech arguably supports such a broader impact.

*Rosenbloom* had been criticized because of the ambiguity of the public interest standard. How does a court determine if the publication involves a "matter of public concern?" Justice Powell says courts should focus on the "context, form and content" of the publication. In *Dun & Bradstreet*, the limited circulation and the commercial character of the speech—which "is hardy and unlikely to be deterred by incidental state regulation"—seemed to be important to the plurality, although the plurality acknowledged that not all commercial speech is private speech. The absence of any "public issue" in controversy—perhaps distinguishing "public concern" from "public interest"—also was stressed. Justice Brennan, dissenting, claimed that the Court provided almost no guidance on the ambit of speech involving "matters of public concern." For the four dissenting Justices, questions of corporate solvency and bankruptcy fell well within the public's concern.

Justice White, concurring in *Dun & Bradstreet*, not only renewed his criticism of the *Gertz* rules, he attacked the balance struck in *New York Times* itself. False statements of fact about public officials do not serve First Amendment interests in the flow of intelligence concerning government. The *New York Times* privilege summarily disposes of libel actions, preventing the issue of truth or falsity from being decided. The public is prevented from ever discovering what is true. Limiting damages would provide ample protection to the press while allowing public officials to vindicate their reputation. He also spoke sympathetically of a vindication remedy, *i.e.*, permitting courts to simply determine—in lieu of a damage remedy—the truth or falsity of the defendant's statement.

Thus far, Justice White's call for a reconsideration of *New York Times* and its progeny has been unsuccessful. In *Masson v. New Yorker Magazine, Inc.*, 501 U.S. 496 (1991), even deliberate alteration of a quotation was deemed insufficient to constitute actual malice. Only if the alteration "results in a material change in the meaning conveyed by a statement" is it a "calculated falsehood." And, in *Milkovich v. Lorain Journal Co.*, 497 U.S. 1 (1990), even while the Court rejected a First Amendment based privilege for statements of opinion, it reaffirmed the constitutional privilege protecting the media. No opinion privilege was needed given the requirement that the plaintiff prove fault, falsity, and that the libelous publication constitutes a defamatory statement of fact (*e.g.*, satire, parody and hyperbole do not provide the basis for libel). The possibility that the *New York Times* privilege will be eroded by decisions limiting its effectiveness, or abandoned altogether, remains a central fear of the media.

## E. PRIVACY

A century ago, in a famous article, Samuel Warren and Louis Brandeis called for recognition of the "inviolate right of privacy against the exposures of a yellow press." Warren and Brandeis, *The Right to Privacy*, 4 Harv. L. Rev. 193 (1890). Today, all jurisdictions recognize privacy in some form. In fact, there are four forms of the privacy tort: intrusion, false light, disclosure, and appropriation. In intrusion, the remedy is directed against the unreasonable invasion of the seclusion of another. Publicity or publication isn't directly involved but First Amendment concerns are incidentally implicated in the protection of newsgathering. Appropriation is concerned primarily with protecting the commercial or property value of one's identity and likeness, *i.e.*, a "right of publicity." While First Amendment problems do arise, they do so infrequently. *See Zacchini v. Scripps–Howard Broadcasting Co.*, 433 U.S. 562 (1977) [award of damages against television station for unauthorized broadcast of performer's entire act does not violate First Amendment]. On the other hand, damage actions based on "false light" privacy and the public disclosure of private facts often generate First Amendment concerns.

False light privacy involves publicity concerning another which places him in a false light. Since the speech must be false, it is closely related to libel.

While defamation seeks to protect reputation (a relational interest), false light privacy is concerned with a person's emotional well-being. Nevertheless, the Court imported the actual malice standard of *New York Times* into false light privacy in *Time, Inc. v. Hill*, 385 U.S. 374 (1967). Life magazine ran a story which provided an inaccurate portrayal of the ordeal of the Hill family, who had been held hostage by escaped convicts. The Supreme Court set aside a damage award, remanding the case to determine if the plaintiff could prove actual malice. Justice Brennan, for the Court, reflected the same concern over media self-censorship from basing liability on negligence that he had exhibited in *New York Times*. Discussing the privacy interest, Brennan characterized exposure of the self as "a concomitant of life in a civilized community." Privacy had to yield "in a society which placed a primary value on freedom of speech and the press."

The fact the Hills were private figures was of no moment to Justice Brennan. As he had indicated in *Rosenbloom*, it was the public interest in the subject matter that was controlling. But the position of the *Rosenbloom* plurality has been repudiated in *Gertz*; the status of the plaintiff, not the nature of the issue, controls the availability of the *New York Times* privilege in libel law. Does *Times, Inc. v. Hill* survive *Gertz*? It could be argued that the harm is not as serious if the speech is not defamatory; the state interest should weigh less in the balance. But the self-help and normative rationale of *Gertz* appear fully applicable. Thus far the Court has not addressed the question. See *Cantrell v. Forest City Pub. Co.*, 419 U.S. 245 (1974) [issue not before the Court since no objection had been made when jury was instructed that actual malice is required for recovery].

The area of privacy law of greatest First Amendment concern involves unreasonable disclosure of private facts. Since the tort requires proof that the invasion of privacy would be highly offensive to a reasonable person and is not "newsworthy" [Restatement (Second) of Torts, § 652D], there is substantial common law protection for press interests. But it is also established that the First Amendment significantly limits the ability of a state to award damages for *truthful* publication of private facts. Truthful publication of information disclosed in public proceedings and open public records is constitutionally protected. *Cox Broadcasting Corp. v. Cohn*, 420 U.S. 469 (1975) [publication of rape victim's name obtained from the public record is protected]. Similarly, "[i]f a newspaper lawfully obtains truthful information about a matter of public significance then state officials may not constitutionally punish publication of the information absent a need to further a state interest of the highest order." *Smith v. Daily Mail Publ'g Co.*, 443 U.S. 97 (1979).

In *Florida Star v. B.J.F.*, 491 U.S. 524 (1989), the Court overturned a damage award against the *Florida Star* for publishing the name of a rape victim in violation of a state statute making such publication negligence *per se*. Since the *Star* had lawfully obtained the truthful information from a publicly released police report, the First Amendment barred damages unless it serves "a need to further a state interest of the highest order." Justice Marshall, for the Court, held that the law was not narrowly tailored to further the state's compelling interest in the protecting the privacy and safety of rape victims and encouraging them to report offenses. The government itself could take steps to prevent public disclosure. Negligence *per se*, added Marshall, prevents a case by case determination whether disclosure is reasonable under the circumstances. Finally, the Florida law at issue was limited to media disclosures, thereby impermissibly discriminating against the press.

In *Bartnicki v. Vopper*, 532 U.S. 514 (2001), privacy concerns arose in the context of federal and state wiretap laws prohibiting not only nonconsensual eavesdropping, but also use and disclosure of the intercepted communications if the user has knowledge or reason to know of their illegal source. When the press published the contents of such an illegally intercepted communications between union officials discussing a strike during which the possibility of violence was discussed, the union official sued under the wiretap laws. The Court, per Justice Stevens, held, 6–3, that the disclosures were protected by the First Amendment and the wiretap laws, as applied, were unconstitutional. While the wiretap laws was content–neutral regulation, Justice Stevens said it involved a direct regulation of speech, not conduct. Relying on *Florida Star v. B.J.F.*, 491

U.S. 524 (1989), he stressed that the information disclosed was true, lawfully obtained by the media, and of significant public concern. While recognizing the possible adverse effect on privacy interests, this case implicated "the core purposes of the First Amendment," because it involved sanctions "on the publication of truthful information of public concern."

Justices Breyer and O'Connor, concurring, went even further in emphasizing the Court's "narrow holding." On the circumstances in this case, the disclosure was reasonable. While the wiretap laws "directly enhance private speech," the media had not participated in the illegal intercept and there was little or no legitimate privacy interest in protecting speech involving the threat of potential violence. While clearly concerned with the effects of technology on privacy, the concurrences concluded that the public interest in disclosure in this case trumped any privacy interests. See Smolla, *Information as Contraband: The First Amendment and Liability for Trafficking in Speech*, 96 Nw. U.L. Rev. 1099, 1116 (2002) ("The concurring opinions . . . in *Bartnicki* may well be used to spin a constitutional doctrine that would empower the government to forbid trafficking in privacy contraband, despite a majority opinion that on its surface seems to deny it.").

Do the above cases mean that the press enjoys an absolute privilege to publish the truth? Media advocates have regularly pressed this argument to the Court. But, thus far, the Court has chosen to decide the cases on narrower grounds. See *Landmark Communications, Inc. v. Virginia*, 435 U.S. 829 (1978) [sanctions against newspaper for publishing confidential information concerning state judicial disciplinary proceedings held invalid]; *Butterworth v. Smith*, 494 U.S. 624 (1990) [state cannot prohibit grand jury witness from disclosing own testimony after end of grand jury term]. The media cites its role as agent of the public to provide truthful reports on matters of public concern and the dangers of self-censorship. Opponents stress the importance of privacy interests that can be harmed even by truthful information, *e.g.*, names of juveniles, identities of victims and witnesses of crimes. Supreme Court decisions have extended substantial constitutional protection to the press against privacy-based claims but they have not extended the broader protection sought by the media.

## F. INTENTIONAL INFLICTION OF MENTAL DISTRESS

Like privacy, the tort of intentional infliction of mental distress is designed to protect the personal interest in emotional well being. The widely adopted Restatement (Second) of Torts, § 46, provides: "One who by extreme and outrageous conduct intentionally or recklessly causes severe emotional distress to another is subject to liability [for damages]." But what if the "extreme and outrageous conduct" takes the form of expression? Does the First Amendment protect patently offensive speech intended to cause emotional distress? The Court addressed this issue in *Hustler Magazine v. Falwell*, 485 U.S. 46 (1988).

Parodying a liquor advertisement, *Hustler* carried an alleged interview with Rev. Jerry Falwell describing his "first time" as a drunken episode with his mother in an outhouse. The article indicated that it was an ad parody, not to be taken seriously. While Falwell's libel action failed, his claim for mental distress was successful below. The Supreme Court unanimously reversed: "We conclude that public figures and public officials may not recover for the tort of intentional infliction of emotional distress by reason of publications such as the one here at issue without showing in addition that the publication contains a false statement of fact which was made with 'actual malice,' *i.e.*, with knowledge that the statement was false or with reckless disregard as to whether or not it was true."

Chief Justice Rehnquist acknowledged that bad motives resulting in harm often yield civil liability. But, he continued, "in the world of debate about public affairs, many things done with motives that are less than admirable are protected by the First Amendment." Political satire and parody are meant to be offensive and cause distress. Debate cannot be "uninhibited if publishers must risk liability based on bad motives." In the context of "public debate about public figures," bad motives cannot be controlling. In responding to Falwell's argument that the "outrageousness" of Hustler's conduct provided a basis for liability, the Chief Justice agreed that public discourse would not suffer if such speech could be regulated under a principled standard. However, " '[o]utrageousness' in the area of political and social discourse has an inherent subjectiveness about it which would allow a jury to impose liability on the basis of jurors' tastes or views, or perhaps on the basis of their dislike of a particular expression."

The decision in *Falwell* is limited to public figures. But is its rationale so limited? It has been suggested that the real problem posed by the case is not to provide a supporting rationale, "but rather how to articulate limits on that rationale that will permit suits for emotional distress inflicted through speech in other contexts to survive." Smolla, *Emotional Distress and the First Amendment*, 20 Ariz. St. L.J. 423 (1988). If the outrageousness takes the form of speech by a private figure concerning public affairs, the rationale used by Chief Justice Rehnquist in *Falwell* is still applicable. On the other hand, why should the First Amendment protect outrageous speech intended to do harm? Like obscenity, the parameters of which are similarly ambiguous, outrageous conduct, intentionally done to cause severe mental distress, is arguably of little value in the marketplace of ideas or in the workings of the political process. Rehnquist in *Falwell* cites *Dun & Bradstreet* for the proposition that "not all speech is of equal First Amendment importance." But this is the same argument used against giving full constitutional protection to offensive and indecent speech. *Hustler Magazine v. Falwell*, 485 U.S.

46 (1988) was a ringing endorsement of the constitutional protection afforded offensive speech, even when it is intentionally harmful, at least in the context of "public debate about public figures." The governing principles of *Falwell* echo the rationale of *New York Times v. Sullivan* and *Cohen v. California*. And, like *New York Times* when it was rendered, the limits of the *Falwell* holding remain uncertain.

# CHAPTER VII

# COMMERCIAL SPEECH

## A. COMMERCIAL SPEECH IN THE *CHRESTENSEN* ERA: A CATEGORICAL APPROACH

Does speech devoted to buying and selling have the same protected First Amendment status as speech which directly involves the political process? A formative decision on this question, *Valentine v. Chrestensen*, 316 U.S. 52 (1942), involved an exhibitor who distributed handbills soliciting people to visit a submarine for a fee. When the exhibitor was told that the handbill violated a New York City anti-litter ordinance, he sought to insulate his handbill from regulation by adding a protest on the backside of the circular concerning the city's decision with respect to wharfage facilities for his submarine. Could the New York City anti-litter ordinance be enforced consistent with the First Amendment? Although Justice Douglas, for the Court, observed that government may not unduly burden freedom of speech in the public forum, he declared: "We are equally clear that the Constitution imposes no such restraint on government as respects purely commercial advertising."

*Chrestensen* did not accord commercial speech First Amendment protection. But it provided no rationale nor did it attempt to provide a definition of commercial speech. A rationale for the conclusion that commercial speech was not protected speech might be found in the self-government model of the First Amendment. What is protected is what contributes to self-government and, arguably, commercial speech does not. More particularly, Alexander Meiklejohn's distinction between "public" speech and "private" speech could rationalize the exclusion from First Amendment protection of commercial speech. Commercial speech in Meiklejohn's analysis arguably would fall under the "private" speech category.

Commercial speech analysis today has moved far from the rigid approach to commercial speech represented by a literal reading of *Chrestensen*. However, some important aspects of the no or low value approach still endure. For example, false and misleading advertising, securities transactions, and consumer protection are all regulated to this day even though expression is either being severely restricted or prohibited altogether. Moreover, the commercial speech subject to such regulation cuts a wider swath than the examples just mentioned.

## B.   THE PROBLEM OF DEFINING COMMERCIAL SPEECH

One sticking point for commercial speech doctrine is the definitional problem. When is speech commercial and when isn't it? Do all advertisements constitute commercial speech? In *New York Times v. Sullivan*, 376 U.S. 254 (1964), Justice Brennan held that an editorial advertisement protesting treatment of civil rights leaders by Alabama authorities did not lose its protected First Amendment status simply because it was a paid advertisement. A contrary conclusion would inhibit newspapers from carrying "editorial advertisements" and would close outlets for the interchange of ideas to those who wished to exercise freedom of speech "even though they are not members of the press."

Years later, in *Virginia State Board of Pharmacy v. Virginia Citizens Consumer Council, Inc.*, 425 U.S. 748 (1976), commercial speech was narrowly defined as speech which "proposes a commercial transaction." In *Central Hudson Gas & Electric Corp. v. Public Service Commission*, 447 U.S. 557 (1980), the definition of commercial speech was broadened to include "expression related solely to the economic interests of the speaker and its audience." A combination approach to the definitional problem was employed in *Bolger v. Youngs Drug Products Corp.*, 463 U.S. 60 (1983), which considered whether an unsolicited advertisement promoting a brand of contraceptives, which also discusses venereal disease and family planning, constitutes commercial speech. The Court held that the informational material did not become commercial speech simply because it was included in a commercial advertisement and the speaker had an economic motivation. But the combination of such factors coupled with the offer to sell led the Court to label the mailings as commercial speech. The federal regulation of the mailing was, nevertheless, held unconstitutional.

The foregoing discussion of the case law make it clear that the difficulties in defining commercial speech as a category greatly contributed to the demise of the rigid categorical approach taken in the *Chrestensen* case. The problem of defining commercial speech continues to bedevil this area of First Amendment doctrine to the present day.

## C.  *VIRGINIA PHARMACY* AND NEW PROTECTION FOR COMMERCIAL SPEECH

In the early 1970s, the Court began to reconsider the commercial speech doctrine and moved toward an approach which would extend some First Amendment protection to commercial speech. A significant weakening of the application of the two-tier approach to commercial speech occurred in *Bigelow v. Virginia*, 421 U.S. 809 (1975), where the Court repudiated the idea that commercial advertising was not entitled to any First Amendment protection. In *Bigelow*, the Court reversed the Virginia conviction of an editor who had accepted an ad which indicated the availability of low-cost abortions in New York state. *Bigelow* rejected the contention that any reasonable state regulation of advertising was permissible under the commercial speech doctrine. Instead, the Court reasoned that since the First Amendment gave some protection to commercial speech, the interests of the publisher, the reader and the consumer would have to be balanced against the state interest in prohibiting the dissemination of publications promoting or encouraging abortions. The Court held that the Virginia statute under which the editor was convicted was invalid since the activity which Virginia proscribed had been rendered legal by *Roe v. Wade*, 410 U.S. 113 (1973).

The watershed case which marked the advent of a new, more broadly protective approach to commercial speech was *Virginia State Board of Pharmacy v. Virginia Citizens Consumer Council, Inc.*, 425 U.S. 748 (1976). In *Virginia Pharmacy*, a state statute which prohibited pharmacists from advertising the price of prescription drugs was held unconstitutional. The Court held, per Justice Blackmun, that even classic commercial speech, which did "no more than propose a commercial transaction," warranted First Amendment protection.

Why did speech which involved only the price of prescription drugs merit First Amendment protection? The advertiser, the consumer and the society each had a First Amendment interest in the untrammeled flow of commercial information. Although the advertiser's interest was an economic interest, that did not "disqualify him from First Amendment protection." The consumer's interest in the free flow of information "may be as keen, if not keener by far, than his interest in the day's most urgent political debate." Indeed, those who were most hurt by the ban on dissemination of prescription drugs were the poor, the sick, and, especially, the aged: "When drug prices vary as strikingly as they do, information as to who is charging what becomes more than convenience. It could mean the alleviation of physical pain or the enjoyment of basic necessities."

Finally, Justice Blackmun asserted that society itself had a "strong interest in the free flow of information." Concededly, some advertisements might have more of a public interest component than others. But that was not the point. Rather, there exists a generalized public interest in information about the price of goods which merits First Amendment protection: "Advertising, however tasteless and excessive it sometimes may seem, is nonetheless dissemination of information as to who is producing and selling what product, for what reason, and at what price. So long as we preserve a predominantly free enterprise economy, the allocation of our resources in large measure will be made through numerous private economic decisions. It is a matter of public interest that those decisions, in the aggregate, be intelligent and well informed. To this end, the free flow of commercial information is indispensable." Blackmun in this passage manages to explain the First Amendment interest in commercial speech in a way that connects it to the self-government model of the First Amendment. Indeed, his rationale echoes Meiklejohn's conception of protected "public speech."

The doctrinal somersault in the First Amendment approach to commercial speech represented by *Virginia Pharmacy* has not been uniformly applauded. A powerful critique of the new commercial speech doctrine is provided by Professors Thomas Jackson and John Jeffries. Speech which does nothing more than propose a commercial transaction, they argue, is almost self-evidently not concerned with democratic self-governance. Nor does it "implicate the traditionally accepted meanings of freedom of speech." The real consequence of the misguided reliance on the First Amendment in *Virginia Pharmacy*, the authors contend, is the resurrection of the substantive due process doctrine of *Lochner v. New York*, 198 U.S. 45 (1905). The drug price advertising ban is just another form of economic market regulation the propriety of which should be left to the discretion of popularly elected legislatures. Jackson & Jeffries, Jr., *Commercial Speech: Economic Due Process and The First Amendment*, 65 Va. L. Rev. 1 (1979).

## D. COMMERCIAL SPEECH DIFFERENTIATED FROM OTHER FORMS OF PROTECTED SPEECH

From the foregoing, it might appear that the protection accorded commercial speech by *Virginia Pharmacy* would be equivalent to the full protection accorded political speech. *Virginia Pharmacy* did not go that far. Commercial speech, although meriting some First Amendment protection is nonetheless still subject to a greater measure of regulation than would be tolerable for more social or political speech.

Why are some forms of protected speech more equal than others? Justice Blackmun in *Virginia Pharmacy* says there are "commonsense differences" between commercial speech and other kinds of protected expression justifying different levels of legal protection. For example, the accuracy of commercial speech is more easily verifiable than news or political commentary. Further, Justice Blackmun saw as critical "the greater objectivity and hardiness of commercial speech." Since advertising was so intertwined with the profit motivation, it was unlikely that commercial speech would be "chilled by proper regulation and foregone entirely." The greater hardiness of commercial speech made it less necessary for the state "to tolerate inaccurate statements for fear of silencing the speaker." Similarly, the "greater hardiness of commercial speech" might make it appropriate for regulation of advertising to require "additional information, warnings and disclaimers."

*Virginia Pharmacy* extended some First Amendment protection to commercial speech but the protection it afforded was hardly all-encompassing. Some forms of commercial speech are still clearly unprotected, such as commercial speech that involves an illegal activity or activity contrary to public policy. In *Pittsburgh Press Co. v. Pittsburgh Commission on Human Relations*, 413 U.S. 376 (1973), the Court had held, per Justice Powell, that a prohibition of the Pittsburgh Human Relations

Commission against use of sex-designated columns in the help wanted pages of the city's newspapers did not violate the First Amendment. The Human Relations Commission had concluded that the sex-designated help wanted columns constituted illegal sex discrimination. When illegal activity is involved, the commercial expression does not enjoy First Amendment protection. *Virginia Pharmacy* cited with apparent approval the *Pittsburgh Press* doctrine that advertisements proposing illegal transactions could be prohibited.

Similarly, the new measure of protection accorded commercial speech by *Virginia Pharmacy* did not mean that false and misleading expression enjoyed First Amendment protection. Justice Blackmun noted that false speech "commercial or otherwise, has never been protected for its own sake." Given the hardiness of commercial speech, it was unlikely that truthful commercial speech would be incidentally deterred when false commercial speech is regulated. Nor did the demise of the commercial speech doctrine mean that deceptive and misleading advertising was in a more protected status.

In *Friedman v. Rogers*, 440 U.S. 1 (1979), the Court held that a Texas statute which prohibited the practice of optometry under a trade name does not violate the First Amendment. How could a state be precluded under *Virginia Pharmacy* from preventing the publication of the price of prescription drugs and at the same time be allowed to prohibit the practice of optometry under a trade name? The answer was that trade names presented opportunities for deception that advertising about prescription drug prices did not. *Friedman* was consistent with *Virginia Pharmacy* because the Texas statute did not "prohibit or limit the type of information protected in *Virginia Pharmacy.*" In *Friedman*, the Court, per Justice Powell, also noted that since the decision to extend First Amendment protection to commercial speech was relatively new, the Court was going to be cautious in evaluating First Amendment challenges to state economic legislation serving valid regulatory interests such as the prevention of deceptive and misleading advertising.

The greater objectivity and hardiness of commercial speech is the rationale that has justified a number of distinctions between even protected commercial speech and other forms of protected speech. For example, in *Virginia Pharmacy*, the Court specifically stated that the greater objectivity and hardiness of commercial speech might also "make inapplicable the prohibitions against prior restraints." In *Pittsburgh Press*, the newspaper had asserted that the Human Rights Commission's ban on sex-designated help—wanted columns was an invalid prior restraint. But the assertion was rejected. The Court held that the narrowness of the restraint and the illegal character of the expression restrained presented no danger to "arguably protected speech."

Similarly, the overbreadth doctrine does not apply to commercial speech. In *Bates v. State Bar of Arizona*, 433 U.S. 350 (1977), Justice Blackmun said that the usual justification for the application of overbreadth analysis "applies weakly, if at all, in the ordinary commercial context." Why? The answer appears to lie once again in the hardiness rationale: "Since advertising is linked to commercial well-being, it seems unlikely that such speech is particularly susceptible to being crushed by overbroad regulation." Overbreadth is a doctrinal tool used where there is anxiety about determining the frontiers of protection. But the advertiser is less in need of such protection than is normally the case with other forms of protected speech. Overbreadth would only be relevant in a First Amendment challenge to a regulation of commercial speech to the extent that the regulation affected non-commercial speech. *Board of Trustees of State University of New York v. Fox*, 492 U.S. 469 (1989).

## E. THE *CENTRAL HUDSON* TEST: SPECIAL OR DIMINISHED PROTECTION FOR COMMERCIAL SPEECH?

*Virginia Pharmacy* did not exhaust the differences between protected commercial speech and other forms of protected speech. There is still a more significant distinction. The usual strict scrutiny standard of review which is usually applied to content regulation is not used. Instead, the Court uses a test set forth in *Central Hudson Gas & Electric Corp. v. Public Service Comm'n of New York*, 447 U.S. 557 (1980). In *Central Hudson*, the issue was whether a regulation of the state public utility commission, which completely banned promotional advertising by an electric utility violated the First Amendment. The public utility, commission thought the advertising promoting the use of electricity was contrary to national energy conservation policy. The *Central Hudson* Court, per Justice Powell, quickly concluded that the expression being regulated was commercial speech. *Central Hudson* emphasized the informational function of commercial speech as the basis for extending First Amendment protection to it. The test in *Central Hudson* was, therefore, developed to protect information which did in fact inform society and to exclude protection for those commercial messages which did not.

The *Central Hudson* test—designed to indicate when commercial speech is protected and when it is not—has four parts. (1) *The commercial speech must not be misleading or involve illegal activity.* If a commercial message is false, illegal, or deceptive, then there is no informational value in it. Understandably, therefore, the first part of the test set forth in *Central Hudson* involves this question: Does the speech in question mislead or involve illegal activity? (2) *The governmental interest advanced by the regulation must be substantial.* The latitude allowed the state to regulate commercial expression which is neither illegal, false nor deceptive is far more limited than is the case with respect to commercial messages which bear these infirmities. Therefore, for regulation to be valid with respect to such protected speech, the asserted governmental interest must be a substantial one. (3) *The regulation must directly advance the asserted governmental interest.* (4) *The government regulation must not be more extensive than is necessary to serve the governmental interest at stake.* These last two parts of the *Central Hudson* test basically ask whether the governmental interest is narrowly tailored to serve the state's substantial interest.

Application by the Court in *Central Hudson* of its four part test provides the student with some guidance on how the test works. First, since the utility company's message promoting the use of electricity was not misleading or illegal, the advertising at issue was commercial speech protected by the First Amendment. The second part of the test dealing with the issue of the substantiality of the governmental interest behind the regulation was also satisfied since government clearly had a substantial interest in the conservation of energy and in the preservation of a fair rate structure. The ban on promotional advertising by the utility met the third part of the *Central Hudson* test since it directly advanced the state's interest in energy conservation. But the fourth part of the *Central Hudson* test was not met by the ban. Justice Powell said this fourth part of the test was the "critical inquiry" in the case—"whether the Commission's complete suppression of speech ordinarily protected by the First Amendment is no more extensive than necessary to further the state's interest in energy conservation." The Commission's ban was not narrowly tailored. It extended to all promotional advertising by a utility whether or not the particular service advertised by the utility had any impact on energy conservation. Moreover, the Commission had failed to show that a more limited regulation of the utility's commercial expression could not have satisfied its interest in conservation. Justice Powell suggested that the Commission might have required instead "that the advertisements include information about the relative efficiency and expense of the offered service."

*Central Hudson* has been subject to considerable criticism. Professor Steven Shiffrin argues that there is a critical distinction between *Virginia Pharmacy* and *Central Hudson*: "In *Virginia Pharmacy*, by way of *ipse dixit*, the Court said that the choice between the dangers of suppressing information and the dangers of its misuse had already been made by the First Amendment. Paternalistic suppression of information was not permitted—period." *Central Hudson*, on the other hand, ushered in "an approach that ultimately allows paternalistic suppression of true commercial information so long as the government has a substantial government interest." Shiffrin, *The First Amendment and Economic Regulation: Away From a General Theory of the First Amendment*, 78 Nw. U.L. Rev. 1212 (1984). In short, the *Central Hudson* test is capable of providing less First Amendment protection for commercial speech than *Virginia Pharmacy* had appeared to provide or promise. On the other hand, if we cast the *Central Hudson* test in its most favorable First Amendment light, it approximates an intermediate standard of review. As such, it provides far greater protection for commercial speech than the rationality standard of the *Chrestensen* era. Indeed, Justice Stevens in *44 Liquormart v. Rhode Island*, 517 U.S. 484 (1996) called for applying the *Central Hudson* test with "special care."

## F.   THE *FOX* AND THE *CENTRAL HUDSON* TEST REVISED

*Central Hudson* did not represent the end of the erosion of substantial First Amendment protection for commercial speech promised by *Virginia Pharmacy*. In *Board of Trustees of State University of New York (SUNY) v. Fox*, 492 U.S. 469 (1989), the Court considered a SUNY regulation governing use of school property, including dormitories, which provided that no authorization should be given to private commercial enterprises to operate on state university campuses or in facilities provided by the university other than to provide for certain specified services. In the *Fox* case, a company offering Tupperware products was asked to leave a SUNY dormitory because it was not one of the services authorized to operate in a campus dorm. Did the SUNY regulation violate the First Amendment? The Court, per Justice Scalia, held that it did not. The state university had a substantial interest in regulating commercial speech such as Tupperware parties, *i.e.*, "promoting an educational rather than commercial atmosphere on SUNY's campuses, promoting safety and security, preventing commercial exploitation of students, and preserving residential tranquility."

The real significance of the *Fox* case was in its revision of the fourth part of the *Central Hudson* test, which inquires into whether the regulation reaches further than is "necessary" to serve the substantial governmental interest at issue. Justice Scalia conceded that "the word 'necessary' [if] interpreted strictly ... would translate into the 'least restrictive means test' " and that the language of *Central Hudson* itself would support this formulation. But Justice Scalia observed that "other formulations in our commercial speech cases support a more flexible meaning for the *Central Hudson* test" and that "something short of a least-restrictive means standard" is required. Accordingly, the Court concluded in *Fox* that a regulation is narrowly tailored within the meaning of the fourth part of the *Central Hudson* test if the regulation at issue "is absolutely the least severe that will achieve the desired end." The *Fox* case considerably watered down the fourth part of the *Central Hudson* test. Justice Scalia described the new approach to this part of the test as follows: "What our decisions require is a 'fit' between the legislature's ends and the means chosen to accomplish those ends, ... a fit that is not necessarily perfect, but reasonable." *Fox,* therefore, represents a further weakening of the full First Amendment status for protected commercial speech seemingly offered by *Virginia Pharmacy*, since it further weakens the *Central Hudson* test—a test which itself has been criticized by defenders of commercial speech as insufficiently protective.

*Cincinnati v. Discovery Network, Inc.*, 507 U.S. 410 (1993) was testimony both to the Court's doctrinal allegiance to the *Fox* test and to the fact that its application did not necessarily mean that commercial speech regulation would prevail. Cincinnati imposed a ban on newsracks distributing commercial publications but not on newspaper newsracks. Authorized by an "outdated ordinance" forbidding distribution of handbills, the ban was justified by the city on the basis of its interests in safety and esthetics on its sidewalks. Justice Stevens, for the Court, invalidated the ban on commercial newsracks using the *Fox* revision of *Central Hudson*. The "reasonable fit" required by *Fox* was not met. In light of the city's "recently developed" interest in newsracks and its failure nonetheless to regulate their "size, shape appearance or number," it was clear that the city had not " 'carefully calculated' the costs and benefits associated with the burden on speech imposed by its prohibition." Since the ban would remove 62 commercial newsracks from the city's streets but leave 1500–2000 newspaper newsracks in place, the safety and esthetic benefit to be derived from banning the commercial newsracks was deemed marginal.

The city attempted to show that a "close fit" existed by arguing that every decrease in the total number of newsracks had the effect of increasing safety and improving the attractiveness of the city.

But discrimination against commercial newsracks that are no more harmful than the permitted newspaper newsracks would in fact have only the slightest impact on the city's sidewalks. The real basis of the ban, said Justice Stevens, was the premise that "commercial speech has only a low value." The city's position, however, "attaches more importance to the distinctions between commercial and noncommercial speech than our cases warrant and seriously underestimates the value of commercial speech." The banned commercial publications shared important characteristics with the permitted newspapers and illustrated the difficulty of drawing "bright lines" cabining the commercial speech category. Furthermore, the city's distinction between commercial and noncommercial speech had no "relationship *whatsoever* to the particular means the city has asserted." The content-based ban on commercial newsracks was an impermissible means of furthering the city's legitimate interests. The Court stressed that its holding was narrow and left open the question whether under other circumstances "differential treatment of commercial and noncommercial newsracks" could be justified.

Justice Blackmun, concurring, said it was little wonder that Cincinnati had limited its ban to commercial newsracks. *Central Hudson*, as refined in *Fox*, gave too little protection to commercial speech: "In this case, *Central Hudson's* chickens have come home to roost." Taking the polar opposite position, Chief Justice Rehnquist in dissent, joined by Justices White and Thomas, said that the majority had not understood the significance of the alteration by *Fox* of the fourth prong of *Central Hudson*. Cincinnati had, in fact, burdened less speech than necessary to accomplish its objectives.

In summary, *Discovery Network* did not signify new protection for commercial speech since the case for a "close fit" between the regulation and the goal to be achieved by it was deemed so clearly lacking by the Court. Instead, *Discovery Network* indicated, with the exception of Justice Blackmun, a continued adherence by the Court to the *Fox* revision of *Central Hudson*—disagreement about its application notwithstanding. Thus, relying on *Central Hudson* and *Fox, United States v. Edge Broadcasting Co.*, 509 U.S. 418 (1993), upheld federal legislation regulating broadcasting lottery advertising.

## G. LAWYER ADVERTISING

### 1. ROUTINE SERVICES

An arena where the new protected status for some commercial speech has had great impact while at the same time generating considerable litigation is that of lawyer advertising. *Bates v. State Bar of Arizona*, 433 U.S. 350 (1977) held that a blanket ban on lawyer advertising in newspapers for routine legal services violated the First Amendment. The routine legal services at issue in *Bates* involved newspaper advertisements which described the price and nature of services offered for matters such as uncontested divorces, uncontested adoptions, personal bankruptcies, and changes of name. A state interest stressed by the state bar of Arizona in favor of the ban was the adverse effect lawyer advertising would have on professionalism. Justice Blackmun found the asserted nexus between a ban on lawyer advertising and protection of lawyer professionalism to be a tenuous one. He noted that in *Virginia Pharmacy*, maintenance of the professionalism of pharmacists had been rejected—in light of the state professional standards applicable to pharmacists and enforced by the state—as a state interest sufficient to justify the prohibition on advertising about the prices of prescription drugs. Similarly, the "highly paternalistic approach" of a flat ban on truthful lawyer advertising of routine services predicated on an asserted need to protect the professionalism of lawyers was repudiated.

Nor was it an argument in favor of the ban that the advertising at issue failed to give potential clients a complete basis on which to choose an attorney: "The alternative—the prohibition of advertising—serves only to restrict the information that flows to consumers." Justice Blackmun criticized the premise "that the public is best kept in ignorance than trusted with correct but incomplete information." *Bates*, therefore, rejected any justification of the disciplinary rule "based on the benefits of public ignorance."

The *Bates* decision was significant since the American legal profession had long enforced a ban on legal advertising. However, lawyer advertising was not accorded across-the-board First Amendment protection in *Bates.* State restraint would be permissible where false and misleading advertising was concerned. In addition, the Court reserved judgement on whether lawyer advertising in the broadcast media "merited special consideration." Further, in a significant *dictum, Bates* distinguished between advertising for routine legal services and advertising about the quality of legal services, *e.g.,* claims that one lawyer's training, experience, or success rate was superior to that of other lawyers. Although the quality issue was not before the Court, *Bates* indicated that quality claims might well be regulated or even restricted: "Such claims are probably not susceptible to precise measurement or verification, and, under some circumstances, might well be deceptive or misleading to the public, or even false."

## 2.  IN–PERSON SOLICITATION

Another commercial speech issue involving lawyer advertising which was left for resolution for another day was "in-person solicitation of clients—at the hospital room or the accident site." Although *Bates* did not itself raise the issue of such in-person solicitation, Justice Blackmun observed that such an activity "might well pose dangers of over-reaching and misrepresentation not encountered in newspaper announcement advertising." A year after *Bates,* the Court, per Justice Powell, in *Ohralik v. Ohio State Bar Association,* 436 U.S. 447 (1978), confronted the in-person solicitation issue left open in *Bates* and ruled that in-person solicitation could be regulated: "[T]he Bar—acting with state authorization—constitutionally may discipline a lawyer for soliciting clients in person, for pecuniary gain, under circumstances likely to pose dangers that the State has a right to prevent."

Ohralik, an Ohio lawyer, had gone to a hospital where he obtained the consent of an auto accident victim to represent her. Although Ohralik was subsequently discharged by his client, he obtained part of the insurance recovery as settlement for a breach of contract action that he had brought against her. The accident victim filed a grievance complaint which resulted in an order of the Ohio Supreme Court that he be suspended. The Supreme Court, per Justice Powell, affirmed the Ohio Supreme Court and rejected Ohralik's contention that the First Amendment shielded his conduct.

*Ohralik* rejected the contention that in-person solicitation of clients should be treated like the advertisements protected in *Bates*. *Bates* was distinguished because in-person solicitation tended to discourage people needing counsel from comparing legal services. In-person solicitation might in fact frustrate the "individual and societal interest, identified in *Bates*, in facilitating 'informed and reliable decisionmaking.'" In sum, the advertising in *Bates* served to inform the public while the in-person solicitation in *Ohralik* tended to frustrate the consumer's need for information. In-person solicitation was essentially a business transaction. Speech was certainly part of the transaction but it was only a subordinate part. This did not mean that the speech was not entitled to First Amendment protection but it did mean that the level of judicial scrutiny should be lowered. The state interest in preventing harmful activity by prohibiting solicitation was strong and proof of harm was not essential. The state could prohibit such in-person solicitation solely as a prophylactic measure.

*Ohralik* should be contrasted with *In re Primus*, 436 U.S. 412 (1978) which involved a South Carolina lawyer who was a cooperating attorney with a local branch of the ACLU. A South Carolina lawyer spoke to a group of women who had been sterilized as a condition for receiving public assistance and advised them of the legal redress available to them. She then informed a woman in the group by letter that free legal assistance would be available to her from the ACLU. The South Carolina Supreme Court ordered a public reprimand of the lawyer. The United States Supreme Court reversed. *Ohralik* was distinguished: "Unlike the situation in *Ohralik*, [the lawyer's] act of solicitation took the form of a letter to a woman with whom [the lawyer] had discussed the possibility of seeking redress for an allegedly unconstitutional sterilization. This was not in-person solicitation for pecuniary gain."

*Primus* stressed that the lawyer who was being disciplined had not sought financial gain but rather was seeking to advance an association's civil liberties objectives. Therefore, unlike *Ohralik*, the level of scrutiny should not be lowered. In dissent, Justice Rehnquist complained that the approach in *Primus* was basically dependent on an examination of the "content of the speech or the motive of the speaker." He argued that the appropriate focus should be on the character of the conduct which the state wished to proscribe. In sum, in *Primus*, the political or ideological solicitation case, the strict scrutiny standard of review was applied. In *Ohralik*, the "ambulance chaser" solicitation case, the Court held that the standard of review must be lowered. Looking at *Ohralik* and *Primus* back to back, the vaunted new protection for commercial speech—*qua* commercial speech—began to look a trifle fragile.

But note that in *Edenfield v. Fane*, 507 U.S. 761 (1993), a state ban on in-person solicitation by Certified Public Accountants (CPAs) was struck down as violative of the First Amendment. *Ohralik* was distinguished. CPA in-person solicitation, unlike more persuasive lawyer in-person solicitation, is "not inherently conducive to overreaching and other forms of misconduct." CPAs are not trained in the art of persuasion and there is slight risk, therefore, that innocent people will be misled. Subsequent decisions have emphasized the Court's statement that government burdens on commercial speech are not satisfied "by mere speculation or conjecture." The harms addressed must be real and the regulation must actually and materially alleviate them.

### 3.  SOLICITATION THROUGH PRINT ADVERTISING AND TARGETED MAILINGS

*Zauderer v. Office of Disciplinary Counsel of the Supreme Court of Ohio*, 471 U.S. 626 (1985) illustrated that the Court continued to make fine distinctions in lawyer advertising cases. Ohio sought to discipline a lawyer who advertised in the newspapers soliciting business from women who had used the Dalkon Shield. The Ohio Supreme Court construed its disciplinary rule prohibiting self-recommendation and solicitation to preclude lawyers from soliciting business through advertisements "containing information or advice on a specific legal problem." Since the ads in this respect were not false or misleading, the burden was on the state to show that a substantial governmental interest was served as in *Ohralik*. But the situation was not the same as in-person solicitations.

Print advertising was unlikely to put the same pressure on a client to agree to the offer of representation as would be the case where the offer of solicitation was made by the lawyer in person— particularly where the offer was made in a stressful situation such as a hospital. Print advertising was more likely to provide an opportunity for reflection and sufficient time to make an informed choice. As a result the state interests that justified the ban on in person solicitation in *Ohralik* were deemed not to be as substantial in *Zauderer*. The same ad which had indicated the lawyer's wish to represent women who had used the Dalkon Shield contained an illustration, which also violated Ohio disciplinary rules prohibiting illustrations. The rule against illustrations was defended as serving the state's interest in ensuring that lawyer advertising was dignified as well as to prevent confusion, manipulation and misleading of the public. The Court held that illustrations bearing these infirmities should be dealt with on a case by case basis. These state interests were simply too minimal to justify a blanket ban.

The Court, per Justice White, however, concluded that the Ohio Supreme Court's decision to discipline the lawyer in *Zauderer* for incomplete disclosure was valid. The lawyer's Dalkon Shield newspaper advertisement stated that representation was on a contingent fee basis and that, if there was no recovery, the client owed no fee. However, the ad did not disclose that clients might be liable "for significant litigation costs even if their lawsuits were unsuccessful." Rejecting the contention that the disclosure requirements should be invalid as the blanket bans had been, Justice White responded that there were "material differences between disclosure requirements and outright prohibitions on speech."

Ohio had not sought to prevent lawyers from providing information to the public. Indeed, it had merely required *more* information. Was this compulsory speech which had been prohibited by *Wooley v. Maynard*, 430 U.S. 705 (1977) and *Miami Herald Publishing Co. v. Tornillo*, 418 U.S. 241 (1974)? No. Ohio had not tried to prescribe what should be orthodox in politics. Instead, it had "attempted only to prescribe what shall be orthodox in commercial advertising." Justice White justified this difference in treatment as follows: "Because the extension of First Amendment protection to commercial speech is justified principally by the value to consumers of the information such speech provides, [the lawyer's] constitutionally protected interest in *not* providing any particular factual information in his advertising is minimal." This was not to say that an advertiser could never raise First Amendment objections to disclosure requirements. But such First Amendment interests were satisfied as long as the disclosure requirements were "reasonably related to the state's interest in preventing deception of consumers."

In *Shapero v. Kentucky Bar Ass'n*, 486 U.S. 466 (1988), the Court held that Kentucky could not prevent lawyers from sending truthful non-deceptive letters soliciting legal business about a specific legal issue. Kentucky's total ban on targeted mailed solicitations by lawyers violated the First Amendment. Justice Brennan, for the Court, reasoned that *Zauderer*, the print advertising case, governed the targeted mail issue: "In assessing the potential for overreaching and undue influence, the mode of communication makes all the difference. Like print advertising, [targeted direct-mail solicitation] 'poses much less risk of overreaching or undue influence' than does in-person solicitation. Neither mode of written communication involves the 'coercive force of the personal presence of a trained advocate' or the 'pressure on the potential client for an immedi-

ate yes-or-no answer to the offer of representation.' " Targeted mail solicitation was analogized to
the use of illustrations by lawyers in newspaper
advertisements in *Zauderer*. It could be restricted
only if a substantial governmental interest was
present and the restriction at issue directly advanced that interest. The facts of *Shapero* did not
meet this test. Just because direct-mail solicitation
is capable of abuse or presents an opportunity for
making mistakes did not justify a total ban in the
absence of specific findings that the solicitation was
false or misleading.

In *Florida Bar v. Went For It, Inc.*, 515 U.S. 618
(1995), the Court, per Justice Stevens, upheld (5–4)
a ban imposed by the Florida Bar on targeted
direct-mail solicitations to victims and their relatives for 30 days after an accident or disaster. The
Bar ban satisfied the *Central Hudson* test. Unlike
*Edenfield v. Fane*, the harms targeted were concrete
and nonspeculative. Unlike *Shapero*, privacy was a
major concern. The purpose of the ban was to
prevent "the outrage and irritation" with the legal
profession that direct solicitation immediately after
an accident provokes. Mail solicitation as well as
face-to-face solicitation can be regulated to serve
the Bar's substantial interest in protecting injured
persons from intrusive conduct by lawyers and the
resulting loss of faith in the legal profession. The
ban imposed by the Bar was narrow both in length
and scope. Justice Kennedy in dissent said *Central
Hudson's* second prong was not satisfied. The state
interest in protecting the victims and their relatives

was not advanced in a direct and material way. The 30 day ban was essentially directed to protecting the reputation of the bar. How this aided persons suffering injury and loss was hardly clear.

## 4.  STATEMENTS OF CERTIFICATION AND SPECIALIZATION

In *Peel v. Attorney Registration and Disciplinary Commission of Illinois*, 496 U.S. 91 (1990), the Court invalidated an Illinois state rule categorically barring a lawyer from advertising his certification as a trial specialist. Justice Stevens for a plurality said the issue was whether a lawyer's letterhead which proclaimed his certification as a trial specialist was misleading. But a statement of certification was capable of verification. It was not an unverifiable opinion of a lawyer's ultimate quality. The lawyer's letterhead in *Peel* was not misleading. There was no evidence of deception. Therefore, the assertion that the letterhead was misleading must be rejected.

The ban on certification and specialization could not be justified because such statements had a potential to mislead. A potential to mislead "does not satisfy the State's heavy burden of justifying a categorical prohibition against the dissemination of accurate factual information to the public." Less categorical means of dealing with potential deception were available to the state, such as "screening certifying organizations or requiring a disclaimer about the certifying organization or the standards of a specialty." As in *Shapero*, the blanket bar of the state rule restricting lawyer's advertising in *Peel* was broader than reasonably necessary to address the interest with which the state was concerned.

In *Ibanez v. Florida Department of Business and Professional Regulation, Board of Accountancy*, 512 U.S. 136 (1994), the censure by the Florida Board of Accountancy of an attorney who had used the words Certified Public Accountant (CPA) and Certified Financial Planner (CFP) in attorney yellow page listings and on her law office stationery was held to be incompatible with the First Amendment. The attorney was in fact a CPA and a CFP. But the Board contended, *inter alia*, that the CFP designation was misleading when used with the term CPA because it implied state recognition and certification as a CFP. Relying on *Edenfield,* the Court concluded the Board had shown no real harm that flowed from the use of this commercial speech. The attorney's use of the CFP designation, like the trial specialist designation in *Peel*, was not inherently misleading. Concern that the word certified in CFP implied state recognition was not sufficient to surmount "the constitutional presumption favoring disclosure over concealment."

## H.   TRUTHFUL ADVERTISING ABOUT LAWFUL BUT HARMFUL ACTIVITY

Can truthful advertising about activity which is legal but potentially harmful be regulated? The short answer to this question is—"Yes." An unusual case which raised the issue was *Posadas de Puerto Rico Assoc. v. Tourism Co. of Puerto Rico*, 478 U.S. 328 (1986). Puerto Rico legalized casino gambling and, at the same time, prohibited advertising about casino gambling to the Puerto Rican public. Yet it permitted restricted advertising about casino gambling on media in mainland United States. Applying *Central Hudson*, Justice Rehnquist, for the Court, held that the ban on casino gambling to Puerto Rico residents did not violate the First Amendment. Clearly, the first part of *Central Hudson* was satisfied. The advertising concerned lawful activity and was neither false nor misleading. The second part—the substantiality of the governmental interest—was also met. The interest served by the ban was to reduce casino gambling by the residents of Puerto Rico. Identical concerns had prompted most of the 50 states to ban casino gambling.

The third and fourth parts of the *Central Hudson* test basically involved "the 'fit' between the legislature's ends and the means chosen to accomplish those ends." The third part of the test was satisfied. The legislature's ban directly advanced the governmental interest in reducing casino gambling by Puerto Rico residents. The legislature's belief that this would be the result of the ban was a reasonable one. The fourth part of *Central Hudson*—"whether the restrictions on commercial speech are no more extensive than necessary to serve the government's interest"—was satisfied "beyond peradventure."

The ban's challengers contended that the First Amendment "requires the Puerto Rico legislature to reduce demand for casino gambling among the residents of Puerto Rico not by suppressing commercial speech that might *encourage* such gambling, but by promulgating speech designed to *discourage* it." Apparently, the theory was that promoting speech that would discourage casino gambling was a less restrictive means to achieve the legislative end. Justice Rehnquist responded that it was for the legislature to decide whether such a "counterspeech" policy would be more effective. In sum, the Puerto Rico ban satisfied each of the four prongs of the *Central Hudson* test.

Additionally, the challengers relied on *Carey v. Population Services International*, 431 U.S. 678 (1977) and *Bigelow v. Virginia*, 421 U.S. 809 (1975). *Carey* had invalidated a ban on the advertisements of contraceptives and *Bigelow* had set aside a criminal conviction based on the advertisements for an abortion clinic. But *Carey* and *Bigelow* dealt with situations where the underlying activity, about which advertising was banned, was constitutionally protected. This was not true of casino gambling. Puerto Rico could have banned casino gambling by its residents entirely: "[T]he greater power to completely ban casino gambling necessarily includes the lesser power to ban advertising of casino gambling, and *Carey* and *Bigelow* are hence inapposite." Justice Rehnquist reasoned that it would be "a Pyrrhic victory" for the casino owners to succeed in their argument that the First Amendment protected their right to advertise casino gambling if in the end the legislature banned casino gambling altogether. The legislature's power over harmful activity ranged from prohibition to legalization "with restrictions on stimulation" of demand for the activity. Ruling out intermediate responses short of prohibition "would require more than we can find in the First Amendment."

Justice Rehnquist's "greater-includes-the-lesser" argument was challenged by Justice Brennan, joined by Justices Marshall and Blackmun, in dissent: "[T]he 'constitutional doctrine' which bans Puerto Rico from banning advertisements concerning lawful casino gambling is not so strange a restraint—it is called the First Amendment." In Brennan's view, strict scrutiny, rather than the *Central Hudson* test, was the appropriate standard of review for truthful advertising about lawful activity. Indeed, Brennan charged Rehnquist in *Posadas* had not been faithful to the *Central Hudson* test which he professed to use in evaluating the First Amendment validity of the Puerto Rico ban: "While tipping its hat to [the *Central Hudson* standards] the Court does little more than defer to what it perceives to be the determination by Puerto Rico's legislature that a ban on casino advertising aimed at residents is reasonable." The criticism was that, in Rehnquist's hands, the *Central Hudson* test, arguably an intermediate standard of review, had become a *de facto* rationality standard.

The promise of *Virginia Pharmacy* that whole categories of truthful commercial advertising, such as the prices of prescription drugs, could not be totally prohibited consistent with the First Amendment was severely undermined by the validation in *Posadas* of the ban on advertising of casino gambling to Puerto Rico residents. Furthermore, Rehnquist's "the-greater-includes-the lesser" theory had the capacity to throw even a rigorous approach to *Central Hudson* into eclipse. Since so much of economic and commercial activity could be banned if the legislature chose, this theory could authorize a ban on advertising these activities as well—thereby dramatically shrinking the domain of protected commercial speech.

Although *Posadas* might have had the potential to transform *Central Hudson* into an approximation of the rationality standard of review, subsequent cases have moved *Central Hudson* in the opposite direction. In *Rubin v. Coors Brewing Co.*, 514 U.S. 476 (1995), a unanimous Court, per Justice Thomas, invalidated a federal law prohibiting the disclosure of the alcohol content of beer on labels holding that it failed to satisfy the *Central Hudson* test. *Central Hudson*'s second prong requiring a substantial governmental interest was met because of the social harm that might follow if breweries competed for business on the basis of a higher alcohol content than their competitors. But the third prong requiring that the regulation directly advance the governmental interest was not satisfied.

Federal law prohibited the disclosure of alcohol content on *labels* unless required by state law. Yet federal law prohibiting disclosure of alcohol content in *advertising* applied only in the 18 states that affirmatively prohibited such advertising. This left brewers free to disclose alcohol content in advertising but not on labels in much of the country. Since curbing the advertising of the alcohol content of various beers would seem to be a more potent weapon to cope with strength wars than regulating labels, the government regulatory scheme was so irrational as to make it unlikely that it would directly and materially advance its objective. Furthermore, the federal law prohibiting disclosing alcohol strength on beer labels was not sufficiently tailored to its goal and thus violated the fourth prong of *Central Hudson*. The government clearly had other alternatives available, *e.g.* government could directly limit the alcohol content of beer. There was an insufficient fit between means and ends. Finally, *Posadas* did not require validation of the law prohibiting disclosure of alcohol content in beer. Although *Posadas* had indeed said that government could ban promotional advertising casino gambling because it could prohibit gambling altogether, the *Posadas* Court had reached that point "only *after* it had already found that the state regulation survived the *Central Hudson* test."

In *44 Liquormart v. Rhode Island*, 517 U.S. 484 (1996), the declining fortunes of *Posadas* were made emphatically clear. The Court struck down a Rhode Island statute prohibiting the advertising of retail liquor sales anywhere but at the point of sale. Although the Court was unanimous in result, there was disagreement on the proper rationale. Justice

Stevens for a plurality of four observed: "The First Amendment directs us to be especially skeptical of regulations that seek to keep people in the dark for what the government perceives to be their own good." Where prohibitions on truthful nonmisleading commercial messages are involved, there was little reason to depart from the "rigorous review" associated with the First Amendment. In such circumstances, *Central Hudson* should be applied with "special care" and with an awareness that such prohibitions "rarely survive constitutional review." An issue the Stevens opinion raised was whether the plurality was using *Central Hudson* to approximate the strict scrutiny standard. Justice Thomas, concurring, called for the abandonment of *Central Hudson* and the resurrection of *Virginia Pharmacy*. Justice Scalia, concurring, also indicated his displeasure with *Central Hudson* but, since he did not know what to replace it with, he decided to apply the existing law.

Justice Stevens believed that *Posadas* and its "greater-includes-the lesser" rationale should be repudiated. The text of the First Amendment itself showed that "attempts to regulate speech are more dangerous than attempts to regulate conduct." Finally, the argument that a ban on price advertising of liquor sales was defensible because it dealt with regulation of a vice was also rejected. A vice exception to First Amendment protection would be difficult, if not impossible, to define.

Justice O'Connor, in a concurrence joined by three other Justices, contended that the established

*Central Hudson* test was sufficient to support the result. The state ban was more extensive than necessary, *e.g.*, a tax would more directly discourage alcohol consumption than a restriction on speech. In an implicit rebuttal to the call by Justice Stevens for more rigorous review under *Central Hudson*, Justice O'Connor said there was no need for a new analysis since the Rhode Island law failed the established "less stringent" *Central Hudson* test. Beyond remarking that the post-*Posadas* Court had given a "closer look" to commercial regulation, Justice O'Connor did not call for the reversal of *Posadas*.

A group of New Orleans area broadcasters brought suit to challenge the validity under the First Amendment of a federal law, 18 U.S.C. Sec. 1304, which prohibited the advertising of casino gambling on radio and television. The law applied even to jurisdictions where casino gambling was legal. A unanimous Supreme Court held, per Justice Stevens, that the law could not be applied to broadcast ads of casino gambling by stations in Louisiana where casino gambling was legal. *Greater New Orleans Broadcasting Association, Inc. v. United States*, 527 U.S. 173 (1999). Justice Stevens refused to repudiate *Central Hudson* and adopt a more direct and stringent test to evaluate regulation of commercial speech. Two features of *44 Liquormart* were reiterated: (1) post-*Posadas* case law applied *Central Hudson* "more strictly" and (2) the idea "that the power to restrict speech about socially harmful activities was as broad as the power to prohibit such conduct" was no longer accepted. Two interests were said to meet the substantiality prong of *Central Hudson:* the broadcast advertising ban (1) reduced the social costs of gambling and (2) aided the enforcement of state antigambling policies. But Sec. 1304 did not satisfy the third and fourth prongs of *Central Hudson*. Federal law was riddled with exceptions to 1304's antigambling policy. Even assuming that state antigambling policy was more coherent than its federal counterpart, the amount of truthful speech about lawful conduct which was sacrificed by the ban, compared to any reasonably expected benefits, was intolerable. The speaker and the audience rather than the government should be the ultimate arbiters of truthful and nonmisleading information about legal activity.

Once again expressly refusing to reject the *Central Hudson* test, the Court in *Lorillard Tobacco Co. v. Reilly*, 533 U.S. 525 (2001) struck down Massachusetts regulations outlawing outdoor tobacco advertising of smokeless tobacco or cigars within 1000 feet of schools or playgrounds. The regulations also banned indoor point-of-sale advertising of these same tobacco products unless the advertising was set more than 5 feet from the floor. This was to prevent children from seeing the advertising. The tobacco companies brought suit contending that the regulations violated the First Amendment. They argued unsuccessfully that *Central Hudson* should be abandoned in favor of the strict scrutiny standard of review. The Court responded that the third and fourth prongs of the *Central Hudson* test were in play. The third prong of *Central Hudson* required that the regulations at issue must advance the government interest. Here that interest was limiting the access of children to tobacco products. The outdoor advertising regulations satisfied the third prong of *Central Hudson*. The Court disagreed with the tobacco companies that there was no evidence that limiting the exposure of the young to tobacco products would "decrease underage use of smokeless tobacco and cigars." The Court said it had previously accepted that product advertising would stimulate demand for the product and that banning such advertising would decrease that demand. But the indoor 5–foot rule failed to meet the third prong of *Central Hudson*. "Not all children are less than 5 feet tall, and those who are certainly have the ability to look up and take in their surroundings."

The fourth prong of *Central Hudson* required a reasonable fit between ends and means. Both sets of advertising regulations failed to meet *Central Hudson's* fourth prong. The fit here was not reasonable. The 1000–foot radius prohibition with respect to outdoor advertising was unduly broad. After all, the sale of tobacco products to adults was a legal activity. And as far as the restriction on on-site advertising was concerned: "A retailer in Massachusetts might have no other means of communicating to passersby on the street that it sells tobacco products." Justice Kennedy, joined by Justice Scalia, concurring, objected to the Court's retention of *Central Hudson* "in view of the substantial objections" that can be made to that test. Justice Thomas, concurring, contended that when government seeks to regulate "truthful speech in order to suppress the ideas it conveys," the strict scrutiny standard of review should be used whether or not the speech was commercial.

In *Thompson v. Western States Medical Center*, 535 U.S. 357 (2002), the Court, per Justice O'Connor, continued to assert its aversion to government prohibitions on truthful commercial speech. In *Thompson*, a federal drug regulation law prohibiting the advertising of compounded drugs was struck down 5–4. Drug compounding is a process which "alters ingredients to meet the needs of the individual patient." The regulation at issue exempted compounded drugs from the exacting standards of the FDA drug approval process so long as the providers of compounded drugs did not advertise them. The Court agreed that the drug approval process and drug compounding served substantial government interests. But the Court ruled that the advertising ban failed the final prong of *Central Hudson*. The regulation was "more extensive than necessary to serve those interests." Alternatives less stringent than a ban on advertising were available. For example, government could ban the use of "commercial scale manufacturing or testing for compounding drug products." Similarly, government could limit the number of compound drug prescriptions any one pharmacist or pharmacy could sell. As for the concern that the advertising of compounded drugs would cause patients to pressure their doctors to prescribe unnecessary prescriptions, the Court had an answer worthy of Adam Smith: "We have previously rejected the notion that the government has an interest in preventing the dissemination of truthful commercial information in order to prevent members of the public from making bad decisions with the information."

Justice Breyer, dissenting, conceded that the law at issue restricted the dissemination of some truthful information but he insisted that commercial speech did not merit the application of the "strictest most speech protective tests." The majority had not given enough weight to the government's public health and safety rationale for the advertising ban. In the past, the Court had applied a more flexible approach and had properly focused on the "fit between ends and means." The Court's approach could end up preventing legislative and regulatory action necessary to protect public health and safety.

In summary, the Court's approach to commercial speech regulation still professes to use the *Central Hudson* test. But *44 Liquor Mart, Greater New Orleans Broadcasting, Lorillard and Thompson* all demonstrate that the test the Court actually uses is far closer to the rigorous review associated with the strict scrutiny standard. As a result, truthful commercial information is now being reviewed at a level of scrutiny just short of that accorded to fully protected speech.

# CHAPTER VIII

# NEW CATEGORIES?

## A. RACIST SPEECH

Speech that is offensive, abusive, insulting or annoying is still protected: "[I]f there is a bedrock principle underlying the First Amendment, it is that the Government may not prohibit the expression of an idea simply because society finds the idea itself offensive or disagreeable." *Texas v. Johnson*, 491 U.S. 397 (1989) [Texas flag desecration law held violative of First Amendment]. But what if the speech is nothing more than a racial epithet? Or what if the idea conveyed is simply that a particular racial, ethnic or religious group is inferior and not worthy of respect or even the protections of citizenship? Is such expression protected under the First Amendment or is it a category of low value expression largely excluded from First Amendment protection?

Issues such as the foregoing highlight the competing demands of the Equal Protection Clause and the First Amendment. Those advocating hate speech laws place emphasis on the Nation's commitment to equality for all persons. Those who believe that laws restricting expression, no matter how well-intentioned, threaten the future of untrammeled public discourse, appeal to the Nation's commitment to free expression and liberty. In sum, the racist speech law controversy is at bottom one more chapter in the ancient battle between liberty and equality.

There was early support for the constitutionality of group vilification laws in *Beauharnais v. Illinois*, 343 U.S. 250 (1952), upholding 5–4 an Illinois criminal libel statute. The law proscribed publications which portray the "depravity, criminality, unchastity, or lack of virtue of a class of citizens, of any race, color, creed, or religion [where the publication] exposes [them] to contempt, derision, or obloquy or which is productive of breach of the peace or riots." In affirming a conviction for distribution of a racist leaflet which violated the statute, Justice Frankfurter invoked several theories in justification of the law. First, he relied on a libel theory. *Chaplinsky* had indicated that libel was not part of the freedom of speech protected by the First Amendment. But it should be noted that *Beauharnais* was decided prior to *New York Times v. Sullivan* which extended substantial First Amendment protection to libellous publications. Second, Frankfurter used a danger theory, citing the tendency of such hate speech to produce interracial violence. But again *Beauharnais* preceded *Brandenburg* and *Cohen*, both of which demanded greater showings of imminent danger from incitement than Frankfurter required in *Beauharnais*. Third, he developed what may be called a human dignity theory. The Court could not deny that the legislature "may warrantably believe that a man's job and his educational opportunities and the dignity accorded him may depend as much on the reputation of the racial and religious group to which he willy-nilly belongs, as on his own merits." This theme comes much closer to the contemporary justifications offered by the proponents of hate speech laws.

*Beauharnais* has long been considered to be a discredited decision. Indeed that is how the lower courts characterized *Beauharnais* in the Skokie cases when the Nazis were permitted to march in Nazi uniform bearing the swastika through the village of Skokie, Illinois, a predominantly Jewish suburb of Chicago. *Village of Skokie v. National Socialist Party*, 373 N.E.2d 21 (Ill.1978); *Collin v. Smith*, 578 F.2d 1197 (7th Cir. 1978). In striking down various village ordinances designed to prevent the march, the Seventh Circuit concluded that such hate speech is "indistinguishable in principle from speech that '[invites] dispute ... induces a condition of unrest, creates dissatisfaction with conditions as they are, or even stirs people to anger.' *Terminiello v. Chicago*, 337 U.S. 1 (1949). Yet these are among the 'high' purposes of the First Amendment." *Collin*.

During the 1980s, academic critics of classical First Amendment theory began to revive some of the ideas which Frankfurter had employed in *Beauharnais* and develop new arguments to justify hate speech legislation. The renewed interest in providing a rationale for such hate laws reflected a concern for securing equality for members of minority groups, particularly those which occupied a subordinate power position in society. Another source of renewed interest in hate speech laws was concern over an alarming increase in racist speech and racially motivated crimes. For the new proponents of hate speech laws, freedom of expression was a value in society but it was not necessarily the ultimate value.

Professor Mari Matsuda has stressed the connection between the message of hatred and ferocity conveyed by hate speech with the subordinate power position of minorities in society: "[F]rom the victims' perspective, all of these implements inflict wounds, wounds that are neither random or isolated. Gutter racism, parlor racism, corporate racism, and government racism work in coordination, reinforcing existing conditions of domination. Less egregious forms of racism degenerate easily into more serious forms." Matsuda, *Public Response to Racist Speech: Considering the Victim's Story*, 87 Mich. L. Rev. 2320 (1989). In Matsuda's view, racist speech helps to entrench the existing power relationships of society. In this view, the classical First Amendment position which would preclude suppression of hate speech becomes a weapon for the forces of inequality.

Professor Charles Lawrence III similarly emphasizes the immediate injurious impact of racist insult as justifying hate speech laws. Such intentional racial epithets are the "functional equivalent" of fighting words. But unlike traditional fighting words, these verbal assaults do not engender vio-

lence but rather silence and submission on the part
of the minority victim. In Lawrence's view, this
effect of silencing the victim's speech provides a
First Amendment rationale in *favor* of the validity
of racist speech laws. Lawrence contends that "as-
saultive racist speech" operates like a preemptive
strike: "[T]he racial invective is experienced as a
blow, not as a proffered idea, and once the blow is
struck, it is unlikely that dialogue will follow."
Lawrence, *If He Hollers Let Him Go: Regulating
Racist Speech On Campus*, 1990 Duke L.J. 431.

Professor Robert Post finds the preemptive silencing argument the most disturbing of the defenses of laws punishing racist speech. But he concludes
that "even if the empirical claim of systematic
preemptive silencing were accepted (and I am not
sure that I do accept it), it is in my view most
directly the result of the social and structural conditions of racism, rather than specifically of racist
speech." Post, *Racist Speech, Democracy, and the
First Amendment*, 32 Wm. & Mary L. Rev. 267
(1991). He concludes that the argument for banning
racist speech is "fundamentally irreconcilable with
the rationale for First Amendment freedoms." But
Professor Richard Delgado argues that there is no
reason that free speech values should subordinate
equality values. Addressing the problem of campus
hate speech, Professor Delgado says: "[judges and
university administrators] could coin an exception
to free speech, thus giving primacy to the equal
protection values at stake or, they could carve an
exception to equality, saying in effect that universi-

ties may protect minority populations except where this abridges speech. Nothing in constitutional or moral theory requires one answer rather than the other." Delgado, *Campus Antiracism Rules: Constitutional Narratives in Collision*, 85 Nw. U.L. Rev. 343 (1991).

In 1992, the Supreme Court was provided an opportunity for making such a choice. However, in *R.A.V. v. City of St. Paul*, 505 U.S. 377 (1992), the Court, per Justice Scalia, avoided making the choice but, nonetheless, cast serious doubt on the future of hate speech laws. A St. Paul hate speech ordinance had been given a narrow savings construction by the Minnesota courts limiting it to fighting words. The Supreme Court unanimously reversed the court below and concluded that the ordinance was unconstitutional. But the Justices split sharply as to the reason for this result.

Justice Scalia, speaking for a bare majority, reasoned that the Minnesota court's interpretation created a content-based classification within the category of fighting words. Not all fighting words were proscribed by the St. Paul ordinance but only those which aroused "anger, alarm, or resentment in others on the basis of race, color, creed, religion, or gender." For example, Scalia pointed out that the use of fighting words to denigrate persons or classes in terms of their political affiliation, union status, or sexual preference would not be prohibited by the St. Paul ordinance. The law was impermissibly underinclusive. Scalia rejected the argument that such ideologically-based discrimination could be justified under the strict scrutiny standard of review employed for content-based legislation. While acknowledging that the governmental interest in protecting the basic human rights of historically disadvantaged groups is a compelling interest, the St. Paul ordinance was not necessary to serve that interest. There existed adequate content-neutral alternatives, *i.e*, a law proscribing all fighting words "not limited to the favored topics."

Four concurring justices, in an opinion authored by Justice White, rejected Scalia's underinclusiveness analysis. First, fighting words are totally excluded from First Amendment protection, regardless of subcategories. Second, even if strict scrutiny is appropriate, Justice Scalia's use of it was not: "Under the majority's view, a narrowly drawn, content-based ordinance could never pass constitutional muster if the object of that legislation could be accomplished by banning a wider category of speech." The concurring justices thought that the St. Paul ordinance was unconstitutional because it was overbroad. The Minnesota court had ruled "that St. Paul may constitutionally prohibit expression that 'by its very utterance' causes 'anger, alarm or resentment.'" But the Supreme Court's fighting words cases had rejected the principle that such generalized public reaction to speech would justify its repression: "The mere fact that expressive activity causes hurt feeling, offense, or resentment does not render the expression unprotected."

What is the future of racist speech laws after *R.A.V.*? Arguably, had the Minnesota courts limited the St. Paul ordinance to the classic definition of fighting words when used in a racial, ethnic, religious or gender context, the ordinance would have been upheld by the justices who concurred with Justice White. A hate speech law not limited to fighting words would have to satisfy the overbreadth concerns of the concurring Justices. The law could not focus on hurt feelings or offensiveness; the law would have to be narrowly drawn to combat the harms associated with discrimination against the identified groups. But such a narrowly drawn hate speech law might pass constitutional muster.

As for the majority who joined Justice Scalia's opinion, a general prohibition on fighting words would be constitutional. Such a law could be enforced against hate speech as long as there was no selective enforcement. Would the Court majority approve a pure hate speech law not limited to fighting words? It seems unlikely in light of Justice Scalia's condemnation of the underinclusiveness of the St. Paul ordinance. Such a law would still be limited only to certain forms of hate speech. It seems unlikely that the majority would find a justification for such underinclusiveness. The difficulty with the Scalia view is that to reach hate speech one is required to shrink the domain of protected expression. Further, the state is required to reach speech which does not produce the same level of harm associated with racist speech. Critics of the Scalia opinion have speculated that the subtext of the opinion is predicated on a desire to bash p.c.—

"political correctness." Whether this is true or not, the majority opinion in *R.A.V.* has greatly limited the future of racist speech laws—if, indeed, they have a future.

Even though laws that punish hate speech itself may not have a bright future, the Supreme Court has indicated that there is a constitutional way for the states to deal with hate crimes. Penalty enhancement statutes for criminal conduct inspired by racial bias are consistent with the First Amendment. In *Wisconsin v. Mitchell*, 508 U.S. 476 (1993), the Court upheld a Wisconsin statute which enhanced criminal penalties when the victim is selected because of race. When a group of black men and boys attacked and beat a white boy severely, the two-year sentence of one of the perpetrators was enhanced to seven years because the perpetrator had selected the victim because of the victim's race.

The defendant contended that since the rationale for enhancing the criminal penalty was his discriminatory motive in selecting the victim, the Wisconsin law punished thoughts and beliefs in violation of the First Amendment. The Court rejected this contention since the motive for a crime can be an important factor in sentencing. In addition, motive played the same role under the Wisconsin penalty enhancement law as it does under the antidiscrimination laws directed against employers. Such laws are aimed at unprotected conduct, not activity protected by the First Amendment. In *Wisconsin v. Mitchell*, the Court took great pains to distinguish *R.A.V.*: "[W]hereas the ordinance struck down in

*R.A.V.* was explicitly directed at expression (*i.e.,* 'speech' or 'messages'), the statute in this case is aimed at conduct unprotected by the First Amendment."

Penalties for bias-inspired conduct were enhanced because the state could reasonably believe that such crimes are "more likely to provoke retaliatory crimes, inflict distinct emotional harms on their victims, and incite community unrest." The state interest involved, therefore, far more than just disagreement with the offender's belief system. Further, there was no First Amendment barrier against the "evidentiary use of speech" in order to prove motive, intent, or the elements of a crime. And any "chilling effect" on protected speech arising from a fear that such speech would be used to enhance penalties was deemed too speculative to support an overbreadth claim. But the racial bias motive must be established beyond a reasonable doubt. *Apprendi v. New Jersey*, 530 U.S. 466 (2000).

The use of the speaker's intent to intimidate to reach racist speech is supported by *Virginia v. Black*, 538 U.S. 343 (2003). Unlike many other cross burning laws, the Virginia statute was limited to proscribing cross burning "with the intent of intimidating" persons. Burning a cross as a means of intimidation, the Court held, can constitutes a "true threat"—a category of expression which the state can regulate consistent with the First Amendment. Even though the Virginia statute was limited to only one form of true threat, it was "a particularly virulent form of intimidation" where fear of bodily harm was most likely. While the state law unconstitutionally presumed intent to intimidate from the act of cross burning itself, *Virginia v. Black* indicates another means whereby states can constitutionally proscribe racist speech.

## B.  PORNOGRAPHY AND FEMINISM

In the early 1980s feminists Andrea Dworkin and Catherine MacKinnon proposed an anti-pornography ordinance premised on the theory that pornography is a form of sex discrimination. According to this theory, women are victimized by being forced to perform pornographic acts, by acts of violence stimulated by pornography, and by the sexual attitudes and roles resulting from such sex discrimination. "Pornography, unlike obscenity, is a discrete, identifiable system of sexual exploitation that hurts women as a class by creating inequality and abuse." Dworkin, *Against the Male Flood: Censorship, Pornography and Equality*, 8 Harv. Women's L.J. 1 (1985).

Just as proponents of obscenity laws confronted the problem of defining obscenity, the anti-pornography theorists had to define the concept of constitutionally unprotected pornography. Their problem is especially difficult. Since most of what they view as regulable or prohibitable pornography has not been defined as obscenity in the past, under conventional First Amendment theory, the material is protected speech. In short, the concept of pornography, at least as described by its feminist advocates, requires nothing less than a radical revision in traditional First Amendment thinking.

As defined in an Indianapolis anti-pornography ordinance, pornography includes "the graphic sexually explicit subordination of women whether in pictures or in words," portraying women in at least one of a variety of different ways, *e.g.*, as sexual objects who enjoy pain or humiliation, or rape, or physical brutality, or casting women in scenarios of degradation or as sexual objects for domination or exploitation. Professor Thomas Emerson castigated the sweep of the Indianapolis ordinance as breathtaking: "It would subject to governmental ban virtually all depictions of rape, verbal or pictorial, and a substantial proportion of other presentations of sexual encounters. It would embrace much of the world's art." Emerson, *Pornography and the First Amendment: A Reply to Professor MacKinnon*, 3 Yale L. & Pol'y Rev. 130 (1985).

An Indianapolis anti-pornography law was enacted which proscribed coercion of persons into performing pornographic acts, trafficking in pornography, and forcing pornography on a person. It also gave victims of conduct directly traceable to pornography a cause of action against the disseminator. In *American Booksellers Ass'n v. Hudnut*, 771 F.2d 323 (7th Cir. 1985), the Indianapolis ordinance was declared unconstitutional and the Supreme Court summarily affirmed. Judge Easterbrook for the Seventh Circuit in *Hudnut* accepted the premises of harm from pornography underlying the ordinance but nonetheless held that the remedy afforded by the ordinance violated the First Amendment. Pornography is not limited, he noted, to obscenity as defined in *Miller* or child pornography as defined in *Ferber*. Indeed, the presence of literary, artistic or scientific value of the regulated material is irrelevant under the anti-pornography law. For Judge Easterbrook, the Indianapolis ordinance was simply viewpoint discrimination based on the content of the speech: "This is thought control. It establishes an approved view of women, of how they may react to sexual encounters, of how the sexes may relate to each other. Those who espouse the approved view may use sexual images; those who do not, may not."

Professor Frank Michelman criticizes Judge Easterbrook's opinion in *Hudnut* for failing to undertake "a direct comparison of the magnitude or rank of the social evils consequent upon regulation with those consequent upon leaving pornography unregulated." For Michelman, this is an area where a cost-benefit analysis could usefully be employed; he formulated the issue as follows: "Which is worse— to leave pornographers subject to the vicissitudes of silencing by the lawmaking activities of political majorities, or to leave women subject to the vicissitudes of silencing by the private publishing activities of pornographers?" Michelman, *Conceptions of Democracy In American Constitutional Argument: The Case of Pornography Regulation*, 56 Tenn. L. Rev. 291 (1989).

Indianapolis had argued that pornography is low value speech which can be proscribed under decisions such as *Young v. American Mini Theatres* and

*Pacifica*. Professor Cass Sunstein apparently would agree. He would validate such anti-pornography laws by bringing them within the category of low value speech, and therefore, subject to the diminished protection accorded such speech. Low value speech, according to Professor Sunstein, "has little or nothing to do with public affairs" and "has purely noncognitive appeal." Moreover, the speaker's purpose is not to communicate a message. Finally, in enacting such laws, "government is unlikely to be acting for constitutionally impermissible reasons or producing constitutionally troublesome harms." Pornography, in his view, shares these characteristics. Sunstein, *Pornography and the First Amendment*, 1986 Duke L.J. 589. Judge Easterbrook in *Hudnut* would have none of this. *Pacifica* and *American Mini Theatres* did not sustain statutes that embody viewpoint discrimination: "Indianapolis has created an approved point of view and so loses the support of these cases."

As was the case in hate speech, there are equal protection foundations behind the movement in favor of anti-pornography laws. In this view, pornography is a discriminatory act rather than expression. As such, it cannot be tolerated since it offends a civil right—the right to gender equality. The victimization of women as a class which pornography fosters justifies the enactment of an anti-pornography ordinance. In this view, the ordinance is not censorship but promotion of civil rights.

Unlike the conservative censors of obscenity who emphasize morality, the feminist censors of pornography emphasize the harm to women produced by pornography. Some critics of anti-pornography laws remain skeptical even assuming that the feminist premises about the consequences of pornography are correct and even assuming that such legislation presents no fundamental First Amendment barrier: "[P]ermitting greater censorship of pornography reinforces paternalistic attitudes that have only recently been identified as constitutionally suspect in the equal protection area. The notion that women must be protected from visual or aural representations of male sexual dominance ironically allows the (usually male) judge to play the far more insidious role of father-figure, protecting his weak charge from the hostile environment of the outside world." Gey, *Apologetics Of Suppression: The Regulation of Pornography As Act and Idea*, 86 Mich. L.Rev. 1564 (1988). In short, anti-pornography laws foster the very paternalistic attitudes and values they seek to combat.

What is the present First Amendment status of feminist sponsored anti-pornography legislation? In light of the summary affirmance of *Hudnut* by the Supreme Court, one could argue that the future for such legislation is dim. Moreover, the *R.A.V.* case, with its distaste for selective prohibitions on speech and its implicit aversion to politically correct restrictions on speech, does not augur well for the future of anti-pornography laws. On the other hand, *R.A.V.* did suggest an exception for the possible First Amendment validity of sexual harassment laws involving speech in the employment context, such as Title VII. Perhaps, more narrowly drawn anti-pornography laws emphasizing specific harms to women such as coercion into pornography or damages for physical injury caused by pornography might pass constitutional muster, although even this is doubtful.

# PART THREE

# GENERAL APPROACHES

---

## CHAPTER IX

## THE PUBLIC FORUM

### A. REGULATING THE PUBLIC FORUM

Who owns the streets and the parks? In *Massachusetts v. Davis*, 39 N.E. 113 (Mass.Sup.Jud.Ct. 1895), Justice Oliver Wendell Holmes, writing at a time when the First Amendment had not yet been held to apply to the states through the due process clause of the Fourteenth Amendment, answered the question this way: "For the legislature absolutely or conditionally to forbid public speaking in a highway or public park is no more an infringement of the rights of a member of the public than for the owner of a private house to forbid it in his house." However, city parks like the Boston Common had traditionally been perceived as appropriate sites for speech. Nevertheless, on appeal, the Supreme Court unanimously accepted Holmes' premise. The power of the state to exclude its citizens from using the

Common necessarily included the lesser power to define the conditions under which it could be used. *Davis v. Massachusetts*, 167 U.S. 43 (1897).

In *Hague v. C.I.O.*, 307 U.S. 496 (1939), Justice Roberts, writing in a different era, took a broader perspective than Holmes: "Wherever the title of streets and parks may rest, they have immemorially been held in trust for the use of the public and, time out of mind, have been used for purposes of assembly, communicating thoughts between citizens, and discussing public questions. Such use of the streets and public places has, from ancient times, been a part of the privileges, immunities, rights, and liberties of citizens." The common law tradition was that speech on the public ways could be regulated but access to it could not be denied. In 1965, Professor Harry Kalven described these public places and public access to them as the public forum: "They are in brief a public forum that the citizen can commandeer; the generosity and empathy with which such facilities are made available is an index of freedom." Kalven, *The Concept of the Public Forum: Cox v. Louisiana*, 1965 Sup. Ct. Rev. 1.

While emphasizing access to the streets and parks, Kalven acknowledged the state's ability to fashion a Robert's Rules of Order to reconcile competing uses of the public places. Thus, in *Cox v. New Hampshire*, 312 U.S. 569 (1941), the Court upheld the conviction of some Jehovah's Witnesses for parading without a permit. The licensing system was a reasonable content-neutral method to permit proper policing and to minimize the risk of disorder. But in *Schneider v. New Jersey*, 308 U.S. 147 (1939), the Court overturned various laws prohibiting leafletting in the public forum. The interest in keeping the streets free of litter was insufficient to justify a law prohibiting handing literature to a person willing to receive it. While the state might prohibit littering, it could not prohibit the expressive activity of leafletting.

Even as the Court was developing a public's *right of access* to the traditional public forums of streets and parks, it was also struggling to craft *a right of equal access* to the traditional public forum. Increasingly, the Court rejected as a prerogative of government the allocation of access to public property for some speakers or messages while denying it for others. Such content-based government action demanded heightened judicial scrutiny: "But above all else the First Amendment means that government has no power to restrict expression because of its message, its ideas, its subject matter, or its content. [U]nder the Equal Protection Clause, not to mention the First Amendment itself, [it] may not select which issues are worth discussing or debating in public facilities. [S]elective exclusions from a public forum may not be based on content alone, and may not be justified by reference to content alone." *Police Department of Chicago v. Mosley*, 408 U.S. 92 (1972) [a law directed to preventing picketing within 150 feet of a school building while school is in session could not validly make an exception for labor picketing].

Is the right of access and the right of equal access to the public forum limited to the public streets or parks? Or does it extend to public property generally? In some early cases, the Court forged a First Amendment right to use public places for speech purposes even though speech and protest were not the primary function of the property. *Edwards v. South Carolina*, 372 U.S. 229 (1963) [convictions of civil rights demonstrators conducting a protest on state house grounds overturned]; *Brown v. Louisiana*, 383 U.S. 131 (1966) [First Amendment protection given to brief silent sit-in at public library to protest library's racial segregation policies]; *Grayned v. Rockford*, 408 U.S. 104 (1972) [ordinance upheld prohibiting noisy demonstrations in areas adjacent to school grounds while classes were in session]. At the least, these cases seemed to mean that speech is protected if, under the circumstances then existing, the protest is not inconsistent with the normal functioning of the property. In *Grayned*, the Court stated: "The nature of a place, 'the pattern of its normal activities, dictate the kinds of regulations of time, place, and manner that are reasonable.' [The] crucial question is whether the manner of expression is basically incompatible with the normal activity of a particular place at a particular time. Our cases make clear that in assessing the reasonableness of a regulation, we must weigh heavily the fact that communication is involved; the regulation must be narrowly tailored to further the State's legitimate interest."

In the above cases, the public forum concept was used as a tool to extend the reach of First Amendment protection. So long as the expressive activity was not inconsistent with the normal functioning of the public property, it was protected under the public forum doctrine. But increasingly the Court adopted a more formalistic, categorical approach to public forum analysis. Outside the traditional public forum, where speech had historically been an accepted purpose, public property had to be dedicated to the public's use for it to be characterized as part of the public forum. Thus was born the "limited" or "designated" public forum—public property which the government had designated as open to speech activity.

The Court has fashioned a set of rules for regulating the two types of public forums—the traditional public forum and the limited public forum. If government seeks to enforce a content-based exclusion, the strict scrutiny standard must be satisfied. The state must show that the regulation at issue "is necessary to serve a compelling state interest and that it is narrowly drawn to achieve that end." *Perry Educ. Ass'n v. Perry Local Educators' Ass'n,* 460 U.S. 37 (1983). Or the state must show that the expressive activity in question falls into a low value speech category not accorded full First Amendment protection. The state may also impose content-neutral time, place and manner regulations if they are "narrowly tailored to serve a significant government interest and leave open ample alternative channels of communication." *Perry.* To be narrowly drawn, the regulation need not be the least restrictive means of achieving the state interest. It is sufficient if the government interest would be achieved less effectively absent the state regulation. *Ward v. Rock Against Racism*, 491 U.S. 781 (1989) [law designed to regulate volume of amplified music at Central Park bandshell held constitutional as a content-neutral, reasonable regulation to protect citizens from unwelcome noise].

In *Heffron v. International Society for Krishna Consciousness*, 452 U.S. 640 (1981), the Court ruled that state fair grounds constitute a limited public forum. A state requirement limiting the sale or distribution of Krishna materials to fixed locations was valid. The fixed location rule was content-neutral, narrowly tailored to further the important state interests in managing traffic flow at the crowded fair grounds, and there were ample alternative forums open to the Krishnas such as speech at the fixed locations and the availability of personal encounters off the fair grounds. See *United States v. Grace*, 461 U.S. 171 (1983) [total ban on all leafletting and picketing on sidewalks adjoining the Supreme Court held unconstitutional]. In *Thomas v. Chicago Park District*, 534 U.S. 316 (2002), the Court upheld Chicago's content-neutral permit system for use of public parks. The 13 grounds allowing the Park District to deny a permit permitted preservation and coordination of multiple uses of public space, prevented dangerous and unlawful uses and ensured compensation for damage. The grounds for denial were sufficiently specific, definite and objective to ensure that decisions were not left to the whim of administrators and judicial review was provided.

But there is an important distinction between the traditional public forum and the limited public forum. In the case of the traditional public forum, government may not prohibit all communicative activity. The state is not required to create the limited public forum and may choose to prohibit future public use of the particular public premises for public speech activity. In a sense, then, the limited public forum is public in terms of access rights for the public as a matter of sufferance on the part of the state. The limited public forum, therefore, in this respect is to be sharply distinguished from the traditional public forum which involves public premises where the right of access and the right of equality of access is guaranteed.

## B.  THE NONPUBLIC FORUM

Are there some public places which cannot serve as a public forum—limited or otherwise? Arguably, all public premises should be open to the public so long as the basic function of the entity is not disrupted. The law, however, has not gone in this direction. In *Adderley v. Florida*, 385 U.S. 39 (1966), the Court upheld the trespass conviction of students engaged in a demonstration on jailhouse grounds. During the civil rights upheaval of the '60s, the students had gathered to protest the arrest of their fellow students who had sought to racially desegregate public theaters. There was no violence arising from the protest nor was there any threat of violence. Justice Black, for the Court, rejected the claim that "people who want to propagandize protests or views have a constitutional right to do so whenever and however and wherever they please." Jailhouse grounds were not part of the public forum: "The State, no less than a private owner of property, has power to preserve the property under its control for the use to which it is lawfully dedicated."

But is the State, even when controlling property not normally open to protest, properly analogized to a private property owner? Admittedly, the private owner exercises broad prerogatives over his property but the State has broad duties and responsibilities to the citizenry. Justice Douglas in dissent rejected the analogy: "To say that a private owner could have done the same if the rally had taken place on private property is to speak of a different case, as an assembly and a petition for redress of grievances run to government not to private proprietors." The jailhouse, like the state capitol grounds in *Edwards,* is a seat of government that is "an obvious center for protest."

*Adderley* provided the foundation for the creation of a nonpublic forum doctrine. If public property is designated as part of the nonpublic forum, the government can discriminate between speakers and messages. All that is required is that government regulations based on speech content or speaker identity must be viewpoint-neutral. Further, any regulation of the nonpublic forum must be reasonable in light of the normal use of the property. In fact, this standard has proven highly deferential with the Court applying little more than a demand of rationality in regulation. Using this standard of review, the Court has upheld general and selective restrictions on access to military bases [*United States v. Albertini*, 472 U.S. 675 (1985); *Greer v. Spock*, 424 U.S. 828 (1976)]; a refusal to sell advertising space on public buses to political candidates [*Lehman v. City of Shaker Heights*, 418 U.S. 298 (1974)]; a ban on access to home mail boxes for unstamped mail [*United States Postal Serv. v. Council of Greenburgh Civic Ass'ns*, 453 U.S. 114 (1981)]; the denial of access to teachers' school mail boxes for a union challenging the designated collective bargaining representative [*Perry Educ. Ass'n v. Perry Local Educators' Ass'n*, 460 U.S. 37 (1983)]; a ban on the posting of signs on utility poles [*Members of the City Council of the City of Los Angeles v. Taxpayers for Vincent*, 466 U.S. 789 (1984)]; the exclusion of legal defense and political advocacy groups from participation in the federal employee charity fund drive [*Cornelius v. NAACP Legal Defense & Educ. Fund*, 473 U.S. 788 (1985)], and the exclusion of candidates from a publicly-sponsored debate [*Arkansas Educational Television Comm'n (AETC) v. Forbes*, 523 U.S. 666 (1998)].

In each of the foregoing cases, the public property at issue was held not to be a public forum. What common characteristics did these public premises share? None of the public premises involved were primarily devoted to, or dedicated to, the public interchange of ideas. While the public may have been freely admitted to the premises, they were not admitted for the purposes of expression. But what has emerged as the dominant factor in nonpublic forum doctrine is the intent or purpose of the government—did the government intend to create a public forum? Did the policies governing the public facility reveal a willingness on the part of government to have it used by the general public for speech purposes?

In *United States v. Kokinda*, 497 U.S. 720 (1990), the Court upheld application of a postal service regulation to bar solicitation of contributions on a post office sidewalk. Was the post office sidewalk a public forum? Justice White said for a plurality that it was not. It lacked the characteristics of a general public sidewalk since it connected only the parking lot to the post office. While some individual groups had been permitted to engage in expressive activity, there were regulations in effect controlling the expression; selective access for some speakers and messages did not transform the post office sidewalk into a public forum. Previously, selective access to public premises served as a rationale to open the premises to all on a First Amendment–Equal Protection principle against discrimination by government. Now selective access was used as a vehicle for establishing government's rejection of general access. Having triggered the nonpublic forum doctrine, the Court had little difficulty in determining that a prohibition on solicitation of funds on the post office sidewalk was reasonable. In-person solicitation can be a highly disruptive form of speech activity. Traffic entering the post office would be slowed; disagreements about the cause being solicited could distract from the post office's mission. The solicitation ban was viewpoint-neutral since all in-person solicitation was prohibited, not solicitation for particular causes.

Justice Kennedy concurred in *Kokinda* and provided the crucial fifth vote. He did not agree, however, that the postal sidewalk was a nonpublic forum. Given the wide range of activities regularly permitted on the sidewalk, he felt there was a powerful argument for judging the postal anti-solicitation regulation by the more demanding standards applicable to a public forum. Nevertheless, he concluded that the regulation was a content-neutral, reasonable time, place and manner regulation. Justice Kennedy based his concurrence on the narrow character of the ban, *i.e.*, in-person solicitation of funds and the availability of alternative means for communicating the solicitation message.

The appropriate forum status of public facilities such as railroad, bus and airport terminals has been a matter of extensive litigation and confusion in the courts. In *International Society for Krishna Consciousness, Inc. v. Lee*, 505 U.S. 672 (1992), the Court grappled with the forum status of an airport terminal. The Court held, 5–4, per Chief Justice Rehnquist, that an airport terminal is a nonpublic forum. Chief Justice Rehnquist rejected characterizing terminals as traditional public forum since "the

tradition of airport activity does not demonstrate
that airports have historically been made available
for speech activity." Airport terminals only recently
achieved their modern size and character. Only in
recent times have groups attempted to use airports
as forums for expressive activity. Efforts by the
litigants to broaden the question to an inquiry into
whether transportation places should be viewed as
public forums was also rejected. Bus and rail terminals had historically been under private rather than
public ownership. Moreover, Rehnquist did not
want to deal with transportation facilities generical-
ly, but rather preferred to take up each mode of
transportation and its compatibility with speech
activity on a case by case basis. The difficulty with
this analysis, however, is that although it sounds
like a dynamic approach, actually it is static. Rehnquist's method is to ask whether historically the
transportation facility at issue was used for speech.
Since most transportation facilities were not used
historically for speech activity—and indeed some of
today's facilities like airports did not exist—the
answer to the inquiry is foretold.

Nor could an airport facility be categorized as a
limited public forum. There was no intention on the
part of the airport authorities to dedicate the terminal to expressive activity since "the frequent and
continuing litigation evidencing the operators' objections belies any such claims." Rather the airport
terminal is a nonpublic terminal which the airport
authority "owns and controls": "Where the government is acting as a proprietor, managing its inter-

nal operations, rather than acting as lawmaker with the power to regulate or license, its action will not be subject to the heightened review to which its actions as a law-maker may be subject."

The private property foundations of the nonpublic forum doctrine recognized in *Adderley* are clearly apparent here. Acting in its proprietary capacity, the government is analogized to the private property owner. Therefore, when the government is acting as a proprietor, it operates relatively free from First Amendment restraints. The problem is that the analogy to private property ownership is destructive of the public forum concept altogether since the private owner has no First Amendment obligations. The First Amendment does not run to private actors.

Justice Kennedy, joined by Justices Blackmun, Souter and Stevens, did not agree that the airport terminal was not a public forum. While acknowledging that airports were of recent vintage, the place in history, or the lack thereof, or the government's intent, or lack of intent to dedicate public property to expressive activity, should not control. The test instead should be an objective one focusing on the actual characteristics and uses of the property: "Under the proper circumstances, I would accord public forum status to other forms of [public] property, regardless of its ancient or contemporary origins, and whether or not it fits within a narrow historic tradition. If the objective, physical characteristics of the property at issue and the actual public access and uses which have been permitted by the government indicate that expressive activity would be appropriate and compatible with those uses, the property is a public forum." At a time when public parks in many cities are no longer safe, or even widely used, when the population has spread far into the suburbs and beyond, new modes of land use and new places of public congregation should be capable of being characterized as public forums if that concept is to have a future. Kennedy's analysis is directed to the original inquiry set forth in the public forum doctrine. Is the public property's primary use compatible with speech activity? His approach expresses a preference for a public forum concept which has a capacity for growth in terms of the public facilities to which it might apply.

The difference between the Rehnquist conception of the public forum doctrine and the Kennedy conception is that the latter is a dynamic conception and the former a static one. The Kennedy conception broadens the reach of the First Amendment whereas the former assumes that, unless history clearly dictates to the contrary, government may choose to exclude expression. Moreover, in Rehnquist's view, unless government has clearly indicated that expression may take place, the assumption is that the property is not dedicated to speech activity. The essence of Justice Kennedy's public forum analysis is a plea for recognition of the new role that new public facilities play, and should play, in the marketplace of ideas. Today the metropolitan airport through which thousands pass daily is the equivalent of the village green of another era: "It is the very breadth and extent of the public's use of airports that makes it imperative to protect speech rights there."

Having characterized the airport terminal as a nonpublic forum, the *Lee* Court now had to consider the validity of the regulations being challenged. The Port Authority of New York and New Jersey had adopted a regulation forbidding the repetitive solicitation of money or distribution of literature within the terminals. Chief Justice Rehnquist spoke for six members of the Court in upholding the ban on in-person solicitation of money. Relying on *Kokinda*, he stressed the disruptive effect such in-person solicitation would have on the functioning of ordinary business. Further, such face to face solicitation involved risks of duress to airport passengers seeking to catch a plane. As a consequence, a prohibition of in-person solicitation in such circumstances was reasonable. Justice Kennedy applying the heightened scrutiny appropriate to a public forum also deemed the regulation a reasonable time, place and manner restriction.

However, when it came to considering the validity of the ban on distribution of literature, Justices O'Connor and Kennedy switched sides. In *Lee v. International Society for Krishna Consciousness, Inc.*, 505 U.S. 672 (1992), the Court held, 5–4, *per curiam*, that the distribution ban violated the First Amendment. Justice O'Connor applying nonpublic forum standards held the ban to be unreasonable. In light of the multi-purpose environment of the airport terminal, a total ban on distribution of materials—peaceful pamphleteering or leafletting— was unacceptable absent proof that it was inconsistent with airport activities. Justice Kennedy, joined by Justices Souter, Stevens and Blackmun, applying public forum standards, similarly determined that the distribution ban was an unreasonable time, place and manner regulation. The distribution ban was not narrowly drawn and did not leave open alternative channels of communications. Problems of congestion could be dealt with by a more narrowly drawn regulation. It is worth noting that, under *Heffron*, the airport might have prevailed if it had merely limited distribution to a fixed location. Chief Justice Rehnquist, now writing in dissent, joined by Justices White, Scalia and Thomas, saw no difference between the risks and burdens of in-person solicitation and distribution: "The weary, harried, or hurried traveler may have no less desire to avoid the delays generated by having literature foisted upon him than he does to avoid delays from a financial solicitation." Chief Justice Rehnquist would have upheld both bans.

The Court drew an important distinction between general and selective access in *Arkansas Educational Television Comm'n (AETC) v. Forbes*, 523 U.S. 666 (1998). Ralph Forbes, a candidate for Arkansas' third congressional district, who had qualified for the ballot, was excluded from a debate sponsored by a public broadcasting station (AETC) on grounds that he lacked sufficient popular support. The Court 6–3, per Justice Kennedy, upheld AETC's action.

While expressing doubt that public broadcasting generally was amenable to forum analysis, Justice Kennedy concluded that public television *debates* are subject to forum analysis because the debates were created as a forum for political speech by candidates and have exceptional significance in the electoral process.

The Court then determined that this debate was a nonpublic forum. To create a designated public forum, the government must intend to make the property generally available to a class of speakers. "[The] government does not create a designated public forum when it does no more than reserve eligibility for access to the forum for a particular class of speakers, whose members must then, as individuals, 'obtain permission to use it.'" The debate was not generally open to all candidates for Arkansas' third congressional district seat. The candidates for the seat were eligible to apply and AETC then made candidate-by-candidate decisions as to which candidates would participate. Kennedy said that this distinction between general and selective access furthered First Amendment interests by encouraging government to open property for at least some expressive activity where the property might otherwise be totally closed to speech. Applying nonpublic forum standards, the government action was held to be reasonable and viewpoint-neutral. Forbes had been excluded because of his lack of public support, not the unpopularity of his views. Given the time constraints of televised debates, AETC's action was a reasonable exercise of discretion.

In sum, public forum analysis in the Supreme Court at this point has become a jurisprudence of labels. In place of careful, candid weighing of competing free speech and public order values, the Court has adopted a conceptualistic categorical analysis. Legal outcomes depend on whether the speech is placed in the public or the nonpublic category, on what pigeonhole of law is determined to apply. The situation is further compounded by the Court's insistence that the traditional public forum categorization is dependent on whether history has treated the forum in question as a public forum. This static conception of the public forum denies it any a capacity for growth and prevents the extension of First Amendment protection to the ever-expanding domain of public property. In the nonpublic forum, free speech values tend to be minimized or ignored; government proprietary interests are emphasized and exaggerated.

## C. PRIVATE PROPERTY

Does the public forum doctrine extend to expression that is directed not at the government but at a private homeowner? The answer to this question was provided in *Frisby v. Schultz*, 487 U.S. 474 (1988). In response to continuing anti-abortion picketing of the home of a doctor who performed abortions, the town enacted an ordinance prohibiting picketing "before or about" any residence. The protesters challenged the ordinance as facially unconstitutional. The Supreme Court, per Justice

O'Connor, interpreted the ordinance not to bar residential picketing but only as a prohibition on "focused picketing taking place solely in front of a particular residence."

In *Frisby*, Justice O'Connor applied the traditional public forum standards: "A public street does not lose its status as a traditional public forum simply because it runs through a residential neighborhood." The fact, however, that the street was considered a public forum, however, did not invalidate the ordinance because the ordinance met the applicable test. It was narrowly tailored to serve a significant governmental interest—to preclude the picketing of "captive" householders—and it left open ample alternative channels for communicating with local neighborhood residents. In upholding the ban on focused picketing in *Frisby*, the Court noted that "the type of focused picketing prohibited by the ordinance is fundamentally different from more generally directed means of communication that may not be completely banned in residential areas."

Whereas the residential picketing ban in *Frisby* was narrowly tailored to protect the unwilling homeowner, bans on canvassing, handbilling and solicitation of homeowners have been held unconstitutional. Such bans impede the flow of information not simply to a particular household but to the public generally. *Martin v. City of Struthers*, 319 U.S. 141 (1943) [ban on door-to-door solicitation held unconstitutional]. On the other hand, a reasonable regulation designed to protect the privacy of the homeowner or prevent fraud does not violate the First Amendment. *Breard v. City of Alexandria*, 341 U.S. 622 (1951) [ordinance prohibiting door-to-door solicitation without advance consent of homeowner which was applied to prevent house-to-house magazine solicitation was held to be reasonably related to protecting the privacy of the homeowner]; *Rowan v. United States Post Office Department*, 397 U.S. 728 (1970) [federal statute authorizing homeowner to stop offensive mailings to his home held constitutional].

Even regulations rather than outright bans of such door-to-door activities, however, must be clear, narrowly drawn and not vest excessive discretion in administrative officials. In *Hynes v. Mayor of Oradell*, 425 U.S. 610 (1976), an ordinance requiring advanced written notice by solicitors and canvassers prior to undertaking door-to-door activity was held unconstitutionally vague and overbroad. The ordinance invalidly vested standardless authority in officials allowing them to determine what kinds of message could be communicated to residents. See also *Village of Schaumburg v. Citizens for a Better Environment*, 444 U.S. 620 (1980) [ordinance prohibiting door-to-door solicitation of contributions by organizations not using at least 75% of their receipts for charitable purposes held facially overbroad].

In *Watchtower Bible & Tract Society of N.Y., Inc. v. Village of Stratton*, 536 U.S. 150 (2002), the Court, 8–1, invalidated a local ordinance prohibiting door to door advocacy to explain or promote any "cause" without first registering and receiving a permit. While there was no charge for the permit and it was routinely issued, the permit, which identified the canvasser, had to be carried and exhibited on request. Jehovah's Witnesses who proselytize rather than sell, successfully challenged the law as violative of the First Amendment.

Justice Stevens, writing for the Court, began by emphasizing that door to door canvassing and pamphleteering had historically been protected by the courts "as vehicles for the dissemination of ideas," and was "essential to the poorly financed causes of little people." He did not formally adopt intermediate review because "the breadth of speech affected by the ordinance and the nature of the regulation" were determinative. The regulation subjected a broad range of speech to government permits, burdening anonymity, the speech of citizens holding religious or patriotic views, and spontaneous speech. The law was not narrowly tailored to the Village's claimed interests in preventing fraud and crime and protecting resident's privacy. It was not limited to commercial transactions and solicitation of funds. Privacy interests could be protected by no solicitation signs and the rights of residents to refuse to speak to canvassers. The absence of a permit would not stop criminals and the Village did not argue that crime prevention motivated the ordinance.

Chief Justice Rehnquist, applying intermediate scrutiny, dissented. He noted the minimal burden from the nondiscretionary regulation of home solicitation. The law narrowly served significant interests and applied to everyone who canvassed door to door. Permits result in fewer knocks disturbing privacy. They deter and help detect wrongdoing. There are ample alternatives for the solicitor, e.g., securing a permit for door-to-door solicitation or using the public forum.

Are there circumstances whereby private property can become a public forum? Since the state action requirement has been held to limit the scope of First Amendment obligation, private actors have generally not been held subject to First Amendment restraints. However, in *Marsh v. Alabama*, 326 U.S. 501 (1946), the Court confronted the question of whether the general view that private actors are not subject to constitutional duty applied as well when a private corporation owned an entire town. In *Marsh*, the company owning the town shut off entry to Jehovah's Witnesses who wished to engage in solicitation on the streets. When the solicitor was arrested by the sheriff and convicted under the Alabama trespass law, she lodged a First Amendment challenge to that application of the state trespass law. The Court, per Justice Black, reversed the conviction and held that a citizen's First Amendment rights could not be denied simply because a private corporation held legal title to every house, street and sidewalk in the town: "Ownership does not always mean absolute dominion. The more an owner, for his advantage, opens up his property for use by the public in general, the more do his rights become circumscribed by the statutory and constitutional rights of those who use it." In short, the private property rights of the corporation were insufficient to justify denial of the citizen's fundamental rights where the property owner had dedicated the property to a public use. In Black's view, when a private company operates a town, it undertakes such a dedication.

In *Amalgamated Food Employees Union v. Logan Valley Plaza, Inc.*, 391 U.S. 308 (1968), the Court expanded the *Marsh* concept and held that a privately owned shopping center would have to admit picketers because it had opened up the property to public entry. Justice Marshall, for the Court, stated: "The shopping center here is clearly the functional equivalent to the business district of [the company town] involved in *Marsh*." The roadways and sidewalks within the shopping center were similar to the streets and sidewalks of the business district of a town—the traditional public forum. Therefore, imposing a limitation on picketing would "substantially hinder" the effort of the picketers to communicate with the public. But Justice Black, the author of *Marsh*, dissented in *Logan Valley* since the private property had not been dedicated to the public use. "[Only] when that *property* has taken on *all* the attributes of a town" could that property be treated as public. Justice Black required a total dedication of the private property to the public use before the private property owners would have First Amendment obligations.

In *Logan Valley*, the union picketers were protesting labor practices at a food market located in the shopping mall where the picketing took place.

In *Lloyd Corp., Ltd. v. Tanner*, 407 U.S. 551 (1972), some anti-Vietnam War protesters sought to distribute handbills in a completely enclosed mall in Portland, Oregon. The mall operator wished to exclude them on the ground that the protesters had no free expression rights on its privately owned property. A majority of the Court agreed. Justice Powell, for the Court, in *Lloyd* called attention to the fact that in *Logan Valley* the object of the protest was related to the site of the protest. Picketers had objected to the labor practices of a food market in the shopping center. This could not be said of the protesters in the *Lloyd* case. More generally, Justice Powell stressed that the shopping center had not extended any open-ended invitation to the public to use it for any and all purposes. He adopted Justice Black's position in *Logan Valley*: "In the instant case [unlike *Marsh*] there is no comparable assumption or exercise of municipal functions or power." It was now Justice Marshall's turn to dissent since he could find "no valid distinction" from *Logan Valley*.

The idea that shopping centers could be viewed as dedicated to the public use for First Amendment purposes was brought to a halt altogether in *Hudgens v. NLRB*, 424 U.S. 507 (1976). Justice Stewart, for the Court, overruled *Logan Valley* and upheld the power of the shopping center to exclude picketing even when the object of the picketing was in fact directed to activity on the site. Why? Stewart said that inquiry into the subject of the picketing—whether the site of the protest was related to the object of the protest—involved a court in content-based discrimination which was inconsistent with its First Amendment task.

Once again, Justice Marshall dissented: "The roadways, parking lots, and walkways of the modern shopping center may be as essential for effective speech as the streets and sidewalks in the municipal or company-owned town. [The] shopping center has assumed the traditional role of the state in its control of historical First Amendment forums." In the Court's zeal to avoid making subject matter distinctions about different kinds of speech in shopping centers, the Court ended up precluding all speech in shopping centers—at least as a matter of First Amendment right. In the aftermath of *Hudgens*, there is neither a right of access, or a right of equality of access, to privately owned shopping centers.

# CHAPTER X

## EXPRESSIVE CONDUCT

Symbolism can be a powerful mechanism for communicating ideas. While conduct can be a vehicle for communicating messages—for example, handbilling or picketing—expressive conduct or symbolic speech involves conduct which is itself communicative. The conduct is the idea or the message. As Justice Jackson put it in *West Virginia State Bd. of Educ. v. Barnette*, 319 U.S. 624 (1943), symbols are "a short cut from mind to mind." Even if a speaker can communicate a message orally, expressive conduct can be a more powerful and persuasive means of reaching and influencing an audience. Expressive conduct may convey an emotive significance that spoken words lack. Further, symbols have often been referred to as the poor man's printing press. Draft card or flag burning attract media and public attention in a way that is seldom available to the soap box orator.

Not all conduct that might be understood by someone to convey a message is necessarily expressive conduct. Nor is the intent of the speaker decisive. The Supreme Court has said: "We cannot accept the view that an apparently limitless variety of conduct can be labeled 'speech' whenever the person engaging in the conduct intends thereby to express an idea." *United States v. O'Brien*, 391 U.S. 367 (1968). An initial question, therefore, is fashioning a definition of expressive conduct; it is necessary to identify when the First Amendment is implicated. If the conduct does implicate the First Amendment, should it be protected in the same way as verbal speech by the courts? A vivid illustration of the problem occurred when Puerto Rican Nationalists attempted to shoot President Truman while he was addressing Congress. Doubtless, the attempted assassination was designed to call attention to the cause of Puerto Rican independence. However, this did not make it First Amendment speech nor did it entitle the conduct to protection. The government's interest in punishing attempted murder would override any First Amendment claim.

## A. STANDARDS FOR EXPRESSIVE CONDUCT

### 1. THE DEFINITIONAL PROBLEM

Professor Thomas I. Emerson argued that full First Amendment protection should be given to speech. Action, on the other hand, should be subject to government regulation free of First Amendment constraints. Obviously, action primarily undertaken to communicate presented a problem for his theory. His answer was that "the guiding principle must be to determine which element is predominant in the conduct under consideration." Emerson, *The System Of Freedom Of Expression* (1970). For example, for Emerson the burning of a draft card in opposition to the Vietnam War was clearly speech. But Professor John Hart Ely responded that "burning a draft card to express opposition to the draft is an undifferentiated whole, 100% action and 100% expression." Ely, *Flag Desecration: A Case Study in the Roles of Categorization and Balancing in First Amendment Analysis*, 88 Harv. L. Rev. 1482 (1975). More generally, Professor Louis Henkin commented: "A constitutional distinction between speech and conduct is specious. Speech is conduct, and actions speak. [The] meaningful constitutional distinction is not between speech and conduct but between conduct that speaks, communicates, and other kinds of conduct." Henkin, *Foreword: On Drawing Lines*, 82 Harv. L. Rev. 63 (1968).

In *Spence v. Washington*, 418 U.S. 405 (1974), the Supreme Court attempted the difficult task of defining expressive conduct, or symbolic speech. In a *per curiam* opinion, the Supreme Court reversed Spence's conviction for affixing a peace symbol to his American flag and displaying it from his window in violation of the state flag misuse statute. Spence was protesting the invasion of Cambodia and the killings at Kent State University during the Vietnam War years. The Court concluded that there was no question that Spence was communicating "through the use of symbols." Such symbolic speech was defined on the basis of a two-part inquiry. First, was there an intent to communicate a specific message? Second, given the circumstances, was it probable that the message would be so understood by its audience? Spence's act was not "mindless nihilism" but rather a "pointed expression of anguish and protest that would be understood by the public."

The *Spence* test provides a guide for identifying symbolic speech or expressive conduct. But it has been criticized for insufficient attentiveness to the social context in which First Amendment issues arise: "The fundamental difficulty with the *Spence* test is that it locates the essence of constitutionally protected speech exclusively in an abstract triadic relationship among a speaker's intent, a specific message, and an audience's potential reception of that message. [But] the constitutional recognition of communication as possibly protected speech also depends heavily on the social context within which this relationship is situated." Robert Post, *Recuperating First Amendment Doctrine*, 47 Stanford L. Rev. 1249 (1995). In the years since *Spence*, the Supreme Court has vacillated in using the test. Sometimes the *Spence* approach has been bypassed when one would think it would have been helpful. Nonetheless, as the first step in deciding an expressive conduct case, the Court may still invoke the two-part test of *Spence*. See *Texas v. Johnson*, 491 U.S. 397 (1989) [conviction under flag desecration statute overturned].

In *Rumsfeld v. Forum for Academic and Institutional Rights (*FAIR*)*, 547 U.S. 47 (2006), the Court did not use *Spence* in holding that the expressive nature of the conduct regulated by the Solomon Amendment, which withholds education funds from higher education institutions that deny military recruiters access equal to that provided other recruiters, is insufficient to bring the conduct within the First Amendment's protection. Chief Justice Roberts, speaking for a unanimous Court, reasoned that the Amendment "neither limits what law schools may say nor requires them to say anything." It "regulates conduct, not speech. It affects what law schools must *do*—afford equal access to military recruiters—not what may or may not *say*." Nor was the conduct "inherently expressive." Rather "[t]he expressive component of a law school's action is not created by the conduct itself but the speech that accompanies it." Any message from the conduct comes from the law school's explanation of why access is denied. "If combining speech and conduct were enough to create expressive conduct, a regulated party could always transform conduct into "speech" simply by talking about it." Precedent would not support such a result. The Court went on to indicate that, even if the Solomon Amendment did regulate expressive conduct, it would not violate the First Amendment since any incidental burden on speech was no greater than is essential, and promotes a substantial government interest that would be served less effectively absent the regulation—disadvantaging military recruiting would impair Congress ability in raising and supporting the Armed Forces. In short, it satisfied the *O'Brien* test.

## 2.　THE *O'BRIEN* TEST

Even if conduct is determined to be speech implicating the First Amendment, the question remains whether the expressive conduct merits First Amendment protection. In *United States v. O'Brien*, 391 U.S. 367 (1968), the Court was presented with an opportunity to formulate standards that would be protective of symbolic speech. It declined the opportunity. David O'Brien was convicted for having burned his draft card on the steps of the federal courthouse in South Boston in violation of a 1965 amendment to the Selective Service Act which provided criminal penalties for knowingly mutilating or destroying one's draft card. Some members of Congress had urged enactment of the amendment as a way of curbing Vietnam War protest.

The 1965 amendment did not curb free speech on its face. But O'Brien argued that the First Amendment was violated by the 1965 amendment as enacted and applied to his symbolic activity. The Court did not agree. Chief Justice Warren was willing to accept that the First Amendment was implicated but stressed that when speech and non-speech elements are combined, "a sufficiently important governmental interest in regulating the non-speech element can justify incidental limitations on First Amendment freedom." *O'Brien* set forth a new and influential four-part test designed to accomplish this task: "[A] government regulation is sufficiently justified [1] if it is within the constitutional power of the Government; [2] if it furthers an important or substantial governmental interest; [3] if the governmental interest is unrelated to free expression; and [4] if the incidental restriction on alleged First Amendment freedoms is no greater than is essential to the furtherance of that interest."

Applying this test to O'Brien's conviction, the Court concluded that the 1965 amendment was properly designed to serve the legitimate and substantial governmental interest in the maintenance and integrity of the selective service system. On its face, the *O'Brien* test appears highly protective of free speech interests, but at least on the Supreme Court level, it has not resulted in protection of expressive conduct. Indeed, in *O'Brien* itself, the conviction for draft card burning was upheld. This result was achieved because the Court gave the component elements of the test a highly deferential interpretation. Further, the Court refused to characterize the law as related to free expression by probing Congress' motive in enacting the 1965 Amendment. In this case, there was a legitimate governmental purpose for the law, unrelated to any legislative effort to curb anti-war dissent.

The second criterion of *O'Brien* requiring a substantial governmental interest was deemed satisfied by the allegation that draft card burning would interfere with the administration of the selective service system, even though federal law already required possession of a draft card. The Court's application of *O'Brien*'s demand for an important or substantial government interest was given limited independent significance in curbing government's regulatory power. From a speech-protective point of view, therefore, one of the surprises—maybe one of the disappointments—about *O'Brien* is that the Supreme Court took such a deferential approach to the government's assertion of its interests.

Even more important, criterion [4], which appears to invoke the least onerous alternative doctrine, was severely watered down by the Court in application. Chief Justice Warren did not require that the means used by the government be the least burdensome on First Amendment values. In applying criterion [4] (the requirement that restriction of First Amendment freedoms be no greater than essential to further the government's interest), Chief Justice Warren merely recited the conclusion that the amendment effectively furthered the government's interest. Professor Ely has referred to Warren's approach to [4] as a requirement that there should be no "gratuitous inhibition" of freedom of speech. Even if another regulation would be more speech protective, government need not use it if it would be less effective. In short, criterion [4] also turned out to have no teeth.

The years since *O'Brien* have seen the test it set forth assume steadily increasing importance. Indeed, in *Clark v. Community for Creative Non–Violence*, 468 U.S. 288 (1984), the Court collapsed two lines of doctrine—its content-neutral time, place and manner rules for the public forum and the four-part *O'Brien* test for expressive conduct. The occasion for this merger was a case which involved a National Park Service regulation prohibiting sleeping in Lafayette Park. The regulation, which was applied to protesters for the homeless, was upheld even though the Court was willing to assume that sleeping in the park to protest treatment of the homeless would constitute First Amendment expressive conduct. The Court, per Justice White, stated that the four-factor standard of *O'Brien* "is little, if any, different from the standard applied to time, place and manner restrictions." The National Park Service regulation banning camping was reasonably designed to prevent wear and tear on the parks, preserving them for their primary recreational function. Protesters had ample alternative channels for communicating their protests.

Justice Marshall, joined by Justice Brennan, in dissent, castigated the deferential character of the Court's application of the *O'Brien* test: "[T]he Court has dramatically lowered the scrutiny of government regulations once it has determined that such regulations are content-neutral." In balancing the free speech and governmental interests, the Court's application of the *O'Brien* test, even though the formal statement of the test may suggest otherwise, has been begrudging in the protection it has actually extended to expressive conduct. See also *Members of City Council of Los Angeles v. Taxpayers for Vincent*, 466 U.S. 789 (1984) [*O'Brien* used in upholding a ban on the posting of signs on public property—utility poles].

But the student should note that the *O'Brien* test applies only if the regulation under review is content-neutral. Under criterion [3] in *O'Brien*, the government interest in regulating the conduct must be "unrelated to the suppression of free expression." Professor Tribe has argued that this has introduced a two-track system into First Amendment analysis. If government is regulating the conduct without regard to the message being communicated, it is content-neutral and the less demanding *O'Brien* standard applies. If government is regulating because of some harm associated with the speaker's message, the law is content-based, and *O'Brien* is inapplicable. Presumably, the strict scrutiny standard would then be applied—assuming that the speech is otherwise entitled to full First Amendment protection.

Professor Ely attempted to clarify this categorization approach: "The critical question would therefore seem to be whether the harm that the state is seeking to avert is one that grows out of the fact that the defendant is communicating, and more particularly, out of the way people can be expected to react to his message, or rather would arise even if the defendant's conduct had no communicative significance whatever." Ely, *Flag Desecration*. In *O'Brien*, for example, the Court refused O'Brien's invitation to label the law as content-based by probing Congress' motives.

In sum, the two-track approach functions as a way of analyzing expressive conduct cases. The flag burning cases *Texas v. Johnson*, 491 U.S. 397 (1989) and *United States v. Eichman*, 496 U.S. 310 (1990), discussed below, while initially invoking *O'Brien*, were found to be content-based regulations and the Court invoked strict scrutiny review. The statutes were held unconstitutional. See also *Tinker v. Des Moines Independent Community School Dist.*, 393 U.S. 503 (1969) [suspension of high school students for wearing black armbands to protest Vietnam War held unconstitutional. Conduct was "akin to pure speech" and could not be proscribed absent evidence that it interfered with work of the school or rights of other students]. On the other hand, in the nude dancing case, *Barnes v. Glen Theatre, Inc.*, 501 U.S. 560 (1991), discussed below, the challenged law was upheld since it was viewed as content-neutral with only incidental burdens on free speech. The Court invoked *O'Brien* and upheld regulation of the expressive conduct.

## B.  FLAG BURNING

The American flag is a potent and revered symbol of the nation, protected under both federal and state law. Similarly, destruction of the flag, its misuse or its desecration, is a powerful means of expressing protest against the policies of the nation. These two realities came into conflict in *Texas v. Johnson*, 491 U.S. 397 (1989). While the 1984 Republican National Convention was taking place in Dallas, Texas, some political demonstrators were engaged in protesting the policies of the Reagan administration as well as the evil consequences of nuclear war. In the course of this demonstration, a protestor, Johnson, unfurled the American flag, doused it with kerosene, and set it afire. While the flag burned, the protesters chanted: "America, the red, white and blue, we spit on you." Johnson was charged with the crime of violating a Texas statute which prohibited desecration of a venerated object. Desecration under the statute included any physical mistreatment "in a way that the actor knows will seriously offend one or more persons likely to observe or discover his action."

Had Johnson been prosecuted simply for the words he spoke, the conviction would have been set aside on the authority of *Street v. New York*, 394 U.S. 576 (1969) [conviction under law prohibiting public defiling of flag reversed since defendant may have been convicted for words alone]. But Johnson was not prosecuted for the insulting words he uttered but for his desecration of the American flag. While Johnson raised a facial challenge to the Texas law, his conviction was overturned, 5–4, by the United State Supreme Court on the ground "that the statute as applied to him violates the First Amendment." Justice Brennan, who wrote for the Court in *Johnson*, had little difficulty in invoking the First Amendment. Applying the *Spence* definitional test, Johnson's conduct involved an intent, as Texas conceded, to communicate a particular message that was likely to be understood by those viewing it. Since Johnson was involved in expressive conduct, Brennan first considered the applicability of the *O'Brien* test. Applying the third criterion in the *O'Brien* test, he inquired whether the interest of the state in convicting Johnson was "unrelated to the suppression of expression." Brennan concluded that the interest asserted by the state—preventing breach of the peace—was not implicated on the facts. The other interest asserted by Texas—the preservation of the flag as a national symbol—Brennan declared, was related to the suppression of expression.

Brennan considered the applicability of various First Amendment doctrines used when the state seeks to justify a law because of the threat of public disturbance or breach of the peace. On the *Johnson* facts, there was no actual or threatened public disturbance. The *potential* for disturbance, or even violence, he concluded, would be insufficient under the revised danger doctrine of *Brandenburg v. Ohio*, 395 U.S. 444 (1969), which requires consideration of the actual danger created by the expression in question. Nor did Johnson's expressive conduct constitute "fighting words": "No reasonable onlooker would have regarded Johnson's generalized expression of dissatisfaction with the policies of the Federal Government as a direct personal insult or an invitation to exchange fisticuffs."

The interest of Texas in preserving the flag as a symbol was based on the apprehension of the state that Johnson's conduct would thwart the communicative message of the flag. Johnson was interfering with government speech by destroying our national symbol of unity. Brennan responded to this assertion of state interest: "These concerns blossom only when a person's treatment of the flag communicates some message, and thus are related 'to the suppression of free expression' within the meaning of *O'Brien*. We are thus outside of *O'Brien's* test altogether." The Texas law was not aimed at protecting the physical integrity of the flag in all circumstances, Brennan said, but only at protecting the flag against mistreatment giving serious offense to others. The measure of misuse in this context is determined by the indignation of the onlooker. For the Court majority in *Johnson*, Texas was concerned with the communicative harm—public offense—that would flow from Johnson's expressive conduct. Johnson's conviction, therefore, was content-based and subject to the "most exacting scrutiny." Applying such a standard, the conviction had to be set aside: "If there is a bedrock principle underlying the First Amendment, it is that the Government may not prohibit the expression of an idea simply because society finds the idea itself offensive or disagreeable."

Chief Justice Rehnquist wrote in dissent: "[T]he public burning of the American flag by Johnson was no essential part of any exposition of ideas, and at the same time it had a tendency to incite a breach of the peace." Johnson's conduct was analogized to "fighting words," the slight social value of which is clearly outweighed by the state's interest in preventing a "probable breach of peace." In short, Rehnquist argued that flag burning should be categorized as low value speech not entitled to normal First Amendment protection. Rehnquist sought to bolster this argument by emphasizing the unique character of the American flag as a symbol of the nation. The flag was a shared symbol which transcended political differences; it could not be appropriated for protest. Justice Brennan, on the other hand, rejected the idea that there were any sacred symbols. If the flag was to be exempted from use as a symbol in demonstrations or protests, what was to prevent other symbols in national life from being similarly conscripted? The American flag could not be meaningfully differentiated from the Presidential Seal or the Constitution itself. Government cannot decide for the people the symbols that they will use for the controversies that beset them.

*Texas v. Johnson* prompted enormous controversy. President Bush declared that the Court was wrong and that a constitutional amendment was needed to protect the flag. In an effort to forestall the mushrooming demand for a constitutional amendment, Congress enacted a new law. The Flag Protection Act of 1989 prohibited the knowing mutilation, defacement, burning, maintaining on the floor or ground, or trampling upon any flag of the United States. This statute was an effort to exploit Justice Brennan's critique of the Texas statute as directed at punishing flag burning because of its offense to others. The new federal statute was portrayed by its defenders as just directed at protecting the physical integrity of the flag in all circumstances whether offense was given to others or not. Perhaps the hope was that Justices Scalia and Kennedy, who had joined Justice Brennan in forming the majority in *Texas v. Johnson*, might be persuaded to validate the new federal law since, arguably, it, unlike the Texas statute, was not content-based. If that was the hope, it did not succeed.

In *United States v. Eichman*, 496 U.S. 310 (1990), Justice Brennan spoke for the same five justices who had formed the majority in *Johnson* and struck down the federal Flag Protection Act of 1989. While Justice Brennan acknowledged that the new Act was not explicitly content-based, the government's asserted interest was still clearly related to the suppression of free expression and concerned with the content of the message. The governmental interest in the physical integrity of a privately owned flag ultimately rested on the need to preserve the flag's status as a symbol of the nation. Brennan's theory on this point appears to be that one would not care about the physical integrity of a piece of cloth—the flag—except for the communicative message which, at bottom, was what really was being protected. In dissent, Justice Stevens, for himself and three others, continued to emphasize that the flag burner was being convicted regardless of the political message he sought to convey to others. In their view, then, a statute punishing flag burning was not a content-based restraint on expression. Rather, it simply removed one method of communicating protest from the public forum. Stevens' dissent, however, failed to provide an answer to the Court's question of why removal of a particular symbol, carrying a particular message, was not itself a form of content-based regulation.

In summary, Professor Steven Heyman has observed that the "Ely–Tribe approach," [see discussion of the O'*Brien* test, *supra*] was accepted by the Supreme Court in the two flag-burning cases:

"[T]he Court equated the 'content' of expression with its 'communicative impact.'" Heyman, *Spheres of Autonomy: Reforming the Content–Neutrality Doctrine in First Amendment Jurisprudence*, 10 Wm. & Mary Bill of Rights Journal 647 (2002).

## C. NUDE DANCING

Not all symbolic speech cases involve political protests such as flag burning and draft card destruction. A group of cases involving a less political form of expressive conduct are the nude dancing cases. The Court has held that a state can prohibit nude dancing in establishments licensed to sell liquor for on-premises consumption consistent with the First Amendment. *California v. LaRue*, 409 U.S. 109 (1972); *New York State Liquor Auth. v. Bellanca*, 452 U.S. 714 (1981); *City of Newport v. Iacobucci*, 479 U.S. 92 (1986). These cases emphasize the state's enhanced power to regulate liquor under the Twenty–First Amendment. On the other hand, the First Amendment was held to prohibit the state from using a zoning ordinance excluding all commercial live entertainment including non-obscene nude dancing, while permitting other commercial activity. *Schad v. Mount Ephraim*, 452 U.S. 61 (1981). The zoning ordinance in *Schad* was not limited merely to liquor control but was an overbroad intrusion on protected First Amendment activity. In all the foregoing nude dancing cases, the Court accepted, without too much enthusiasm, the principle that First Amendment concerns were implicated even by barroom nude dancing.

A case where expressive conduct was arguably given diminished protection than had been the case in the past was *Barnes v. Glen Theatre, Inc.*, 501 U.S. 560 (1991). Two Indiana establishments wished to provide totally nude dancing. One of these establishments, the Kitty Kat Lounge, Inc., sold alcoholic beverages and featured "go-go-dancing." The other establishment, Glen Theatre, Inc., furnished so-called "adult entertainment" such as movie showings and live entertainment at an enclosed bookstore consisting of nude and seminude performances by females behind glass panels. The two establishments sought to enjoin enforcement of the state public indecency law. The Supreme Court, per Chief Justice Rehnquist, upheld, as applied to nude dancing, the Indiana public indecency law which prohibited knowingly or intentionally appearing in a state of nudity in a public place. Given the specific language of Indiana's statutory definition of nudity, a nude dancer would have to wear a G-string and pasties. This, the Court said, was the "bare minimum" necessary to achieve the state's purpose.

Chief Justice Rehnquist conceded "that nude dancing of the kind sought to be performed here is expressive conduct within the outer perimeters of the First Amendment, though only marginally so." While Chief Justice Rehnquist gave lip service to the protected status of expressive conduct such as nude dancing, the begrudging acceptance of this premise raises serious questions about the whole-heartedness of the Court's application of First

Amendment doctrine in the expressive conduct context of nude dancing. Many critics see in *Barnes* a judicial willingness to create new categories of low value speech to which diminished First Amendment protection is accorded even while the Court's expressive conduct doctrine is formally given homage. In *Barnes*, a three Justice plurality opinion for the Court—Rehnquist, Kennedy, and O'Connor—professed to apply the *O'Brien* test. The Indiana law did not ban nude dancing as such but was instead directed at public nudity. The question for Justice Rehnquist was whether application of the public indecency law to nude dancing as a form of public nudity was justified despite the incidental restriction on some expressive activity. The Court found that the public indecency law furthered a substantial governmental interest in order and morality. On the other hand, one might have thought that the First Amendment exists to prevent the enforcement of state ordained conceptions of morality.

Nor did the plurality opinion in *Barnes* find any impediment to the application of the Indiana statute stemming from the third criterion of the *O'Brien* test. The state's interest in order and morality was deemed unrelated to the suppression of free expression. Indiana was proscribing nude dancing, not because of any erotic message conveyed by the dancers, but because of the state's more general interest in protecting morality. Erotic messages could still be conveyed by dancers with pasties and G-strings even if that made the message slightly less graphic: "The perceived evil that Indiana seeks

to address is not erotic dancing but public nudity."
It was public nudity that was barred regardless of
whether or not it conveyed an erotic message. Finally, applying *O'Brien*'s fourth criterion, the plurality
held that the incidental restriction on First Amendment activity was narrowly tailored. The student
should recall, however, that the narrowly tailored
inquiry of *O'Brien* is a highly diluted version of the
less onerous alternative test. It requires only that
the means used directly and effectively further the
state's substantial interest. *Ward v. Rock Against
Racism*, 491 U.S. 781 (1989).

The *Barnes* case provided a valuable snapshot of
the post-Brennan Court's First Amendment divisions. Justice Souter, who replaced Justice Brennan, concurred only in the judgement. (Justice
Brennan would not have done even that). Like the
plurality, Justice Souter accepted that the nude
dancing engaged in by the plaintiffs "is subject to a
degree of First Amendment protection." But he did
not accept that morality could be a substantial
government interest sufficient in itself to justify the
limitation embodied in the Indiana law as applied.
Instead, the state's action was justified on a secondary effects rationale of the type associated with *City
of Renton v. Playtime Theatres, Inc.*, 475 U.S. 41
(1986). Indiana could rely on the public interest in
deterring prostitution, sexual assault, and associated criminal conduct.

Justice Souter's approach, however, does seem to
raise some problems with regard to *O'Brien*'s third
criterion. Weren't the pernicious secondary effects a

product of the persuasive effect of the erotic message of nude dancing? In other words, nude dancing was not so clearly unrelated to the harms the state was seeking to curtail. Justice Souter's answer to this problem was to deny any chain of causation between the secondary harms and the persuasive effect of the nude dancing's expressive message: "Because the State's interest in banning nude dancing results from a simple correlation of such dancing with other evils, rather than from a relationship between the other evils and the expressive component of the dancing, the interest is unrelated to the suppression of free expression." In that case, one might ask how could secondary effects constitute a substantial governmental interest?

Rehnquist and Souter said that the nude dancing was expressive conduct entitled to some measure of First Amendment protection. Scalia did them one better. Scalia said the First Amendment was not implicated at all: "[A]s a general law regulating conduct and not specifically directed at expression, [the Indiana law] is not subject to First Amendment scrutiny at all." There was no showing that Indiana in practice had targeted only expressive nudity. Presumably, such a showing would have implicated the First Amendment. On this point, Scalia continued the campaign he began in *Employment Division v. Smith*, 494 U.S. 872 (1990) (*Smith II*). In *Barnes*, Scalia describes *Smith II* as holding that "general laws not specifically targeted at religious practices did not require heightened First Amendment scrutiny even though they diminished some people's ability to practice their religion."

Since the First Amendment was not involved, Scalia felt no need to apply *O'Brien*. Scalia simply justified the state statute on the ground of the state's interest in morality. Nor did the application of the law to public nudity require any First Amendment inquiry. When a law restricts speech, reasoned Scalia, the Court employs a high First Amendment standard of justification: "But virtually *every* law restricts conduct, and virtually *any* prohibited conduct can be performed for an expressive purpose. [It] cannot reasonably be demanded, therefore, that every restriction of expression incidentally produced by a general law regulating conduct pass normal First Amendment scrutiny, or even—as some of our cases have suggested—see *e.g. O'Brien*, that it be justified by an 'important, or substantial' government interest."

Unlike the flag burning cases, the purpose of the Indiana public indecency law was not designed to suppress communication. A difficulty with Scalia's position, and indeed in this respect with Rehnquist's, is that they simply assume that public nudity is just conduct. They do not grapple with the problem that nudity itself may convey an idea—and an erotic one at that. Insofar as Rehnquist even considers this problem, he does so from the basis that nudity is symbolic speech but that nudity is only incidentally or secondarily regulated under the *O'Brien* framework. Justice White, joined by Blackmun, Marshall and Stevens, made this very point in a vigorous dissent: "The nudity is itself an expressive component of the dance, not merely incidental 'conduct.'" For the dissent, application of the Indiana law was content-based regulation requiring strict First Amendment scrutiny. Stimulating ideas, emotions and thoughts is what communication is all about. In White's view, the nudity element of nude dancing could not be pigeonholed outside of First Amendment protection by a formalistic application of *O'Brien* which simply categorized nudity as conduct.

In *Erie v. Pap's A.M.*, 529 U.S. 277 (2000), the Court upheld an Erie, Pennsylvania ordinance which prohibited nude appearances in public and required the use of a G-string and pasties in nude dancing establishments. As in *Barnes*, no one opinion commanded a majority of the Court. In a plurality opinion, Justice O'Connor, joined by Chief Justice Rehnquist and Justices Kennedy and Breyer, declared that nude dancing of the type at issue in this case was "expressive conduct" which fell within the "outer ambit" of First Amendment protection.

The plurality opinion used the *O'Brien* approach and deemed the law to be content-neutral. Rejecting the contention that the aim of the ordinance was to target the erotic message conveyed by nude dancing, the plurality viewed the law as a general prohibition banning all nude dancing regardless of "whether that nudity is accompanied by expressive activity." The ordinance on public nudity was designed to prevent harmful secondary effects unrelated to the suppression of free expression. On the basis of *City of Renton* and *American Mini Theatres, Inc.*, the city was justified in its view that even one adult entertainment business in a neighborhood was likely to produce harmful secondary effects. These secondary effects satisfied the substantial governmental interest prong of the *O'Brien* test.

Justice Scalia, joined by Justice Thomas, concurred in the judgement on the ground that the law was not subject to "First Amendment scrutiny at all" since the law was not targeted against expressive conduct and was generally applicable. Justice Stevens, joined by Justice Ginsburg, protested the "dramatic changes" in First Amendment doctrine "that the Court endorses today." In the past, the secondary effects doctrine had been used only to justify the regulation of the location of indecent entertainment businesses but here the secondary effects doctrine was being used to justify the "total suppression of protected speech." Justice Stevens also criticized the "dramatic" reduction in the degree to which "the State's interest must be furthered by the restriction imposed on speech."

The *Barnes* and *Pap's A.M.* opinions vividly illustrate the chaotic condition of First Amendment doctrine in the context of expressive conduct and symbolic speech. *Barnes* and *Pap's A.M.* also demonstrate the uncertainty and manipulability of the *O'Brien* standard. It is hard to escape the feeling that the aversion of the Court in these cases to the indecent message conveyed by nude dancing significantly affected the *O'Brien* analysis. While indecent speech is supposedly given full First Amendment protection, the plurality's approach to the *O'Brien* test in both cases indicates that it was not a very effective guarantor of First Amendment protection. *Barnes* and *Pap's A.M.* dismissed burdens on First Amendment speech as either incidental or secondary effects, justifying diminished First Amendment protection. This suggests an increasing deference to state regulation—First Amendment challenges notwithstanding.

# CHAPTER XI

# FREEDOM OF ASSOCIATION AND BELIEF

While there is no express mention of any right of association in the text of the First Amendment, the freedom of association is an implied First Amendment right. Further, the Court has held "that freedom to engage in association for the advancement of beliefs and ideas is an inseparable aspect of the 'liberty' assured by the Due Process Clause of the Fourteenth Amendment, which embraces freedom of speech." *NAACP v. Alabama*, 357 U.S. 449 (1958). Why is freedom of association protected as an implied right under the First Amendment? The Constitution speaks of the rights, privileges, and immunities of persons and citizens, not of groups or associations. Typically, the concern in due process cases is individual liberty, not freedom of group activity. In short, there is little attention directed to the interests of groups, associations or even political parties in the constitutional text.

But even the great eighteenth century exponent of individualism, John Locke, realized the importance of private associations and the force they represent in restraining what Thomas Hobbes called the great Leviathan, the State. Today there is little doubt that political parties and interest groups are vital in pursuing political objectives and checking political power. The relevance of associational rights to freedom of assembly has been noted by the Court: "Effective advocacy of both public and private points of view, particularly controversial ones, is undeniably enhanced by group association." *NAACP v. Alabama*, 357 U.S. 449 (1958). And even effective participation in the marketplace of ideas makes association vital if private individuals are to compete with private concentrations of power.

Social association is not itself protected under the implied right of freedom of association; association in its generic form is not within the implied right. In *City of Dallas v. Stanglin*, 490 U.S. 19 (1989), the Court held that a city ordinance which limited the ability of adults to gain entrance to teenage dance halls did not affect the associational rights of either minors or adults. The coming together of adults and teenagers in dance halls was neither "intimate association" nor "expressive association." It is the right to associate for First Amendment purposes that is constitutionally protected by expressive association.

The freedom to organize to pursue economic interests through a voluntary association can be within the ambit of First Amendment protection. Thus, neither the NAACP nor its members could be held liable for damages resulting from a legal civil rights boycott of white merchants even though the association had sponsored the boycott. *NAACP v. Claiborne Hardware Co.*, 458 U.S. 886 (1982). On the other hand, a boycott violative of the antitrust laws,

organized by lawyers representing indigents to secure increased compensation, was held to be unprotected activity. The expressive dimension of the
boycott was insufficient to invoke First Amendment
protection given its fundamentally economic and
non-political character. *FTC v. Superior Court Trial
Lawyers Ass'n*, 493 U.S. 411 (1990). Further, government has no affirmative obligation to further
associational activity. *Regan v. Taxation With Representation of Washington*, 461 U.S. 540 (1983) [de-
nial of tax breaks to groups that lobby does not
violate the First Amendment]; *Lyng v. International
Union, UAW*, 485 U.S. 360 (1988) [limitation on
ability of strikers to claim food stamp benefits does
not "directly or substantially" interfere with associational rights].

Nor is there any express protection in the First
Amendment for freedom of belief—at least in a non-
free exercise sense. Yet freedom of belief is nonetheless protected under the First Amendment. In *West
Virginia State Bd. of Educ. v. Barnette*, 319 U.S.
624 (1943), Justice Jackson declared for the Court:
"If there is any fixed star in our constitutional
constellation, it is that no official, high or petty, can
prescribe what shall be orthodox in politics, nation-
alism, religion, or other matters of opinion or force
citizens to confess by word or act their faith there-
in." From this principle flowed the holding in *Barnette* that Jehovah's Witnesses could not be forced
by the state to salute the flag in the public schools
in violation of their freedom of belief. Freedom from
compelled orthodoxy is a vital component of the

personal dignity, self-fulfillment, and self-determination protected by due process liberty.

What standard of review is appropriate when courts review government regulations burdening the implied rights of association and belief? This is a difficult question because these rights include both expression and activity. As expression, strict scrutiny would seem appropriate. As activity, some lesser standard would appear to obtain. Further, Supreme Court response to the implied rights has travelled a vacillating course as the Court has been called upon to deal with the associational claims of diverse groups such as the Communist Party in the 1950s, civil rights organizations such as the NAACP in the '50s and '60s, and—in our own time—private clubs practicing gender discrimination. Today, however, the Court generally applies a heightened standard of scrutiny when reviewing government burdens on the right to associate for purposes of political expression: "Infringements [may] be justified by regulations adopted to serve compelling state interests, unrelated to the suppression of ideas, that cannot be achieved through means significantly less restrictive of associational freedoms." *Roberts v. United States Jaycees*, 468 U.S. 609 (1984).

## A.  REGULATION OF GROUP MEMBERSHIP

Many countries in the world have imposed bans on the Communist Party, the National Socialists

(Nazis), and other groups. Membership in such organizations has been made a crime. How would such government regulations fare in our country governed as it is by the First Amendment? While the Supreme Court has never been required to deal with such a total ban, the Court has had to grapple with the imposition by government of severe infringements on such organizations. From these cases, Professor Tribe has concluded that an organization could not be declared illegal in the absence of a showing that the group is engaged in illegal activity sufficient to satisfy the modern clear and danger test. Tribe, *American Constitutional Law* (2d ed. 1988).

Could membership in a terrorist organization committed to illegal conduct be criminally proscribed? Associations and parties have multiple objectives, some legal and some illegal. Association in such a group may be intended to further only the legal objectives of the group. Guilt by association is antithetical to the guarantee of freedom of association and belief. Thus, membership in an organization advocating illegal conduct cannot be punished unless the law is limited to active membership with knowledge of the organization's illegal objectives coupled with specific intent to further the illegal objectives. In *Scales v. United States*, 367 U.S. 203 (1961), the membership clause of the Smith Act was upheld by interpreting, and therefore limiting, it to require *scienter* and specific intent to engage in illegal conduct. In *Noto v. United States*, 367 U.S. 290 (1961), the Court reversed a conviction for membership in the Communist Party on the ground that the evidence was insufficient to establish the requisite *scienter* and specific intent.

## B. GOVERNMENT EMPLOYMENT AND BENEFITS

Citizens cannot be punished solely for their membership in a party or association. Guilt by association has been rejected. But can a citizen be denied public benefits and privileges, such as a government job, which are not provided as a matter of right? Justice Holmes in one of his famous, and in this case mischievous, one-liners said: "The petitioner may have a constitutional right to talk politics, but he has no constitutional right to be a policeman." *McAuliffe v. Mayor of New Bedford*, 29 N.E. 517 (Mass.Sup. Jud.Ct.1892). At one time, the courts accepted this so-called right-privilege dichotomy as a basis for denying government employees associational rights. The right-privilege dichotomy was also used where public benefits were concerned.

Today this dichotomy has been generally abandoned. Government cannot condition either employment or other aspects of its largesse on the surrender of First Amendment rights. In *Schware v. Board of Bar Examiners*, 353 U.S. 232 (1957), the Court overturned a state refusal to admit an applicant to the bar solely because of past associations. Similarly, in *United States v. Robel*, 389 U.S. 258 (1967), the Court invalidated a provision of a federal statute prohibiting members of Communist-action organizations from employment in defense facilities regardless of the sensitivity of the position. Under this provision, the cryptographer and the cook were treated alike. Instead of using a balancing approach, the Court held the law unconstitutionally overbroad. Chief Justice Warren declared for the Court: "Our decision today simply recognizes that when legitimate legislative concerns are expressed in a statute which imposes a substantial burden on protected First Amendment activities, Congress must achieve its goal by means which have a 'less drastic impact' on the continued vitality of First Amendment freedoms." In sum, absent *scienter* and specific intent, civil penalties cannot be imposed solely because an individual has exercised the right of association.

While the courts have severely restricted the ability of government to deny public benefits to those exercising associational rights, the courts have recognized that the government has a significant interest in the qualification and loyalty of its employees. During the Cold War era, the Court was obliged to balance the interest of the government as employer against the burden imposed by the regulation on associational rights. For example, it was established that loyalty programs could not be so sweeping as to undermine the basic right of association. Thus, in *Keyishian v. Board of Regents*, 385 U.S. 589 (1967), the Court held unconstitutional a loyalty program punishing knowing membership in a seditious organization without requiring specific intent. The state was required to legislate using less drastic means: "Because First Amendment freedoms need breathing space to survive, government may regulate in the area only with narrow specificity."

## C.  REGISTRATION AND DISCLOSURE

The previous section dealt with direct prohibitions on group organization and group membership. What if the government regulation is indirect, *e.g.*, requiring that the organization register and disclose its membership lists? Anonymity has historically been protected; the anonymous pamphleteer enjoys First Amendment protection. In *Talley v. California*, 362 U.S. 60 (1960), the Court invalidated, on its face, a city ordinance prohibiting anonymous handbilling, applied to distribution of unsigned handbills urging an economic boycott. Justice Black, for the Court, warned that "persecuted groups and sects from time to time throughout history have been able to criticize oppressive practices and laws either anonymously or not at all."

This concern for anonymous leafletting found modern expression in *McIntyre v. Ohio Elections Commission*, 514 U.S. 334 (1995). The Court invalidated an Ohio statute prohibiting the distribution of anonymous material designed to influence the voters in any election. Justice Stevens, writing for the Court, reaffirmed *Talley*. While the present law applied only in the electoral context, the Court's reasoning in *Talley* had "embraced a respected tradition of anonymity in the advocacy of political causes."

The challenged law was a regulation of the content of core political speech. Applying strict scrutiny, the Court held that the State "interest in providing voters with additional relevant information does not justify a state requirement that a writer make statements or disclosures she would otherwise omit." While the State also has a legitimate interest in preventing fraud in elections, the Ohio law extended to materials that were not even arguably false and misleading. Further, the State had other laws dealing with this problem. The State's efforts to cite the Court's approval of mandatory disclosure laws in the electoral spending context (see Ch. 12, B), were rejected. Such laws are "a far cry from compelled self-identification on all election-related writings." Justice Stevens concluded: "Under our Constitution, anonymous pamphleteering is not a pernicious, fraudulent practice, but an honorable tradition of advocacy and of dissent. Anonymity is a shield from the tyranny of the majority."

The threat of intimidation and the chilling of associational freedom, sometimes quite deliberate, is also bound up with requests by the state for registration and disclosure of the membership lists of unpopular and controversial organizations. In a number of cases earlier in this century, involving first the Ku Klux Klan and later the Communist Party, the Court balanced the government's need for information against the rights of association and belief. In *New York ex rel. Bryant v. Zimmerman*, 278 U.S. 63 (1928), it was held that the membership list of KKK members in the state must be disclosed pursuant to the state interest in controlling the Klan's illegal activities. In *Communist Party of America v. Subversive Activities Control Board*, 367 U.S. 1 (1961), the Court similarly upheld forced disclosure of the Communist Party's membership list based on the Board's conclusions regarding the danger posed by expansionist world-wide Communism. In both cases, the Court's balancing analysis displayed marked deference to the legislature's findings of fact. The judicial inquiry was little more than a rationality inquiry.

On the other hand, in *NAACP v. Alabama ex rel. Patterson*, 357 U.S. 449 (1958), the Court struck down state disclosure requirements imposed on the NAACP. The case was distinguished from *Bryant* because the Klan, unlike the NAACP, was engaged in illegal activities. Justice Harlan for the Court in *NAACP* stated: "Inviolability of privacy in group association may in many circumstances be indispensable to preservation of freedom of association, particularly where a group espouses dissident beliefs." Absent from Harlan's analysis was the marked deference to the legislative judgment that had characterized the decisions involving the Klan and the Communist Party.

What can be made of this quite uneven judicial treatment of burdens on associational rights? Perhaps, the answer lies simply in the Court's determination that the activities of the Klan and the Communist Party were illegal. However, in Alabama during the civil rights protests of the '50s and '60s, the activities of the NAACP were deemed inimical to the public well-being by the state. Nevertheless, it can be argued that these cases reflect the principle that the right of association and belief is limited to a right to associate for purposes furthering First Amendment objectives. On the other hand, the Court's differing balancing analysis as applied to one organization as compared to another may simply reflect political realities. The NAACP enjoyed popular acceptance; the Klan and the Communist Party did not. In more recent times, the Court has been moving toward greater scrutiny of laws burdening associational privacy. In *Brown v. Socialist Workers '74 Campaign Committee*, 459 U.S. 87 (1982), the Court struck down application of a state disclosure requirement providing for disclosure of campaign contributors and recipients to the Socialist Workers Party. There was sufficient evidence that disclosure would subject contributors and recipients to threats, harassment and reprisals. The government's interests in disclosure of the information from a weak minor party was deemed minimal.

The judicial ambivalence reflected in the handling of the group disclosure cases is also reflected in cases involving the efforts of legislative investigative committees to force individuals to disclose information concerning their associational activities. In early cases involving congressional probes of the Communist Party, the Court adopted a highly deferential balancing approach. In *Barenblatt v. United States*, 360 U.S. 109 (1959), the Court, per Justice Harlan, upheld the contempt conviction of a young instructor at the University of Michigan who refused to disclose whether he was a member of the Communist Party. In balancing the interests, Justice Harlan stressed the broad power of Congress "to legislate in the field of Communist activity in this Country, and to conduct appropriate investigations in aid thereof." For Harlan, the congressional investigatory power "rests on the right of self-preservation 'the ultimate value in any society.'" Against the interests of government in self-preservation, the associational claims of Lloyd Barenblatt paled. In dissent, Justice Black protested that the Court's mode of balancing led to a preordained result. The balancing was stacked in favor of the government: "[I]t completely leaves out the real interest in Barenblatt's silence, the interest of the people as a whole in being able to join organizations, advocate causes and make political 'mistakes' without later being subjected to governmental penalties for having dared to think for themselves."

In contrast to *Barenblatt* was the Court's treatment of a state legislative investigation of the NAACP in *Gibson v. Florida Legislative Investigation Committee*, 372 U.S. 539 (1963). Justice Goldberg, for the Court, characterized the disclosures sought as involving a substantial abridgement of freedom of association. Such a burden on freedom of association required "that the State convincingly show a substantial relation between the information sought and a subject of overriding and compelling state interest." But in *Gibson* the Court could find no compelling interest on the part of the state that would justify the forced disclosure of information concerning the membership of a "wholly legitimate organization."

On a doctrinal level, the differing results in *Barenblatt* and *Gibson* can be explained by saying that the former used the deferential ad hoc balancing test and *Gibson* used the demanding non-deferential strict scrutiny test. On a political level, one could argue that the Court was sympathetic to the NAACP while, in 1959, it was highly unsympathetic to the Communist Party. Today the strict scrutiny standard would most probably be applied in this area. The continued movement toward this approach is illustrated by *DeGregory v. Attorney Gen. of New Hampshire*, 383 U.S. 825 (1966). *Gibson* was cited as the basis for curbing a state investigation of the affiliation of DeGregory with the Communist Party. As in *Gibson*, the state had failed to make a showing of overriding and compelling state need for the disclosure.

## D.  COMPELLED ASSOCIATION

Just as there is freedom to speak, to associate and to believe, so also there is freedom not to speak, associate or believe. "The right to speak and the right to refrain from speaking are complementary components of the broader concept of 'individual freedom of mind.'" *Wooley v. Maynard*, 430 U.S. 705 (1977). Freedom of conscience dictates that no individual be forced to espouse ideological causes with which he disagrees: "[A]t the heart of the First Amendment is the notion that the individual should be free to believe as he will, and that in a free society one's beliefs should be shaped by his mind and by his conscience rather than coerced by the State." *Abood v. Detroit Bd. of Educ.*, 431 U.S. 209 (1977).

Freedom from compelled association is a vital component of freedom of expression. Indeed, freedom from compelled association illustrates the significance of the liberty or personal autonomy model of the First Amendment. As a general constitutional principle, it is for the individual and not for the State to choose one's associations and to define the *persona* which she holds out to the world. Important as the freedom from compelled association is, it is, nonetheless, not absolute. Here as in other areas of contemporary First Amendment law, the strict scrutiny standard appears dominant: "Infringements on that right may be justified by regulations adopted to serve compelling state interests, unrelated to the suppression of ideas that cannot be achieved through means significantly less restrictive of associational freedoms." *Roberts v. United States Jaycees*, 468 U.S. 609 (1984).

In determining whether the freedom from compelled association is significantly burdened, the Court will consider factors such as whether the government is prescribing a particular message which the individual is required to avow. Illustrative is *Wooley v. Maynard*, 430 U.S. 705 (1977). A Jehovah's Witness objected to New Hampshire's requirement that licensed motor vehicles carry license plates upon which was emblazoned the state motto "Live Free or Die." The Jehovah's Witness contended that requiring him to carry this message on his license plate conflicted with his moral, political, ethical and religious convictions. Accordingly, he covered up the offending motto. New Hampshire prosecuted him and the Supreme Court in *Wooley*, per Chief Justice Burger, set aside his conviction: "Here [the State] forces an individual as part of his daily life—indeed constantly while his automobile is in public view—to be an instrument for fostering public adherence to an ideological point of view he finds unacceptable." The state interests—state pride, state history and the ability to distinguish New Hampshire license plates from others—were insufficiently compelling to override the First Amendment interest in freedom from compelled association: "Such interests cannot outweigh an individual's First Amendment right to avoid becoming the courier for such a message." In dissent, Justice Rehnquist, joined by Justice Blackmun, contended that the state had not forced the Jehovah's Witness to make any affirmation of belief: "For First Amendment principles to be implicated, the State must place the citizen in the position of either appearing to, or actually, 'asserting as true' the message."

The principle of no-compelled affirmation of belief was upheld once again in *Abood v. Detroit Board of Education*, 431 U.S. 209 (1977). The Court considered a Michigan statute which permitted an agency shop arrangement whereby nonunion public employees paid service charges in lieu of union dues.

Insofar as these charges were used to finance the collective bargaining activities of the union they were constitutionally permissible. True the non-union employees were being obliged to cooperate with unionism, with which they presumably disagreed. Nonetheless, the charges were constitutionally justified given the importance of the governmental interest in union membership as evidenced by federal labor legislation protecting such membership. On the other hand, the use of service charges from the nonunion employees to fund ideological causes with which these members might totally disagree was impermissible. The union, of course, can spend funds to further its views on ideological issues: "[The] Constitution requires only that expenditures be financed from [charges] paid by employees who do not object to advancing those ideas and who are not coerced into doing so against their will by the threat of loss of government employment."

In *Davenport v. Washington Education Association*, 127 S.Ct. 2372 (2007), the Court, per Justice Scalia, upheld a state of Washington law which barred public sector unions from using the agency shop fees of non-members for political or electoral matters without the non-union member's consent. The Supreme Court of Washington below had taken a contrary position and had ruled that in reconciling the constitutional rights of unions and non-unions members "a non [union] member must shoulder the burden of objecting before a union can be barred from spending his fees for purposes impermissible under *Abood*." That court concluded that since the Washington state law departed from this approach, "heightened First Amendment scrutiny" should be invoked. But Justice Scalia declared that the Supreme Court of Washington had pushed the Court's agency fee cases far beyond what they actually require. The short of the matter was that "[w]e have never suggested that the First Amendment is implicated whenever government places limitations on a union's entitlement to agency fees above and what beyond what *Abood* and [related cases] require."

The principle of *Abood* was reaffirmed in *Keller v. State Bar*, 496 U.S. 1 (1990). *Keller* held that the use of mandatory membership dues by the California state bar to further ideological causes with which some members might disagree violated the First Amendment. Only if the state bar could show that the challenged expenditures are "necessarily or reasonably incurred for the purpose of regulating the legal profession or 'improving the quality of legal service'" would the imposition of charges be justified.

But *Abood* and *Keller* were distinguished in *Board of Regents of University of Wisconsin v. Southworth*, 529 U.S. 217 (2000), upholding compulsory student fees, without any showing that the mandatory fees were germane to the educational mission. "If it is difficult to define germane speech with ease or precision where a union [*Abood*] or bar association [*Keller*] is the party, the standard becomes all the more unmanageable in the public

University sitting, particularly where the State undertakes to stimulate the whole universe of speech and ideas."

In *PruneYard Shopping Center v. Robins*, 447 U.S. 74 (1980), the freedom from compelled association principle did not prevail. The California courts, interpreting the state constitutional guarantee of freedom of expression, held that a private shopping center could be required to grant access for expressive activity, including distribution of pamphlets, despite the objections of the owners of the shopping center. The shopping center owners unsuccessfully protested that the views of those seeking access would be wrongfully identified with them in violation of their First Amendment right to be free of compelled association. In *PruneYard,* the Court, per Justice Rehnquist, factually distinguished prior cases. California was compelling access to business establishments open to the public, making it unlikely that the shopping center owners would be identified with the message of those seeking access. Further, unlike *Wooley*, there was no specific message dictated by the state which the owners where being required to display on their property. "There consequently is no danger of government discrimination for or against a particular message." Finally, there was nothing to prevent the shopping center owners from disavowing any connection with messages with which they disagreed.

In *Pacific Gas & Electric v. Public Utilities Commission*, 475 U.S. 1 (1986), the Court distinguished *PruneYard* and reaffirmed the basic principle that the First Amendment prohibits compelling expression with which one disagrees. A public utility commission, in order to achieve a more balanced presentation of views on energy issues, sought to require a privately owned utility company to include inserts in the company's billing envelope along with the company's newsletter. The Supreme Court, per Justice Powell, invalidated the order: "Compelled access like that ordered in this case both penalizes the expression of particular points of view and forces speakers to alter their speech to conform with an agenda they do not set."

In *Pacific Gas & Electric*, *PruneYard* was distinguished on grounds that the shopping center owners had not contended that they disagreed with the contents of the pamphlets being distributed. In *Pacific Gas & Electric*, the utility objected that the inserts it would be forced to include contained ideas to which it was hostile. Further, the access right at issue in *Pacific Gas & Electric* was content-based. Access was awarded because the group seeking to respond objected to what the utility had said in its newsletter. Finally, the Court in *Pacific Gas & Electric* also invoked *Miami Herald Publishing Co. v. Tornillo*, 418 U.S. 241 (1974). The public utility commission order might chill speech since the utility company, rather than having to include a response with which it disagreed, might simply refrain from making statements that would trigger a response. In sum, the government failed to offer adequate justification for its viewpoint discrimination and its compulsory speech order. The order was simply not narrowly tailored to serve any compelling state interest.

A potentially divisive context for the First Amendment right of no compelled association arises when the right conflicts with the constitutional interest in promoting equality. The right not to associate is rooted in the due process guarantee of liberty—the right of the individual or group to exercise freedom of association free from government regulation. But what if the exercise of freedom of association is based on race or gender grounds? What if a group or association denies membership to a person because of her race, gender, religion or sexual preference? In such circumstances, can the state constitutionally provide relief to the individual discriminated against?

Issues such as the foregoing were raised in *Roberts v. United States Jaycees*, 468 U.S. 609 (1984). The Jaycees is a national organization whose by-laws limit regular membership to males between the ages of 18 and 35. Two local Jaycees chapters in Minnesota violated the national by-laws by admitting women. When the national organization threatened revocation of the charters of the Minnesota chapters, both chapters filed discrimination charges under state law prohibiting gender discrimination in public accommodations. The United States Jaycees filed suit in federal court alleging that requiring the organization to accept women would infringe the rights of speech and association of its membership.

Justice Brennan for the Court in *Roberts* distinguished two aspects of freedom of association. The first aspect is the right to enter and maintain intimate human relationships which is protected as a fundamental element of personal liberty. The second aspect is the right to associate for the purpose of the expressive activities protected by the First Amendment. The first aspect—intimate human relationships—was not affected by the Minnesota anti-discrimination law. The second aspect—expressive association—was significantly burdened but that burden was justified by the state's compelling interest in promoting equality.

Justice Brennan began his *Roberts* opinion by stressing the importance of intimate association in our constitutional tradition. Maintenance of close personal ties or bonds serves to transmit our culture and traditions. As John Locke noted, small groups promote diversity and serve to buffer the individual from the power of the state. Moreover, they are instruments for achieving and securing a pluralistic society. But these values of intimate association apply only to groups which manifest smallness, a high degree of selectivity in decision-making regarding policy and membership, and "seclusion from others in critical aspects of the relationship." On this point, it should be noted that these aforementioned characteristics are employed to define the private club exemption of Title II of the 1964 Civil Rights Act prohibiting racial discrimination in public accommodations. But the United States Jaycees did not share the distinctive intimate small group characteristics which would justify First Amendment protection.

The Court next considered expressive association. Justice Brennan had no doubt that the expressive association aspect of the right was plainly implicated since "[t]here can be no clearer example of an intrusion into the internal structure or affairs of an association than a regulation that forces the group to accept members it does not desire." But the right of expressive association is not absolute: "Infringements on that right may be justified by regulations adopted to serve compelling state interests, unrelated to the suppression of ideas, that cannot be achieved through means significantly less restrictive of associational freedoms." There was no doubt that the state interest in eliminating gender discrimination provided compelling justification for curbing the associational freedom of the Jaycees. Nor did the mode of regulation sweep unnecessarily into the right of expressive association. There was no showing by the Jaycees that the admission of women would impose any serious burden on its ability to express organizational ideas and values. Or, to put it in more philosophic terms, in this context, equality trumped liberty.

In a sense, *Roberts* was an easy case and it is not surprising that its principles controlled the outcome of several other compelled association cases as well. *Board of Dirs. of Rotary Int'l v. Rotary Club of Duarte*, 481 U.S. 537 (1987) [application of non-discrimination principles to Rotary Club membership does not violate intimate association given the size, purpose and membership policies of the organization. Nor was expressive association violated absent evidence demonstrating that admitting women to the Rotary would significantly impair the organization's humanitarian, social and ethical objectives]; *New York State Club Ass'n v. City of New York*, 487 U.S. 1 (1988) [First Amendment overbreadth challenge to city law prohibiting gender discrimination in clubs with over 400 members and which charge fees for services to non-members was rejected. Once again, the law did not unconstitutionally burden either aspect of the right of association].

The foregoing cases did not involve the right of intimate association. What if regulation embracing an anti-discrimination principle did in fact do so? For example, what if a city requires a very small association or place of employment to accept members of a racial minority. If a religious group, a church or synagogue, for example, refused to allow participation in its programs to non-members, would the equality principle of *Roberts* continue to prevail against the associational interest of the non-member? This is a difficult question for a society such as ours which values pluralism and which also values equality. Indeed, similar questions arise when the state undertakes to regulate hate speech or female pornography. Thus far, the Court has provided few answers for resolving this fundamental constitutional conflict between equality and the liberty dimension of freedom of association.

When Massachusetts courts applied state antidiscrimination laws to force the private sponsor of

Boston's St. Patrick's Day parade to include a group of gay, lesbian and bisexual marchers of Irish descent, the Court in *Hurley v. Irish–American Gay, Lesbian and Bisexual Group of Boston (GLIB)*, 515 U.S. 557 (1995) unanimously held that the First Amendment was violated. Justice Souter, for the Court, reasoned that parades are a form of expression even if they don't seek to communicate a particularized message and even if a variety of groups are allowed to participate. But GLIB also sought to communicate a message. By participating in the parade as a group, rather than as individuals, it sought to celebrate its members' identity in the Irish community. By requiring inclusion of this message, state courts forced the parade sponsors to alter the expressive content of their parade. "But this use of the State's power violates the fundamental rule of protection under the First Amendment, that a speaker has the autonomy to choose the content of his own message." A parade is not a mere conduit for the speech of others, since there is a danger that the sponsor would be identified with the marchers. Inclusion of GLIB in the parade was likely to be perceived as having resulted from the sponsor's determination that the group's message was worthy of communication and even of support. A moving, expressive parade was not a context similar to the shopping centers in *PruneYard* where the sponsors could easily disassociate themselves from the GLIB message.

The Court in *Boy Scouts of America v. Dale*, 530 U.S. 640 (2000), relied on *Hurley* in upholding the right of the Boy Scouts to expel an assistant scouts-master who publicly declared that he was homosexual and a gay rights activist. The Court held 5–4 that New Jersey could not apply its public accommodations law to admit Dale consistent with the organization's right of expressive association. Chief Justice Rehnquist, for the Court, reasoned from the premise that Boy Scouts is an association that engages in expressive activity by seeking to transmit a system of values. The Court accepted the Scout's assertion that Dale's presence in the association would significantly burden its message "that homosexual conduct is not straight" and would interfere with its desire not "to promote homosexual conduct as a legitimate form of behavior." Dale's presence would force the organization to send a message "that the Boy Scouts accepts homosexual conduct as a legitimate form of behavior." The Court rejected application of the *O'Brien* test, holding: "the state interests embodied in New Jersey's public accommodations law do not justify such a severe intrusion on the Boy Scouts' rights to freedom of expressive association." Justice Stevens, writing for the four dissenters, argued that the New Jersey law "does not 'impose any serious burdens on [the Boy Scouts'] 'collective effort on behalf of [its] shared goals,' nor does it force [the Boy Scouts] to communicate any message that it does not wish to endorse."

In *Rumsfeld v. Forum for Academic and Institutional Rights*, 547 U.S. 47 (2006) *(FAIR)*, the Court distinguished these compelled speech and association cases in rejecting a First Amendment challenge to the Solomon Amendment which withholds federal funds from institutions of higher education which deny military recruiters equal access. Chief Justice Roberts, for a unanimous Court, said that, unlike *Hurley*, forcing law schools to accommodate the military's speech does nothing to affect the law schools own message, "because the schools are not speaking when they host interviews and recruiting receptions." Unlike the selection of parade contingents, law school recruitment services lack any expressive quality—"accommodation of a military recruiter's message is not compelled speech because the accommodation does not sufficiently interfere with any message of the school." Distinguishing *Dale*, the Court held that the Solomon Amendment did not violate the right of expressive association. It does not have a comparable effect of the law school's ability to express its message. "Students and faculty are free to associate to voice their disapproval of the military's message; nothing about the statute affects the composition of the group by making group membership less desirable."

## E.  THE ELECTORAL PROCESS

Speech, association and voting in the electoral process lie at the core of our First and Fourteenth Amendment freedoms. Certainly, the citizen participation rationale for First Amendment protection must view the electoral process as occupying the very heart of protected expression in our democratic society. "[T]he First Amendment 'has its fullest and most urgent application' to speech uttered during a campaign for political office." *Eu v. San Francisco Cty. Democratic Cent. Comm.*, 489 U.S. 214 (1989). Similarly, freedom of association includes both the rights of the individual voter to associate with the party of her choice as well as the right of the political party to identify the people who will constitute the association. *Tashjian v. Republican Party of Connecticut*, 479 U.S. 208 (1986). Furthermore, the constitutional protection accorded voting similarly implicates First Amendment rights of political expression and association.

If the legal restriction on the right is "severe," it must satisfy strict scrutiny. *Norman v. Reed*, 502 U.S. 279 (1992). On the other hand, a less intense standard of review will obtain when the burden on the protected right is less destructive: "But when a state election law provision imposes only 'reasonable, non-discriminatory restrictions' upon the First and Fourteenth Amendment rights of voters, 'the State's important regulatory interests are generally sufficient to justify' the restrictions." *Burdick v. Takushi*, 504 U.S. 428 (1992), quoting *Anderson v. Celebrezze*, 460 U.S. 780 (1983).

In *Republican Party of Minnesota v. White*, 536 U.S. 765 (2002), the Court held, 5–4, that Minnesota's "Announce Clause," prohibiting candidates for judicial election from announcing their views on disputed legal or political issues, violated the First Amendment. The Clause did not require that the candidate bind himself to maintain the position

after election. That was covered by a separate
"pledge or promises" prohibition. Justice Scalia, for
the Court, applied strict scrutiny since the Clause
prohibited speech based on content and burdened
"a category of speech that is 'at the core of our
First Amendment freedom'—speech about the qualification of candidates for public office." Justice
Scalia questioned the meaning of the claimed state
interest on preserving the impartiality of the state
judiciary and the appearance of impartiality. The
Clause was not narrowly tailored to the interest in
impartiality in the sense of avoiding bias for against
either party to a proceeding since the Clause does
not address speech for or against particular parties
but rather speech for or against particular issues.
Impartiality in the sense of lack of preconceptions
for or against a particular legal view is not a compelling state interest. Avoiding judicial preconceptions, reasoned Justice Scalia, "is neither possible
nor desirable." The state interest in impartiality,
understood as openmindedness—to remain open to
persuasion—was not the purpose of the Announce
Clause. Further, the Clause is "woefully underinclusive" if that were its purpose since candidates
often announce positions on legal issues either before becoming a candidate or after election. Justice
Scalia concluded that the state had failed to carry
its burden under the strict scrutiny test.

Justice Ginsburg, for the dissent, argued that
"judges perform a function fundamentally different
from that of the people's elected representatives."
While elected political officials represent their con-

stituents, judges represent the law. While Minnesota chose to elect judges, it tailored its election process to reflect this difference and maintain judicial integrity. The "pledges and promises" clause advances the compelling interest in protecting due process for litigants and promotes public confidence in the states judges. The Announce Clause is necessary to prevent the pledges and promises clause from being circumvented by statements that do not technically constitute promises.

A vital dimension of freedom of political association is the ability of the political association to determine its structure, choose its members, and fashion its policies. When a state undertakes to regulate political parties operating at the national level in matters such as selecting presidential candidates, its interests are minimal and are likely to be insufficient to justify any significant burden on the associational right.

*California Democratic Party v. Jones*, 530 U.S. 567 (2000) stressed the limitations on state regulation of the parties' internal processes, holding, 7–2, that a California law requiring a blanket primary violated the First Amendment. The blanket primary allowed voters to vote for any candidate regardless of political affiliations; the candidates of each party who wins the most votes becomes the nominee. Justice Scalia, for the Court, said that the California law was "forced association" requiring political parties to adulterate their candidate-selection process by opening it up to persons unaffiliated with the party. This significant burden on associational freedom required strict scrutiny. But the Court found no compelling state interest in privacy or fairness which was narrowly served by the law and which could not be served by a nonpartisan blanket primary.

But in *Washington State Grange v. Washington State Republican Party*, 128 S.Ct. 1184 (2008), the Court 7–2 upheld a Washington state voter initiative (I–872) providing that candidates for office could designate their party preference on the ballot; that voters could vote for any candidate; and that the top two votegetters for each office, regardless of party preference, would advance to the general election. The Court, per Justice Thomas, used a deferential standard of review "[b]ecause I–872 does not on its face impose a severe burden on political parties' associational rights" and claims that I–872 had the affect of imposing a severe burden "rest on factual assumptions about voter confusion that can be evaluated only in the context of an as-applied challenge."

Unlike *Jones*, Justice Thomas reasoned "the I–872 primary did not, "by its terms, choose party nominees." Rather, the law identified the top two candidates for the general election regardless of party designation. The claim of the political parties challenging I–872 that it nevertheless burdened associational rights was based on the belief that voters would be confused by the candidates' own party preference designations. Justice Thomas said this was "sheer speculation" and a facial challenge cannot rest "on the mere possibility of voter confusion." The State's asserted legitimate interest in providing voters with relevant information about the candidates was easily sufficient to sustain the law under the deferential standard of review.

Justice Scalia, joined by Justice Kennedy, dissented, arguing that I–872 significantly undermined political association by causing "a party to be associated with candidates who may not fully (if at all) represent its views." The law resulted in forced association by allowing the self-identified party supporter to distort the party's message and hijack its goodwill. There was no opportunity on the ballot for the party to repudiate the candidate or to identify the candidate the party in actually favored. Because Washington failed to satisfy strict scrutiny, the dissent would find the law unconstitutional.

The above cases establish that a political party has a First Amendment right to limit its membership and to define its candidate selection process to reflect its political message. But in *New York State Board of Elections v. Lopez–Torres*, 128 S.Ct. 791 (2008), the Court rejected extending this into an associational right for a person to have a fair chance of prevailing in the parties' candidate selection process. The Court unanimously upheld a New York election law requiring that political parties select their nominees for Supreme Court Justice at a convention of delegates chosen by party members in a primary election.

# CHAPTER XII

# GOVERNMENT SPONSORED ENVIRONMENTS

The protected status of freedom of speech has come to mean that courts closely scrutinize government regulations burdening protected speech. Meeting a rationality standard of review is insufficient justification for such laws. But there are exceptions. When government regulates speech in nonpublic forums, the only conditions for the validity for such regulation are viewpoint neutrality and meeting the rationality standard of review. (see Ch. IX, B). And when government regulates speech in government sponsored environments—speech by government employees, students, military personnel, prisoners— courts regularly depart from traditional First Amendment standards. Similarly, government is accorded marked deference in prescribing regulations concerning the use of funds provided grantees when expression is thereby curtailed. Government, like most donors, can define the terms under which it is willing to make a grant. *Rust v. Sullivan*, 500 U.S. 173 (1991).

In these contexts, the courts employ balancing which often becomes essentially a deferential rationality review. For example, in upholding a prison policy that prevented prisoners from fulfilling their

Islamic religious obligations, the Court stated: "To ensure that courts afford appropriate deference to prison regulations, we have determined that prison regulations alleged to infringe constitutional rights are judged under a 'reasonableness' test less restrictive than that ordinarily applied to alleged infringements of fundamental constitutional rights." *O'Lone v. Estate of Shabazz*, 482 U.S. 342 (1987). See *Goldman v. Weinberger*, 475 U.S. 503 (1986) [application of Air Force regulation to prevent airman, who was an ordained rabbi, from wearing his yarmulke, held constitutional]; *Parker v. Levy*, 417 U.S. 733 (1974) [court-martial conviction of army physician for making statements critical of certain personnel and urging resistance to Vietnam War upheld].

Is this deference appropriate? Arguably, the values underlying the principle of freedom of speech are still applicable in these contexts. Millions of people spend a significant part of their lives in these government sponsored environments. A significant amount of expression is thus curtailed when the courts avoid meaningful scrutiny of speech restrictive policies in such environments. On the other hand, the laws being reviewed are not generally applicable regulations. They restrict the speech activity of only a sector of the public having a special relationship to the government. The laws are directed to the ongoing operation of that relationship and the sanctions usually are limited to ending the relationship. Further, those regulated have often voluntarily entered into the special relationship, *e.g.*, government employees, nonconscripted military personnel, recipients of government grants. In the past, in justification of a hands-off policy denying constitutionally-based relief to individuals in government sponsored environments, the courts spoke of the regulated party as enjoying a privilege or benefit rather than a right. Under this now generally discredited doctrine, what government granted was a matter of grace in the first place. No rights, therefore, accrued to the claimant.

In the case of many of these government sponsored environments, courts often feel they lack the ability to assess the justifications for the regulation. In military and prison cases especially, the courts often express a reluctance to second-guess administrative expertise. More generally, the courts emphasize the vital interests of government in maintaining restrictions in such environments. But the student should note that the government interests are being used to justify a lower standard of review in all cases involving the specific government sponsored environment. The government interests are not being examined in applying a heightened standard of review to determine if the particular regulation being challenged is justified. The government interest thus does double duty. It is used to justify a lower standard of review in the government sponsored environment class of cases generally and then to justify the particular regulation in question.

## A. STUDENT SPEECH

The student speech cases reflect the tension between two competing paradigms. The liberal paradigm stresses the classroom as "peculiarly the 'marketplace of ideas.' " *Tinker v. Des Moines Independent Community School Dist.*, 393 U.S. 503 (1969). The academic forum should foster a free exchange of ideas, even though the ideas may be offensive, nonconformist or disputatious. Children can contribute to the marketplace and both children and the society grow from the resulting dialogue. See *Board of Educ. v. Pico*, 457 U.S. 853 (1982) [Court reversed summary dismissal of suit challenging removal of offensive books from school library; plurality of Court stressed student's right of access to even those ideas which are offensive].

The alternative communitarian paradigm used in the student speech cases emphasizes the schools as the place for "inculcating fundamental values necessary to the maintenance of a democratic political system," *Ambach v. Norwick*, 441 U.S. 68 (1979), and for teaching the "shared values of a civilized social order." *Bethel School Dist. No. 403 v. Fraser*, 478 U.S. 675 (1986). The educational mission is to transmit the community's basic values to its young. School administrators must be given broad discretion to pursue this educational mission, including the regulation of speech deemed inconsistent with that mission.

The leading case extending broad First Amendment protection to student speech using the liberal paradigm is *Tinker v. Des Moines Independent Community School District*, 393 U.S. 503 (1969). Three public high school students who were suspended for wearing black armbands to protest the Vietnam War successfully challenged a school rule prohibiting the wearing of the armbands. Students are "persons" possessed of fundamental rights, Justice Fortas observed for the Court. Further, "[s]tudents or teachers [do not] shed their constitutional rights to freedom of speech or expression at the schoolhouse gate." The students were engaged in symbolic conduct "closely akin to 'pure speech,'" which had been accorded "comprehensive protection" by the Court.

*Tinker* did not adopt any of the traditional judicial standards for reviewing content regulation. Instead, it fashioned a new formulaic test which would require government to prove that the regulated speech "materially and substantially interfere[s] with the requirements of appropriate discipline in the operation of the school" or that it "impinge[s] upon the rights of other students." This is not the language of strict scrutiny. The "material and substantial disruption" test of *Tinker* lacks the immediacy of harm associated with the clear and present danger test. Moreover, Justice Fortas called for courts to balance the competing interests "in light of the special characteristics of the school environment."

Still, *Tinker* clearly requires the state to provide significant justification for limiting free debate. The "un-differentiated fear or apprehension of disturbance would not suffice." Nor would the offensiveness of the student speech justify suppression. In *Tinker*, there was only "a silent, passive expression of opinion, unaccompanied by any disorder or disturbance." The language and spirit of *Tinker* did not reflect judicial avoidance nor judicial deference to school administrators nor even a simple balancing of interests. Instead, the Court demanded substantial justification when student speech is significantly burdened. Evidence supporting the need for the restriction is judicially examined. It is in its adherence to free speech principles that *Tinker* reflects the use of the liberal paradigm in student speech problems.

For Justices Black and Harlan in dissent, the ultimate question in school speech cases was, "Who should govern?" Should it be the school authorities? The students? The courts? In their view, there could only be one answer—the school authorities. For Justice Black, the school environment was simply inconsistent with judicially protected free speech. Justice Hugo Black, famous First Amendment absolutist, took the position in *Tinker* that no one has a right to speak, in a particular manner, at a particular place. Government creates schools as places for learning, not as forums for freedom of expression. Justice Black's nonpublic forum analysis in *Tinker* was to provide a touchstone for a more restrictive approach to student speech in future cases.

A more communitarian approach was taken by the Court in *Bethel School Dist. No. 403 v. Fraser*,

478 U.S. 675 (1986). A public high school disciplined a student who delivered an indecent and inappropriate speech at a school assembly. The assembly in question was school-sponsored but student-run. Matthew Fraser, a 17 year old high school senior, delivered a nominating speech on behalf of a classmate running for a student government office making use of humorous sexual innuendos in his speech. Some students hooted and hollered and simulated sexual actions during the speech. Other students and teachers were offended and upset. Fraser was suspended for three days and barred from being a graduation day speaker. Fraser brought suit against the school authorities challenging the sanctions as a violation of his First Amendment rights.

Chief Justice Burger, for the Court in *Fraser*, provided two justifications for upholding the school disciplinary action. First, the Chief Justice emphasized the governmental interest in pursuing its educational mission by controlling the curriculum and protecting other children. Second, when indecent speech of a sexual character is at issue in a public school context, the First Amendment interest does not weigh heavily in a balancing analysis.

The Court's first theme emphasizing what might be called communitarian values in pursuing the educational mission is not necessarily inconsistent with *Tinker*. It can be argued that a school's educational mission can be disrupted not only by physical disorder, as recognized in *Tinker*, but also by inappropriate expressive behavior inconsistent with norms of civility. Thus, for Justice Brennan, who concurred in *Fraser*, it was critical that the speech which was subject to discipline occurred at a school-run assembly that was part of the school program. If the speech had taken place in the cafeteria or during a school break, Brennan might have extended protection to it. Alternatively, the notion of what would be required to show material disruption was simply broadened in *Fraser* to include expression that would conflict with the community's values even though the expression did not actually disrupt, or threaten to disrupt, the educational program. From this vantage point, which emphasizes order and discipline in the schools, *Fraser* represents a new direction, a direction which deviates from *Tinker*'s liberal paradigm.

The second theme—the focus on indecent sexually oriented speech—reflects different standards of judicial scrutiny in the government sponsored school environment. Chief Justice Burger's balancing approach is far less protective of free speech values than the analysis adopted in *Tinker*. Why is this so? Presumably, because in the school environment the educational program and its furtherance is weighted more heavily than a high school student's free expression rights. Further, in First Amendment analysis indecent speech in ordinary civil society is constitutionally protected expression. But, for Chief Justice Burger in *Fraser*, indecent speech in the school context is either given no protection or only minimal value in balancing the interests: "[I]t is a highly appropriate function of public school education to prohibit the use of vulgar and offensive terms in public discourse."

The Chief Justice then added: "The determination of what manner of speech in the classroom or school assembly is inappropriate properly rests with the school board." At least in the context of speech involving the curriculum, judicial deference to school authorities is the norm. Under *Fraser*, a school board's label on curricular speech by students as inappropriate removes it from meaningful First Amendment protection. This judicial deference to school authorities reflects a communitarian paradigm and represents a substantial departure from the liberal paradigm applied in *Tinker*. Sensitive to this departure, Justice Brenann concurring in *Fraser* warned: "Courts have a First Amendment responsibility to insure that robust rhetoric is not suppressed by prudish failures to distinguish the vigorous from the vulgar."

The communitarian approach to school speech issues received a further boost in *Hazelwood School District v. Kuhlmeier*, 484 U.S. 260 (1988), which upheld the power of school principals to censor school-sponsored student newspapers so long as such censorship serves valid educational purposes. Members of a journalism class at a public high school wrote and edited *Spectrum*, the school newspaper. The school principal, however, objected to two articles scheduled for publication. One article discussed teenage pregnancy at the high school. The principal feared the article would deprive students of vital anonymity and, indeed, might be inappropriate altogether for young students. The second article discussed divorce and criticized the student writer's father. This article raised such problems as privacy, libel and general propriety. Without prior notice to the students, the principal deleted two entire pages from the newspaper. The students were subsequently informed that the articles were "inappropriate, personal, sensitive, and unsuitable." Three former *Spectrum* staff members brought suit and contended that the principal's action violated the First Amendment.

Justice White, speaking for the Court, upheld the school administration and rejected the First Amendment challenge. Justice White's rationale in *Hazelwood* is a hybrid of the school as nonpublic forum theme that had been suggested by Justice Black in *Tinker* and the no-protection-for-curricular-speech theme of *Fraser*. What was crucial for Justice White was that the newspaper was a part of the curriculum. First, the paper was a nonpublic forum. Justice White emphasized that the school had not "by policy or by practice" created a limited public forum. As a nonpublic forum, all that was required under the First Amendment for the censorship of the newspaper to be valid was that the principal's action be viewpoint neutral and reasonable. The nonpublic forum analysis taken by White in *Hazelwood* basically amounts to little more than the most deferential kind of rationality review. What is the scope of the nonpublic forum context in public education? Is it limited to the school newspaper? Arguably, the students in *Tinker* were operating in a nonpublic forum when they wore their armbands into the classroom. In fact, if designation of the forum depends on the school's policy and practice, *i.e.*, the intent of school officials, it is difficult to think of any part of the educational enterprise that could qualify as a public forum. At the very least, Justice White's approach would allow school officials to exclude free expression from the program simply by designating the activity as a nonpublic forum.

Justice White's second theme in *Hazelwood* is even more deferential to school authorities than his use of nonpublic forum doctrine. He creates a whole new category of student speech that is outside the ambit of *Tinker* by distinguishing between "personal expression that happens to occur on the school premises" and "school sponsored publications, theatrical productions, and other expressive activities that students, parents and members of the public might reasonably perceive to bear the imprimatur of the school." Only the former category is governed by *Tinker*. In the latter category of curricular speech, regulations by school authorities will be upheld "so long as [school officials'] actions are reasonably related to legitimate pedagogical concerns." Action by school officials lacks such a reasonable relation only if it has "no valid educational purpose."

The curricular speech doctrine of *Hazelwood* raises many difficult questions. Most fundamentally, when *is* student expression part of the educational program? Is the decisive factor whether or not academic credit is awarded for the expression at issue? Suppose one receives recognition at graduation for membership in an activity even though no credit was awarded? If the school provides financial support but no credit, it is difficult to determine on which side of the line the activity falls. Is the critical element, as Justice White suggests, how the activity is viewed by the public—does the public identify the activity with the school? Besides the difficulty of deciding whether an activity is part of the educational program, another problem with the *Hazelwood* doctrine is that the means of evasion are apparent. If the school wishes to suppress student expression, the school authorities need only rule that the activity is now part of the educational program. Finally, *Hazelwood* presents the vexing question of whether its doctrine applies to state university students as well as high school students.

Justices Brennan and Marshall dissented in *Hazelwood*; they accused the Court of abandoning *Tinker*. Justice White pled guilty to this charge. The teaching of *Hazelwood* is that *Tinker* does not apply to the educational program. This is an amazing doctrine since *Tinker* itself was conceived in the classroom. *Tinker* emphasized the role of First Amendment values in the schoolhouse and in the educational program. Justice Brennan declared in dissent in *Hazelwood*: "[The] mere fact of school sponsorship does not, as the Court suggests, license such thought control in the high school, whether through school suppression of disfavored viewpoints or through official assessment of topic sensitivity."

The Roberts Court continued the erosion of *Tinker* in *Morse v. Frederick*, 127 S.Ct. 2618 (2007). The principal of Juneau–Douglas High School (JDHS) had permitted staff and students to leave school to observe the Olympic Torch Relay. As the torchbearers and cameras passed by, Frederick joined some fellow students in unfurling a 14–foot banner bearing the phrase "BONG HiTS 4 JESUS." Morse, the principal, confiscated the banner and subsequently suspended Frederick.

The Court rejected Frederick's claim that his First Amendment rights had been violated. Even though Frederick's speech was neither "offensive" (*Fraser*) nor could it be understood as bearing the school's imprimatur (*Hazelwood*), the Court held that the speech was unprotected, since the principal could reasonably interpret it as advocating or promoting the use of illegal drugs. Looking at the context, the Court noted that, unlike *Tinker*, Frederick's speech was not political, and the threat posed by illegal drug use by students was "far more serious and palpable" then that posed by the armbands in *Tinker*. Unfortunately, the Court did little more to provide guidance on the limits of this new exception to the *Tinker* standard.

The need for limitations was also illustrated by a concurring opinion by Justice Alito, joined by Justice Kennedy. They joined the Court's opinion but only on the understanding that "(a) it goes no further than to hold that a public school may restrict speech that a reasonable observer would interpret as advocating illegal drug use and (b) it provides no support for any restrictions of speech that can plausibly be interpreted as commenting on political or social issue, including speech on issues such as 'the wisdom of the war on drugs or of legalizing marijuana for medical use.' " Their concurrence adopted a very narrow understanding of the Court's new exception to *Tinker* and an unwillingness to encourage any other viewpoint based on restrictions on student speech. This case stood "at the far reaches of what the First Amendment permits."

Justice Stevens, joined by Justices Souter and Ginsburg, dissenting, argued that the majority violated two cardinal First Amendment principles animating *Tinker*. First, content-based regulation, "is subject to the most rigorous burden of justification." Second, punishing advocacy is constitutional "only when the advocacy is likely to provoke the harm that the government seeks to avoid." Instead, the majority's approach "invites stark viewpoint discrimination." Even assuming that the concern over the consequences of pro-drug speech justifies some restrictions on speech, it would not justify a prohibition on "an obscure message with a drug theme that a third party subjectively—and not very reasonably—thinks is tantamount to express advocacy." For the dissent, Frederick's speech was "a nonsense message; not advocacy."

*Morse v. Frederick* introduces still another categorical exception to the First Amendment limitation forged in *Tinker*. Unfortunately the new departure is even more ill-defined than its predecessors. Is the exception for advocacy of illegal drug use *sui generis* or does it reflect some broader range of illegal activities? How about alcohol use? Is there any viable limitation on a school's ability to censor drug-related speech? Doesn't any speech questioning government policy on drug use, "encourage" drug use? The majority's approach sounds very much like the "bad tendency" test of another era. And when does speech qualify for Justice Alito's caveat of commentary on social or political issues? Why wasn't Frederick's "BONG HiTS 4 JESUS"— within the protected caveat?

*Fraser, Hazelwood* and *Frederick* have moved the Court a long way from the road marked by *Tinker*. *Tinker* emphasized First Amendment values in the schoolhouse. The later cases emphasized the need for school authorities to determine how best to pursue the educational mission. *Tinker* stressed the need for judicial sensitivity in reviewing censorship of student speech by school authorities. *Fraser, Hazelwood* and *Frederick* stress judicial deference to those same authorities.

This cleavage between the cases may be explained by a disenchantment with the student protest and social upheavals of the 1960s. It may also reflect the appointment of new justices to the Court; justices committed to conservative or communitarian values in place of liberal justices who gave primacy to free speech against authority. Further, *Tinker* represented an egalitarian view that high school students, no less than adults, merited broad First Amendment protection. The *Fraser, Hazelwood* and

*Frederick* majorities take a more paternalistic view when the rights of those who are not quite adults are presented. Finally, the evolution of doctrine from *Tinker* to *Frederick* may reflect the tension inherent in reconciling the mission of schools to inculcate societal values in the young with the need to avoid the pall of orthodoxy and the suppression of dissent in the classroom. In short, it is little wonder these cases are often decided by a bitterly divided Court. They raise issues on which society itself is also deeply divided.

## B.  GOVERNMENT EMPLOYMENT

In an aphorism which unfortunately proved so quotable that it was too influential for too long a time, Justice Oliver Wendell Holmes remarked when he was still a judge on the Massachusetts Supreme Judicial Court: "[A police officer] may have a constitutional right to talk politics but he has no constitutional right to be a policeman." *McAuliffe v. Mayor of New Bedford*, 29 N.E. 517 (Mass. Sup. Jud. Ct. 1892). For Holmes, it followed that "the servant cannot complain as he takes the employment on the terms on which they are offered to him." It apparently was of no consequence that the employer was the government rather than a private party. Since the government employer controlled the job, it could define the conditions of the employment offer.

The theory underlying the Holmes approach is that government employment is a privilege not a right. Although once a powerful doctrine, the right-privilege doctrine today has been largely rejected. In *Perry v. Sindermann*, 408 U.S. 593 (1972), the Court stated, per Justice Stewart: "For at least a quarter century, this Court has made clear that even though a person has no single 'right' to a valuable governmental benefit and even though the government may deny him the benefit for any number of reasons, there are some reasons upon which the government may not rely. It may not deny a benefit to a person on a basis that infringes his constitutionally protected interests—especially his interest in freedom of speech." If government could penalize or inhibit free expression by its control over the public workplace, government could "produce a result which [it] could not command directly."

Just as a student does not completely lose her constitutional rights upon entering the schoolhouse, so also the government employee retains, to some degree, the constitutional rights of a citizen even when she takes on the status of a public employee. Both in the workplace and the community, the government employee still is entitled to some measure of First Amendment protection. Furthermore, it is important to recognize the critical information about government activities possessed by government employees. The whistle-blower has become a valuable adjunct of the public's right to know. Finally, the total workforce that is in the public sector, whether federal state or local, is now enormous. A hands-off policy by the courts with respect to constitutional claims by public employees would leave too large a slice of the populace with no constitutional protection.

Nonetheless, there are differences between the government as regulator and the government as employer. "[The] State has interests as an employer in regulating the speech of its employees that differs significantly from those it possesses in connection with regulation of the speech of the citizenry in general." *Pickering v. Board of Education*, 391 U.S. 563 (1968). Government must be able to accomplish the public's business. The Court in *Pickering* described the fundamental issue: "The problem in any case is to arrive at a balance between the interests of the [government employee], as a citizen, in commenting upon matters of public concern and the interest of the State, as an employer, in promoting the efficiency of the public services it performs through its employees."

## 1.   DEFINING PUBLIC INTEREST SPEECH

When the government undertakes to discipline its employees for expressive activities critical of government policy, the Court has employed a two part inquiry. The Court asks if the employee's speech involves a matter of public concern or is instead a private matter. In the latter case, the Court will usually defer to the government's personnel decision. Essentially, in this instance, the Court takes a hands-off policy. If the speech is determined to be a of matter of public interest, the Court proceeds to the second part of the test, which is a balancing determination.

In *Pickering*, a teacher had been dismissed by the local Board of Education for publishing in a newspaper a letter critical of the Board's school funding policies. The Board claimed that many statements in the letter were false and detrimental to the administration of the schools. The Illinois courts upheld the dismissal and Pickering sought Supreme Court review. In reversing, the Supreme Court, per Justice Marshall, applied a balancing test. The expression at issue involved no impairment of the ability of superiors to maintain discipline nor did it pose any threat of disharmony among co-workers. The teacher's employment relationships with the Board did not involve "the kind of close working relationships for which it can persuasively be claimed that personal loyalty and confidence are necessary to their proper functioning." Thus even to the extent that the teacher's comments, critical of the Board, were substantially correct, they still did not furnish grounds for dismissal.

As far as the statements made by the teacher that were found to be false, the Court again held on balance that the teacher should be protected. There was no threat to the professional reputation of the school administrators since the teacher's letter had generally been greeted by apathy and disbelief. There was no reason that the Board could not rebut the teacher's charges through counter-speech. The school administration's interest in controlling the speech of the teacher was not significantly greater than its interest in limiting similar speech by the general public. Not surprisingly, the Court considered the case as involving criticism by Pickering the citizen rather than criticism by Pickering the government employee. The Court, therefore, invoked the defamation standard of *New York Times Co. v. Sullivan*, 376 U.S. 254 (1964). Using the *Times* standard, applicable to the citizen-critic of government, the Court found no proof that the statements were made knowingly or recklessly.

The plaintiff in a *Pickering*-type case must establish that she was disciplined because of her First Amendment expressive activity. If the government employee establishes a sufficiently strong case that her speech was the basis for the government's disciplinary action against her, the government may respond by showing that it would have taken the disciplinary action even apart from the employee's expressive activities. In that instance, the First Amendment will not provide a successful defense for the employee. *Mt. Healthy City School Dist. Bd. of Educ. v. Doyle*, 429 U.S. 274 (1977).

In *Connick v. Myers*, 461 U.S. 138 (1983), the Court held that the *Pickering* balancing test is to be used only for speech involving matters of public concern, not matters of purely personal interest. In understanding this distinction, it should be noted that private conversations involving matters of public concern are given protection under *Pickering*. In short, a matter can be confidential and still be of public concern. *Givhan v. Western Line Consolidated School Dist.*, 439 U.S. 410 (1979).

In *Connick*, an assistant district attorney strongly objected to her transfer to another section of the court. She circulated a questionnaire within the office concerning transfer policies, office morale, the handling of grievances, employee confidence in supervisors, and pressure to work on political campaigns. Myers was terminated. She brought suit claiming that the discharge violated her free speech rights. The Supreme Court, per Justice White, disagreed 5–4. While speech on private matters was not devoid of any First Amendment protection, the state as a public employer enjoyed broad discretion: "We hold only that when a public employee speaks not as a citizen upon matters of public concern, but instead as an employee upon matters of personal interest, absent the most unusual circumstances, a federal court is not the appropriate forum in which to review the wisdom of a personnel decision taken by a public agency allegedly in reaction to the employee's behavior." How can we distinguish between speech that concerns the public and personal speech that does not? While there is no bright line, the *Connick* Court offered the following formulation: "Whether an employee's speech addresses a matter of public concern must be determined by the content, form, and context of a given statement as revealed by the whole record." Applying this test, the Court held that most of Myers' statements simply reflected the dissatisfaction of an employee with her transfer.

One of the items involved in the questionnaire circulated by the assistant district attorney in *Connick* concerned pressure to work in political campaigns. Applying the *Pickering* test, this item was held to involve a matter of public concern. Nevertheless, given the close working relationships in the D.A.'s office, greater deference to the public employer's judgment was necessary. Relevant also to a determination of the validity of government disciplinary action is the time, manner and place of the expressive activity. The questionnaire, for example, was prepared, distributed and completed during working hours. Finally, the context in which the dispute arose was deemed significant. The questionnaire was in response to a dispute over transfer policy. The *Connick* Court concluded: "The limited First Amendment interest involved here does not require that [the public employer] tolerate action which he reasonably believed would disrupt the office, undermine his authority, and destroy close working relationships. Myers' discharge, therefore, did not offend the First Amendment."

Significant attention in Justice Brennan's dissent was directed to the Court's conclusion that Myers' questionnaire did not generally involve a matter of public concern. The Court's conclusion to the contrary was simply a matter of fiat: "Based on its narrow conception of which matters are of public concern, the Court implicitly determines that information concerning employee morale at an important government office will not inform public debate. To the contrary, the First Amendment protects the dissemination of such information so that the people, not the courts, may evaluate its usefulness." For the dissenters, the majority's decision in *Connick* could only deter public employees from making critical comments concerning the operation of government which is at the heart of the First Amendment. In short, *Connick* presented a major obstacle to whistle-blowers.

The two part inquiry of *Pickering* and *Connick* was applied in *Rankin v. McPherson*, 483 U.S. 378 (1987). Upon hearing of an attempt on the life of President Reagan, Ardith McPherson, a clerical employee in a Texas county constable's office, said to a fellow employee, "If they go for him again, I hope they get him." Subsequently, Constable Rankin discharged McPherson. McPherson brought suit contending that her discharge violated the First Amendment. The Supreme Court, per Justice Marshall, upheld her claim 5–4.

First, McPherson's speech could be fairly characterized as satisfying the *Connick* inquiry—the statement *was* a matter of public concern. The statement was made in the context of a conversation discussing the Reagan administration's policies. The statement was not a punishable threat on the President. The controversial and inappropriate character of the statement was irrelevant on the basic *Connick* issue. In dissent, Justice Scalia, joined by Chief Justice Rehnquist and Justices White and O'Connor, argued for a much narrower conception of speech on matters of public concern. The dissent would limit protection to speech involving self-governance. Philosophical discourse on presidential policies would be protected; Ardith Rankin's death wish would not.

Having found that McPherson's speech involved a matter of public concern, Justice Marshall, for the Court, applied the *Pickering* balancing test. The state failed to show that McPherson's statement interfered with the effective functioning of the public employer's enterprise. Since the statement was not made to the public, the constable's office ran no risk of being discredited in the public eye. Most important for the Court was the purely clerical character of McPherson's job. Her position had no impact on the law enforcement activities of the constable's office: "Given the function of the agency, McPhersons's position in the office, and the nature of her statement, we are not persuaded that Rankin's interest in discharging her outweighed her rights under the First Amendment."

For the dissent, Scalia declared that this balancing analysis was wrong-headed. The issue was not whether Rankin's interest in discharging McPherson outweighed her First Amendment rights. Instead, the issue was "whether his interest in preventing the expression of such statements in his agency outweighed her First Amendment interests in making the statement." By deemphasizing—indeed, ignoring—the sanction imposed by the state, Scalia chose a terrain where the First Amendment interest is much harder to defend. For Scalia, the Constable's interest in maintaining an *esprit de corps* and a public image consistent with the law enforcement responsibilities of his office outweighed the minimal First Amendment interest embodied in McPherson's death wish.

The Court was sharply divided in *Rankin v. McPherson* and the Court's composition has since changed. Further, in *Waters v. Churchill*, 511 U.S. 661 (1994), a plurality held, per Justice O'Connor, that, even if the employee speech would be a matter of public concern, an employer could discharge an employee based on the facts as he reasonably believed them to be after investigation, even if it later turns out that he was mistaken.

But in *United States v. National Treasury Employees Union*, 513 U.S. 454 (1995), the Court 6–3 adopted a strong pro-employee position in holding unconstitutional a provision of the Ethics in Government Act prohibiting numerous federal employees from accepting an honorarium "for an appearance, speech or article (including a series of appearances, speeches, or articles if the subject is directly related to the individual's official duties or the payment is made because of the individual's status with the Government.)" The law was challenged by a class of federal employees below Grade GS–16. *Pickering*, rather than *Connick*, was deemed controlling since the law applied to "citizen" comments on matters of public concern rather than "employee" comment on workplace matters. Justice Stevens, for the Court, stressed that the speech controlled by the policy was generally addressed to a public audience, was made outside the workplace and involved content largely unrelated to the government employment. While covered employees could still speak, the denial of compensation was a significant burden on expression.

Government sought to justify the ban as needed to prevent misuse of power or the appearance of misuse of power. But it cited no evidence of misconduct related to honoraria by lower level federal employees below GS–16. There was no reasonable basis, said Justice Stevens, for extending the law to "an immense class of workers with negligible power to confer favors...." Nor could administrative convenience justify the complete ban on individual speeches and articles. Congress had required a nexus to government employment for a *series* of speeches and articles; such unrelated expression was exempted from the ban. Justice Stevens noted: "Absent such a nexus, no corrupt bargain or even appearance of impropriety appears likely." If the government could administer the exemption for unrelated speech in a series, it could enforce the nexus for individual expressive activity. The "speculative benefits" of a blanket ban on honoraria were insufficient to justify the "crudely crafted" burden on employee speech. Over the objections of the dissent and Justice O'Connor concurring, the Court held that invalidation of the law as to the class of plaintiffs was the appropriate remedy, leaving to the Congress the decision whether a law with a nexus requirement should be enacted.

Chief Justice Rehnquist, joined by Justices Scalia and Thomas, dissenting, argued that the law was only a limited burden on employee rights. Employees could still speak or write without penalty; the honoraria ban was content-neutral. The government interests, on balance, he claimed, justified this limited burden.

In a *per curiam* opinion, the Court ruled that the First Amendment does not protect a police officer who was terminated because he engaged in and sold explicit sexual videos of himself. *City of San Diego v. Roe*, 543 U.S. 77 (2004). The police officer contended that the employment termination violated his free speech rights. Although Roe's activities did not take place in the workplace and did not relate to his job, Roe used his uniform and his website indicated he was in law enforcement. The result was a "debased parody of an officer performing indecent acts in the course of his employment." Such activity reflected adversely on the professionalism of the police force and its officers. *Treasury Employees* was not applicable but *Pickering* and *Connick* were. Since the police officer was not speaking on a matter of public concern, the *Pickering* balancing test did not apply. The subject matter of the video was a matter of private concern and, under *Connick*, it was not protected by the First Amendment.

In *Garcetti v. Ceballos*, 547 U.S. 410 (2006), a newly constituted Court introduced a *per se* rule into its already confused jurisprudence on government employee speech. Justice Kennedy wrote for a 5–4 majority stating: "We hold that when public employees make statements pursuant to their official duties, the employees are not speaking as citizens for First Amendment purposes, and the Constitution does not insulate their communication from employer discipline.''

Richard Ceballos, a deputy district attorney, wrote a memorandum to his supervisors, arguing that an affidavit used by an attorney in his office to obtain a search warrant contained inaccuracies. He recommended dismissal of the prosecution, but his supervisors decided to continue. Ceballos told defense counsel of his views and he was subpoenaed to testify. Ceballos testified but the trial court rejected the challenge to the warrant. Subsequently Ceballos brought an action claiming that he had been subjected to retaliatory action because of his constitutionally protected speech.

The Court held that Ceballos was speaking as an employee and not as a citizen when he wrote his memorandum. Therefore, he was not engaged in speech protected by the First Amendment. It was not critical that he spoke in his office rather than publicly. Nor was it dispositive that the subject of his speech concerned his employment. The controlling factor was that his expressions were made pursuant to his duties as a calendar deputy advising his supervisors about how to proceed in a pending case. To hold that such speech is protected would "commit state and federal courts to a new, permanent, and intrusive role, mandating judicial oversight of communication between and among government employees and their supervisors in the course of official business. The displacement of managerial discretion by judicial supervisors finds no support in our precedents."

Since the present case involved no issue on the scope of employment, the Court said that it had no occasion "to articulate a comprehensive framework for defining the scope of an employee's duties." But it rejected the argument that a government employer could control employee speech by broadly defining the scope of employment. Further, it noted that its holding did not necessarily apply to public employees' scholarship or teaching. Finally, the Court expressed it's belief that adequate protection for public employees existed in whistle-blower laws, labor codes, rules of conduct and other constitutional safeguards.

Justice Stevens, dissenting, urged that the First Amendment "sometimes, not never," protects speech made pursuant to employee's duties. Stevens denied "that there is a categorical difference between speaking as a citizen and speaking in the course of one's employment."

*Garcetti* continues the movement away from applying *Pickering* balancing to public employee speech. Even though the issue of official misconduct is clearly of public significance, the employee speech was not protected. It can be expected that *Garcetti* will spawn a new wave of litigation as efforts are made to define the scope of official duty and to probe the limits of the Court's new categorical rule. Further, the student should remember that the *Pickering* balancing inquiry itself involves a less demanding form of judicial review of content-based regulation than would be applied to political speech undertaken by ordinary citizens who are not public employees.

In *Tennessee Secondary School Athletic Association v. Brentwood Academy*, 127 S.Ct. 2489 (2007), the Court considered whether a rule of the TSSAA prohibiting high school coaches from using "undue influence" in recruiting middle school athletes violates the First Amendment. Earlier the Court had held that enforcement of the Association's rules against member schools constituted state action. A unanimous Court, per Justice Stevens, now held that enforcement of the rule against Brentwood Academy based on a pre-enrollment letter sent by its football coach to eighth-grade boys inviting them to attend spring practice sessions did not violate the First Amendment. Assuming, without deciding, that the coach was speaking as a citizen about a matter of public concern, the Court, relying on *Garcetti v. Ceballos*, held that TSSAA could "impose only those conditions on such speech that are necessary to managing an efficient and effective state-sponsored high school athletic league." Justice Stevens said that such necessity was obviously present in the case. "We need no empirical data to credit TSSAA's common sense conclusion that hard-sell tactics directed at middle school students could lead to exploitation, distort competition between high school teams, and foster an environment in which athletics are prized more highly than academics."

Brentwood had voluntarily decided to join TSSAA and to abide by its antirecruiting rule. Just as the government's interest in running an effective workplace can sometimes outweigh employee free speech rights, the athletic league's interest in enforcing it's rules sometimes justifies curtialing the speech of its voluntary participants. See *Pickering*.

## 2.   POLITICAL ACTIVITY

Distaste for the spoils system traces back to the post-Civil War period and ultimately to the reform of the federal civil service and the enactment of the Hatch Act in 1940. In *United Public Workers v. Mitchell*, 330 U.S. 75 (1947), the Court upheld a provision of the Hatch Act prohibiting federal employees in the executive department from taking "any active part in political management or in political campaigns." In *Mitchell*, the Court deferred to the Congress and the president who bear responsibility for assuring efficient public service: "If, in their judgement, efficiency may be best obtained by prohibiting active participation by classified employees in politics as party officers or workers, we see no constitutional objection." There was no restraint upon public employees voting or engaging in non-partisan civic affairs. The prohibition of the Hatch Act was directed to partisan political activities.

The holding of *Mitchell* was reaffirmed in *United States Civil Service Comm'n v. National Ass'n of Letter Carriers*, 413 U.S. 548 (1973). The issue presented in *Letter Carriers* was whether the prohibition in the Hatch Act which precludes federal employees from taking an "active part in political management or in political campaigns" violated the First Amendment. The Supreme Court, per Justice White, answered "No" to this question. Invoking *Pickering*, the Court in *Letter Carriers* balanced the interests of the government employee against the interests of the government employer. The interests in favor of the prohibition were many. Government employees should not administer government according to the "will of a political party." Further, not only the reality but the appearance to the public that government employees were not political partisans was important. The vast army of government employees should not be seen as fodder for the construction of a "powerful, invincible, and perhaps, corrupt political machine." Finally, it was also important that government employees be insulated "from pressure to vote in a certain way or to perform political chores in order to curry favor with their superiors rather than to act out their own belief."

Justice White explained the necessity for judicial deference to Congress and the president: "[P]artisan political activities by federal employees must be limited if the Government is to operate effectively and fairly, elections are to play their proper part in representative government, and employees themselves are to be sufficiently free from improper influences." The government employees argued that the language of the prohibition in question was unconstitutionally vague and fatally overbroad. The Court disagreed. The regulations promulgated by the Civil Service Commission were sufficiently clear and were not substantially overbroad.

Justice Douglas in dissent did not agree that the overbreadth and vagueness claims were cured. Indeed, he thought they had a chilling effect on the exercise of political rights by government employees. Moreover, for Douglas it was important to stress that government did not own the entire life of a government employee: "[I]t is no concern of Government what an employee does in his spare time, whether religion, recreation, social work, or politics is his hobby—unless what he does impairs efficiency or other facets of the merits of his job."

## 3. POLITICAL PATRONAGE

Believers in political patronage might argue, "To the victors belong the spoils." But Justice Brennan responded during his tenure on the Court: "To the victor belong only those spoils which may be constitutionally obtained." *Rutan v. Republican Party of Illinois*, 497 U.S. 62 (1990). Justice Brennan might have added that those spoils that may be constitutionally awarded by the victorious political party have been substantially diminished as a result of Supreme Court opinions.

In *Elrod v. Burns*, 427 U.S. 347 (1976), the Court held that the discharge of Republican non-civil service employees of Cook County, who occupied non-confidential, non-policymaking positions, for the sole reason of their political affiliation violated the First and Fourteenth Amendments. The decision was in some respects a bombshell. Patronage had been considered a perquisite of the winning political party and a key ingredient for the maintenance of the two party system. Moreover, historically, it had always been an accepted practice. Justice Brennan, in a plurality opinion, joined by Justices White and Marshall, emphasized the heavy cost that patronage exacted from the exercise of freedom of belief and association. As he argued later in *Rutan*, "conditioning employment on political activity pressures employees to pledge political allegiance to a party with which they prefer not to associate, to work for the election of political candidates they do not support, and to contribute money to be used to further policies with which they do not agree." Such coercion of political belief and association, the *Elrod* plurality concluded, merited examination by strict scrutiny.

The *Elrod* plurality considered three possible justifications for discharge of non-civil service government employees on political grounds. One was the need to assure efficiency in government. Second was the need to assure the political loyalty of employees so that the victors' policies would be implemented. Third was the need to preserve the democratic process and maintain the integrity of the political party system.

The *Elrod* plurality rejected the first or efficiency argument, as indeed, the Court has in subsequent cases. The Court questioned "that the mere differ-

ence of political persuasion motivates poor performance." Even if it were assumed that such a relationship existed there would be less drastic means
available for insuring effective job performance
such as discharge for good cause. The second interest—the need for loyal employees to implement new
policies—was rejected as well: "Limiting patronage
dismissals to policymaking positions is sufficient to
achieve this governmental end. Non-policymaking
individuals usually have only limited responsibility
and are therefore not in a position to thwart the
goals of the in-party." The third and final interest—preserving the democratic process and the integrity of party politics—was also considered an insufficient justification for dismissal. The Court was
unpersuaded that the elimination of patronage
would bring about the demise of party politics.
Even though patronage has been reduced as the
merit system spread through the federal, state and
local civil service, political parties and indeed the
two party system have survived. In sum, none of
the interests offered to support the political dismissals in *Elrod* satisfied the demanding standard
of review that was applied by the plurality to evaluate the infringements on the freedoms of association and belief of the government employees.

In *Branti v. Finkel*, 445 U.S. 507 (1980), the
Court held that the discharge of a Rockland County,
New York assistant public defender who was satis-
factorily performing his job solely because of his
political beliefs was unconstitutional. The county
defended by distinguishing *Elrod* and insisting that

an assistant public defender was a higher-echelon policymaking position. With respect to such positions, the local government contended that political party affiliation was a proper basis for dismissal. Indeed, it was a requirement if the electoral will was to have any meaning. The whole idea of political victory was that policy-making positions would be occupied by members of the victorious political party. Justice Stevens rejected this rationale since "party affiliation is not necessarily relevant to every policymaking or confidential position." Justice Stevens then reformulated an exception left open in *Elrod* as to when political affiliation could be used as a basis for discharge: "[T]he ultimate inquiry is not whether the label 'policymaker' or 'confidential' fits a particular position; rather, the question is whether the hiring authority can demonstrate that a party affiliation is an appropriate requirement for the effective performance of the public office involved." Applying this standard, the Court concluded that the job of assistant public defender did not depend on partisan political considerations.

In *Rutan v. Republican Party*, 497 U.S. 62 (1990), yet another First Amendment challenge to patronage practices was successful. The Republican governor of Illinois promulgated an order establishing an employment freeze on all state governmental units under his control. No employees could be hired, promoted, transferred, etc., without the governor's express approval. Personnel decisions, the employees charged, were being made by the governor's office on the basis of factors such as whether the employee had voted in Republican primaries, given financial contributions to the Republican Party or been supported by Republican Party officials. In sum, in *Rutan* state employees challenged the governor's order on the ground that state employment was being unconstitutionally used to establish a patronage system to benefit the Republican Party. The Supreme Court agreed. *Rutan* extended the principles of *Elrod* and *Branti* to promotion, transfer, recall and hiring decisions. Patronage, which had received major body blows in *Elrod* and *Branti* as far as dismissals were concerned, now received virtually the *coup de grace*.

The attempt of the political defendants in *Rutan* to distinguish the prior cases failed since all these employment decisions constituted a serious privation of protected political rights: "The First Amendment prevents the government, except in the most compelling circumstances, from wielding its power to interfere with its employees' freedom to believe and associate, or to not believe and not associate." Justice Brennan simply reiterated the principles of his *Elrod* plurality opinion on the insufficiency of the government interests used to justify patronage-based employment practices.

Justice Scalia wrote a scathing dissent. Joined by Rehnquist and Kennedy, Scalia contended that *Elrod* and *Branti* should be overruled: "Given [the] unbroken tradition [of patronage] regarding the application of an ambiguous constitutional text, there was [n]o basis for holding that patronage-based dismissals violated the First Amendment." For Justice Scalia, the traditional acceptance of patronage from the earliest days of the Republic until *Elrod* established the constitutionality of the practice.

Further, now joined also by Justice O'Connor, Scalia argued that if *Elrod* and *Branti* were not to be overruled at least their principles should not be extended to reach the personnel decisions before the Court in *Rutan*. Scalia objected to the use of strict scrutiny in reviewing patronage practices. Government was not engaged in regulating a practice or profession but rather was operating as a proprietor or employer. In such restricted environments, the Court has regularly employed a less demanding balancing of the competing interests. For the dissenters, patronage "is a political arrangement that may sometimes be a reasonable choice and should therefore be left to the judgment of the people's elected representatives." Patronage decisions can have systemic effects that promote political stability by energizing political parties and preventing excessive political fragmentation. Patronage can also facilitate "the social and political integration of previously powerless groups."

In spite of the strong protests in the dissents to these patronage cases, and the close division of the Court in *Rutan*, in *O'Hare Truck Service, Inc. v. City of Northlake*, 518 U.S. 712 (1996), the Court, 7–2, extended First Amendment protection for "the exercise of rights of political association or the expression of political allegiance" to independent contractors. A tow truck company had been removed from the rotation list of companies approved to provide towing services when its owner refused support and campaign contributions to the mayor. Justice Kennedy, for the Court, reasoned that drawing a distinction between government employees and contractors would invite government manipulation by attaching different labels to particular jobs. There had been no convincing showing that patronage demands are less coercive for contractors than government employees. The absolute right to enforce a patronage scheme to maintain control, claimed by the government, had not been shown "to be a necessary part of a legitimate political system in all instances."

Justice Scalia, joined by Justice Thomas, dissenting, castigated the majority for not only adhering to *Elrod*, *Branti* and *Rutan*, but for extending those decisions to cover government contracting. For the dissent, political favoritism is a traditional and inevitable feature of government. Even if the First Amendment were applied to cabin patronage for government employees, it was unnecessary to extend protection to contractors, which are usually corporations, usually facing only a loss of part of its business.

## C.  SUBSIDIZED SPEECH: SPONSORSHIP OR CENSORSHIP?

Millions of federal, state and local dollars flow annually to private beneficiaries. Grantees of government largesse are often heavily dependent on the continued flow of these subsidies so that termination of the funds, or the threat of termination, can be expected to have a significant impact on the behavior of the grant recipients. Professor Robert Post, *Subsidized Speech*, 106 Yale L.J. 151, 152 (1996), has said that subsidized speech challenges two fundamental assumptions of ordinary First Amendment doctrine. First, "[i]t renders uncertain the status of speakers." Are they independent participants in the formation of public opinion or instrumentalities of government? Second, "it renders uncertain the status of government action, forcing us to determine whether subsidies should be characterized as government regulations imposed on persons or instead as a form of government participation in the marketplace of ideas."

In defending regulation of subsidized speech, government contends that it is a participant and not a regulator. Further, government argues that the stringent standard of review should apply only when the government acts as censor or regulator of private expression. When government acts as a voluntary participant in the marketplace, either by means of subsidies or tax exemptions, government action should be upheld unless for some reason it fails to meet the deferential rationality standard of review. Another way to reach the same result in this area is to view grants, subsidies and exemptions as nonpublic fora which government can regulate as long as it acts rationally and in a viewpoint neutral fashion. A speaker is free to speak in another forum but not in the nonpublic forum that government has created. On the other hand, government cannot achieve indirectly what it is prohibited from doing directly. The use of government monies can be a covert means of achieving regulatory objectives when regulation would be barred by the First Amendment. In short, government can buy up rights. The threat of termination of funds if grantees do not agree to abide by certain governmentally imposed conditions can operate to coerce and penalize the exercise of protected freedoms.

Two lines of analysis have tended to dominate the area of government sponsored speech. The first approach, greatly influenced by Justice Brennan, may be called the First Amendment approach. While government may not have an obligation to provide funds, it must operate in a content-neutral and non-discriminatory manner. It cannot condition the receipt of benefits on the surrender of constitutional rights without compelling justification.

The doctrine of unconstitutional conditions is, perhaps, more accurately called the doctrine of no-unconstitutional-conditions. The doctrine has been justly described as reflecting "the triumph of the view that government may not do indirectly what it may not do directly over the view that the greater power to deny a benefit includes the lesser power to impose conditions on its receipt." Sullivan, *Unconstitutional Conditions*, 102 Harv. L. Rev. 1415 (1989). Professor Sullivan contends that if government would have to meet a strict scrutiny standard of review to prevent individuals from undertaking a certain form of advocacy, it should not be permitted to circumvent searching judicial scrutiny by phrasing its law so that it can make silence the price of receiving government largesse.

The second line of analysis, greatly influenced by Chief Justice Rehnquist, might be called the government-as-participant approach. In this view, government is simply creating various environments through granting subsidies or providing tax exemptions. When government acts in this fashion, it is merely making allocational decisions concerning its resources. Furthermore, in this view such allocational decisions are in the public interest. For, after all, was it not the electorate who voted in the government which is making these policy choices? Individuals are free to accept or reject the government grants and any conditions attached to them. Since government is not obliged to make grants in the first place, this theory contends government may choose the conditions upon which it wishes to make grants. If the student thinks this is the right-privilege dichotomy reborn, the student would probably be right. Under the government-as-participant theory, it follows that government can fund some views and not others. Otherwise the majority in a democracy would be voiceless. If government funds democracy, it is not obliged to fund Fascism or Communism. If government uses public monies to discourage cigarette smoking—and it does—the cigarette industry has no constitutional basis for protest that its pro-smoking message is not funded by government.

An example of the government–as–participant approach is *Regan v. Taxation With Representation (TWR)*, 461 U.S. 540 (1983). *Regan* involved a challenge to provisions of the Internal Revenue Code which granted tax benefits to veterans' groups engaged in lobbying. But similar benefits were denied to the lobbying activities of other charitable organizations. Was this distinction in the tax code favoring expressive activity of some groups but not of others an unconstitutional discrimination among speakers by government? The Court, per Justice Rehnquist, held that the distinction was constitutional: "It is not irrational for Congress to decide that tax exempt charities such as TWR should not further benefit at the expense of taxpayers at large by obtaining a further subsidy for lobbying. It is also not irrational for Congress to decide that, even though it will not subsidize substantial lobbying by charities generally, it will subsidize lobbying by veterans' organizations."

Why was rationality the appropriate standard of review in *Regan*? No fundamental right of free expression or of equal protection was burdened or penalized. Charities could still lobby. Government was not obliged to provide tax advantages to lobbying activities. The fact that government had chosen to provide tax advantages to some groups did not penalize those not so favored. The situation would be different, the Court noted, if Congress had discriminated invidiously in its subsidies in order to suppress ideas deemed dangerous. But the veterans groups received a tax advantage without regard to the content of their lobbying.

An example of the First Amendment approach to government sponsored speech is found in *FCC v. League of Women Voters*, 468 U.S. 364 (1984). The Supreme Court considered a First Amendment challenge to a provision of the Public Broadcasting Act of 1967 that prohibited noncommercial educational broadcasting stations receiving funds from the Corporation for Public Broadcasting from engaging in editorializing. The Supreme Court, per Justice Brennan, declared that the statutory prohibition against editorializing was a content-based violation of the First Amendment. Because broadcasting was involved, the Court did not apply strict scrutiny, but asked if the restriction was narrowly tailored to further a substantial governmental interest. Justice Brennan concluded: "The specific interests sought to be advanced by [the ban on editorializing] are either not sufficiently substantial or are not served in a sufficiently limited manner to justify the substantial abridgement of important journalist freedoms which the First Amendment jealously protects."

Unlike Rehnquist in *Regan*, Brennan in *League of Women Voters* did not apply rationality review to the challenged statute. Why did the statute in *League of Women Voters* merit a more stringent form of review? Justice Brennan distinguished *Regan* by emphasizing the penalty imposed on public broadcasters in *League of Women Voters*. Even though the station received only 1% of its overall income from government grants, it was absolutely barred from all editorializing, even with private funds. There was no way in which the grantee could continue to engage in editorializing since there was no way by which the station could match up its editorial programming with its revenue sources.

Predictably, Justice Rehnquist dissented. For him, *Regan* was not distinguishable and its principles should be followed: "Congress has rationally concluded that the bulk of taxpayers [would] prefer not to see the management of public stations engage in editorializing. [Because] Congress' decision to enact [the ban] is a rational exercise of its spending powers and strictly neutral, I would hold that nothing in the First Amendment makes it unconstitutional." Rehnquist's approach was simple. If Congress had a reason for funding some speech and not other speech, the courts should defer at least as long as there was no breach of viewpoint neutrality. But viewpoint discrimination was not a problem in *League of Women Voters*; all editorializing—regardless of content—was banned.

The Court continued to adopt the First Amendment heightened scrutiny approach in *Arkansas Writers' Project, Inc. v. Ragland*, 481 U.S. 221 (1987). The principle that government cannot discriminate based on content or viewpoint in conferring benefits such as subsidies or grants was reaffirmed. A state sales tax on general interest magazines which exempted religious, professional, trade, and sports journals was held unconstitutional: "Our cases clearly establish that a discriminatory tax on the press burdens rights protected by the First Amendment." Justice Marshall, for the Court, applying strict scrutiny, concluded that, while an interest in encouraging fledgling publications might be compelling, the tax scheme was not narrowly tailored. The state's distinction for granting or withholding its tax subsidy was based entirely on the content of the publication. This distinction ran counter to the First Amendment principle that makes content-based regulation presumptively unconstitutional. The fact that the content-based regulation involved tax subsidies did not render this principle inapplicable.

Justice Scalia, joined by Chief Justice Rehnquist, in dissent, argued that the strict scrutiny standard of review was inappropriate since no fundamental right was burdened. The tax exemption was not limited to publications adopting a particular viewpoint nor was there any evidence that the tax scheme "was meant to inhibit, or have the effect of inhibiting, [a particular] publication." There was no significant coercive effect.

Despite use of the First Amendment approach in *League of Women Voters* and *Arkansas Writers'*, the Court returned to the government-as-participant approach in the much publicized and controversial abortion-counselling case, *Rust v. Sullivan*, 500 U.S. 173 (1991). In *Maher v. Roe*, 432 U.S. 464 (1977), the Court had held that government is under no obligation to fund abortions for indigent women even though government provided funds for normal childbirth for such women. In *Harris v.*

*McRae*, 448 U.S. 297 (1980), the Court held further that legislation prohibiting the use of federal funds for medically necessary abortions was valid. This was so even though other medically necessary benefits were made available to indigent women. The fact that indigent women had a constitutional right to choose not to go forward with a pregnancy did not mean that government was obliged to fund that right. The ban on federal funding for abortions was rationally related to the legitimate government interest—indeed, preference—for potential life.

In *Rust*, federal family planning grantees, and doctors supervising the grants, challenged the facial validity of federal regulations that prohibited federally funded projects from engaging in counselling concerning referrals for activities advocating abortion as a means of family planning. The regulations also required that the projects be physically and financially separate from any abortion activities. Those challenging the regulations argued that the regulations discriminated on the basis of viewpoint because they prohibited discussion about abortion while compelling grantees to provide information promoting pregnancy.

The Court, per Chief Justice Rehnquist, rejected this contention because government has not practiced viewpoint discrimination. Rather, the government had made a presumptively valid decision on how to allocate its limited resources. There was no penalty involved simply because government chose not to fund the exercise of a fundamental right. The restrictions on abortion counseling were designed to assure that all funds were used to further the program objectives. The regulations were germane to assuring that only family planning other than abortion was provided. This was significant because if the restriction were not germane it would be evidence of viewpoint-bias by government.

*Arkansas Writers' Project* was distinguished: "[We] have here not the case of a general law singling out a disfavored group on the basis of speech content, but a case of the Government refusing to fund activities, including speech, which are specifically excluded from the scope of the project funded." This analysis exemplified the government-as-participant approach. Government in this view was interested in funding non-abortion type family planning. Government's decision not to fund anything in connection with abortion was permissible since it was simply outside the scope of what government had decided to fund. It had nothing to do with the deprivation of First Amendment rights since government was not restraining the doctors from performing abortions or even advocating abortion. Government was just refusing to fund those activities in its federally funded projects.

The challengers also contended that the restrictions on abortion-related speech violated the unconstitutional conditions doctrine. The regulations conditioned a benefit, the receipt of family planning funding, on the surrender of a constitutional right—abortion advocacy and counseling. Not so, said Chief Justice Rehnquist: "[T]he government is not denying a benefit to anyone, but is instead simply insisting that public funds be spent for the purposes for which they were authorized." The regulations did not force grantees to give up abortion related speech but simply prevented federal funds from being used to support the speech. Rehnquist stressed that the condition was not imposed on the recipient of the grant but instead on the project itself. Thus federal monies were prevented from being used for an activity outside the scope of the project, *i.e.*, non-abortion family planning.

*League of Women Voters* was distinguishable from the facts in *Rust* since the condition in that case was directed at the recipient and barred all editorializing activities by the grantee even though obtained from private funds. Indeed, *Rust* was like *Regan* since the beneficiary there remained free to engage in lobbying activities. In *Rust* grantees and doctors could still engage in abortion advocacy. However, the federally funded projects in which they worked could not provide such advocacy.

Chief Justice Rehnquist provided a caveat to the principle that government could control speech in government sponsored environments. In areas that have been traditionally open to public expression or have been dedicated to speech activity, government cannot unduly restrict speech even through the use of a subsidy. In short, in these public forums, First Amendment principles remain dominant. By way of illustration, a university, Chief Justice Rehnquist explained, is "a traditional sphere of free expression so fundamental to the functioning of our society that the Government's ability to control speech within that sphere by means of conditions attached to the expenditure of Government funds is restricted". Outside of these public forums government sponsored environments are nonpublic forums where government can regulate subject only to the requirement that it act rationally and with viewpoint-neutrality. This, indeed, was the approach the Court used in *Hazelwood* with respect to the student newspaper.

Justice Blackmun, joined Justices by Marshall and Stevens, dissenting, argued that the government's challenged regulations constituted viewpoint discrimination and the imposition of unconstitutional conditions. For the dissent, the government was plainly engaged in purposeful ideological viewpoint discrimination. The dissent also argued that the regulations imposed an unconstitutional condition on project staff members. The limitation on employee free speech was the consequence of accepting employment at a federally funded project. Chief Justice Rehnquist's response that the employee need not accept employment at such a project was inadequate. Justice Blackmun said in rejoinder: "But it has never been sufficient to justify an otherwise unconstitutional condition upon public employment that the employee may escape the condition by relinquishing his or her job."

Nor was Justice Blackmun impressed that the employee remained free to advocate abortion outside the federally-funded workplace: "Under the majority's reasoning, the First Amendment could be read to tolerate *any* governmental restriction upon an employee's speech so long as that restriction is limited to the funded workplace. This is a dangerous proposition, and one the Court has rightly rejected in the past." In public employment cases, the Court had used a balancing test when government undertook to regulate employee speech. In *Rust*, the Court does not even balance the free speech interests of those employed by the grantee against the government interest in assuring that federal funds are spent only for purposes within the scope of the program.

In the above cases, the Court had indicated that, in funding the speech of others, government could not "aim at the suppression of dangerous ideas." This prohibition again viewpoint discrimination found expression in *Rosenberger v. Rector and Visitors of the University of Virginia*, 515 U.S. 819 (1995). Although the University of Virginia used mandatory student fees to pay printing costs of student publications, guidelines prevented funding any "religious activity," defined to include any activity that "primarily promotes or manifests a particular belief in or about a deity or an ultimate reality." The Court held 5–4 that denial of funding to a Christian student newspaper was forbidden viewpoint discrimination.

Justice Kennedy, for the Court, characterized the subsidy program as a limited or designated public forum. While content discrimination consistent with the purposes of the limited forum might be permissible, he said viewpoint discrimination is presumptively impermissible. The university regulation does not simply prohibit discussion of religion as a subject matter "but selects for disfavored treatment those journalistic efforts with religious editorial viewpoints." *Rust* was distinguished as involving government speech using private grantees. "When the government disburses public funds to private entities to convey a governmental message, it may take legitimate or appropriate steps to ensure that its message is neither garbled nor distorted by the grantee." But Justice Kennedy reasoned that it did not follow that "viewpoint-based restrictions are proper when the University does not itself speak or subsidize transmittal of a message it favors but instead expends funds to encourage a diversity of views from private speakers." While government as *speaker* (i.e., as a participant in the marketplace) may engage in viewpoint discrimination, government as *patron* of the private speech of others may not silence targeted viewpoints. Applying strict scrutiny, the Court held that Establishment Clause concerns did not justify the viewpoint discrimination since funding religious speakers would not violate the Clause's mandate of government neutrality. Justice Souter, writing for the four dissenting justices, denied that the University had engaged in viewpoint discrimination. The guidelines were not limited to Christian advocacy, but extended to the entire subject matter of religious apologetics.

The prohibition against viewpoint discrimination in public subsidies programs when government is acting as patron rather than as speaker was again involved in *National Endowment for the Arts v.*

*Finley*, 524 U.S. 569 (1998). But in this instance the Court rejected 8–1 a facial challenge to a federal law requiring NEA, in making grants, to ensure that "artistic excellence and merit are the criteria by which applications are judged, taking into consideration general standards of decency and respect for the diverse beliefs of the American public."

In rejecting the claim that the "indecency and respect" provision was substantially overbroad viewpoint discrimination, Justice O'Connor reasoned that the law imposed no categorical ban on funding indecency. Rather, the law was only hortatory and set forth "considerations" to be used in determining artistic merit. Indecent art could still be funded. The risk of censorship was not significant given the lack of consensus on what is indecent. Unlike the university funding in *Rosenberger* which was available to student groups generally, NEA funding does not indiscriminately "encourage a diversity of views from private speakers." Arts funding necessarily involves content-based aesthetic judgments and choice among numerous applicants for limited funds. Vagueness challenges to the law were dismissed, since harms caused by imprecision are of less concern in subsidy programs. While rejecting the facial challenge, Justice O'Connor did not rule out the possibility of an as-applied challenge to particular grants as the product of invidious viewpoint discrimination. Government may not "ai[m] at the suppression of ideas". Relief would be appropriate if subsidies are "manipulated" to have a "coercive" effect. If government funding were calculated to drive "certain ideas or viewpoints from the marketplace," the First Amendment would be violated.

Justices Scalia and Thomas, concurring only in the judgment, would uphold the "indecency and respect" provisions even though they concluded they were mandatory and viewpoint-based. While indecency and respect need not be determinative under the challenged law, they must be considered in funding and this is discrimination based on viewpoint. But such discrimination is not an "abridgment of speech"—"Those who seek to create indecent and disrespectful art are as unconstrained now as they were before the enactment of the statute." For Justice Scalia, it was "preposterous to equate the denial of taxpayer subsidy with measures 'aimed at the suppression of dangerous ideas' " He rejected any "coercion" from denial of government funding as both insufficient in general and inapplicable where, as here, other sources of funding are available. As in other contexts, for Justice Scalia, incidental, indirect burdens on First Amendment rights simply don't implicate the constitutional right. Further *Rosenberger* was distinguished as involving a limited public forum, different from a context such as the NEA where it is the business of government to favor and disfavor points of view on various subjects. Finally, Justice Scalia argued that government can discriminate in its subsidy programs even if it is not speaking but funding the speech of others.

Justice Souter was the only dissenter. Like Justices Scalia and Thomas, he concluded that the funding limitation was viewpoint discrimination. Like the Court, he believed viewpoint discrimination in funding private speech where government is patron rather than speaker violates the First Amendment. "So long as Congress chooses to subsidize expressive endeavors at large, it has no business requiring the NEA to turn down funding applications of artists and exhibitors who [defy] our tastes, our beliefs, or our values."

In *Legal Services Corp. v. Velazquez*, 531 U.S. 533 (2001), the Court, per Justice Kennedy, held, 5–4, that a federal law prohibiting legal representation funded by recipients of Legal Services Corporation moneys if the representation involves an effort to amend or otherwise challenge existing welfare law violated the First Amendment. The Court rejected the effort of the United States and LSC to characterize the expression as government speech as in *Rust v. Sullivan*. Rather, as in *Rosenberger*, "the LSC program was designed to facilitate private speech, not to promote a governmental message." The LSC-funded attorney speaks on behalf of the private client in a welfare claim against the government. Government was seeking "to use an existing medium of expression and to control it, in a class of cases, in ways which distort its usual functioning." The government cannot use a subsidy to effect a "serious and fundamental restriction on advocacy of attorneys and the functioning of the judiciary." The restriction would force LSC-funded attorneys to cease representation if a question of the validity of a welfare statute arose and would threaten a severe impairment of the judicial function by insulating welfare laws from judicial inquiry. Justice Scalia, for the dissent, argued that "[t]he LSC subsidy neither prevents anyone from speaking nor coerces anyone to change speech, and is indistinguishable in all relevant respects from the subsidy upheld in *Rust v. Sullivan*." Government simply declined to subsidize a certain class of litigation, which does not infringe the right to bring such litigation.

What is the teaching of these cases which are marked by such uncertainty and ambiguity and such sharp conflict in approach? First, a distinction should be drawn between government-as-regulator and government-as-participant. Second, in the context of government-as-regulator, the Court is more responsive to First Amendment claims. These claims embrace the unconstitutional conditions doctrine, the concern that government not penalize or coerce the exercise of First Amendment rights, and an exacting demand for precision and clarity. Third, if the government acts as a participant-speaker in the marketplace, communicating a particular message directly or through others as in *Rust*, it need not fund competing ideas or viewpoints. Even though critics might argue that government is in a position to skew marketplace debate, the cases indicate government can engage in viewpoint discrimination. Fourth, if the government acts as a patron, funding the speech of others, it may not selectively fund only certain views or ideas. Professor Frederick Schauer, *Principles, Institutions and the First Amendment*, 112 Harv. L. Rev. 84, 96 (1998), says: "When government is operating in its subsidizing mode and not in its speaking mode, the existing caselaw supports the view that viewpoint-based distinctions are impermissible, even though content-based distinctions that are not viewpoint-based [i.e., subject matter discrimination] are both inevitable and constitutional." It should be noted, however, as *Finley* suggests, the determination of whether the selection process constitutes viewpoint discrimination may well be controversial. Perhaps, the more that the context requires government to make subjective judgments among competing applicants, the less likely is it that the program will be held to be viewpoint-based.

## D. SUMMARY

In a sense the distinctions discussed in this chapter reflect a dichotomy. Government has two roles—one private and one public. When government acts in its private role as proprietor, employer, educator, or participant, the First Amendment restraints on its activities are often subordinated. When government acts in its public role as regulator, the First Amendment applies with all its force. But the truth is that this is not really a dichotomy. The public and private roles of government are more of a continuum. There is no sharply marked line of demarcation between these roles.

The more government action controls the behavior of citizens, the more government should be viewed as having a regulatory role. But government never ceases to be government and is always subject to the First Amendment. For the courts to abdicate judicial review in these government sponsored environments simply invites government to pursue impermissible regulatory objectives through indirect means.

There is a final matter which requires comment. Many cases present fact patterns where determining whether the government is acting in its private role or its public one will hardly be clear. The student should be aware that in such cases those justices who think that deference to the legislature is the appropriate role in the main for the non-elected judiciary will be more inclined to view the matter as private. Those justices who see the role of the Court as the defender of individual liberties will, on the other hand, be more likely to characterize the facts in a way which emphasizes the government's public role. In the end, doctrine is in the hands of people and, therefore, outcomes are uncertain.

# CHAPTER XIII

# FREEDOM OF THE PRESS

## A. THE PRESS CLAUSE—
## "OR OF THE PRESS"

The First Amendment contains both a free speech clause and a free press clause. In the main, the Supreme Court has not distinguished between the two clauses. Instead, freedom of speech and freedom of the press have been treated as inter-changeable terms. In 1974, Justice Potter Stewart delivered a speech at Yale Law School offering a different vision of the press and a discrete meaning for the press clause: "The primary purpose of the constitutional guarantee of a free press was [to] create a fourth institution outside the Government as an additional check on the three rival branches." Stewart, *"Or of the Press,"* 26 Hastings L.J. 631 (1975). For Justice Stewart, the press is a fourth branch of government providing a separate element in the checks and balances system. The press is the only private business that is given explicit constitutional protection. The First Amendment is not simply a guarantee of freedom of expression for citizens with the press as their agent. The press clause is a structural provision of the Constitution extending to the press a special protection as an institution. The press

clause in this perspective extends different and perhaps greater protection than does the free speech
clause.

In a concurring opinion in *First National Bank of
Boston v. Bellotti*, 435 U.S. 765 (1978), Chief Justice
Burger considered the merits of the Stewart thesis.
He rejected the proposition that the two clauses
should have separate and distinct meanings for two
reasons. First, the press was singled out in the text
of the First Amendment only because it had been
the special object of official wrath and censorship in
the Anglo–American past. Second, who or what is
the press? See *Developments in the Law—The Law
of Media*, 120 Harv. L. Rev. 990, 993 (2007) ["[T]he
Internet has expanded access to traditional media
sources and facilitated a proliferation of new information sources, many of which take novel approaches and raise difficult questions about what
even counts as media."] Does the press encompass
only the institutional media? What of the lonely
pamphleteer or the underground newspaper? Moreover, there is a related difficulty—who decides who
is the press? If it is government, the government
ends up being a licensor. Basically, Chief Justice
Burger concludes that the two clauses state a textual distinction without any real difference between
them. As he put it, "Because the First Amendment
was meant to guarantee freedom to express and
communicate ideas, I can see no difference between
the right of those who seek to disseminate ideas by
way of a newspaper and those who give lectures or

speeches and seek to enlarge the audience by publication and wide dissemination."

The view that the speech and press clauses are essentially interchangeable has generally prevailed. The Court has indicated on a number of occasions that the press does not enjoy privileges and immunities beyond those available to the ordinary citizen. The fact that a law burdens the ability of the press to publish and gather news does not necessarily mean that it is unconstitutional. Justice White, an ardent exponent of the view that the journalist is just another citizen, stated: "Generally applicable laws do not offend the First Amendment simply because their enforcement against the press has incidental effects on its ability to gather and report the news. [E]nforcement of such general laws against the press is not subject to stricter scrutiny than would be applied to enforcement against other persons or organizations." *Cohen v. Cowles Media Co.*, 501 U.S. 663 (1991).

Nonetheless, Stewart's view regarding the unique role of the media in our constitutional system does find continued expression in the case law. The press are the eyes and the ears of the citizen-critic of government. The public cannot be present whenever government acts. It lacks the competence and the capability to actively scrutinize the government. But mass media in a mass age are peculiarly equipped to take up the role of the citizen-critic. In a post-Watergate view of the press, popularized by Professor Vincent Blasi, the press serves as a kind of countervailing power to government. One behemoth, mass media, is a worthy opponent for the other, big government. The First Amendment value of the press in this perspective is its checking value against official abuse: "The checking value is premised upon a different vision—one in which the government is structured in such a way that built-in counter-forces [including the press] make it possible for citizens in most, but not all, periods to have the luxury to concern themselves with private pursuits." Blasi, *The Checking Value in First Amendment Theory*, 1977 Am. B. Found. Res. J. 521.

The student should note that the courts draw a distinction between restrictions on media publication and restraints on newsgathering. While the former are treated as direct restraints on the First Amendment subject to traditional stringent judicial scrutiny, restraints on newsgathering are viewed as incidental burdens on freedom of expression and subject to less demanding standards of review. It has been correctly observed that "a right to gather the news, *of some dimension*, must exist," but "[t]he dimensions of the newsgathering right are, nevertheless, decidedly uncertain." Dienes, Levine & Lind, *Newsgathering and the Law* (3d ed. 2005). While constitutional privilege is available to the press in the context of defamation, disclosure privacy and mental distress torts, there are no First Amendment press defenses or privileges available against tort or contract liability for newsgathering activity. See, *e.g.*, *Cohen v. Cowles Media, Inc.*, 501 U.S. 663 (1991) (Ch. XIII B, 2). Similarly, in *Wilson v. Layne*, 526 U.S. 603 (1999), the Court held that media ride-alongs, where journalists accompany the police when the latter execute an arrest warrant, violate the Fourth Amendment. While acknowledging the important role played by the press in informing the public about the operations of government, the Court stressed that the Fourth Amendment also protects important rights. Further, the need for accurate reporting "bears no direct relation to the Constitutional justification for the police intrusion into a home in order to execute a felony arrest warrant."

## B.  JOURNALIST'S PRIVILEGE

### 1.  PROTECTING CONFIDENTIALITY

In the late 1960s, the ferment generated by Vietnam, the domestic civil rights movement, and the advent of the counter-culture gave rise to a new role for journalists. The press now saw itself as the adversary of government. The age of investigative journalism had begun, dramatically illustrated by the Watergate scandal in the mid–1970s. Government sought to identify the confidential sources and secure unpublished materials which had been garnered by journalists during the newsgathering process. But journalists often refuse to make the disclosures sought by government, basing their refusal on a number of legal grounds.

Journalists contend that the common law extends a privilege to them analogous to the attorney-client privilege or the doctor-patient privilege. However, the courts have been reluctant to recognize a new common law privilege to protect the confidences obtained by journalists from their sources. The press also relies on so-called state shield laws which authorize journalists to resist government efforts to compel disclosure. Sometimes journalists are successful in relying on these shield laws. But often they are not. Since shield laws are in derogation of the common law, they are frequently construed strictly. Further, only about 35 of the states have such laws and they differ significantly. Finally, there is no federal shield law (although proposals are pending) and the state laws vary markedly in the scope of protection they afford. Therefore, often the solution for the journalist who refuses to be conscripted to do the state's investigative work has been to seek judicial recognition of a qualified First Amendment-based journalist's privilege.

At the beginning of the 1970's, three cases came to the Supreme Court which together presented the following questions: Do reporters called by a grand jury investigating criminal matters have to give testimony like other citizens? Or does the special role of the press entitle reporters to at least a qualified constitutional privilege? The Supreme Court, per Justice White, in *Branzburg v. Hayes*, 408 U.S. 665 (1972) answered: There was no First Amendment-based privilege—at least with respect to the duty of reporters to appear and respond to the demand for evidence by a grand jury.

At the outset of the *Branzburg* opinion, Justice White did accept that newsgathering is protected by the First Amendment. The guarantee of freedom of expression cannot be limited only to protection of publishing but must extend to the processes which make publishing possible: "[W]ithout some protection for seeking out the news, freedom of the press could be eviscerated." This recognition by Justice White that freedom of the press encompassed not only the freedom to publish but the freedom to acquire information was extremely important. In the past, the focus on the meaning of the freedom of the press had been almost entirely on the freedom to publish and the problem of censorship. But denial of a journalist's privilege, reasoned Justice White, imposes only an incidental burden on freedom of expression. Reporters still could seek out the news from legal sources and report their findings. There was no restraint on their freedom to publish. Incidental burdens on the press resulting from generally applicable laws did not in themselves violate the First Amendment.

Justice White offered four different grounds for his rejection of a First Amendment-based journalist's privilege. The first one we have already noted. The press, no less than others, is bound by generally applicable laws. In the past it had been held that the press, like other businesses, was bound by the Fair Labor Standards Act and the antitrust laws. Similarly, its representatives—reporters—must give evidence when called upon to do so by a grand jury in the same manner required of other citizens. "Citizens generally are not constitutionally immune from grand jury subpoenas; and neither the First

Amendment nor any other constitutional provision protects the average citizen from disclosing to a grand jury information that he has received in confidence." The press enjoys no greater privileges and immunities than does the ordinary citizen even though the newsgathering process is thereby incidentally burdened.

The second ground for refusing to establish a privilege was related to the media's assertion that refusal to do so would seriously limit the flow of news to the public. Indeed, it was argued that forced disclosure of information given by sources in confidence might dry up the flow of news altogether. Justice White's response to these contentions was dismissive—they lacked empirical support. "[W]e remain unclear how often and to what extent informers are actually deterred from furnishing information when newsmen are forced to testify before a grand jury." Even though there were statistical surveys offered to the Court as well as depositions by journalists, the Court remained unconvinced that sources would not disclose information absent a constitutional privilege to protect the journalist. Basically, White believed sources and reporters needed each other too much for anything to destroy their symbiotic relationship. The student should note, however, that even if it could be proven that denial of a privilege would dry up news sources, this would not have persuaded Justice White to create a privilege. The public interest in pursuing and prosecuting crime which exists here and now prevails over "the public interest in possi-

ble future news about crime from undisclosed, un-
verified sources."

This latter point led Justice White to the third
basis for rejecting the claim for privilege in *Branzburg*, which related to the historic importance of
the grand jury in American law enforcement. There
was a strong and unbroken historical tradition that
gave grand juries the right to subpoena witnesses:
"[T]he public has a right to every man's evidence."
When this tradition was measured against a novel
claim for the creation of a new testimonial privilege,
the appropriate response was that claims of the
grand jury should prevail. Justice White was not
prepared to create "a virtually impenetrable constitutional shield" designed "to protect a private system of informers operated by the press to report on
criminal conduct." The government has a compelling or paramount interest in securing the safety of
persons and the property of citizens. The grand jury
plays a vital part in furthering this interest in
effective law enforcement which requires that reporters give testimony to the grand jury on the
same basis as other citizens.

The fourth and final ground which Justice White
relied upon was definitional and administrative.
Even if the courts were willing to fashion such a
privilege, who should be embraced within it? The
short of the matter was that Justice White, to say
the least, thought it would be unseemly—and perhaps unconstitutional—for courts, an arm of the
state, to define who would qualify to benefit from a
privilege it had just created. Further, problems of

defining who was a journalist aside, administering such a privilege would surely create new dilemmas. Courts would be required to determine whether the proper predicate had been laid for the invocation of the privilege. Is the subpoenaed information relevant and necessary to effective law enforcement? Are alternative sources available to the government? In short, Justice White concluded: "The administration of a constitutional newsman's privilege would present practical and conceptual difficulties of a high order."

Justice White did leave the door to First Amendment relief slightly open. Since newsgathering does enjoy First Amendment protection, a grand jury investigation not instituted and conducted in good faith might well violate the First Amendment guarantee. The grand jury did not have *carte blanche* to trample on the rights of the press: "Official harassment of the press undertaken not for purposes of law enforcement but to disrupt a reporter's relationship with his news sources would have no justification. [We] do not expect courts will forget that grand juries must operate within the limits of the First Amendment as well as the Fifth."

A majority of the justices joined the Court's opinion in *Branzburg* rejecting even a qualified First Amendment-based journalist's privilege. Further, the Supreme Court has yet to acknowledge that such a First Amendment-based journalist's privilege exists. Nevertheless, at the present time, most federal circuits and most state jurisdictions, recognize a qualified First Amendment-based journalist's privilege in at least some contexts. What is more remarkable is that *Branzburg* is regularly cited as authority for the proposition that such a First Amendment-based privilege exists. This unusual situation has resulted from a laconic but extremely important concurrence written by Justice Powell in *Branzburg*. Justice Powell concurred in Justice White's opinion for the Court but gave aid and succor to the dissent's acceptance of a First Amendment-based journalist's privilege.

In dissent, Justice Stewart, joined by Justices Brennan and Marshall, accepted Justice White's premise that newsgathering is a protected First Amendment activity. "News must not be unnecessarily cut off at its sources, for without freedom to acquire information the right to publish would be impermissibly compromised." But unlike Justice White, Stewart argued in dissent that this First Amendment right to acquire information is significantly burdened if government can subpoena the testimony and other materials gathered by the journalist. Journalists need informants for newsgathering; confidentiality is the price the reporter must pay if informants are to continue to talk. An unbridled subpoena power in government, Stewart argued, will deter sources from confiding in journalists and will lead the press to engage in self-censorship about what will be published. While concrete evidence and common sense support the existence of such a deterrence, Stewart noted that the Court had never required such empirical evidence. Indeed, in *New York Times Co. v. Sullivan*,

376 U.S. 254 (1964), the chilling effect of state libel law on vigorous and robust public debate to the detriment of First Amendment interests had simply been assumed. No empirical proof had been required.

Given the significant burden on First Amendment rights that result from government subpoenas of reporters, government must satisfy a demanding standard of justification before the courts will require journalists to testify or produce documents. If the government provided such justification, the journalist's motion to quash the subpoena would be denied. Otherwise, the First Amendment would protect the journalist's refusal to make disclosure. Justice Stewart's test had three components—relevancy, no alternative sources, and a compelling interest by government in obtaining the information. 1) *Relevancy*—government must show that there is probable cause to believe that the journalist possesses information which "is clearly relevant to a specific probable violation of law." 2) *No Alternative Sources*—government must demonstrate that the relevant and material information sought from the reporter cannot be obtained by alternative means that would be less destructive of First Amendment rights. 3) *Compelling Interest by Government*—government must show an interest that is compelling and which overrides the First Amendment interest of the reporter in non-disclosure.

Justice Douglas also dissented. It is hard to decide whether he had more contempt for the majority's position or for Stewart's. Douglas thought that the

First Amendment extended journalists an absolute privilege. "A newsman has an absolute right not to appear before a grand jury [and] a journalist who voluntarily appears before that body may invoke his First Amendment privilege to specific questions." All the balancing that needed to be done had been done by those who wrote the First Amendment in the first place. Douglas excoriated the position of Alexander Bickel, counsel for the New York Times, who had urged a qualified privilege, as adopting a "timid, watered-down, emasculated" version of the First Amendment.

But it was Justice Powell's crucial concurring opinion that led to the unexpected aftermath of *Branzburg*. While Powell joined the opinion of the Court, he concurred to emphasize the "limited nature of the Court's holding." In the process, Powell arguably went significantly further than Justice White. White had said the First Amendment would protect against harassment of reporters. But Powell seemed to say that a privilege for journalists based on the First Amendment could be invoked even in cases where there was no harassment. Powell urged a case-by-case balancing of the interests: "The asserted claim to privilege should be judged on its facts by the striking of a proper balance between freedom of the press and the obligation of all citizens to give relevant testimony with respect to criminal conduct. The balance of these vital constitutional and societal interests on a case-by-case basis accords with the tried and traditional way of adjudicating such questions."

In the years that followed *Branzburg*, Justice Stewart's dissenting opinion proved more influential than Justice White's majority opinion. Why was this so? For one thing, in the light of Powell's concurrence, there were only four votes for the really negative view of a First Amendment–based journalist's privilege taken in Justice White's opinion. Why was Stewart's approach to privilege preferred by the lower courts to those taken by Powell or Douglas? The answer appears to be that Douglas's position was deemed too disregarding of the interests that sometimes favor—indeed demand (as in the case of a criminal defendant seeking vital evidence to establish innocence)—disclosure. The Powell position, with its plea for ad hoc balancing, lacked any predictability; it did not furnish sufficient guidance for the judicial inquiry. The Stewart dissent's three part test, on the other hand, provided lower courts with tools with which to work. The Stewart test was also more predictably supportive of the interests of journalism and the First Amendment.

But the student should not assume that acceptance of a constitutional privilege necessarily means that reporters will be able to resist compelled disclosure. In this area, the interests favoring disclosure sometimes triumph. Especially in the grand jury context, where the *Branzburg* opinion is most relevant, journalists are generally required to disclose sources and produce materials or suffer sanctions. Journalists also frequently lose when a criminal defendant invokes constitutional rights granted by the Fifth and Sixth Amendments, binding on the states through the Fourteenth Amendment, in an effort to secure evidence to establish her innocence. It is in the civil context that the claim of journalist's privilege most often prevails. Even in this context, however, this is not always the case. For example, if the reporter refuses to divulge sources or materials necessary to a plaintiff's defamation claim against her media employer, the price of nondisclosure may be defeat for the media defendant on the libel claim. Efforts to invoke constitutional privilege for non-confidential material often fail.

Despite the fact that the lower courts have, on the whole, responded sympathetically to the claim for a qualified First Amendment-based journalists privilege, it must nonetheless be acknowledged that the Supreme Court has in terms of its formal opinions loftily ignored these developments. The Court has remained obdurate in its distaste for the creation of any new First Amendment-based privileges. In *Herbert v. Lando*, 441 U.S. 153 (1979), the Court, per Justice White, refused to create a First Amendment-based editorial privilege that would shield the editorial process from the rigors of intrusive and chilling discovery. More recently, in *University of Pennsylvania v. EEOC*, 493 U.S. 951 (1989), the Court, in a Title VII case, in the course of rejecting an academic freedom privilege for peer review material, per Justice Blackmun, stated: "We were unwilling [in *Branzburg*], as we are today, 'to embark the judiciary on a long and difficult journey to an uncertain destination.' " There is no reason to believe that the present Supreme Court would be more sympathetic to the First Amendment claims of journalists seeking to resist forced disclosure of confidential information than it has been in the past. And a significant new development is an increasing objection in lower federal courts to recognition of a qualified journalist privilege. See *In re Grand Jury Subpoena, Judith Miller*, 397 F.3d 964 (3d Cir. 2005).

## 2.   BURNING THE SOURCE

A man bites dog case in the journalist's privilege area was *Cohen v. Cowles Media, Inc.*, 501 U.S. 663 (1991). Reporters for two newspapers in the Twin Cities had promised confidentiality to a source in return for his promise to reveal information about the prior arrest record of a Democratic candidate for state office. The source, Dan Cohen, was a Republican Party operative. The editors of the paper thought his partisan identity was more newsworthy than the trivial arrests he had disclosed. Accordingly, they burned the source and published the stories including Cohen's identity. Cohen was fired and sued the newspaper defendants under state law for, among other things, breach of contract. The Minnesota Supreme Court said that the only claim Cohen might have would be based on promissory estoppel, but the First Amendment precluded recognition of that claim.

In the *Cohen* case, the Supreme Court, 5–4, per Justice White, returned to the *Branzburg* theme that the press, like other citizens, was bound by generally applicable law—including the law of promissory estoppel. The press argued that prior law had established that there can be no liability for publishing truthful information lawfully obtained absent compelling justification. *See Smith v. Daily Mail Publishing Co.*, 443 U.S. 97 (1979) [a state does not have power, consistent with the First Amendment, to punish truthful publication by a newspaper of the name of a juvenile offender that it had lawfully acquired]; *The Florida Star v. B.J.F.*, 491 U.S. 524 (1989) [award of damages against a newspaper for publishing the name of a rape victim when the name had been lawfully obtained violated the First Amendment]. White responded that information has not been lawfully acquired if, as in *Cohen*, the press has violated state law in obtaining it. Of course, it could be argued that when the promise was made to secure the information, there was no breach of state law. The breach of the promise occurred only after the information was in the possession of the newspapers.

Justice Souter argued in a strong dissent that the burden imposed on the media in this instance was not an incidental burden as had been the case in *Branzburg*. Instead, the media was being held liable based on the content of the publication. Further, the publication involved core political speech concerning public officials involved in an election. There was no subordinating state interest which would justify such content-based regulation. Justice Souter asserted, relying on *Miami Herald Pub. Co. v. Tornillo*, 418 U.S. 241 (1974), that it was for the publisher, not the government, to decide what should be published. Justice White responded that paying damages to Cohen for the breach of the promise to him was simply a cost of doing business. The newspaper had gotten what it bargained for— the information that Cohen had provided. It was the parties, not the government, that defined their legal obligation in this instance.

Justice White also rejected the proposition that the press should be given any special immunity from the law of promissory estoppel. But Justice Blackmun said that this misconceived the First Amendment issue presented. It was the nature of the speech that merited First Amendment protection and not the media identity of the speaker. Even a non-media defendant would be allowed to claim a First Amendment defense. Not a word in *Cohen* acknowledged the growth of a qualified First Amendment-based privilege in the lower courts. White refused to see the case in First Amendment terms either from the point of view of the plaintiff or the media defendants. In other words, the plaintiff's contention that refusal to protect the source would be detrimental to the First Amendment because it would dry up sources was ignored. The media defendant's argument that there was a First Amendment interest in publication of truthful information was also not involved because the newspapers had in fact published what they wished.

The *Cohen* case was a difficult one for the press. In *Branzburg*, they had argued that the First Amendment should be interpreted to provide a privilege to protect journalists possessing confidential information. In *Cohen*, they had to argue the unat-

tractive position that the First Amendment permitted the press to ignore that which in *Branzburg* the
press had asked the Court to protect. The media
responded that an award of damages for breach of
promissory estoppel based on the content of a publication was more akin to *New York Times Co. v.
Sullivan*, 376 U.S. 254 (1964) than to *Branzburg*.
Rejection of a First Amendment-based journalist's
privilege may be only an *incidental* burden on the
First Amendment right attached to newsgathering.
The award of contract damages based on the content of the publication especially involving core
political speech is a *direct* burden on the First
Amendment right to publish. For the layman, however, *Cohen* stands for the proposition that the First
Amendment does not allow the press both to promise confidentiality and then to repudiate it.

It remains an open question whether the recurring theme sounded by Justice White in these
cases—the press is bound by generally applicable
law—will be extended from the contract context of
*Cohen* to tort contexts such as the field of negligent
publication. Negligent publication involves publication of material which the publisher arguably
should reasonably have foreseen would produce
physical, emotional, or economic injury to another.
Should the First Amendment be a bar to recovery
on such a theory? The state awards damages in
negligence based on its generally applicable law.
The argument, therefore, would appear to be that if
contract law applies to the press like anyone else, so
does negligence law. On the other hand, contract

law involves duties to others which are voluntarily assumed. Tort law involves duties or obligations which are imposed by the state regardless of the agreement of the parties.

In some other tort areas involving liability for publication, the "generally applicable [tort] law" rationale has not been accepted. In *New York Times Co. v. Sullivan*, 376 U.S. 254 (1964), the state was prevented from applying its generally applicable libel law when to have done so would have been equivalent to allowing state censorship of the press. Even in the post-*New York Times* libel case, *Gertz v. Robert Welch, Inc.*, 418 U.S. 323 (1974), which allowed states to use a negligence standard in private plaintiff libel cases, the Court refused to allow a state to adopt a rule of strict liability or to apply its general rules regarding damages. Moreover, in *Hustler Magazine v. Falwell*, 485 U.S. 46 (1988), the Court held that at least in a public figure case, a state could not apply its general laws regarding intentional infliction of emotional distress to the media absent actual malice. A problem with applying the generally applicable law argument of *Cohen* and *Branzburg* to the tort context is that it provides the means for an end run around *New York Times Co. v. Sullivan*. See also *Time, Inc. v. Hill*, 385 U.S. 374 (1967) [actual malice test of *New York Times* applied to privacy claim]. Most of the lower courts that have dealt with the issue of negligent publication have held that negligence alone cannot support a cause of action against a media defendant. Most courts have required a showing of incitement to illegal conduct for such content-based regulation. But the issue remains an open one.

## C.  GAGGING THE PRESS

### 1.  INTRODUCTION

Restraints on media publication are at the historical core of the First Amendment. As early as the seventeenth century, John Milton condemned prior restraints against publication imposed by the King's licensors. Milton was inveighing against administrative censorship of criticism of government. But restraints against publication also arise in other contexts. What if the restraints imposed by a court against media publication are issued to protect the fair trial rights of the accused? The Fifth and Sixth Amendments to the Constitution guarantee to the criminal defendant that guilt or innocence will be determined by an impartial judge or jury in a fair proceeding. Publicity before and during a trial often threaten these guarantees. The problem becomes most intense and visible in sensational cases such as the murder trial of O. J. Simpson. Even the leaking of incriminating evidence prior to trial can threaten the impartiality of the jury. A major concern is that information, and sensational information at that, will so saturate a community that it will be impossible to select a disinterested jury. Of course, if a defendant has been convicted by a biased jury, he can seek to have the conviction reversed on appeal. But another response would be to prevent the prejudice, or the potential for prejudice, in the first place.

In *Sheppard v. Maxwell*, 384 U.S. 333 (1966), the Court cataloged a number of options available to a trial judge to prevent publicity from interfering with the fair administration of justice. Justice Clark, for the Court, suggested that the trial judge could participate actively in the *voir dire* in order to guard against selection of jurors who might have become excessively influenced by pre-trial media publicity about a case to the point of pre-judging it. Further, trial judges could take steps to insulate witnesses and could sequester juries. Another step available to the trial judge confronted with prejudicial media publicity is use of a continuance until community passions abate. In addition, if the community is clearly permeated by hostility to the accused as a result of media publicity, the trial venue can be changed.

But can a trial judge determined to prevent undue publicity about a criminal proceeding go further and take action against the media itself? For example, could the judge use her contempt powers to punish publications that interfere, in the court's opinion, with the administration of justice? The contempt sanction is regularly used against the media in the United Kingdom. But in *Bridges v. California*, 314 U.S. 252 (1941) and its progeny, the Court has held that only a clear and present danger to the fair administration of justice would justify contempt sanctions against the media for out-of-court publications. In *Bridges,* the Court substituted the more rigorous clear and present danger standard for the earlier, more lenient reasonable tendency test, thereby making the task of prosecutors seeking contempt citations against the media more difficult. Indeed, the Supreme Court has never upheld such a contempt citation for out-of-court publications, regardless of how critical or unfair the publication.

## 2.   THE *NEBRASKA PRESS* CASE

There are other possible alternatives to using contempt citations against media personnel. Instead of punishing the media for publications prejudicial to the fair administration of justice, a trial court may issue orders prohibiting the press from publishing anything about a particular case either before or after the trial. These orders—called restrictive orders by courts and "gag" orders by the media—were the subject of a major Supreme Court case, *Nebraska Press Association v. Stuart*, 427 U.S. 539 (1976). In 1975, Erwin Simmons walked into his neighbor's yard in a small Nebraska farming community of 800 people and murdered a ten year old girl and members of her family. Simmons was arrested and incarcerated pending trial. A state trial judge issued an order that, after modification by the state supreme court, prohibited the media from publishing any confessions or admissions against interest made by the defendant. The media appealed the order and the case ultimately went to the United States Supreme Court which overturned the "gag" order.

Chief Justice Burger, speaking for a unanimous Court in *Nebraska Press*, held that there was a heavy presumption in the Anglo–American law against the validity of prior restraints—a category in which he placed judicial "gag" orders. While Chief Justice Burger declared that gag orders were presumptively invalid, the Court did not hold that these gag orders were *per se* invalid. Gag orders would be valid if there was a clear and present danger to the administration of justice. Clear and present danger, however, was defined by the Chief Justice, not in the terms of the famous Holmes–Brandeis formulation, but in the more lenient terms of *Dennis v. United States*, 341 U.S. 494 (1951).

If, as an abstract matter, the verbal formulation used in *Nebraska Press* appeared to edge towards allowing gag orders in some circumstances, close analysis of the opinion indicates otherwise. Chief Justice Burger declared that a gag order on the press publication could issue only after a trial judge conducted a hearing and determined that certain demanding conditions were satisfied. First, the court had to determine that there *would* be intense and pervasive pre-trial publicity concerning the case which *might* impair the defendant's right to a fair trial. Chief Justice Burger acknowledged that such findings were necessarily speculative since they dealt with factors unknown and unknowable. Second, the trial judge must determine whether alternative remedies short of a prior restraint would protect the defendant's rights. The student should note the speculative character of this determination which depends on calculating the effect of options that in fact were not chosen. Finally, the trial judge must determine that the requested order will be effective in controlling the feared prejudicial publicity. On the basis of the application of these demanding standards, Chief Justice Burger concluded that the gag order issued by the trial court was impermissible in the factual context of the *Nebraska Press* case.

Looked at overall, the *Nebraska Press* case has to be regarded as a virtual death knell for gag orders by courts against media publication. It is true that the Court left the door slightly open; gag orders were not declared *per se* invalid prior restraints. But the First Amendment standards set down in *Nebraska Press* are indeed demanding. Moreover, the use of the clear and present danger test in this context is itself indicative of the Court's negative attitude toward gag orders against the media. If any case presented a clear and present danger to the administration of justice, the barrage of national publicity targeted at a tiny farming hamlet in Nebraska where a brutal and sensational murder had occurred was such a case. Yet the Court held that the requirements of the clear and present danger test were not met. It becomes clear, therefore, that the reference to clear and present danger is not to be taken literally. The real test flows from the demanding standards the opinion sets forth and the Court's insistence that there is a heavy presumption against the validity of all prior restraints, including gag orders. It is not surprising that, in the post-*Nebraska Press* era, gag orders against the media are seldom issued and rarely upheld on appeal. Nevertheless, the principle that "gag" orders are not *per se* invalid remains true.

## D.   SILENCING THE BAR AND OTHER TRIAL PARTICIPANTS

The virtual invalidation of "gag" orders against media personnel announced in *Nebraska Press* has left trial judges searching for alternatives in order to resolve the conflict between free press and fair trial. One alternative is issuing silencing orders directed to lawyers and other courthouse personnel. These orders may arise in different contexts, such as standing rules developed for the governance of the bar. Another context is in the form of judicial "gag" orders issued during court proceedings precluding those subject to the order—lawyers, court clerks, witnesses and others—from talking to the press. Those silenced assert a variety of constitutional objections. Some raise their own First Amendment rights to criticize the law enforcement and the criminal justice system. Criminal defense lawyers often assert the rights of their clients to a full and meaningful defense including the ability to counter the charges of the prosecutor in the media. The media itself challenges these "gag" orders on lawyers and other trial participants as abridgments of the First Amendment right of journalists to gather news. The right of the media not to be gagged in what it chooses to publish is ultimately not worth much if others are prohibited from giving the media the information it needs to publish. See Dienes, *Trial Participants in the Newsgathering Process*, 34 U. Rich. L. Rev. 1107 (2001) (arguing "for strict scrutiny review of direct restraints on lawyer speech and of indirect restraints on newsgathering based on the personal and societal interests implicated.").

The courts have responded to these claims by lawyers and other trial participants in two major ways. In some instances, the courts have treated the "gag" order as a content-based restraint on speech and have invoked the clear and present danger doctrine. Trial participants contend that a "gag" order directed against them is still a prior restraint preventing speech and publication. If *Nebraska Press* mandates satisfying the clear and present danger doctrine before a "gag" order against the press can issue, then, under this view, silence orders directed to others should be subject to the same standard. On the other hand, it is argued that a less demanding standard is appropriate for restrictive orders on trial participants. For example, the court might employ some *ad hoc* balancing test such as a "reasonable likelihood" test or as a "substantial likelihood" test. Under the latter test, a silence order directed against trial participants or lawyers is valid if there is a "substantial likelihood" that permitting out of court statements will materially prejudice the fair administration of justice.

Proponents of these less demanding standards argue for a more classic and limited definition of prior restraint. In the case of silence orders against lawyers, for example, they contend that there is no restraint on publication of material already in the hands of the media. There is only an incidental burden on one of the means whereby the media acquires information; the press cannot use, in these limited circumstances, trial participants as a source for their stories. Proponents of lesser standards similarly argue that trial participants have a special relationship to the court imposing special obligations of trust and confidentiality. Lawyers, for instance, are officers of the court. These special relationships permit a larger scope for regulation of the extrajudicial statements of trial participants than would be permitted to courts with respect to publications by the press. On the other hand, lawyers argue that the result is a hierarchical First Amendment whereby journalists as a craft are given greater protection under the First Amendment than lawyers.

These competing arguments were joined in *Gentile v. State Bar of Nevada*, 501 U.S. 1030 (1991). Attorney Gentile held a press conference on behalf of his recently indicted client in which he sketched out his client's defense. He charged that his client was an innocent "scapegoat" who was being prosecuted instead of the real culprits—"crooked cops" in the police department. Following the acquittal of his client, the State Bar of Nevada filed a complaint against Gentile for violating Nevada Supreme Court rules prohibiting an attorney from making extrajudicial statements to the press that would have a "substantial likelihood of materially prejudicing" an adjudicative proceeding. The rule then listed a number of safe harbors for the attorney where statements could be made without fear of discipline "notwithstanding" the general rule against extrajudicial statements. One such safe harbor was a provision in the standing rules allowing a defense attorney to state without elaboration the nature of the defense upon which he would rely.

A majority of the Supreme Court in *Gentile* held, 5–4, that the "substantial likelihood" test employed in that case satisfied the First Amendment. The Court, per Chief Justice Rehnquist, held that the clear and present danger standard used for reviewing silence orders directed against the press need not be used when attorneys were the subject of such orders: "Lawyers representing clients in pending cases are key participants in the criminal justice system, and the State may demand some adherence to the precepts of that system in regulating their speech as well as their conduct. Because lawyers have special access to information through discovery and client communications, their extrajudicial statements pose a threat to the fairness of a pending proceeding since lawyers' statements are likely to be received as especially authoritative. We agree with the majority of the States that the 'substantial likelihood of material prejudice' standard constitutes a constitutionally permissible balance between the First Amendment rights of attorneys in pending cases and the state's interest in fair trials."

While one group of justices, led by Chief Justice Rehnquist, would have upheld the application of the

state bar standing rule against Gentile, Justice
O'Connor switched sides and joined another group
on the Court who found the rule with its safe
harbor exceptions violative of the void-for-vagueness doctrine. Justice Kennedy who wrote the opinion for the Court on the void-for-vagueness point
concluded that the standing rules failed to provide
sufficient guidance to lawyers like Gentile with respect to what comments were permissible. The up-
shot was that the judgement of the Supreme Court
of Nevada affirming sanctions against Gentile was
reversed.

The *Gentile* case is difficult to evaluate. It may be
that the "substantial likelihood" test approved in
that case will be no more significant for silence
orders directed against lawyers and other trial participants than the clear and present danger test has
been for "gag" orders against the media. The void-
for-vagueness ruling in *Gentile* certainly took the
sting out of the Court's willingness to accept a
diminished standard for silence orders directed
against lawyers. In short, abstract approval of the
"substantial likelihood" test cannot be taken too
literally; it may not silence as much extrajudicial
commentary by lawyers as at first blush might
appear. On the other hand, suppose a state has
standing rules prohibiting extrajudicial commentary
by court personnel including lawyers which is
framed solely in terms of "substantial likelihood"
with no safe harbors at all? Under the logic of
*Gentile*, such rules should presumably be sufficiently clear to avoid vagueness infirmities. Whether

such a rule would then be affirmed against First Amendment challenges remains to be seen. Technically, however, such a rule would appear to meet the standards set forth in *Gentile*. Finally, the relevance of *Gentile* for silence orders against nonlawyers remains to be seen.

## E.  ACCESS TO THE COURTROOM

Another method used by trial judges seeking to avoid prejudice and preserve the fair administration of justice is the use of closure orders. A closure order prevents public access, including the press, to a judicial proceeding or to documents filed in connection with that proceeding. Journalists confronted with such closure orders have argued for a First Amendment-based right of access. Relying on the First Amendment right to acquire information and gather news on behalf of the public, journalists assert a public interest in disseminating information about what transpires behind courtroom doors. Sometimes this is called by the inexact but nonetheless oft-used phrase, the public's right to know.

In the space of a decade, courts have increasingly recognized a First Amendment-based right of access. The right has been extended to an ever wider range of judicial proceedings, criminal and civil. The courts have declared that issues concerning such proceedings should be approached with a presumption of openness. This presumptive right of access has also been extended to a variety of documents and materials associated with judicial proceedings.

Critics of the movement toward greater access to the courtroom for press and public contend that there is no express constitutional right of access to government and judicial proceedings. More particularly, they resist the very notion that there is any constitutionally-based public right to know. Further, they question the scope of any such right. Must the courts remain open even for the testimony of a young girl who has been raped? Does the press have some special right of access to confidential materials required by the discovery process? Does this presumption of openness invariably trump claims of privacy and the interests of law enforcement in on-going investigations?

## 1.  TRIAL PROCEEDINGS

A case which squarely presented the question of whether there was a First Amendment right to open courtrooms was *Richmond Newspapers, Inc. v. Virginia*, 448 U.S. 555 (1980). The question arose whether the public and the press had a right to attend the criminal trial of Stevenson, who was being tried for murder. Before the fourth trial on the matter—there had been earlier mistrials—defense counsel, fearful of outside influences on witnesses, moved that the courtroom be closed and the prosecutor agreed. Relying on a Virginia statute giving him such authority, the trial judge, without a hearing on the matter, closed the proceeding to the press and public. Subsequently, the press moved unsuccessfully to vacate the closure order.

The Supreme Court held that the trial court had been in error in issuing the closure order. Chief Justice Burger, in a plurality opinion, stated: "[T]he right to attend criminal trials is implicit in the guarantees of the First Amendment; without the freedom to attend such trials, which people have exercised for centuries, important aspects of freedom of speech and 'of the press could be eviscerated.'" In arriving at this conclusion, Chief Justice Burger emphasized that historically criminal trials have been routinely open in the Anglo–American law. On the basis of this history, he reasoned that the First Amendment extended a right to attend criminal trials to the press and public. He added that openness was critical to the proper functioning of the trial since it would expose bias or partiality. Furthermore, public trials have significant community therapeutic value; they provide an outlet for community hostility and emotion. In addition, the public criminal trial serves a vital educative function. It enhances the citizen's understanding of the system in general and its workings in the particular case. In the nature of things the public may not always be in a position to pursue this right. The media, therefore, appropriately serve as the surrogate for the public.

Despite Chief Justice Burger's paean to openness, the right to attend a criminal trial is not absolute. There was to be sure a presumption of openness but, in unusual circumstances, closure was still possible: "Absent an overriding interest articulated in findings, the trial of a criminal case must be open to the public." In the *Richmond Newspapers* case, the trial judge had made no findings to support closure. Nor had the trial judge made any inquiry into alternatives that might have assured fairness to the accused without the need for closure.

Justice Brennan, joined by Justice Marshall, concurred in the judgment but saw no reason to inquire into an overriding interest that might justify closure in circumstances not presented by the facts before the Court. Moreover, they appeared to suggest that they would require an even more demanding standard for such closure than the one espoused by Chief Justice Burger. In determining the existence of a right of access to criminal trials, Justice Brennan focused on more than just history and tradition: "[T]he value of access must be measured in specifics. [W]hat is crucial in individual cases is whether access to a particular government process is important in terms of that very process." Public access, Brennan concluded, is essential if the public was to have confidence in the administration of justice.

Justice Brennan spoke for the Court in its next major public trial controversy after *Richmond Newspapers*. In *Globe Newspaper Co. v. Superior Court*, 457 U.S. 596 (1982), a Massachusetts trial judge excluded the press and public from the courtroom during the trial of a defendant charged with the rape of three young girls. The statute under which the trial judge acted required closure as an absolute matter. The Court held that the blanket exclusion authorized by the statute violated the

First Amendment and reversed the closure order. While *Richmond Newspapers* had established that public trials are presumptively open as a constitutional matter, the fragmented character of the Court in that case had left uncertain the appropriate standard of justification required for a closure order. Justice Brennan in *Globe Newspaper* resolved that issue: "Where the State attempts to deny the right of access in order to inhibit the disclosure of sensitive information, it must be shown that the denial is necessitated by a compelling governmental interest, and is narrowly tailored to serve that interest."

*Globe Newspaper* acknowledged that the state interest in the physical well-being of a minor is compelling. But that interest did not justify a mandatory closure rule. A statutory bar to access in all cases, when such closure might not be justified by the circumstances of the particular case, was not narrowly tailored. Nor was the absolute statutory bar justified by the state interest in encouraging minor victims of sex crimes to come forward and cooperate. Not only was there an absence of empirical support that the closure would in fact encourage such cooperation, there were numerous alternative sources of information whereby the press and public would be able to breach the privacy interest without violating the statute.

It was now Chief Justice Burger's turn to dissent. Joined by Justice Rehnquist, Chief Justice Burger returned once more to tradition and history as the guide for openness. There was a long history of

closing the courtroom in the case of sex crimes—
particularly those involving minors. Further, the
law had only a minimal effect on public access to
information since there was closure only during the
actual testimony of the child victim. Therefore, balancing the interests, Burger concluded that the
statutory rule "rationally serves the Common-
wealth's overriding interest in protecting the child."
In short, Burger's standard for justification, at least
in this factual context, was far less demanding than
that of Justice Brennan.

## 2.  PRETRIAL PROCEEDINGS

In the case of pretrial hearings generally, and
preliminary hearings in particular, the courts historically have been more sympathetic to requests
for closure than in reviewing motions to close a
trial. Courts have been fearful that a judge's ruling
that there is probable cause justifying prosecution
of the accused will be misunderstood by the press
and the public as a determination of guilt.

A pre-*Richmond Newspapers* pretrial proceeding
involving pretrial suppression of evidence was *Gannett v. DePasquale*, 443 U.S. 368 (1979), where the
Court, per Justice Stewart, rejected, 5–4, a claim
that the Sixth Amendment gave the press and public a right of access to a pretrial suppression hearing. The pretrial hearing in that case had been
closed by agreement of both the defense and the
prosecution. The *Gannett* Court noted that the
Sixth Amendment guarantee of a public trial was

for the benefit of the defendant, not the press or the public. See *Waller v. Georgia*, 467 U.S. 39 (1984) [closure of a pretrial evidentiary suppression hearing over the objection of the defendants was held to violate the Sixth Amendment guarantee of a public trial]. Not surprisingly, in the year following *Gannett* a great number of closure orders were issued in the United States. How much of *Gannett* survived the subsequent decision in *Richmond Newspapers*? This is a perplexing question. The *Gannett* Court tended to use the words pretrial and trial interchangeably. *Richmond Newspapers* clearly established a First Amendment presumption of openness for the criminal trial and *Gannett* did not rule on the First Amendment questions presented. Did *Richmond Newspapers* change the result *sub silentio* in a pretrial context like *Gannett*?

In *Press–Enterprise v. Riverside County Superior Court*, 464 U.S. 501 (1984) (*Press–Enterprise I*), the Court considered an effort by the press to gain access to the *voir dire* of a defendant charged with the rape and murder of a teenage girl. The public initially was admitted to the *voir dire* for three days. Then the trial judge, relying on the need for jury privacy, closed the *voir dire* for its remaining six weeks. After the jury was empaneled, the judge denied the efforts of *Press–Enterprise* to secure a transcript of the *voir dire*. *Press–Enterprise* sought review and contended that the *voir dire* should have been open to the public and the transcript should have been made available to them. A unanimous Supreme Court agreed that the presumption of openness attached to the *voir dire*. The selection of jurors is part of the trial process itself. Therefore, *Richmond Newspapers* was controlling. The historical evidence demonstrated that the process of selecting jurors had traditionally been open to the public. Closure had been permitted only where good cause could be shown at a hearing. Further, the basic fairness of the criminal trial was enhanced by openness as was the appearance of fairness on which public confidence depends.

*Press–Enterprise I* established a presumption of openness for the *voir dire* and set forth a new standard for reviewing closure orders in a pretrial context: "The presumption of openness may be overcome only by an overriding interest based on findings that closure is essential to preserve higher values and is narrowly tailored to serve that interest." In *Press–Enterprise I*, Chief Justice Burger, trailing echoes of *Nebraska Press*, pointed out that the trial court had failed to articulate findings with the requisite degree of specificity. The trial judge had failed to consider alternatives to closure and total suppression of the transcript. Under the circumstances, closure and suppression of the entire transcript had not been shown to be necessary to protect the anonymity of the potential jurors or the right of the defendants to a fair trial.

Since *Press–Enterprise I* had dealt with the *voir dire*—which may be considered to be part of the trial itself—it was not necessarily controlling on the question of closure for pretrial hearings generally. Nevertheless, in *Press–Enterprise v. Riverside*

*County Superior Court*, 478 U.S. 1 (1986) (*Press–Enterprise II*), the Court, per Chief Justice Burger, held, 7–2, that there is a First Amendment right of access to transcripts of a California preliminary hearing in a criminal proceeding. Robert Diaz, a nurse charged with murdering twelve patients, moved to exclude the public from the preliminary hearing. A California statute required that such proceedings be open unless closure was necessary to protect the defendant's right to a fair trial. The magistrate granted the unopposed closure motion and the 41–day preliminary hearing was closed. At the conclusion of the preliminary hearing, Press–Enterprise asked for the release of the transcript of the proceedings. The magistrate refused and sealed the record.

Chief Justice Burger, for the Court in *Press–Enterprise II*, again went through the two part inquiry. First, has the proceeding historically been open? Second, does public access contribute to the proper functioning of the proceeding in question? This two-pronged inquiry was undertaken to determine if there was a qualified First Amendment right of access for the public and press to the preliminary hearing. Chief Justice Burger placed special emphasis on the nature of the preliminary hearing under California law. First, he observed that there was a "tradition of accessibility to preliminary hearings of the type conducted in California." Second, California preliminary hearings were sufficiently like trials so that it could be fairly concluded that public access does in fact contribute to the proper functioning of the proceeding. The extensive scope of the California preliminary hearing often made it "the final and most important" stage in a criminal proceeding, especially given the absence of any jury at a preliminary hearing.

Having determined that a qualified First Amendment right of access attaches to the preliminary hearings as conducted under California statute, the Court invoked the standard set forth in *Press–Enterprise I*—proceedings cannot be closed "unless specific on the record findings are made demonstrating that 'closure is essential to preserve higher values and is narrowly tailored to serve that interest.' " Applying that standard to the right of the accused to a fair trial, the Chief Justice stated that the hearing could be closed only if there was a specific finding that "first, there is a substantial probability that the defendant's right to a fair trial will be prejudiced by publicity that closure would prevent and, second, reasonable alternatives to closure cannot adequately protect the defendant's fair trial rights."

Justice Stevens, joined by Justice Rehnquist, dissented. Historically, there was not a common law right of access to preliminary proceedings, so the Framers of the First Amendment could not have intended any constitutionally, mandated rule of presumptive openness. Further, the Court's reasoning in *Press–Enterprise II* for opening the preliminary hearing to the public would apply equally to traditionally secret grand juries. The grand jury, the dissenters pointed out, is also a critical step in the criminal proceeding, yet the grand jury is not open to public observation. In short, the Court's logic was inherently boundless: "By abjuring strict reliance on history and emphasizing the broad value of openness, the Court tacitly recognizes the importance of public access to government proceedings generally." Further, the dissent argued that the Court was tacitly overruling *Gannett*, which had allowed closure on a showing of reasonable probability of prejudice—a far less demanding standard than the probability standard employed by the Court.

### 3. SUMMARY

What general conclusions may be drawn about the First Amendment status of closure orders? At the very least, it is clear that a qualified First Amendment right of access to trials and to some pretrial proceedings does exist. Whether a particular proceeding is presumptively open depends on a two part inquiry. First, the Court will examine history and tradition to determine whether the proceedings have been open in the past. Second, the Court will consider whether public access contributes in a positive way to the functioning of the particular proceeding at issue. If so, the presumption of openness will attach and can only be set aside at a hearing where specific findings justifying closure are made.

In examining whether the First Amendment status of closure motions is the same for trial and pretrial, part of the problem is that *Globe Newspaper*, where the Court most clearly articulated a strict scrutiny standard for closure in trials, was authored by Justice Brennan with Chief Justice Burger in dissent. On the other hand, *Richmond Newspapers* and the *Press–Enterprise* cases were authored by Chief Justice Burger who managed to refrain from kind words about a strict scrutiny test for closure orders. The situation is further complicated by the fact that *Gannett*, which approved a closure order in a pretrial hearing, albeit in a Sixth Amendment context, has never been overruled.

## F.  ACCESS TO THE MEDIA

### 1.  ACCESS TO THE ELECTRONIC MEDIA

In 1967, one of the authors of this *Nutshell* wrote the following: "Our constitutional theory is in the grip of a romantic conception of free expression, a belief that the 'marketplace of ideas' is freely accessible. But if ever there were a self-operating marketplace of ideas, it has long ceased to exist. [A] realistic view of the first amendment requires recognition that a right of expression is somewhat thin if it can be exercised only at the sufferance of the managers of mass communication." Barron, *Access to the Press—A New First Amendment Right*, 80 Harv. L. Rev. 1641 (1967).

The First Amendment approach to broadcasting, a new and unique medium, has been particularly responsive to this view. A larger measure of regulation has been permitted and promoted for the electronic media than would be tolerated in the print media. At least two theories have been offered to justify this greater measure of regulation. First is the so-called scarcity theory. The broadcast spectrum has been traditionally seen as technologically limited; the electronic spectrum is finite. Theoretically, at least, newsprint is not. The second theory, the so-called social impact theory, sees the electronic media as having a greater impact on the opinion process than the printed word. The pervasive nature of broadcasting, particularly television, and its profound influence on society has been emphasized by the courts. In some situations—particularly in the area of indecency—the pervasive influence of broadcasting has been used to justify a measure of regulation which would not be permitted in the print media. In *FCC v. Pacifica Foundation*, 438 U.S. 726 (1978), which validated sanctions for indecent expression over the radio, Justice Stevens tellingly observed: "[O]f all forms of communication, it is broadcasting that has received the most limited First Amendment protection."

In *Red Lion Broadcasting Co. v. FCC*, 395 U.S. 367 (1969), the Supreme Court considered the constitutional validity of the fairness doctrine and one of its corollaries, the personal attack rules. The fairness doctrine required that the broadcast licensee provide a balanced presentation of controversial ideas of public importance. The personal attack rules provide that where a person was the subject of a personal attack of a specified character, equivalent reply time has to be furnished by the broadcaster. Clearly, these regulations impinged on the editorial discretion of broadcast journalists. Were these regulations therefore violative of the First Amendment?

In the *Red Lion* case, the Supreme Court, per Justice White, unanimously answered in the negative. Broadcasting was different than the print media. The spectrum could not be licensed to all who might choose to broadcast. It followed that those selected as broadcast licensees were trustees for the public. Justice White declared: "It is the right of the viewers and listeners, not the right of the broadcasters, which is paramount." In this view, it is the function of government to preserve an uninhibited marketplace of ideas and to prevent the monopolization of the opinion making process by those wealthy enough to control it. To the claim of the broadcasters that such government regulation would lead to self-censorship, Justice White responded that this was mere speculation. If it were ever shown that government regulation in fact impeded rather than enhanced the volume and quality of marketplace debate, it might become necessary to reconsider the First Amendment issues presented. In 1987 the FCC reached exactly that conclusion and abolished the fairness doctrine.

In the *Red Lion* case, specific regulations issued by the FCC were before the Court. In *CBS, Inc. v. Democratic National Committee*, 412 U.S. 94 (1973), the Court was confronted with more difficult questions. Did the First Amendment have an affirmative dimension? Did the First Amendment *ex proprio vigore* afford a right of access to the electronic media? In the *CBS* case, the Democratic National Committee and an organization of business people opposed to the Vietnam War asked the FCC to issue a declaratory ruling that the networks could not, consistent with the First Amendment, maintain a blanket policy refusing to sell them substantial time segments to disseminate their political and social ideas. In view of the emphasis in *Red Lion* on the public's right of access to ideas, the groups bringing suit in *CBS* contended that they had a First Amendment right of access to the electronic media. For their part, the networks contended that a right of access, as asserted by the parties, trespassed unconstitutionally on their editorial judgement. The Supreme Court, per Chief Justice Burger agreed: "The [FCC's] responsibilities under a right-of-access system would tend to draw it into a continuing case-by-case determination of who should be heard and when." The FCC was under no First Amendment obligation to impose such a restraint on the editorial discretion of broadcasters.

In dissent, Justice Brennan, joined by Justice Marshall, contended that the First Amendment does have an affirmative dimension and that it serves not only as a limitation on government but as source of individual rights: "The First Amendment values of individual self-fulfillment through expression and individual participation in public debate are central to our concept of liberty. If these values are to survive in the age of technology, it is essential that individuals be permitted at least *some* opportunity to express their view on public issues over the electronic media.''

In *CBS, Inc. v. Democratic National Committee*, Chief Justice Burger had acknowledged that a different case might be presented if the access obligation on the part of broadcasters were imposed by the Congress or the FCC. In *CBS, Inc. v. FCC*, 453 U.S. 367 (1981), the Supreme Court was confronted with just such a situation. The Federal Election Campaign Act of 1971 created a requirement of ''reasonable access'' for *federal* political candidates. This ''reasonable access'' requirement became Sec. 312 (a)(7) of the Federal Communications Act. The Carter–Mondale Presidential Committee requested that the major networks provide time for a 30–minute program in the early part of December 1979. The networks declined to provide such time and the Committee contended that the ''reasonable access'' provision was violated. The FCC and the federal appellate court agreed.

Before the Supreme Court, the networks contended that the ''reasonable access'' provision was an unconstitutional restraint on their editorial judgement and discretion in violation of the First Amendment. Chief Justice Burger rejected the argument and upheld the challenged ''reasonable access'' statutory provision: ''[The statutory provision] makes a significant contribution to freedom of expression by enhancing the ability of candidates to present, and the public to receive, information necessary for the effective operation of the democratic process. [The limited right of 'reasonable access'] does not impair the discretion of broadcasters to present their views on any issue or to carry any particular type of programming. [The statutory right of access for federal political candidates] properly balances the First Amendment rights of federal candidates, the public, and broadcasters."

*Red Lion* and its unruly progeny recognized the constitutionality of federal licensing and regulation, even to the point of approving structural mechanisms of political debate such as the fairness doctrine and the "reasonable access" provision. In the years since *Red Lion* there has been an explosion of new technologies. We have witnessed the emergence of cable television and satellite communications. Soon the regional telephone companies will commence the dissemination and origination of information themselves. In the light of the multiplicity of electronic forums now available, the scarcity rationale, which was used to justify treating the broadcast media differently than the print media, has come under reexamination. Although the Supreme Court has recognized the diminishing force of the scarcity rationale, *FCC v. League of Women Voters*, 468 U.S. 364 (1984), *Red Lion* and *CBS, Inc. v. FCC* are still in force and still reflect the dominant view that the electronic media is unique, justifying a separate and distinct First Amendment approach.

*Turner Broadcasting System, Inc. v. FCC*, 512 U.S. 622 (1994) considered a First Amendment challenge to the must-carry provisions of the 1992

Cable Act obliging cable operators to set aside a specified percentage of their channels for local over-the-air broadcast signals. Justice Kennedy, joined by three other justices, said that the purpose of must-carry was to preserve "access to free television programming for the 40 percent of Americans without cable." Congress feared that the shift in market share from broadcasting to cable would jeopardize the economic base of free local over-the-air broadcasting. The cable operators argued, however, that they were being forced to carry speech they did not want to carry. The Court agreed with the cable operators that they were engaged in speech and that broadcasting's deferential *Red Lion* standard of review should not be applied to cable. The scarcity rationale justifying broadcast regulation was not appropriate for the multi-channel medium of cable. The cable operators argued that that *Miami Herald Publishing Co. v. Tornillo* [see Ch. XIII, F, 2] rather than *Red Lion* should be the governing precedent. Like the newspapers in *Tornillo,* they were being required to speak, *i.e.,* carry programming not of their own choosing. The Court responded that although content-based regulation of cable merited the strict scrutiny standard of review, this was content-neutral regulation to be reviewed under the *O'Brien* test. The must-carry requirements were not triggered by a message transmitted by the cable operator. Must-carry afforded access to all "full power, local broadcasters, whatever the content of their programming."

Government *can* favor one set of speakers over another. But government can not favor one set of speakers because of a government preference for speech of the favored speaker. The must-carry rules were not designed to favor the speech of local over-the-air broadcasters but instead to preserve the economic viability of free local over-the-air broadcasting. Nonetheless, additional findings were necessary. Justice Kennedy, therefore, remanded the case to ascertain (1) whether substantial governmental interests justified must-carry, *i,e.,* whether without must carry local over-the-air broadcasting would be placed in economic peril and (2) whether must-carry suppressed more speech than necessary.

Justice Stevens thought no remand was necessary. But to achieve a disposition of the case commanding the "support of a majority of the Court," he joined Justice Kennedy's opinion, thereby providing a critical fifth vote. For Stevens, the access justification for must-carry was self-evident: "The public interests in protecting access to television for the millions of homes without cable and in assuring the availability of a 'multiplicity of sources' are unquestionably substantial."

On remand, the lower federal court found that substantial evidence supported the Congressional prediction that without must-carry a sizeable number of over-the-air broadcast signals would be denied cable carriage. Applying the intermediate standard of review "enunciated in *O'Brien,*" the Supreme Court affirmed, 5–4. Must-carry advanced important government interests—preserving free local over-the-air broadcasting, providing public access to information from multiple and diverse sources of information, and stimulating competition in the television programming market. Furthermore, absent must-carry the future of free local over-the-air broadcasting would be placed in economic jeopardy. Finally, must-carry provisions did not burden substantially more speech than necessary. The majority of the nation's cable systems had not canceled any programming to satisfy must-carry. Justice Kennedy concluded for the Court: "[T]he burden imposed by must-carry is congruent to the benefit it affords." *Turner Broadcasting System, Inc. v. FCC*, 512 U.S. 622 (1997).

Justice Breyer, concurring in part, ignored the content-based versus content-neutral line of analysis and took a pragmatic approach to the First Amendment issues raised by must-carry. Yes, must-carry exacted some First Amendments costs. To some degree, it suppressed the speech of the cable operator. But that was not decisive. A central First Amendment value for Justice Breyer was assuring public access to the widest variety of information sources. Using a balancing approach, Justice Breyer weighed the "speech-restricting and speech-enhancing consequences" of must-carry and concluded that the burden must-carry imposed on cable system operators and cable programmers was not substantial compared to the heavy burden that would be borne by the over-the-air viewers absent must-carry: "In essence, Justice Breyer concluded that Congress could reasonably determine that must-carry aids the over-the-air viewer more than it hurts the cable subscriber." Barron, *The Electronic Media and the Flight from First Amendment Doctrine: Justice Breyer's New Balancing Approach,* 30 U.Mich.J. L. Reform 817 (1998).

In *Denver Area Educational Consortium, Inc. v. FCC*, 518 U.S. 727 (1996), the Court reviewed a First Amendment assault on three provisions of the 1992 Cable Act regulating indecent programming on leased access and public access channels. [These provisions and the Court's rulings on their validity are set forth in the indecent speech materials in Chapter V.] In a world of ever new electronic media, the various opinions in *Denver Area* confront a perplexing issue: Should the same First Amendment doctrinal standards be applied to all media or should new standards be developed for new media? In a plurality opinion for the Supreme Court, Justice Breyer, joined by Justices Stevens, O'Connor and Souter, applied a new contextual balancing test to cable regulation. Justice Breyer expressly rejected analogizing cable television to established First Amendment categories. Justice Kennedy thought, for example, that leased access channels should be characterized as common carriers and that content regulation of them should be under a strict scrutiny standard of review. The Breyer plurality was standardless. Particularly in the case of new electronic media, it was essential that First Amendment issues be governed by existing and constant doctrine.

Justice Breyer rejected the three-tiered standard of review for cable regulation and used instead as a "guiding principle" the following standard: "Congress may not regulate speech except in cases of extraordinary need and with the exercise of a degree of care that we have not elsewhere required." This sounds like the strict scrutiny standard of review. But on examination the resemblance is only on the surface. The true focus is on the "balance of competing interests and the special circumstances of each field of application." In short, this new balancing approach "weighs the strength of the government interest in the suppression of expression against the strength of the government interests in access for expression." Barron, 31 U. Mich. J .L. Ref. at 840.

Justice Thomas contended that the First Amendment protects the owners of the media and no one else. "Like a free-lance writer seeking a paper in which to publish newspaper editorials, a programmer is protected in searching for an outlet for cable programmers but he has no free-standing First Amendment right to have that programming transmitted." Indeed, Justice Thomas challenged the First Amendment validity of public access channels on cable. Public access requirements were an infringement on the editorial discretion of cable operators. Justice Breyer, on the other hand, would leave open the question of "whether the interests of the owners of communications media always subordinate the interests of all other users of a medium." Justice Stevens made a distinction between leased access and public access channels. Public access channels were created by local governments. The federal government had no more power to censor the programming on public access channels created by local governments than they had power to censor the programming of cable operators on channels they owned. Justice Souter, like Justice Breyer, took a practical rather than a doctrinal approach: "[B]ecause we know that changes in these technologies will enormously alter the structure of regulation itself, we should be shy about saying the final word today about what will be accepted as reasonable tomorrow."

The novel feature of the *Denver Area* opinions, particularly those of Breyer and Souter, is in their suggestion that as new electronic media evolve, the approaches used to govern them should be sufficiently flexible to permit courts to move with changing technology despite existing First Amendment doctrine. Especially noteworthy is Breyer's acceptance, in the context of the must-carry cable requirements, that government has a role to play in securing First Amendment objectives when the contending parties each assert First Amendment interests.

If the failure of the marketplace of ideas thesis has received a measure of acceptance in the electronic media, it has been received with far more hostility in the context of the print media. The watershed case in this area is *Miami Herald Publishing Co. v. Tornillo*, 418 U.S. 241 (1974), which considered a First Amendment challenge to a Florida statute affording a right of reply to personal attacks on political candidates by newspapers.

While Chief Justice Burger, for the Court, accepted many of the arguments of the advocates for access to the media who championed the Florida statute as giving voice to the public-at-large, nevertheless the Court invalidated the statute as inconsistent with the First Amendment. The *Tornillo* Court relied on two principal themes in rejecting Florida's right of reply statute. First, compulsory publication was perceived as imposing a significant penalty on freedom of expression based on the content of the publication thereby chilling speech. Second, the Florida statute was seen as an impermissible restraint on editorial autonomy.

The argument that the Florida statute chilled expression proceeded on an assumption that if a newspaper contemplated publishing a particularly caustic attack on a candidate, it would necessarily contemplate that it might be obliged to surrender valuable space to provide a reply. The consequence, it was feared, was that they might choose not to publish the attack at all: "[Editors] might well conclude that the safe course is to avoid controversy and that, under the operation of the Florida statute, political and electoral coverage would be blunted and reduced."

The argument that the Florida right of reply statute trespassed on editorial autonomy was premised on the principle that the First Amendment guarantees a free press, not a fair one. It is not the function of government to assure press responsibility through regulation of editorial judgement. As Justice White, concurring, put it: "A newspaper or magazine is not a public utility subject to 'reasonable' governmental regulation in matters affecting the exercise of journalistic judgement as to what shall be printed." First Amendment scholar Benno Schmidt has argued that the access controversy exemplified by *Tornillo* represented a conflict between the First Amendment tradition of protection for editorial autonomy and the newer utilitarian philosophy that puts great weight on diversity of expression. *See* Schmidt, *Freedom of the Press v. Public Access* (1976). This utilitarian or instrumental approach to First Amendment problems, says Schmidt, developed as a response to the growth of mass media and the concentration of ownership patterns which it exhibits. The right of access approach rejected in *Tornillo* values debate and diversity over editorial autonomy.

Is *Tornillo* the last word on the issue of a right of access to the print media? There have been no subsequent Supreme Court cases involving the print media that suggest the contrary. On the other hand, Justice Brennan, concurring, went out of his way to observe in *Tornillo* that its rationale did not in any way undermine the validity of retraction statutes in a libel context. Some have contended, therefore, that a statute affording a right of reply to defamatory attack in lieu of damages might still be valid. In any case, it is clear that editorial autonomy receives far greater First Amendment protection in the print media context than it does in the case of the electronic media.

# PART FOUR

# FREEDOM OF RELIGION

---

## CHAPTER XIV

## TEXT, HISTORY AND THEORY OF THE RELIGION CLAUSES

The freedom of religion guarantee of the First Amendment encompasses two clauses. One clause prohibits Congress from interfering with the free exercise of religion. The other clause prevents Congress from enacting legislation respecting the establishment of religion. Both guarantees have been made applicable to the states through the due process liberty clause of the Fourteenth Amendment. *Cantwell v. Connecticut*, 310 U.S. 296 (1940) [free exercise]; *Everson v. Board of Educ.*, 330 U.S. 1 (1947) [antiestablishment]. It is easy to understand the incorporation of the limitation on government coercion of religious belief and practice as reflecting a fundamental liberty in a civilized society. It is more difficult to appreciate why the due process guarantee of personal liberty encompasses the antiestablishment principle. Critics of incorporation of the antiestablishment principle caustically note that some states in fact engaged in the establishment of religion by favoring particular denominations. By the time of the adoption of the Fourteenth Amendment, however, these establishments had been eliminated. *School Dist. of Abington v. Schempp,* 374 U.S. 203 (1963) [Brennan, J., defending the incorporation of the antiestablishment clause]. Defenders of incorporation argue that prohibiting the establishment of religion by government is an essential protection for both personal and institutional religious liberty. "A state-created orthodoxy puts at grave risk that freedom of belief and conscience which are the sole assurance that religious faith is real, not imposed." *Lee v. Weisman,* 505 U.S. 577 (1992).

Today it is clear that both the federal government and state governments are subject to the same constitutional restraints when they take action implicating religion. But fundamental and difficult questions persist. What is establishment? What is free exercise? What is the relationship of the two clauses to each other? What relationship between church and state does protection for freedom of religion contemplate? The inclusion of protection for the free exercise of religion in the Bill of Rights is not surprising. Many of the colonists had come to the new world as religious dissenters seeking to escape religious persecution. Nevertheless, the level of religious tolerance in late nineteenth century America, especially of non-Christian religions and non-religionists, was marginal. The antiestablishment principle of the First Amendment was an even more novel idea. Institutional religion was a vital part of nineteenth century American society and religion was a regular part of public life. If one wished, and some do, to take a narrow view of the antiestablishment principle, it could be argued that it was simply a federalist limitation on the national government. A contemporary exponent of this view is Justice Clarence Thomas who observed in his concurring opinion in *Van Orden v. Perry*, 545 U.S. 677 (2005) that the history and text of the Establishment Clause resists the idea that it was incorporated against the States. In his view, "the Establishment Clause does not restrain the States." States in this view might choose which religion or religions they wished to favor and discriminate against other sects. The states, in short, did not fear what they themselves might do; they feared instead the establishment of a national church as in England.

One could go slightly further and argue that the antiestablishment principle was also meant to prevent Congress from discriminating among religions. In this view, as long as government treated all religions equally, the Establishment Clause would not be a particular restraint on favoring or disfavoring religion in general. Chief Justice Rehnquist has strongly urged this narrow originalist position. See *Wallace v. Jaffree*, 472 U.S. 38 (1985) (Rehnquist, J., dissenting). There are at least three counterarguments to this position. The first is that it is incompatible with the incorporation of the antiestablishment principle into the personal liberty guarantee protected by the Fourteenth Amendment against state invasion. The second is that the changes in the place and character of religion in modern American society challenge reliance on the narrow interpretative position, at least if the values underlying the antiestablishment clause are to be realized. The third is that if one surveys the Supreme Court's freedom of religion jurisprudence over the past more than half a century, the antiestablishment clause, at least for the present, still imposes an ambiguous, uncertain restraint on federal and state government whenever they act to aid and advance religion.

Thomas Jefferson, James Madison and Roger Williams are generally regarded as the formative influences on the concept of freedom of religion in America. While all three accepted a principle of separation of church and state, they wrote from very different premises regarding religion and its proper relation to the state. Jefferson was a child of the eighteenth century Enlightenment. He emphasized reason and was skeptical of religious dogmas. While he championed personal freedom of conscience and religious belief, Jefferson was suspicious of institutional religion and was fearful that it might have a corrupting influence on the body politic. It was necessary to erect a "wall of separation" between church and state so that public life would not be corrupted. James Madison, on the other hand, accepted the importance and value of institutional religion in public life. Religion bolstered the public morality and public morality was an essential part of fostering civic virtue. This did not mean, however, that government should actively support and involve itself in religious life. For Madison, religious freedom was best safeguarded by preserving and encouraging a multiplicity of religious sects. In this way, no one denomination would become dominant. Madison wrote in *The Federalist No. 51*: "In a free government the security for civil rights must be the same as that for religious rights. It consists in the one case in the multiplicity of interests, and in the other in the multiplicity of sects. The degree of security in both cases will depend on the number of interests and sects." For Roger Williams, the separation of church and state was a means to preserve religion from state interference. Jefferson feared religion would corrupt the state; Williams feared the state would corrupt religion. Government action operated to encourage and aid religious ministry was fully acceptable. In short, government could act in support of religion when such support was necessary.

Influenced by these and other ideas, four enduring and sometimes conflicting and overlapping themes emerge in the evolution of the religion clauses of the First Amendment—*strict separation, neutrality, accommodation* and tests such as *endorsement* and *coercion*.

*Strict separation*—This concept is best embodied in Jefferson's metaphor calling for a wall of separation between church and state. Government and religion occupy separate spheres and each must be prohibited from excessive influence on the other. In *Everson v. Board of Educ.*, 330 U.S. 1 (1947), Justice Black, for the Court, invoked Jefferson's wall metaphor when he declared: "The 'establishment of religion' clause of the First Amendment means at least this. Neither a state nor the federal government can set up a church. Neither can pass laws which aid one religion, aid all religions, or prefer one religion over another." Despite the strict separationist rhetoric in *Everson*, the Court upheld a challenged township law that authorized the use of public bus transportation of students to both public and parochial schools. The Court viewed the challenged law as a general program designed to serve a secular public purpose—the safe transportation of school children—and not an impermissible government aid to religion.

For Justice Rutledge, writing for four dissenters, the state was aiding children "in a substantial way to get the very thing which they are sent to the particular school to secure, namely, religious training and teaching." For Rutledge, there was far too little separation in Black's approach and much too much accommodation. Justice Black's public welfare purpose exception to the separationist principle, Rutledge protested, would swallow up the separationist theory altogether. The Supreme Court's decision in *Zelman v. Simmons–Harris*, 536 U.S. 639 (2002), see Ch. XV, rendered a severe, perhaps fatal, blow to the strict separationist understanding of the Establishment Clause. *Zelman* approved government-funded tuition vouchers for private schools which in the main went to religiously-affiliated schools. Arguably, the government thus aided religion in violation of Jefferson's wall of separation. Justice Stevens in dissent appealed to the fear of intra-group conflict and societal divisiveness that undergirds the separationist position and lamented; "Whenever we remove a brick from the wall that was designed to separate religion and government, we increase the risk of religious strife." Justice Souter in dissent in *Zelman* asked: "How can a Court consistently leave *Everson* on the books and approve the Ohio vouchers?" His answer was that it could not. Yet *Everson* has not been reversed. Furthermore, as Justice Souter acknowledged, the Court has not approved "vouchers for religious schools alone" nor has it approved government aid "earmarked for religious instruction."

*Neutrality*—Writing in 1961, Professor Philip Kurland argued that formal neutrality should be the measure of whether government action violated the constitutional guarantee of freedom of religion. The two clauses, he argued, formulated the precept "that government cannot utilize religion as a standard for action or inaction because these clauses read together as they should be, prohibit classification in terms of religion either to confer a benefit or to impose a burden." P. Kurland, *Religion and the Law* (1962). Kurland's position would allow state action regardless of the burden it imposes on religion so long as the state remains indifferent to the religious consequences of its action or inaction. But

Justice O'Connor, concurring in the judgement in *Wallace v. Jaffree*, 472 U.S. 38 (1985), stated: "It is difficult to square any notion of 'complete neutrality' with the mandate of the Free Exercise Clause that government must sometimes exempt a religious observer from an otherwise generally applicable obligation." On the other hand, a general but religiously-neutral aid program providing substantial assistance to religion would be constitutional. At least until recently, the Court had rejected the formal neutrality position.

There are other formulations of neutrality. Certainly, neutrality between religious denominations is a recognized principle of Establishment Clause law. Professor Douglas Laycock argues that the Court's decisions reflect a principle of "substantive neutrality": "The religion clauses require government to minimize the extent to which it either encourages or discourages religious belief or disbelief, practice or non-practice, observance or non-observance." Laycock, *Formal, Substantive, and Disaggregated Neutrality Toward Religion*, 39 DePaul L. Rev. 993 (1990). The student should note the frequent use of the language of neutrality in Supreme Court opinions.

*Accommodation*—The accommodationist position was expressed by Justice Douglas in *Zorach v. Clauson*, 343 U.S. 306 (1952): "When the state encourages religious instruction or cooperates with religious authorities by adjusting the schedule of public events to sectarian needs, it follows the best of our traditions. For it then respects the religious nature of our people and accommodates the public service to their spiritual needs." More recently, Professor Michael McConnell, one of the leading accommodationist theorists, made this statement on the accommodationist approach: "The nation is understood not as secular but as pluralistic. Religion is under no special disability in public life; indeed, it is at least as protected and encouraged as any other form of belief and association—in some ways more so. The idea of accommodation of religion, which is foreign to interpretations of the religion clauses based on strict neutrality or separation follows naturally from the pluralist understanding." McConnell, *Accommodation of Religion*, 1985 Sup. Ct. Rev. 1. McConnell defends the accommodationist approach on the ground that it is more consistent with the liberal pluralist nature of the American democratic state than are its competitor theories. For McConnell, there is no requirement of neutrality between religion and non-religion. He argues that "religious liberty is the central value and animating purpose of the Religion Clauses of the First Amendment." *Id.* Government can and should favor religion: "Any constitutional constraint must arise because the special treatment of religion would have a deleterious effect on religious liberty—not because other activities or systems of thought are of equal constitutional dignity." *Id.*

Critics of McConnell contend that his approach is imbalanced in favor of the Free Exercise Clause: "The case against accommodation is at bottom an Establishment Clause case; because Professor

McConnell offers a weak or undeveloped account of the Establishment Clause, his accommodation principles rest on an unreasonably narrow base of constitutional concern. As a result, his structure of accommodation wobbles under stress." Lupu, *The Trouble with Accommodation*, 60 Geo. Wash. L. Rev. 743 (1992). In short, Professor Lupu contends that in an effort to encourage government to accommodate religion in the name of free exercise, the accommodationists are willing to severely weaken the antiestablishment principle. The student should also consider the view that: "The inevitable tendency of accommodationism as it is currently practiced—on an ad hoc, unprincipled basis—is towards religious favoritism, overt or covert, of mainstream religions, because these religions are in a position to be benefitted by accommodation." *Developments in the Law—Religion and the State*, 100 Harv. L. Rev. 1606 (1987). The accommodationist theme gathered significant strength under the Burger and Rehnquist Courts. But as Justice Souter pointed out in *Board of Education of Kiryas Joel Village School District v. Grumet*, 512 U.S. 687 (1994), [See Ch. XV] the accommodation principle has limits: "[W]hatever the limits of permissible legislative accommodations may be, [i]t is clear that neutrality as among religions must be honored."

*Endorsement*—The endorsement test has steadily attained increasing importance in the Court's Establishment Clause jurisprudence. As early as *Lynch v. Donnelly*, 465 U.S. 668 (1984), Chief Justice Burger had observed that government could celebrate Christmas in some ways but not in ways that endorse religious doctrine. In *Allegheny County v. ACLU*, 492 U.S. 573 (1989) Justice Blackmun held that a solitary Christmas creche not accompanied by any other secular holiday symbols constituted government endorsement. Similarly, in *Lee v. Weisman*, 505 U.S. 577 (1992), [See Ch. XV] the Court held, per Justice Kennedy, that a clergyman's prayer at a public high school baccalaureate exercise constituted state imposed psychological pressure on students to participate. Significantly, four of the Justices who joined Justice Kennedy in *Weisman* wrote separate concurrences whose essence was that endorsement rather than coercion should be the touchstone of an Establishment Clause violation. In *Zelman v. Simmons–Harris*, 536 U.S. 639 (2002), popularly known as the school voucher case, both the neutrality and the endorsement tests were used by the Court to validate the Ohio voucher program. The program did not constitute an implied endorsement of a religious message because the government aid being received was attributable to the individual rather than to the government. Professor Jesse Choper contends that the endorsement test avoids some of the infirmities of both the *Lemon* test and the "strict neutrality" test because it clearly permits "some government accommodations for both minority and mainstream religions" and in this respect "its solicitude for free exercise values" is a "step forward." Yet Professor Choper does not believe endorsement is a satisfactory standard: "By finding a constitutional violation on mere feelings of indignity or offense, the endorsement test proves too restrictive of governmental attempts to acknowledge religious interests." Choper, *The Endorsement Test: Its Status and Desirability*, 18 Journal of Law and Politics 499 (2002). [For discussions of *Lynch*, *Allegheny County*, *Weisman*, and *Zelman*, see Ch. XV.]

*Coercion*—In *Lee v. Weisman, supra*, Justice Kennedy for the Court ruled that the state, by having a clergyman give the benediction and invocation at a public high school graduation ceremony, was creating pressures on students to participate in a religious exercise. If one assumes that coercion is a different measure of an establishment violation than endorsement, how do the two differ? Arguably, the coercion test could be seen as more susceptible to an accommodationist approach than endorsement since, in this view, coercion by the state might be more difficult to prove than endorsement by the state. So far the coercion test has not been used outside the public school context. See *Santa Fe Independent School District v. Doe*, 530 U.S. 290 (2000) [See Ch. XV]. As between endorsement and coercion, endorsement appears to be the more significant test.

The diverse and competing theories and tests discussed above attempt to explain the Free Exercise and Antiestablishment Clauses and explore their relationship. The ferment they reflect in thought about freedom of religion has generated a sense of tentativeness in the Supreme Court's anal-

ysis and a sense of uncertainty about the doctrine
in freedom of religion cases.

A problem common to both religion clauses of the
First Amendment is the dilemma of defining religion. To define religion is in a sense to establish it—
those beliefs that are included enjoy a preferred
constitutional status. For those left out of the definition, the definition may prove coercive. Indeed, it
is in this latter context, which roughly approximates the area covered by the Free Exercise Clause,
where the cases and discussion of the meaning of
religion have primarily centered. The Framers may
well have intended to limit religion to the established traditional theistic varieties. But in our highly pluralistic society, with its cults and nontheistic
belief systems, any such narrow definition is unworkable. Not surprisingly, then, the Court rejected
limiting religion to theistic religions. *Torcaso v.
Watkins*, 367 U.S. 488 (1961) invalidated a provision of the Maryland constitution which required
appointees to public office to declare a belief in the
existence of God. Justice Black, for the Court in
*Torcaso,* concluded that the *Everson* command of
neutrality prohibited government favoritism of traditional religions. Government can neither "aid all
religions against non-believers [nor] can [it] aid
those religions based on a belief in the existence of
God as against those religions founded on different
beliefs." This principle extended protection not only
to the secular humanist who challenged the Maryland law but also to the adherents of other non-

theistic religious beliefs such as Buddhism, Taoism, and Ethical Culture.

In a series of cases involving conscientious objection to military service, the Court again confronted the task of defining religion. A provision of the Universal Military Training and Service Act exempted from military service any person "who, by reason of religious training and belief, is conscientiously opposed to participation in war in any form." At that time, the Act defined "religious training and belief" as requiring belief in a Supreme Being. The Act specifically excluded "essentially political, sociological, or philosophical views or a merely personal moral code." In *United States v. Seeger*, 380 U.S. 163 (1965), the Court, per Justice Clark, interpreted the Act broadly and stated that the relevant test "is whether a given belief that is sincere and meaningful occupies a place in the life of its possessor parallel to that filled by the orthodox belief in God of one who clearly qualifies for the exemption."

The parallel beliefs test of *Seeger* was taken a step further in *Welsh v. United States*, 398 U.S. 333 (1970). A claimant for conscientious objector status had deleted the word "religious" from his application and indicated instead that his belief system came from readings in history and sociology. Justice Black, in a plurality opinion, held that "if an individual deeply and sincerely holds beliefs which are purely ethical or moral in source and content but that nevertheless impose upon him a duty of conscience to refrain from participating in any war at any time, those beliefs certainly occupy in the life of that individual 'a place parallel to that filled [by] God' in traditionally religious persons." On the other hand, in *Gillette v. United States*, 401 U.S. 437 (1971), the Court refused to extend the statutory exemption for conscientious objector to those opposed to particular wars.

Is it possible to define religion? It will be recalled that the parallel beliefs approach adopted in *Seeger* attempts to avoid the problem of defining religion solely in terms of the traditional and familiar by extending the protection of the religion clauses to any equivalent belief system. The great theologian, Paul Tillich, may have captured the parallel beliefs system concept when he defined religion to encompass "matters of ultimate concern." Tillich, *Dynamics of Faith* (1958). Drawing upon this idea, it has been suggested that religion extends "to the underlying concern which gives meaning and orientation to a person's whole life." Note, *Toward A Constitutional Definition of Religion*, 91 Harv. L. Rev. 1056 (1978). The author of this Note contends that the approach requires that any such ultimate concern be protected regardless of how secular it may be. Further, he argues that the only one capable of determining what constitutes an ultimate concern is the individual believer.

In the years since the conscientious objector cases, the Court has continued to avoid providing a formal definition of religion. Similarly, the Court has continued in its refusal to restrict protected religious belief to the tenets of organized religion.

As the Court said in *Frazee v. Illinois Dept. of Emp. Sec.*, 489 U.S. 829 (1989), the protection of the Free Exercise Clause is not limited to those "responding to the commands of a particular religious organization." Nor does the fact that adherents to a particular faith may have different ideas on what their faith requires preclude recognition of a belief on the part of an adherent as religious: "[T]he guarantee of free exercise is not limited to beliefs which are shared by all the members of a religious sect." *Thomas v. Review Board*, 450 U.S. 707 (1981). Instead, *Thomas* stands for the principle that exemption can be granted if the individual acts from "an honest conviction" which springs from his religion even though his co-religionists disagree.

# CHAPTER XV

# THE ANTIESTABLISHMENT CLAUSE

At the very least, it is clear that the Antiestablishment Clause prohibits the establishment of a national church or discrimination between denominations. This is illustrated by *Larson v. Valente*, 456 U.S. 228 (1982) where the Supreme Court invalidated a state law that imposed registration and reporting requirements on religious organizations soliciting more than 50% of their funds from non-members. The Unification Church, popularly known as the Moonies, and other non-traditional sects, were especially hard hit by this legislation. Justice Brennan, for the Court, explained the nature of the disparate impact created by the statute: "[T]he provision effectively distinguishes between 'well-established churches' that have 'achieved strong but not total financial support from their members,' on the one hand, and 'churches which are new and lacking in a constituency, or which, as a matter of policy, may favor public solicitation over general reliance on financial support from members,' on the other hand." Since the law discriminated on the basis of religion, the Court applied strict scrutiny. Justice Brennan stated: "[T]he clearest command of the establishment clause is that one religious denomination cannot be officially preferred over another." While the state had a compelling interest in protecting its citizens from abusive practices during solicitation, there was no showing that the 50% rule was closely fitted to furthering that objective.

But the Supreme Court has not limited the reach of the proscription of the Establishment Clause to state churches or governmental preferences in favor of particular denominations. How broad then is the reach of the Establishment Clause? In *Lemon v. Kurtzman*, 403 U.S. 602 (1971), the Court responded to this question by applying a tripartite test. First, the government action must have a secular legislative purpose. The existence of a purpose to aid religion will not itself doom a law so long as a legitimate public welfare purpose can be invoked to support it. Second, the primary effect of the government action must neither advance nor inhibit religion. The fact that a law incidentally advances or burdens religion will not result in its invalidation. Third, the government action must not foster an excessive government entanglement with religion. The more a law fosters a continuing relationship between church and state or is likely to produce divisiveness in the community, the more likely it will be held to involve an impermissible establishment.

The *Lemon* test has been greatly eroded and its future is not bright. Critics argue with respect to its first criterion—the secular purpose requirement—that it is often difficult to distinguish a secular from a sectarian purpose. Government can argue that it is fostering religious values in order to serve the public welfare. Similarly, the distinction drawn between a primary effect that advances religion and an incidental benefit to religion is often more a conclusory label than the product of persuasive analysis. Critics of the *Lemon* test also have contended that the third prong of the *Lemon* test—the excessive entanglement criterion—is simply a restatement of the primary effect test. Other critics argue that the third prong presents the state with a dilemma—in fashioning a program to avoid a primary religious effect, the government may create an "excessive entanglement."

In the context of legislative prayer, the Court failed to apply the *Lemon* test. *Marsh v. Chambers*, 463 U.S. 783 (1983) held that the opening of a state legislative session with an official prayer was constitutional because such prayer was based on long-accepted practice. In *Marsh*, history and tradition rather than *Lemon* became the measure of constitutionality. Nevertheless, the Court continued to use the *Lemon* test. See, e.g., *Lynch v. Donnelly*, 465 U.S. 668 (1984) [inclusion of a Nativity scene in a municipal Christmas display held not to violate the Establishment Clause]; *Jimmy Swaggart Ministries v. Board of Equalization*, 493 U.S. 378 (1990) [imposition of a state sales and use tax on religious materials sold by a religious organization held not to violate the Establishment Clause]. But defections from the *Lemon* test have become increasingly common, alternative formulations have emerged. One of the most significant is the endorsement test. In *Lynch v. Donnelly*, Justice O'Connor, concurring, urged, as a "refinement" of the purposes and effects prongs of *Lemon*, that the proper Establishment Clause inquiry is "whether the government intends to convey a message of endorsement or disapproval of religion." Government must not send a message to nonadherents of religion that they are outsiders and not full members of the political community.

In *Allegheny County v. ACLU*, 492 U.S. 573 (1989), the Court, per Justice Blackmun, employed the endorsement test in holding that the placement of a creche on the Grand Staircase of the Allegheny County Courthouse constituted a violation of the Establishment Clause. While explaining that the term endorsement is not self-defining, Justice Blackmun stated: "The Establishment Clause, at the very least, prohibits government from appearing to take a position on questions of religious belief or from 'making adherence to a religion relevant in any way to a person's standing in the political community.'" Since there was nothing in the display that suggested that it was anything other than religious in nature, the display carried an unmistakable message that the municipality promoted and protected religion. In short, the display of the creche under these circumstances constituted an impermissible endorsement of religion. Justice Kennedy, joined by three other justices, dissented in *Allegheny County v. ACLU* and attacked the endorsement test as "flawed in its fundamentals and unworkable in practice." The fact that the creche might promote feelings of exclusion from the political community making nonadherents feel like outsiders, he argued, was an inadequate basis for condemning the traditional Christmas practice of displaying the nativity scene. Other critics of the endorsement formulation argue that it is, in fact, a watering down of *Lemon*. State practices adopted for the purpose of supporting religion and having the primary effect of advancing religion might still not be an impermissible endorsement.

In *Lee v. Weisman*, 505 U.S. 577 (1992), Justice Kennedy, now writing for the Court, formulated an alternative to the *Lemon* test and the endorsement variation on it. *Lee* held, 5–4, that the practice of having a clergyman recite an invocation and a benediction at an official public high school graduation baccalaureate ceremony violated the establishment clause. See this chapter, B, 2, Religious Exercise in the Schools. Justice Kennedy focused on the coercive effect of the state's involvement on the students even though the students were not compelled to attend the graduation ceremony. Employing a broad conception of coercion, Justice Kennedy cited the psychological, public and peer pressure on the students to participate in the baccalaureate ceremony and the prayer.

Justice Scalia, joined by three other members of the Court, dissented in *Lee* and took particular exception to Justice Kennedy's concept of coercion on the ground that it was "as infinitely expandable as the reasons for psychotherapy itself."

Justice Kennedy's coercion analysis in *Lee* constitutes a new Establishment Clause test. The difference between the endorsement test and the coercion test presumably is that the latter arguably is even more tolerant of government practices accommodating religion. In short, fewer government practices are likely to fall under the ban of the Establishment Clause under the coercion standard test than would be the case using the endorsement test or the *Lemon* tripartite test.

## A. GOVERNMENT FINANCIAL AID TO RELIGIOUS INSTITUTIONS

One of the most frequently recurring factual contexts involving Establishment Clause challenges concerns government financial support for religious institutions, especially parochial schools. In this context, the *Lemon* tripartite test has been dominant. But in the school voucher case *Zelman v. Simmons–Harris*, 536 U.S. 639 (2002), *infra*, the opinion for the Court did not even mention *Lemon*. While the outcome depends on a case-by-case analysis of the particular facts presented, application of the *Lemon* criteria tended to follow a pattern. The assistance is usually found to be in furtherance of a legitimate secular purpose—for example, the education of children. But when the Court turns to whether the assistance has a primary effect of advancing or inhibiting religious, or whether aid involves an excessive governmental entanglement with religion, predictability of outcome is soon lost.

In determining whether the latter two elements of the *Lemon* test are satisfied, certain factors have had a recurring importance. First, consideration is given to whether the aid is directed at elementary and secondary education or colleges and universities—the pervasive religiosity of the parochial schools creates a potential for advancing religion that often produces a finding of establishment. Second, the type of assistance provided is often important. One-time construction financing provided by government to religious institutions is more likely to be upheld than a governmental program involving a continuing relationship between Church and State. The continuing program simply presents a much greater potential for religious indoctrination and excessive entanglement than a one-time construction grant. Third, analysis of the cases indicates that it is of great importance whether the recipient is the parent or the school child or whether the direct beneficiary of the assistance is the parochial school itself. If it is the parent or child who receives the aid, the likelihood that it will be validated is much greater. Why? It is the individual rather than the religious institution that controls how the government assistance will be used. Fourth, generally the aid must be given to citizens across the board. Thus, bus vouchers can be given to all school children, whether public or parochial. Aid that would simply allocate bus vouchers from public funds to parochial school children would more likely be deemed favoring the religious over the public sphere. Fifth, the place where the assistance occurs can often be a critical criterion. Assistance provided on parochial school grounds offers opportunities for religious indoctrination that might produce a finding of impermissible establishment.

Government assistance to religious institutions in the form of non-ideological benefits such as bus transportation and textbooks on secular subjects is more likely to be upheld than more ideological forms of aid. For example, the landmark decision of *Everson v. Board of Educ.*, 330 U.S. 1 (1947), upheld the provision by the state of bus transportation to all school children even though parochial schools were incidentally benefitted. The law had the secular purpose of aiding education. *Everson* stressed that government should not put religious adherents at a disadvantage by denying them public benefits available to citizens generally.

Consistent with the *Everson* precedent, the Court in *Board of Education v. Allen*, 392 U.S. 236 (1968) upheld a state law authorizing the loan of nonreligious textbooks used in the public schools to students in religious secondary schools. Again the law served the secular public welfare purpose of educating the young. And it was the parents and children rather than the religious institution itself who received the government benefit. On the other hand, *Wolman v. Walter*, 433 U.S. 229 (1977) invalidated the loan of instructional materials (*e.g.*, maps, magazines and tape recorders) and provision of public transportation for field trips for parochial students. The Court said the facts presented made it impossible to tell whether it was the sectarian or the secular that was being benefitted. *See Meek v. Pittenger*, 421 U.S. 349 (1975) [state loan of instructional material and equipment to parochial schools held unconstitutional]. Both *Meek* and *Wolman* were overruled in *Mitchell v. Helms, infra,* to the extent they were inconsistent with *Mitchell.*

Provision of state testing and diagnostic services to religiously sponsored schools has provided another fertile ground for Establishment Clause litigation. In the main, state reimbursement for costs incurred by schools in conforming to state requirements regarding testing and services are upheld. *Wolman v. Walter*, 433 U.S. 229 (1977) upheld state provision of standardized tests and scoring services to children in nonpublic schools even though the site for testing and services was the private schools. The critical factor for the Court was that the public authorities maintained control and supervision over the programs so that there was limited risk of religious indoctrination. *Wolman* also upheld provision of speech, hearing and psychological diagnostic services by public employees to students at religious schools by stressing that such aid offered a minimal potential for religious indoctrination. It should be noted that that part of the *Wolman* holding that barred the state loans of instructional materials to religiously-affiliated schools was reversed in *Mitchell v. Helms, infra.*

These same basic considerations controlled the outcome in *Committee for Public Education and Religious Liberty v. Regan*, 444 U.S. 646 (1980), involving state payments covering the cost of administering and reporting standardized tests made to religiously sponsored schools. These payments were held to be permissible since state control of the tests and the reporting services could not easily be converted into part of the private school's religious training mission.

In *Witters v. Washington Dept. of Services for the Blind*, 474 U.S. 481 (1986), the rationale of *Mueller v. Allen* was united with that underlying the testing and diagnostic services cases. Vocational rehabilitation aid provided to a blind student and used by him at a Christian college was held not to trespass on the Antiestablishment Clause. As in *Mueller*, the aid went directly to the student and the religious institution was only incidentally benefitted. As in the testing cases, the aid was essentially nonideological. There was little likelihood that the assistance would further the school's religious training mission. Indeed, there was no assurance that an aid recipient would even choose to attend a religious school. Finally, *Zobrest v. Catalina Foothills School District*, 509 U.S. 1 (1993) extended *Witters* to hold that a public school district could provide funds for a sign language interpreter for a ninth grader in a Catholic high school.

Not every form of nonideological aid provided on private school grounds will survive an Establishment Clause challenge. In *School Dist. of Grand Rapids v. Ball*, 473 U.S. 373 (1985) and *Aguilar v. Felton*, 473 U.S. 402 (1985), the Court struck down Community Education and Shared Time programs taught by public employees in leased classrooms in nonpublic schools. The courses being offered in the religiously sponsored schools involved secular subjects. Nonetheless, these programs were objectionable from an establishment perspective given the "pervasively religious atmosphere" of the parochial schools. In *Ball*, the Court held, per Justice Brennan, that the programs had the primary effect of advancing religion. First, teachers involved in the program might intentionally or inadvertently skew their courses to further the religious missions of their schools. Second, the program might be viewed by impressionable youngsters as creating "a crucial symbolic link between government and religion." Viewed from this vantage point, the power of government had been placed behind the religious institution. Third, the program could have the effect of directly promoting religion by subsidizing teachers for the school.

In *Aguilar v. Felton*, New York City had attempted to avoid the primary effect failings of *Ball*. The city fashioned an extensive system for monitoring the content of the publicly funded courses in order to safeguard against religious inculcation. The *Aguilar* Court held, per Justice Brennan, that such a supervisory system "inevitably results in the excessive entanglement of church and state." In a vigorous dissent in *Aguilar*, Justice O'Connor took issue with the abstract character of the Court's analysis and its lack of concern with practical realities and consequences. O'Connor noted that there had not been a single documented instance of religious indoctrination concerning these programs despite the thousands of classes that had been held. Nonetheless, in *Aguilar*, the Court had invalidated a program which reached 20,000 educationally disadvantaged and special needs school children: "The Court greatly exaggerates the degree of supervision necessary to prevent public school teachers from inculcating religion and thereby demonstrates the flaws of a test that condemns benign cooperation between church and state."

In *Agostini v. Felton*, 521 U.S. 203 (1997), Justice O'Connor, for the Court, upheld the public school teacher administration in religious schools of the same federal program struck down in *Aguilar:* "*Aguilar* is no longer good law." No Establishment Clause bar prohibited public school teachers from providing remedial services to disadvantaged children in parochial schools. The assumptions upon which *Ball and Aguilar* were based were incorrect. The three-pronged *Lemon* test still applied. But the way the Court evaluates whether government aid to religion has the impermissible effect of advancing religion has changed. Government indoctrination of religious belief has an impermissible effect. But indoctrination is now measured differently in two important ways. First, *Zobrest* disavowed the idea that the Establishment Clause is an "absolute bar to the placing of a public employee in a sectarian school" and that it creates an impermissible " 'symbolic link' between government and religion." Second, *Witters* rejected the precept set forth in *Ball* that any government aid that directly assists the educational program of religious schools is impermissible. Not only *Aguilar* but that part of *Ball* that dealt with the Shared Time Program is no longer good law. After *Zobrest* and *Witters,* the Shared Time Program in *Ball* and the program in *Aguilar* can no longer be viewed as having the impermissible effect of advancing religion through indoctrination. Government aid which is provided according to neutral and secular criteria that neither favor nor disfavor religion, and which is made available to both religious and secular schools on a nondiscriminatory basis, is unlikely to have the effect of advancing religion.

The program reviewed in *Aguilar* was characterized as creating an excessive entanglement between government and religion. But some "interaction between church and state is inevitable" and has always been tolerated: "Entanglement must be 'excessive' before it runs afoul of the Establishment Clause." A federally funded program providing remedial instruction to disadvantaged children on a neutral basis does not violate the Establishment Clause simply because public school teachers provide this instruction on the premises of private sectarian schools. Justice Souter, joined by Justices Stevens, Ginsburg and Breyer, dissenting, asserted that as long as a government program supported religion "in some substantial degree," the fact that the program was neutral as a formal matter did not negate the force of the Establishment Clause or of the *Aguilar* and *Ball* holdings.

A federal program providing for grants of financial aid to state educational agencies to enable them to lend educational resources such as computers and computer software to public and private schools (including private religious schools) for use in "secular, neutral and nonideological" programs does not violate the Establishment Clause. *Mitchell v. Helms*, 530 U.S. 793 (2000). The government aid was granted on the basis of neutral criteria and was secular in content. It was true that some of the government aid went to religiously-sponsored entities under the program. But Justice Thomas, joined by the Chief Justice and Justices Scalia and Kennedy, in a plurality opinion for the Court, declared that result was the consequence of "numerous private choices rather than the single choice of a government." Where such independent individual private choice controlled the grant of government aid pursuant to neutral eligibility criteria, it would be difficult for government to easily "grant special favors that might lead to a religious establishment." Furthermore, *Meek* and *Wolman,* which had invalidated the use by religious schools of taxpayer funds for the purchase of secular instructional material and equipment, were overruled to the extent they conflicted with the Court's opinion.

Justice O'Connor, joined by Justice Breyer, agreed that the precept in *Meek* and *Wolman*—that the possibility of the diversion of government aid to religious uses rendered such aid unconstitutional— should be overruled. However, if plaintiffs could prove that the government aid at issue actually is being used, or has been used for religious purposes, then there would be an Establishment Clause violation. What was unconstitutional, in her view, was actual not possible diversion. Since the government aid here was granted on the basis of neutral and secular criteria, the program at issue was in accord with *Agostini v. Felton*. The program here did not have the "impermissible effect of advancing religion." Justice Souter, joined by Justices Stevens and Ginsburg, dissenting, rejected the plurality view that even-handed neutrality could suffice as the measure of whether government-funded school aid violated the Establishment Clause. They protested the plurality's failure to give any "independent significance" to whether a school's religious mission is aided.

Direct financial aid to religious institutions is likely to be held unconstitutional. Given the pervasively religious atmosphere of the religiously sponsored elementary and secondary school, it is almost impossible to prevent public funds from advancing the school's religious mission. Furthermore, it is in this context that the potential for community divisiveness is greatest. In higher education, on the other hand, the tradition of academic freedom and the maturity of the students makes the potential for religious indoctrination and community divisiveness much less of a concern. In *Lemon v. Kurtzman*, the case where the tripartite test was born, the Court, per Chief Justice Burger, invalidated state salary supplements for teachers of secular subjects in parochial elementary schools. The Court cited the impressionable age of the children and the religious orientation of the school's activities as primary sources of concern. In an effort to prevent public funds from being used for religious indoctrination, the state legislature had provided extensive precautions. But the implementation of these safeguards created a constant danger of excessive entanglement.

On the other hand, government grants to higher education, including sectarian institutions, are regularly upheld. In *Tilton v. Richardson*, 403 U.S. 672 (1971), the Court rejected an Establishment Clause challenge to federal construction grants for college buildings to be used solely for secular activities. Construction aid was given on a one-time basis, was religiously neutral and did not require continuing government surveillance of the use of public monies. Therefore, the grants were deemed permissible. Again in *Roemer v. Board of Public Works*, 426 U.S. 736 (1976), the Court upheld state annual noncategorical grants to religiously sponsored colleges even though the colleges included clearly religious courses and programs in their course offerings. The *Roemer* Court responded that colleges are not pervasively sectarian. Where secular and sectarian activities could be separated, and the aid directed only to the secular, the aid would be valid.

Tax relief and tuition benefits will most likely be upheld when the aid is given to citizens generally rather than to the religious institution itself. *Mueller v. Allen*, 463 U.S. 388 (1983) upheld, 5–4, a state law permitting taxpayers to deduct designated education expenses. Unlike an earlier state law which had been held unconstitutional, *Committee for Pub-*

*lic Education v. Nyquist*, 413 U.S. 756 (1973), the state tax aid at issue in *Mueller* was available to all parents of school children in Minnesota whether the children went to public or private schools. Justice Rehnquist, for the Court, noted that government aid that "neutrally provides state assistance to a broad spectrum of citizens is not readily subject to challenge under the establishment clause." Further, by channeling the state assistance to the parents rather than to the parochial schools, the state reduced the dangers that the establishment clause was designed to prevent. An interesting aspect of Justice Rehnquist's use of the *Lemon* test in *Mueller* arose in his discussion of the secular purpose underlying the Minnesota law. In addition to the usual reference to the important state interest in assuring an educated citizenry, Justice Rehnquist acknowledged "a strong public interest in assuring the continued financial health of private schools, both sectarian and nonsectarian."

The decline of separationism and the ascendancy of neutrality in Establishment Clause jurisprudence was illustrated by *Zelman v. Simmons–Harris*, 536 U.S. 639 (2002), the so-called voucher case. Ohio established a program offering parents of school age children in Cleveland two kinds of assistance. One program offered tuition aid or vouchers for students attending a participating public or private school of the student's choosing. The other program provided tutorial financial aid for students who chose to remain in the public schools. If a parent chose to use the private school tuition aid or voucher program, the check was payable to the parent who then endorsed the check over to the private school the parent selected. Although parents could choose either religious or non-religious schools, the great majority of the private schools participating in the program were enrolled in religiously affiliated schools. The federal court of appeals ruled that the program violated the Establishment Clause because it had the "[primary effect" of advancing religion. The Supreme Court, 5–4, per Chief Justice Rehnquist, reversed, declaring that *Mueller*, *Witters*, and *Zobrest* had set forth the following principle: A government program will not easily yield to Establishment Clause attack if the program is neutral concerning religion and provides direct assistance to a group of citizens who act out of their own private and independent choice to redirect that government aid to private religious schools.

The crucial point about the Ohio program is that any incidental advancement of a religious objective or implied endorsement of a religious message is attributable to the individual receiving government aid and not to the government. The Ohio voucher program had neither the purpose nor the effect of advancing religion. The purpose of the program was clearly secular. It provided vital financial aid to poor children in an inadequate public school system. Nor did the program have the effect of advancing religion. Parents were given a secular option. They could if they chose elect state financed tutoring assistance and remain in the public schools. The fact that the majority of the participating private schools were religiously-affiliated schools was irrelevant from an Establishment Clause perspective. The key fact was that the selection by parents of those schools was the consequence of "numerous private choices, rather than the single choice of government."

Justice Souter, joined by Justices Stevens, Ginsburg and Breyer, dissenting, took aim at the Court's emphasis on neutrality and private choice in validating the program. The program was not neutral as far as religion was concerned. The secular option was in fact no match for the private religiously-affiliated schools. The tutoring aid available for those choosing to remain in the public schools was far less substantial than the tuition vouchers that were available if one elected the private schools that were predominantly religiously-affiliated. The fact that 96.6% of the voucher money went to religious schools did not demonstrate a real choice by families but only that "too few nonreligious school desks" were available and that few but religious schools could "afford to accept more than a handful of voucher students." For the majority of children using vouchers, the only alternative to the public schools was religious schools. Justice Souter concluded: "[A] Hobson's choice is not a choice."

In summary, *Agostini* seriously watered down the *Lemon* test. *Agostini* took a far more accommodationist approach in assessing what constitutes an impermissible effect than did *Ball* and *Aguilar*. Furthermore, the threshold for what constitutes an excessive entanglement between government and religion is considerably higher after *Agostini* than it was before. The plurality opinion in *Mitchell v. Helms* made neutrality its lodestar. *Mitchell* overruled *Meek* and *Wolman* to the extent those cases had held that taxpayer-funded instructional materials could not be loaned to religiously-affiliated schools. But an important and controversial question still remained: Could government-funded tuition vouchers be used by students in religiously-funded schools? *Zelman v. Simmons–Harris* answered that question in the affirmative and approved government-funded vouchers for religiously-affiliated schools so long as individuals were given a choice. In short, *Zelman* moved the Court even further from the path of strict separationism and toward a greater than ever emphasis on neutrality.

## B.  RELIGION IN THE SCHOOLS

### 1.   RELEASED TIME AND EQUAL ACCESS

May the public schools release their students for religious instruction? The Court's answer to this question has been equivocal depending on the site of the instruction. In *McCollum v. Board of Educ.*, 333 U.S. 203 (1948), the Court invalidated a program of released time for religious instruction which was conducted in the public school building. The Court emphasized that the state was providing direct support for the religious message and thereby placing its *imprimatur* on religious instruction. But in *Zorach v. Clauson*, 343 U.S. 306 (1952), the

Court sanctioned a program of released time which allowed the public school students to go outside the school for their religious education.

On the basis of the holdings of these cases, one could conclude that God's Word could be taught in God's house with Caesar's help but God's Word could not be taught in Caesar's house itself. Justice Douglas declared in *Zorach* that the failure of the state to accommodate the religious instruction of children would not be the neutrality mandated by the Establishment Clause but hostility towards religion. It would "prefer those who believe in no religion over those who do believe."

A modern expression of the released time controversy has been the debate over whether public schools and colleges must make their facilities available to religious groups. May state universities which open their doors to groups generally close them to religious groups? Is such closure justifiable in order to avoid the prohibitions of the Establishment Clause? These questions were presented to the Court in *Widmar v. Vincent*, 454 U.S. 263 (1981), which involved a state university policy precluding student religious groups from using state university facilities "for purposes of religious worship or religious teaching." The university had otherwise opened its facilities to a broad variety of student groups. The Court held that the state university policy discriminated against religious speech in a state-created "public forum" and was not justified by the Establishment Clause.

State avoidance of an Establishment Clause violation would be a compelling justification for discriminating against certain speech based on its religious content. But, in these circumstances, an equal access policy which includes religious groups would not violate the Establishment Clause. Using the *Lemon* test, the Court concluded that such an equal access policy would serve the secular purpose of promoting the free exchange of ideas. While there would be incidental benefits for religious groups, the state message would be one of neutrality rather than one of endorsement. Open access does not have a primary effect which advances religion. To deny public facilities to religious speech while making them available to non-religious speech would prefer the secular to the religious; it would constitute hostility to religion. Finally, requiring public institutions to discriminate between religious and non-religious groups with respect to the use of their facilities would in fact foster a greater entanglement of church and state as institutions sought to differentiate groups than would an across-the-board equal access policy.

Does the *Widmar* principle, forged in the context of the state university, apply as well to public elementary and secondary schools? This issue was presented in *Board of Educ. v. Mergens*, 496 U.S. 226 (1990). In the aftermath of *Widmar*, Congress had enacted "The Equal Access Act of 1984" which provided that if public high schools permitted non-curricular related groups to use the school's facilities a "limited open forum" was thereby created. In such circumstances, a public school could not prevent student religious groups from using the school's facilities during times when the facilities were not being used for curriculum related purposes. In *Mergens*, a student Christian club wished to use the facilities of a public high school for meetings. The school refused to permit the use of its facilities for such a purpose contending that, since student activities are an integral part of its educational program, the school would in fact be endorsing the religious activities of the student Christian club. The Supreme Court held that the Equal Access Act had been violated by the school and that the use of the school by the student religious club would not violate the Establishment Clause.

In *Mergens*, Justice O'Connor, speaking for herself, Chief Justice Rehnquist and Justices White and Blackmun, followed the logic of *Widmar*. While the plurality applied the *Lemon* test, it adopted the *endorsement* refinement. Congress had an avowed secular purpose to prevent discrimination against religious and other types of speech; "the Act's purpose was not to 'endorse or disapprove of religion.' " Nor did the Act have a primary religious effect since "secondary school students are mature enough and are likely to understand that a school does not endorse or support student speech that it merely permits on a non-discriminatory basis." While the Establishment Clause precludes *government* speech endorsing religion, *private* speech supporting religion is protected by the Free Speech and

Free Exercise Clauses. The potential for official endorsement and coercion was also controlled by the fact that the Act limited the extent to which school officials could participate in the religious activities of student groups and by the broad spectrum of officially recognized student clubs at the school. The Act's limitation on the role of school officials in the participation of the activities of the religious groups also operated to minimize entanglement concerns.

Justice Kennedy, joined by Justice Scalia, concurred in the result in *Mergens* but rejected an endorsement theory in favor of a two part inquiry. The first inquiry was whether the challenged government practice gave a direct benefit to religion. The second inquiry was whether the practice coerced any student to participate in religious activities. Kennedy and Scalia answered both inquiries in the negative. Any benefit to religion was only incidental. There was no showing of any state pressure on students to participate in the religious activity.

The Court applied the *Lemon* test again in *Lamb's Chapel v. Center Moriches Union Free School District*, 508 U.S. 384 (1993), where the Court, per Justice White, held that the denial by a school board of a church group's application to use public school facilities to show a film series on child rearing violated freedom of speech. A public school board rule which permitted school property—a nonpublic forum—to be used for the presentation of "all views about family issues and child-rearing except those dealing with the subject matter from a religious standpoint" impermissibly discriminated on the basis of viewpoint. In defense of its rule excluding use of school facilities by the church, the school district contended that it had a compelling interest in preventing the use of school property in violation of the Antiestablishment Clause of the First Amendment. Relying on *Widmar v. Vincent,* the Court ruled that no establishment violation would occur if school property were used by religious organizations under the school district's open access policy. The showing of the film in question would not have taken place during school hours, was not sponsored by the school, and was open to the public and not just to church members. As in *Widmar,* there was no "realistic danger" that the community would believe that the school district "was endorsing religion or any particular creed, and any benefit to religion or to the Church would have been no more than incidental." Under these circumstances, the use of school property by a church would not constitute an impermissible establishment under the three part *Lemon* test.

A principle of equal access for private religious speech applies to other public facilities besides schools. In *Capitol Square Review and Advisory Board v. Pinette*, 515 U.S. 753 (1995), the Court overturned a refusal by state officials to permit the Ku Klux Klan to erect a ten foot cross on a public square that adjoined the state Capitol Building in Columbus, Ohio. The Supreme Court, granting review only on the Establishment Clause issue, declared, per Justice Scalia, that the cross display was private religious speech and was as fully protected under the Free Speech Clause as private secular speech: "Our precedent establishes that private religious speech, far from being a First Amendment orphan, is as fully protected under the Free Speech Clause as secular private expression." Content-based regulation of the public square, a traditional public forum, was subject to the strict scrutiny standard of review. Sometimes Establishment Clause compliance can satisfy the compelling government interest demanded of strict scrutiny review but not here. A grant of the permit to display the cross was not a government endorsement of the Klan's expression. The public square was government property open to the public for expression by private groups.

One part of Justice Scalia's opinion, joined in only by Chief Justice Rehnquist and Justices Kennedy and Thomas, responded to the argument that the public square's proximity to the state Capitol might lead the public to believe that the cross display was an impermissible state endorsement. Justice Scalia said this was far too broad a view of the Court's approach to endorsement. The endorsement test has been used in a context involving *"expression by the government itself"* as in *Lynch* or where government is said to *"discriminate in favor* of private religious expression or activity" as in *Allegheny County*. The crucial distinction is between *government* speech that endorses religion and *private* speech that does so. The Free Exercise and Free

Speech Clauses protect the latter. The Establishment Clause is violated only when government gives preferential access to private religious speech. Government *"favoritism"* is not present when as here access is sought to a genuine public forum. Justice Scalia concluded: "Religious expression cannot violate the Establishment Clause where (1) it is purely private and (2) occurs in a traditional or designated public forum, publicly announced and open to all on equal terms."

Justice O'Connor, concurring, said that the endorsement test should be applied and that the measure of endorsement was the hypothetical "reasonable observer." In light of the use of this public space in the past, "allowing the Klan cross, along with an adequate disclaimer" would not be understood by the community as a endorsement by the state. Justice Souter, joined by Justices O'Connor and Breyer, concurring, protested the Scalia plurality's creation of a new two part *"per se"* rule. Under prior precedent, the reasonable observer had been the arbiter of the endorsement test. The Scalia plurality's rule created a "serious loophole" to endorsement test protection. The state has a responsibility to show there is no endorsement either by a disclaimer or by setting up an area for unattended private displays marked as not endorsed by the State. Justice Stevens in dissent said the cross conveyed a religious message which could not be transmitted by the State without violating the Establishment Clause.

In *Rosenberger v. Rector and Visitors of the University of Virginia,* 515 U.S. 819 (1995), the Supreme Court held, 5–4, per Justice Kennedy, that the university was not justified in refusing to allow money from a Student Activities Fund supported by mandatory student fees to pay for student publications that promoted belief in a "deity or an ultimate reality." The University's decision not to pay for the printing costs of a student publication, *Wide Awake: A Christian Perspective,* constituted impermissible viewpoint discrimination in violation of the free speech guarantee. The Establishment Clause did not justify the university's action. *Lamb's Chapel, Mergens,* and *Widmar* all teach that the Establishment Clause does not justify, much less require, the denial of "free speech rights to religious speakers who participate in broad-reaching government programs neutral in design." The Student Activities Fund was neutral toward religion and was thus quite different from a tax or a general assessment imposed for the direct support of a church or churches. This disbursement went to pay for the printing costs of a student publication protected under the free speech guarantee: "There is no Establishment Clause violation in the University's honoring its duties under the Free Speech Clause." Justice O'Connor, concurring, said that aspects of the Student Activities Fund—disbursement of funds directly to third-party vendors, "the vigorous nature of the forum at issue," and the ability of "objecting students" to opt out—persuaded her that government assistance here was not an impermissible endorsement of the religious message voiced by *Wide Awake*.

Justice Souter for the dissenters objected that the Court had for the first time approved "direct funding of core religious activities by an arm of the State." The Court had gone far beyond the scope of *Widmar, Mergens*, and *Lamb's Chapel*. Those cases rested on an analogy between the public street corner and open classroom space. But this holding far exceeds the "literal speaking" with which the forum-access cases were concerned. This case, Justice Breyer asserted, validates the grant of new economic benefits to religion in clear violation of the Establishment Clause ban against such direct aid.

In *Good News Club v. Milford Central School*, 533 U.S. 98 (2001), the Court, per Justice Thomas, ruled that a school district's refusal to permit the after-school use of a public school facility for use by a Christian club for children, the Good News Club, constituted unconstitutional viewpoint discrimination that was not required by the Establishment Clause. The case arose out of a New York state school district program which permitted residents to use public school facilities for a number of after-school activities such as education and arts instruction as well as social, civic and recreational activities. The school district, however, refused to allow the Good News Club to use public school facilities under this same program. The school district contended that the Establishment Clause barred the use of public school facilities to a club which intended to engage in religious activities on public school property. This was different than a club which discussed secular subjects from a religious perspective. The Supreme Court disagreed. Justice Thomas said the case was similar to *Rosenberger* and *Lamb's Chapel*. The Good News Club sought to teach morality and character from a religious perspective. Such teaching was permissible under the school district's use rules. The church in *Lamb's Chapel* sought to do the same through films. The key point was that "both modes of speech use a religious viewpoint." Justice Thomas also observed that the Club's activities were no more religious and no less deserving of First Amendment protection than was the publication of the Christian student publication in *Rosenberger*.

The religious nature of the Club's activities did not distinguish it from *Lamb's Chapel* and *Rosenberger*. It did not matter that the Club's purpose was to teach children " 'how to cultivate their relationship with God through Jesus Christ.' " Even something " 'quintessentially religious' " could also be characterized as the "teaching of morals and character development from a particular viewpoint." A state interest in avoiding Establishment Clause violations can be deemed "a compelling governmental interest justifying content-based discrimination." But that issue did not have to be confronted here because the school district has no "valid Establishment Clause interest." Neutrality is evident since none of the groups were sponsored by the school district. Moreover, the after-hours forum permitted by the program was open to non-religious groups. No coercion is present because the relevant community is the parents not elementary school children: "Because the children cannot attend without their parents' permission, they cannot be coerced into engaging in the Good News Club's religious activities." The possibility that some children might perceive endorsement of religion cannot trump the free speech rights of the club and its members.

Justice Souter, joined by Justice Ginsburg, dissenting, contended that the club did not intend to use public school facilities for discussion of a subject from a Christian perspective but instead the club intended to conduct "an evangelical service of worship calling children to commit themselves in an act of Christian conversion." Justice Stevens, dissenting, thought that speech with a religious viewpoint should be distinguished from religious proselytizing. The Good News Club's involvement in the latter would tend "to separate young children into cliques that undermine the school's educational mission."

In summary, *Widmar* and *Mergens* set forth the principle that granting religious groups equal access with other groups to state university and public school facilities does not violate the Establishment Clause. *Capitol Square* and *Rosenberger* hold that private religious expression is entitled to the same protection in the use of the public forum under the Free Speech Clause as other private speech. Discrimination in the use of the public forum, based on the religious content of the message, can only be upheld by a showing of compelling governmental interest. *Good News Club* teaches that while Establishment Clause compliance can serve as a compelling governmental interest, it was not sufficient in this case. There must be a showing of something in addition, such as, for example, government coercion or government favoritism for the religious content of the message.

## 2.    RELIGIOUS EXERCISE IN THE SCHOOLS

One of the most controversial areas in Establishment Clause jurisprudence has been the Supreme Court's exclusion of prayer and other religious exercises from the classroom. For many, such religious exercises are an essential part of the inculcation of moral and ethical values in our youth, which is an essential mission of the public schools. So long as students are not forced to pray, the argument continues, the public schools are only accommodating religion, not establishing it. From this perspective, to exclude religion from the classroom exalts the secular. Indeed, it establishes a "religion of secularism" and demonstrates a hostility toward traditional religion. Supreme Court decisions invalidating religious practices as violative of the Establishment Clause are sometimes met in parts of the country with non-compliance and even defiance. Nevertheless, the Supreme Court has consistently rebuked state efforts to prescribe prayer, Bible readings, or other religious exercises.

In *Engel v. Vitale*, 370 U.S. 421 (1962), the Court invalidated a twenty-two word non-denominational prayer prepared by the New York State Board of Regents to be read without comment at the opening of the public school day. Justice Black, for the Court, stated: "It is no part of the business of government to compose official prayers for any group of the American people to recite as a part of a religious program carried on by government." A year after *Engel*, the Supreme Court struck again. In *School District of Abington v. Schempp*, 374 U.S. 203 (1963), the Court, per Justice Clark, invalidated a Pennsylvania law requiring that ten Bible verses be read at the beginning of the school day. The Bible reading was a religious exercise required by the state and thus breached the "strict neutrality" required by the First Amendment. It was no defense to say that such readings merely gave voice to the free exercise claims of the majority. Free exercise claims could not be exploited to the point that they constitute an establishment: "While the Free Exercise Clause clearly prohibits the use of state action to deny the rights of free exercise to anyone, it has never meant that a majority could use the machinery of the State to practice its beliefs." The fact that a student could be excused from the Bible reading upon the written request of his parent in *Schempp* did not save the practice: "[A] violation of the Free Exercise Clause is predicated on coercion while the Establishment Clause violation need not be so attended." Coercion was ultimately to become a key Establishment Clause inquiry but, in

*Schempp*, the coercion inquiry was not critical to the result. Rather the focus of the Court was on the religious character of the exercise and its effect on the advancement of religion.

A more difficult issue is presented by "moment of silence" laws. If the law is framed as a truly religiously neutral requirement providing a time for repose and reflection during the school day, it might well withstand Establishment Clause challenge. In *Wallace v. Jaffree*, 472 U.S. 38 (1985), the Court dealt with an Alabama law requiring one minute of silence for purposes of "meditation or voluntary prayer" in the public schools. The Court, per Justice Stevens, invalidated 6–3 the Alabama "moment of silence" law, using Justice O'Connor's endorsement refinement of the *Lemon* test. While a state can have a religious purpose without violating the Establishment Clause, it must be invalidated "if it is entirely motivated by a purpose to advance religion." In *Jaffree*, the state had failed to produce any evidence of secular purpose to justify the Alabama law. The Alabama law had been enacted for the single purpose of endorsing prayer activities: "[T]he State intended to characterize prayer as a favored practice." This endorsement, Stevens concluded, violated the principle "that the government must pursue a course of complete neutrality toward religion."

In a concurring opinion, Justice O'Connor indicated that some "moment of silence" laws might be valid. In so doing, she defended the value of her endorsement test in giving analytic content to the purpose and effect prongs of the *Lemon* test. Even if a statute designed to promote a secular interest has the primary effect of advancing religion, in her view this would not necessarily invalidate it: "The endorsement test does not preclude government from acknowledging religion or from taking religion into account in making law and policy. It does preclude government from conveying or attempting to convey a message that religion or a particular religious belief is favored or preferred." Such an endorsement violates the religious liberty of the non-adherent since it puts government power behind a particular religious belief and indirectly coerces conformity from religious minorities. Applying these standards to the Alabama law, Justice O'Connor concluded that "the conclusion is unavoidable that the purpose of the statute is to endorse prayer." Justice O'Connor made a point, however, of indicating that some "moment of silence" laws would be valid. Unlike the state-sponsored prayer and Bible reading cases, "a moment of silence is not inherently religious" and the participant need not compromise his or her beliefs.

Justice Rehnquist dissented and urged a return to the language and intent of the drafters of the First Amendment: "The evil to be aimed at [appears] to have been the establishment of a national church, and perhaps the preference of one religious sect over another; but it was definitely not concerned about whether the Government might aid all religions evenhandedly." The First Amendment did not command government neutrality between religion and irreligion. Much less did it create a wall of separation between church and state: "[U]nfortunately the Establishment Clause has been expressly freighted with Jefferson's misleading metaphor [about the wall of separation] for nearly forty years [since *Everson*]." Not surprisingly, Justice Rehnquist called for the repudiation of the *Lemon* test.

In *Lee v. Weisman*, 505 U.S. 577 (1992), the Court considered yet another religious exercise in the public schools—a prayer given by a clergyman, a rabbi, at the baccalaureate exercises of a public high school. The case could have provided the opportunity for the interment of the *Lemon* test. Indeed, the Solicitor General of the United States filed a brief urging the Court to abandon the *Lemon* test and uphold the prayer as a noncoercive accommodation of religion. Justice Kennedy, for the Court in *Lee*, neither adopted the *Lemon* test nor repudiated it. Relying on precedents relating to prayer and religious exercises, the Court held, 5–4, that the baccalaureate program violated the Establishment Clause: "[T]he government involvement with religious activity in this case is pervasive, to the point of creating a state-sponsored and state-directed religious exercise."

Justice Kennedy noted that it was the state that decided to include a prayer, chose the clergyman to deliver the prayer, and directed and controlled the content of the prayer. He concluded that the limits imposed by the Establishment Clause were transgressed in these circumstances. In a word, Justice Kennedy looked at the behavior of the state and found coercion. There was a subtle psychological coercive pressure to participate in the prayer. The fact that attendance at the baccalaureate itself was voluntary did not diminish the force of the coercive pressure to attend the event. The high school student has no real choice given the significance of high school graduation in our culture. Justice Kennedy concluded: "It is a tenet of the First Amendment that the State cannot require one of its citizens to forfeit his or her rights and benefits as the price of resisting conformance to state-sponsored religious practice."

All four justices who joined Justice Kennedy's opinion in *Lee v. Weisman*—Blackmun, O'Connor, Souter and Stevens—also joined in separate concurring opinions. The theme of these concurrences was that endorsement rather than coercion should be the primary measure of an Establishment Clause violation. Further, while coercion may sometimes be sufficient to make out an Establishment Clause violation, proof of coercion is not a precondition for an Establishment Clause violation. Indeed, to make coercion the measure of the Establishment Clause "would render the Establishment Clause a virtual nullity" (Souter, J., concurring). Since state action that coerces religious conformity would violate the Free Exercise Clause, proof of an Establishment Clause violation would simply be redundant.

Justice Scalia, joined by Chief Justice Rehnquist and Justices White and Thomas, dissenting, argued that the historical and traditional acceptance of public ceremonies featuring prayers of thanksgiving and petition should have been determinative of the constitutional question. The coercion that matters in an Establishment Clause case, Scalia argued, is only coercion that is backed *"by force of law and threat of penalty."* Finally, Justice Scalia invoked what is sometimes called the civic religion theme. Civic religion refers to ceremonies and exercises that occur throughout our national life which are characterized by their long history and their non-sectarian character. They seek to achieve unity by fostering a sense of community purpose and a common ethics and morality. Responding to Scalia, Justice Kennedy rejected the effort to distinguish a permissible civic religion from an impermissible public involvement in religious exercises as an unacceptable contradiction.

In *Santa Fe Independent School District v. Doe*, 530 U.S. 290 (2000), the Court, per Justice Stevens, held that a school district practice of authorizing student-led and student-initiated prayers over a public address system prior to varsity public high school football games violated the Establishment Clause. The school district had previously had a policy of having a student chaplain deliver prayers at such games. When suit was brought to challenge this practice, a policy of providing for two student elections was instituted. One election was held to determine if there should be an invocation at football games. If the answer was in the affirmative, a second election was held to select the student who would deliver the invocation. This policy was further modified by a federal district court ruling that only nonsectarian, non-proselytizing prayer would be permissible. But even so, the policy was struck down as unconstitutional under *Lee v. Weisman.* The school district's effort to distinguish *Lee v. Weisman* on the ground that the invocation was private student speech was rejected. The invocation was authorized government policy taking place on school district property at school sponsored and school connected events. No effort was made to create a forum for the student body at large. In fact, the forum was only open to one student. Only student messages deemed appropriate by school authorities were permissible. Moreover, the student election scheme did not save the program. Elections did not protect minority views. Elections simply placed students holding minority views "at the mercy of the majority."

Although the school district contended that there was no school involvement, the Court pointed out that, as was the case in *Weisman*, the invocation bore the imprimatur of the state and put school-age children who objected in a difficult position. Responding to the school district defense that the program was designed to encourage good sportsmanship and student safety, the Court declared that "the expressed purposes of the policy encourage the selection of a religious message."

More pointedly, the Court observed that the courts had a duty to distinguish between sham and sincere secular purposes. As for the argument that attendance was voluntary, the Court said that, in fact, this was not true for the football team, cheerleaders, and members of the band. The constitution precluded government from presenting students with a choice whether to attend a high school football game or "risk facing a personally offensive religious ritual." Government policies that have "the purpose and perception of establishment of religion as well as a government sponsored student election that submits the issue of prayer in a public high school fail a facial challenge under the Establishment Clause." Chief Justice Rehnquist, joined by Justices Scalia and Thomas, pointed out that in *Lee v. Weisman* the graduation prayer given by a rabbi was under the control of a school officer. Here the pre-game invocation would have been chosen by a student. The former was public speech but this was private speech. The *Santa Fe Independent School District* case demonstrates that the coercion concerns expressed in *Lee v. Weisman* remain a significant factor in Establishment Clause cases.

## 3. RELIGION AND CURRICULUM CONTROL

*Epperson v. Arkansas*, 393 U.S. 97 (1968) is an example of constitutional protection for the free exercise of scientific speech. Arkansas had enacted an anti-evolution law prohibiting public school teachers from teaching "the theory or doctrine that mankind ascended or descended from a lower order of animals." In *Epperson*, the Supreme Court invalidated the Arkansas law because it "selects from the body of knowledge a particular segment which it proscribes for the sole reason that it is deemed to conflict with a particular religious doctrine."

*Edwards v. Aguillard*, 482 U.S. 578 (1987) went a step further and demonstrated the privileged position of scientific speech in the public schools. In *Aguillard*, the Supreme Court considered a Louisiana statute, "The Balanced Treatment for Creation–Science and Evolution Science in Public School Instruction Act." Under this legislation, if evolution was taught, creationism also had to be taught. This so-called "Creationism Act" was held unconstitutional on grounds that it lacked a valid secular purpose and was designed only to further a particular religious belief.

The state had argued that the purpose of the Act was to protect academic freedom by requiring that all the theories explaining the origin of humanity be presented if any are. While the Court acknowledged that deference to the state's articulated purposes normally is required, the avowed purpose must "be sincere and not a sham." Justice Brennan, for the Court in *Aguillard*, concluded that the preeminent purpose of Louisiana was to advance the religious view that a supernatural being created mankind.

Out of all the possible subjects in the curriculum, the legislature had chosen to legislate with respect to only one—the teaching of scientific evolution, a subject which, of course, was anathema to the creationists. The legislature had not required that all scientific theories concerning the origin of man be taught. Instead, it had mandated that creationism be sufficiently empowered so that it might do battle with "evolution." The legislature had sought to give advantages to the teaching of creationism that were not offered to the teaching of evolution, *e.g.*, the Act required that curricular guides be developed for teaching "creation science." Justice Brennan concluded in *Aguillard*: "The Act violated the Establishment Clause [b]ecause it seeks to employ the symbolic and financial support of government to achieve a religious purpose." See *Stone v. Graham*, 449 U.S. 39 (1980) [state statute requiring the posting of the Ten Commandments in public schools furthers only sectarian purposes, and hence violates the Establishment Clause].

Justice Scalia, joined by Chief Justice Rehnquist, dissented in *Aguillard* and challenged both the Court's application of the purpose inquiry as well as the validity of such an inquiry in the first place. The Act had set forth a legitimate secular purpose in promoting academic freedom and was supported by numerous individuals and groups, most of whom could by no means be characterized as religious fundamentalists. The Court had no basis for characterizing the secular purpose as a "sham" and disregarding it. Furthermore, the inquiry into purpose was itself objectionable. Under the Court's precedents, it was difficult or impossible to discern what in fact was a saving secular purpose.

## C.  GOVERNMENT ACKNOWLEDGEMENT OF RELIGION

The concept of a civic religion has found significant support in a class of cases which turn on the fact that they are perceived to represent an acknowledgement by the state of the place of religion in our society. Our coins bear the phrase, "In God We Trust." The pledge of allegiance to the flag includes the phrase, "One Nation Under God." The sessions of the United States House of Representatives and the United States Senate begin with an invocation given by a chaplain. Even the sessions of the Supreme Court begin with the Marshal saying, "oyez, oyez, oyez, God save the United States and this Honorable Court." Our government gives official acknowledgement to Christmas and Thanksgiving by making them national holidays in spite of their religious significance. When such government recognition of religion is challenged, the courts generally uphold the governmental practices of what are essentially religious ceremonies and displays by invoking history and tradition. The theory is that the sectarian aspects are subsumed by the secular values that can be marshalled to justify the practice.

The issue of the constitutionality of legislative prayer came to the Court in *Marsh v. Chambers*, 463 U.S. 783 (1983). The Nebraska legislature opened each day with a prayer offered by a chaplain who was paid from state funds. The Presbyterian minister who had been employed for eighteen years as the chaplain of the legislature composed nonsectarian Judaeo–Christian "prayers" reflecting "elements of the American civil religion." The Supreme Court, per Chief Justice Burger, upheld the practice against an Establishment Clause challenge without ever mentioning the *Lemon* test. Instead, the Court relied on the unique history of legislative prayer which dated back to the First Congress which had drafted the Establishment Clause.

The presence of a chaplain at the opening of a session of the legislature does not attract the attention of the entire community. What, however, about the display of a Nativity scene on the village green or in front of the city hall or, indeed, in the city hall? Responding to this issue, the Supreme Court has fashioned what is sometimes called the "reindeer rule." The existence of an Establishment Clause violation is made to turn on the overall context of the religious display. While a creche or a cross or a menorah standing alone might well constitute an establishment, the addition of a "reindeer" can save the religious display. Why should this be? As in *Marsh*, the answer lies in tradition and history.

*Lynch v. Donnelly*, 465 U.S. 668 (1984) upheld, 5–4, against an Establishment Clause challenge, the constitutional validity of a Christmas display. A display consisting of Santa Claus and his reindeer, a Christmas tree, and various other symbols of the season, was erected by the city of Pawtucket, Rhode Island, in a park owned by a non-profit organization. The inclusion of a creche, however, provoked litigation. Chief Justice Burger, for the Court, acknowledged that the wall of separation might be a useful figure of speech but asserted that it was not a wholly accurate description of church-state relationships. Chief Justice Burger observed: "Nor does the Constitution require complete separation of church and state; it affirmatively mandates accommodation, not merely tolerance, of all religions, and forbids hostility toward any."

Proceeding from this accommodationist premise, Chief Justice Burger, in drawing the line between an impermissible establishment and a permissible accommodation, acknowledged that the *Lemon* test can be useful. Nonetheless, *Lynch* evidenced that the future of the *Lemon* test was hardly secure by observing that the Court should not be confined to any single test in the sensitive area of religion. In *Lynch*, the Court applied *Lemon* with a focus on "the creche in the context of the Christmas season." Chief Justice Burger found a secular purpose in the city's desire to celebrate the Christmas holiday and to depict the origins of that holiday. The benefit to religion was deemed "indirect, remote and incidental." Finally, there was no excessive entanglement since there was no involvement of city authorities with church leaders concerning the display and minimal public funds were involved in its maintenance.

Writing for the four dissenters, Justice Brennan insisted there was a significant difference between recognizing Christmas day as a public holiday and government involvement in distinctively religious aspects of the holiday. Christmas as a national holiday is a permissible accommodation. Public display of a creche "places the prestige, power and financial support of a civil authority in the service of a particular faith." The student should note that Justice O'Connor, concurring, applied the endorsement test and found no violation of the Antiestablishment Clause. Justice Brennan, in dissent, on the other hand, found a clear endorsement of a particular faith in the public display of a creche. Clearly, the endorsement test is no panacea for the resolution of Establishment Clause issues.

Five years later, in *Allegheny County v. ACLU*, 492 U.S. 573 (1989), the Court was once again presented with the issue of religious holiday displays. The case involved two displays located on public property in downtown Pittsburgh. The case was controlled by the "reindeer rule" of *Lynch*. The first display, a creche placed on the Grand Staircase of the Allegheny County Courthouse, was held to be a violation of the Establishment Clause. The second display, located outside the city-county building, involving a Chanukah menorah accompanied by a Christmas tree and a sign saluting liberty, was held to be permissible under the Establishment Clause. Writing for the Court in *Allegheny County*, Justice Blackmun applied an endorsement test and held that the solitary creche unaccompanied by any other secular holiday symbols was an impermissible establishment. Joining him in this ruling were Justices O'Connor, Stevens, Brennan and Marshall. Unlike *Lynch*, nothing in the display detracted from the religious message of the Nativity scene. The essential teaching of *Lynch* was that "government may celebrate Christmas in some manner and form, but not in a way that endorses Christian doctrine." The solitary display of the creche was such an endorsement and, therefore, constituted a violation of the antiestablishment principle. Endorsement, it should be noted, was not used by Chief Justice Burger in the opinion for the Court in *Lynch*.

Justice Kennedy, joined by Chief Justice Rehnquist and Justices White and Scalia, dissented from the Court's holding that the creche display was unconstitutional. For these dissenters, there were two limiting principles that defined the line between permissible accommodation and impermissible establishment. First, "government may not coerce anyone to support or participate in any religion or its exercise." Second, government may not give direct benefits to religion to such a degree that it establishes a state religion or has a tendency to do so. This is a far more lenient establishment test than the *Lemon* test. Justice Kennedy combined these two limitations to formulate the following principle: "Non-coercive government action within the realm of flexible accommodation or passive acknowledgment of existing symbols does not violate the Establishment Clause unless it benefits religion in a way more direct and more substantial than practices that are accepted in our national heritage." Applying this principle to the creche, the dissenters concluded there was no establishment violation. The government's coercive power had not been used to further the interests of Christianity or

Judaism. No one was compelled to observe or participate in religious activity and no significant amount of tax money was used in support of a particular faith. The creche was only a passive symbol or a religious holiday which passersby could ignore if they chose. Nor was it an impermissible direct benefit to religion. *Lynch* was dispositive that a creche does not represent an effort to proselytize or constitute a first step to establish a state religion.

But what was the status of the menorah? For Justice Kennedy and the accommodationists who joined him, the creche and the menorah enjoy the same constitutional status: "Both are the traditional symbols of religious holidays that over time have acquired a secular component." Neither display involved coercion or a direct benefit to religion. In fact, a majority of the justices validated the city of Pittsburgh's menorah display. This result was obtained by a combination of the four accommodationists led by Justice Kennedy being joined by Justices Blackmun and O'Connor. For Justice Blackmun, it was not sufficiently likely that the residents of Pittsburgh would perceive tree, sign and menorah as an endorsement of a particular religious belief or disapproval of their own religious choices. Justice O'Connor reached a similar conclusion.

But for Justice Stevens, joined by Justices Brennan, and Marshall—the Court's fervent separationists—the antiestablishment principle created a strong presumption against any governmental display of religious symbols on public property. The city government had failed to take sufficient precautions to dilute the religious message of the menorah display: "The overall display manifests governmental approval of the Jewish and Christian religions." But in *Capitol Square Board v. Pinette*, 515 U.S. 753 (1995), the state was required to permit the Ku Klux Klan to erect a ten foot cross on a public square adjoining the State Capitol Building, *Allegheny County* was distinguished on the ground that the display of a privately-sponsored creche on the "Grand Staircase" of the county courthouse violated the Establishment Clause because the staircase, unlike the public square was not "open to all on an equal basis, so the County was *favoring* sectarian religious expression."

The difficult and divisive issue of whether displays of religious documents, symbols or monuments violated the Establishment Clause arose in two cases involving the Ten Commandments—cases where the court reached opposite results. *McCreary County v. ACLU*, 545 U.S. 844 (2005) involved two Kentucky counties which displayed large copies of the Ten Commandments on the walls of the county courthouse. In response to Establishment Clause challenges to the displays, the Counties twice enlarged the displays. The first display included eight smaller historical documents such as the Declaration of Independence but the focus of thee added displays was on the religious element in these documents. A federal district court entered a preliminary injunction against the enlarged displays because they lacked the secular purpose required by

*Lemon*. The counties then revised their displays to include nine framed documents of equal size; these included the King James Bible version of the Ten Commandments, the lyrics of the Star Spangled banner and the Declaration of Independence. The Court held, 5–4, per Justice Souter, that the displays violated the Establishment Clause. The argument of the Counties that only the last display should be considered was rejected. The context was crucial. A reasonable observer could not be expected to ignore the context in which the Ten Commandments display arose.

Rejecting a request to abandon *Lemon's* secular purpose prong, the Court ruled that where the predominant purpose of government actions was to advance religion, the central Establishment Clause precept of religious neutrality was violated. *Lemon's* secular purpose prong helped to assure government neutrality in matters concerning religion. The Court relied on *Stone v. Graham*, 449 U.S. 39 (1980) which held that a Ten Commandments display in a public school violated the Establishment Clause since the pre-eminent objective of the government's action had been religious in purpose. The government's claim of secular purpose is owed deference but courts have the responsibility to distinguish genuine claims from sham ones. In conclusion, Justice Souter declared that "the divisiveness of religion in current public life is inescapable." Therefore, it was essential to interpret the Establishment Clause to require neutrality on the part of government concerning matters of religious belief. *McCreary County v. ACLU*, 545 U.S. 844 (2005).

Justice O'Connor joined in the Court's opinion in *McCreary* but wrote a separate concurrence. A reasonable observer would view the Ten Commandments displays in the two Kentucky county courthouses as an "unmistakable message of endorsement" by government. The fact that many Americans shared the precepts proclaimed by the Ten Commandments was irrelevant. In an implicit rebuttal to Justice Scalia, she declared: "[W]e do not count heads before enforcing the First Amendment."

Justice Scalia, joined by Chief Justice Rehnquist and Justice Thomas and in part by Justice Kennedy, dissented. As he had done in earlier cases, Justice Scalia criticized the majority's result-oriented approach to the *Lemon* test. First, secular purpose was now to be analyzed by the way in which government action appeared to a reasonable observer. Second, a secular purpose must now predominate over any intention to advance religion. Justice Scalia asserted that the vast majority of believers in the United States were adherents of monotheistic religions: "[T]here is a distance between the acknowledgment of a single creator and establishment of a religion." Honoring the Ten Commandments was indistinguishable from "publicly honoring God." Neither practice should be understood as the endorsement of any particular religion.

In *Van Orden v. Perry*, 545 U.S. 677 (2005), the Court ruled on another governmental display of the Ten Commandments. This one involved a six foot monument on the grounds of the Texas state capitol grounds on which the Tenth Commandments was inscribed. Unlike *McCreary*, the Court rejected the Establishment Clause challenge and upheld the Ten Commandments monument display. Chief Justice Rehnquist, joined by Justices Scalia, Kennedy and Thomas, wrote the plurality opinion for the Court. Each of these Justices had been in dissent in *McCreary*. Chief Justice Rehnquist said that the government had an obligation to preserve separation between government and religion. But a policy of disfavoring religion would undermine the very neutrality which the Establishment Clause is designed to assure. The fact that a government display has some religious content or is consistent with religious doctrine does not in itself violate the Establishment Clause. There were sixteen other monuments on the state capitol grounds as well as 21 historical markers. Unlike *Stone v. Graham*, 449 U.S. 39 (1980), where public schools were confronted on a daily basis with the Ten Commandments display, the Texas state capitol Ten Commandments monument constituted a far more passive use.

The decisive vote in *Van Orden* was cast by Justice Breyer's concurring opinion; he declined to join the plurality and concurred only in the result. Breyer declared that the Texas state capitol Ten Commandments monument communicated both a religious and a secular message. But the secular message was the predominant one. The monument was one of many on the capitol grounds and was simply a way of illustrating the variety of values which have influenced the history and citizenry of Texas. The monument had stood on the capitol grounds for forty years without attracting controversy or challenge. This was quite different than the court house displays in Kentucky whose history disclosed a governmental purpose to promote religion. A contrary result would lead to the removal of Ten Commandments displays from government buildings throughout the nation. The consequence of such wholesale removal would be to stimulate that religious divisiveness which the Establishment Clause sought to prevent.

Justice Stevens, joined by Justice Ginsburg, dissenting, contended that the Establishment Clause "has created a strong presumption against the display of religious symbols on public property." Allowing government to use the state capital to disseminate a religious monotheistic message makes non-monotheists and nonbelievers outsiders in the national polity. The guiding principle should be neutrality "between religion and irreligion." To permit government to display religious texts such as the Ten Commandments mocks the neutrality principle. Justice Souter, joined by Justices Stevens and Ginsburg also dissented. Souter did not accept that the Ten Commandments monument should be viewed as simply one of many monuments on the 22 acres of state capitol grounds. Anyone walking on the state capitol grounds would surely consider each monument on its own. Contrary to the contention of the plurality, *Stone v. Graham* was not a less passive use of the Ten Commandments. Certainly, it was true public school children in *Stone* were compelled to see the Ten Commandments display every day and walkers on the state capitol grounds could avoid them if they chose. But citizens should be able to visit the state capitol without having to confront religious displays intended to espouse an "official religious position." Justice O'Connor dissented for reasons stated by Justice Souter's dissent and in her concurrence in *McCreary.*

How does one reconcile *McCreary's* holding that a Ten Commandments display in a county courthouse violated the Establishment Clause with *Van Orden's* holding that a six foot Ten Commandments monument on state capitol grounds does not? A harmonizing approach perhaps can be found by focusing on the critical significance of context. Justice Breyer who was the only Justice who took a different stance on the constitutionality of government displays of the Ten Commandments in each case said these cases were peculiarly fact specific. Inquiry should be directed to whether government was promoting religion by the display or whether the particular religious symbol or document at issue was simply one of many acknowledgments by government of symbols and documents that had influenced the life of the state or nation.

## D.  RELATED ESTABLISHMENT
## CLAUSE PROBLEMS

### 1.  TAXATION AND TAX EXEMPTIONS

Government can aid religion not only by providing direct support or acknowledgement but also by relieving religious institutions of tax burdens. *Walz v. Tax Comm'n*, 397 U.S. 664 (1970) dealt with a New York law providing a tax exemption for real property used for religious, educational or charitable purposes. In *Walz*, the Court, per Chief Justice Burger, upheld the tax exemption for real property used for religious purposes against an Establishment Clause challenge. For the Court, the tax exemption was a form of benevolent neutrality: "The legislative purpose of a property tax exemption is neither the advancement nor the inhibition of religion; it is neither sponsorship nor hostility." *Walz* found that the "exemption creates only a minimal and remote involvement between church and state." The long and deeply entrenched history of tax exemptions for religious property in the United States demonstrated that such benefits do not involve excessive sponsorship of religion. Further, the likelihood of entanglement of the state in the affairs of religion was in fact minimized by the tax exemption for religious property. If religious property was exempt from taxation, government would have no need to assess the property, impose tax liens or foreclose for non-payment, or dispute with religious officials on the appropriate measure of taxation.

The significance of the breadth of the tax exemption provided in *Walz* was perhaps not fully comprehended until Justice Brennan's opinion for the Court in *Texas Monthly, Inc. v. Bullock*, 489 U.S. 1 (1989) made the breadth of the exemption the dispositive factor. Texas had exempted religious periodicals from a general sales and use tax. The publisher of a general interest magazine not entitled to the exemption successfully challenged it on establishment grounds. Justice Brennan, for a plurality of the Court, concluded that the state tax exemption lacked sufficient breadth to pass Establishment Clause scrutiny: "Insofar as [a tax exemption or subsidy] is conferred on a wide array of non-sectarian groups as well as religious organizations in pursuit of some legitimate secular end, the fact that religious groups benefit incidentally does not deprive the subsidy of the secular purpose and primary effect mandated by the Establishment Clause."

In short, the outcome in *Walz* was explained by the fact that the tax exemption there was not directed to religion alone but encompassed a wide array of non-profit organizations. On the other hand, the Texas law, represented special legislation for the benefit of religion. In sum, the Texas tax exemption for religious periodicals was impermissible state sponsorship of religious belief. Justice Scalia, joined by Chief Justice Rehnquist and Justice Kennedy, dissented. They argued that *Walz* was "utterly dispositive" of *Bullock*. Scalia denied that *Walz* had rested on the breadth of the exemption.

Rather, the Court had stressed the danger of government hostility to religion, represented by the opportunity to tax religious institutions. *Walz* had concluded that tax exemptions for religion such as those involved in *Bullock* were a reasonable and balanced accommodation of religion by government.

*Walz* and *Bullock* involved the validity of governmentally conferred tax exemptions. *Hernandez v. C.I.R.*, 490 U.S. 680 (1989) involved the validity of the *refusal* to grant a tax exemption. The I.R.S. had ruled that payments made by members of the Church of Scientology to the church for auditing sessions to enhance spiritual awareness did not qualify as charitable contributions; the payments involved the purchase of services rather than contributions. The church argued that the ruling was an unconstitutional denominational preference since it imposed a disproportionate burden on religions that raise funds by charging for participation in certain religious practices.

The Supreme Court, per Justice Marshall, rejected the Establishment Clause claim. But what of *Larson v. Valente*, 456 U.S. 228 (1982)? There the Court had struck down a tax scheme that imposed a disproportionate burden on certain nontraditional religions. Justice Marshall reasoned that the state statute in *Larson* drew "explicit and deliberate distinctions between different religious organizations." The I.R.S. ruling in *Hernandez*, on the other hand, applied to all religious entities and involved no denominational preference. *Hernandez* held that the I.R.S. ruling passed constitutional muster under the

*Lemon* test. The government action was neutral in design and purpose. Nor was there a significant danger of excessive entanglement even though the I.R.S. was required to examine church practices and financing: "[R]outine regulatory interaction which involves no inquiries into religious doctrine, no delegation of state power to a religious body, and no 'detailed monitoring and close administrative contact' between secular and religious bodies, does not of itself violate the nonentanglement command."

Another case involving *refusal* on the part of the state to grant a tax exemption to a religious group was *Jimmy Swaggart Ministries v. Board of Equalization*, 493 U.S. 378 (1990). The Court held that application of the California sales and use tax to religious materials sold by the Jimmy Swaggart Ministries did not violate the Establishment Clause. Applying the *Lemon* test, the Court concluded that the taxes were neutral and non-discriminatory regarding religion or religious belief. Nor was there an excessive entanglement of church and state. The materials were subject to the tax without the need for any state inquiry into the content of the materials or the motive of the parties involved in the sale.

## 2.   SABBATH DAY OBSERVANCE LAWS

A subject that was at one time a matter of greater controversy in constitutional litigation than it is today is Sunday blue laws. These laws, prohibiting certain kinds of business activity on Sunday, have been challenged on both establishment and free exercise grounds. Those observing a day other than Sunday as their religious day of observance and rest argued that the Sunday blue laws subjected them to an economic burden. Those observing Sunday had to close on that day. But Sabbath observing members of minority religions had to close because of blue laws on Sunday by state decree and on yet another day because of their faith. The Establishment Clause challenge was grounded on at least two concerns. First, such laws constitute an impermissible government preference for the dominant religion consisting of Sunday observers. Second, Sunday blue laws constitute an invalid government benefit favoring religion over non-religion. Both the Establishment and Free Exercise Clause challenges to Sunday blue laws failed.

In *McGowan v. Maryland*, 366 U.S. 420 (1961), Chief Justice Warren, for the Court, rejected an Establishment Clause challenge to a Sunday closing law. Warren acknowledged that blue laws were originally motivated by religious considerations, but he concluded: "The present purpose and effect of most of them is to provide a uniform day of rest for all citizens." Whatever the original purpose of blue laws, today they clearly have a secular purpose. Not every law which allows a worshiper to pursue his religious beliefs on a particular day will withstand Establishment Clause scrutiny. In *Estate of Thornton v. Caldor, Inc.*, 472 U.S. 703 (1985), the Court held that a Connecticut law providing employees with an absolute right not to work on their chosen Sabbath violated the antiestablishment guarantee.

Chief Justice Burger took direct aim at what he considered the primary religious purpose and effect of the Connecticut law. An employee who seeks a day off from his employer for compelling, although secular, reasons can be denied, but the Sabbath observer cannot. The machinery of the state may not be so harnessed to facilitate the religious convictions of a favored group.

But the separationist perspective reflected in *Estate of Thornton* should be contrasted with the accommodationist perspective reflected in *Corporation of the Presiding Bishop of the Church of Jesus Christ of Latter–Day Saints v. Amos*, 483 U.S. 327 (1987). In *Amos*, an employee of the Mormon Church filed a Title VII action alleging religious discrimination in employment. The employee was discharged as a building engineer (a non-religious job), for a gymnasium operated by the Mormon church because of his failure to follow the precepts of the Mormon Church. Title VII exempts from its prohibition against religious discrimination employee discharges by religious organizations. The Supreme Court declared that the Title VII exemption for religious organizations was not a violation of the Establishment Clause.

Justice White refused to hold that *Lemon* required the invalidation of the exemption because of its religious purpose: "Under the *Lemon* analysis, it is a permissible legislative purpose to alleviate significant governmental interference with the ability of religious organizations to define and carry out their religious missions." Nor did the accommodation reflected by the exemption fail the second, or primary effect, requirement of *Lemon*: "For a law to have 'forbidden effects' under *Lemon*, it must be fair to say that the government itself has advanced religion through its own activities and influence." The government exemption for religion in Title VII relieved religion of a burden imposed on it by government itself. Therefore, the exemption was not a government conferred benefit on religion but simply a removal of a government imposed burden. Unlike *Thornton*, the state had not legally required the employee or the employer to take any action; it simply removed a burden from the employer. Nor did the statutory exemption present an entanglement problem. Indeed, the exemption effected a more complete separation of church and state and made unnecessary an intrusive inquiry into religious beliefs.

### 3.  ESTABLISHMENT CLAUSE MISCELLANY

The theme that the machinery of the state cannot be put at the service of religion was sounded again in *Larkin v. Grendel's Den, Inc.*, 459 U.S. 116 (1982). In *Larkin*, the Court employed *Lemon* in invalidating a law barring the granting of liquor licenses to establishments within 500 feet of a church or school if these institutions objected. The practical effect of the law was to give religious institutions an absolute veto over a state function— the distribution of liquor licenses. The state cannot delegate its zoning powers to religious institutions.

While the state law in *Larkin* had a secular purpose of protecting spiritual and educational centers from the hurly-burly accompanying liquor outlets, the law had a primary effect of advancing religion. There was no assurance that the power given by the law to religious institutions would be used in a religiously neutral way, There was a danger that a religious institution could use the powers provided by the statute for "explicitly religious goals." Further, "the mere appearance of a joint exercise of legislative authority by church and state provides a significant symbolic benefit to religion in the minds of some by reason of the power conferred." *Larkin* struck down a law which fused government and religious functions. This was accomplished by delegating "important, discretionary, governmental powers" to religious entities. The consequence was an excessive entanglement of government and religion.

*Larkin's* principles were re-affirmed in *Board of Education of Kiryas Joel v. Grumet*, 512 U.S. 687 (1994), a case involving the the Village of Kiryas Joel in New York state. The villagers were Satmar Hasidim, a strict sect within Orthodox Judaism, who educated their children in private religious schools in the village. But these schools did not offer the special education services that handicapped children need and to which, under state and federal law, they are entitled even if enrolled in private schools. Kiryas Joel children requiring special ed services were required to attend public school outside the village. This arrangement was unsatisfactory to their parents who said the exposure of their children to the unfamiliar secular public schools outside the village caused them to suffer " 'panic, fear and trauma.' " In 1989, a state law took Kiryas Joel out of the school district to which it had belonged and created a new separate school district, which now mirrored the village boundaries. The newly created Kiryas Joel School District only offered a special ed program. The non-handicapped Kiryas Joel children remained in their parochial schools.

New York state taxpayers successfully challenged the law making Kiryas Joel a separate school district as a violation of the Establishment Clause. Under *Larkin,* the 1989 law constituted a prohibited fusion of government and religious functions and went beyond permissible accommodation. The law granted civil power to an electorate defined by a shared religion and did so in a manner that did not "foreclose religious favoritism." There was no assurance that the "next group seeking a school district of its own" would obtain it. An allocation of political power by the state on the basis of a religious criterion lacks the requisite "government impartiality toward religion." *Board of Education of Kiryas Joel v. Grumet,* 512 U.S. 687 (1994).

The claim that a federal statute, the Adolescent Family Life Act (AFLA), was a facially unconstitutional advancement of religion violative of the Establishment Clause was rejected, 5–4, in *Bowen v. Kendrick,* 487 U.S. 589 (1988). The AFLA authorizes federal grants to public and private agencies, including religious organizations, to provide research, services and counseling in adolescent sexuality and pregnancy. Chief Justice Rehnquist for the *Kendrick* Court acknowledged that some of the objectives of the AFLA coincided with the approach taken by certain religions. This did not mean that the AFLA was motivated by religious concerns: "AFLA was motivated primarily, if not entirely, by a legitimate secular purpose—the elimination or reduction of social and economic problems caused by teenage sexuality, pregnancy, and parenthood."

Nor did the inclusion of religious organizations as potential grantees make the primary effect of the law the advancement of religion. Congress could reasonably recognize that religious organizations influence values and family life, thereby making them appropriate grant recipients, given the purposes of the Act. Any benefit to religion was "incidental and remote." The potential risk that public aid would be used for religious purposes "is undercut by the AFLA's facially neutral grant requirements, the wide spectrum of public and private organizations which are capable of meeting the AFLA's requirements, and the fact that, of the eligible religious institutions, many will not deserve the label of 'pervasively sectarian.' " The student should note that some of the themes used by Chief Justice Rehnquist in this passage mirror those employed by the Court in the past in applying *Lemon* in reviewing government financial aid to religious schools. The aid is given to a broad range of organizations, not simply to religious institutions. Further, like private colleges and universities, and unlike parochial elementary and secondary schools, the grantees are not necessarily pervasively religious. Finally, the type of grant monitoring connected with the AFLA did not threaten any excessive entanglement of church and state.

Indeed, the minimal monitoring involved in the use of the AFLA grant funds was what drew the ire of the four dissenters. There was nothing that would prevent the federal monies from being used to further the religious beliefs of the religious grantees regarding sexuality and parenthood. Speaking for the dissenters, Justice Blackmun stated: "Whatever Congress had in mind, it enacted a statute that facilitated, and, indeed, encouraged the use of public funds for [religious] instruction, by giving religious groups a central pedagogical and counseling role without imposing any restraints on the sectarian quality of the participation." Chief Justice Rehnquist responded to this critique by noting that if grants were used to advance religious objectives or flowed to pervasively sectarian institutions, such grants might be unconstitutional as applied. But this did not render the AFLA facially invalid. Indeed, the Supreme Court remanded the case to see if the AFLA was invalid on an "as applied" basis.

A final factual context generating Establishment Clause problems should be noted. Courts are often asked to intervene in internal church disputes. One group of church members may seek to oust another group on the ground it is faithless to the true precepts of the particular denomination. Generally, the courts decline to mediate such disputes since decisions may well turn on inquiries into religious doctrine. Such inquiries are inappropriate for secular courts governed by the principles of the Establishment Clause. On the other hand, if an intra-church dispute can be resolved simply by the application of "neutral principles of law" which do not involve an inquiry into religious doctrine, the Establishment Clause will be no bar to judicial resolution of the dispute. *Jones v. Wolf*, 443 U.S. 595 (1979) [state court could decide which group should control church property as a consequence of a schism within the church].

## E.   THE ESTABLISHMENT CLAUSE TODAY

History and tradition are increasingly employed, especially by accommodationists, to validate measures that might be clearly viewed as religious if governmental practice were to embrace them today for the first time. It must be conceded that it is often difficult in particular fact contexts to predict in advance the outcome of a present day Establishment Clause case. None of the so-called tests provides anything remotely resembling a bright line. Further, there is a tension that exists between accommodationists and separationists on the Court. Finally, the positions of the justices are not static; each justice apparently has a different breaking point.

The *Lemon* test is clearly showing signs of mortality. In a concurrence in *Lamb's Chapel,* Justice Scalia likened *Lemon* to "some ghoul in a late-night horror movie" which "stalks our Establishment Clause jurisprudence." Justice White responded to the attack on *Lemon* by observing that "*Lemon,* however frightening it might be to some, has not been overruled." This remains true. *Lemon,* venerable but not venerated, still survives but it now has formidable rivals in the coercion, endorsement and neutrality tests.

The cases in this chapter demonstrate the ferment in contemporary Establishment Clause doctrine. At various times, justices invoke the *Lemon* test, the endorsement refinement of *Lemon*, or the coercion test. All these tests in varying degrees have weakened the strict separationist position exemplified in the wall of separation metaphor. While the Court has been unwilling to adopt the narrow view limiting the Establishment Clause to a ban on denominational preferences, it has been increasingly willing to accept state support of religion as a permissible accommodation.

# CHAPTER XVI

## THE FREE EXERCISE CLAUSE

The First Amendment provides that "Congress shall make no law ... prohibiting the free exercise" of religion. What constitutes a prohibition of free exercise? The answer to this question is as uncertain as what constitutes an establishment of religion. Can government regulate religious belief and opinion? In regulating conduct, can government require an individual to perform acts that his religion prohibits? Can government prohibit her from engaging in conduct required by her religious beliefs? If government offers benefits to citizens generally, can it impose conditions to receipt of the benefits which a religious adherent cannot meet consistent with his religious beliefs? If government voluntarily undertakes to benefit religion by removing burdens on free exercise, does this violate the Establishment Clause? These are the questions that perplex the student of the Free Exercise Clause. The problems raised by these questions provides the content for the present chapter.

As we shall see, once again separationists and accommodationists vie for dominance. In the free exercise context, however, the lines become even more uncertain. Accommodationists are divided. Is it appropriate for the courts to fashion constitutionally-required religious exemptions from general laws? Some advocates of religious accommodation argue that exemptions from hardships created by religious objections to conforming to general laws must come from the legislature. The Free Exercise Clause does not authorize judicial excusal of religious objectors from conformity to a religiously neutral law.

The judicial response to the Free Exercise Clause has changed markedly over the years. First, there was a distinction drawn between belief/opinion and conduct that made the Free Exercise Clause largely irrelevant to the practice of religion. Then, beginning in the 1960s, the judicial focus turned to the nature and severity of the burden imposed on religious conduct. At times, the Court distinguished between direct and indirect burdens but ultimately largely abandoned this conceptualist distinction. Increasingly, the Court focused on whether the state had a compelling justification for any significant burden imposed on religion, whether direct or indirect. Finally, starting in 1990, the Court came almost full circle and returned to the principle that an incidental burden on religious conduct imposed by a religiously neutral law normally does not require any special compelling justification by the state. General laws designed to achieve secular objectives will not violate the Free Exercise Clause simply because they significantly burden religious conduct.

A precondition for invoking the Free Exercise Clause depends on showing that it is a religion or religious belief that is burdened. Further, the claim for protection of free exercise is dependent on the ability of the claimant to establish that his religious belief is sincerely held. Courts have been willing to probe the sincerity of the religious claim in determining the burden on free exercise. Courts have been willing in the past to inquire into the centrality of a belief or practice to a religion in assessing the free exercise claim. See *Wisconsin v. Yoder*, 406 U.S. 205 (1972). But, more recently, the Court stated: "It is no more appropriate for judges to determine the 'centrality' of religious belief before applying a 'compelling interest' test in the free exercise field, than it would be for them to determine the 'importance' of an idea before applying the 'compelling interest' in the free speech field." *Employment Div. v. Smith*, 494 U.S. 872 (1990) (*Smith II*). While judicial probes of sincerity or centrality have been, in the past, deemed permissible, inquiries into the truth or falsity of the claimant's religious beliefs are not. *United States v. Ballard*, 322 U.S. 78 (1944) [jury should not be allowed to consider the truth or falsity of the religious claims of two persons accused of mail fraud that they had spoken with Jesus and were delegated by St. Germain to serve as divine messengers to provide cures for the sick].

## A. BELIEF/OPINION OR CONDUCT

A number of early cases drew a distinction between religious belief/opinion which was protected by the Free Exercise Clause and government regulation of religious conduct which was subject to regulation in spite of the guarantee. The early free exercise cases limited the Free Exercise Clause to little more than protection of religious belief or opinion; religious conduct could be regulated on the same basis as any other conduct.

In *Reynolds v. United States*, 98 U.S. 145 (1878), Reynolds, a Utah Mormon, was charged with violating a federal law prohibiting polygamy. Reynolds' defense that his conduct was protected by the Free Exercise Clause was rejected. Chief Justice Waite, for the Court, drew a sharp distinction between protected belief/opinion and the conduct of polygamy: "Congress was deprived of all legislative power over mere opinion, but was left free to reach actions which were in violation of social duties or subversive of good order. Laws are made for the government of actions, and while they cannot interfere with mere religious beliefs and opinions, they may with practices." *Reynolds* indicated that regardless of the burden that government regulation might impose on the religious adherent, the Free Exercise Clause was not violated if the regulation did not interfere with religious belief or opinion. As far as Chief Justice Waite was concerned, Reynolds could believe in polygamy but he could not practice it. It has been said that "*Reynolds* drained the free exercise clause of its primary constitutional function. As long as the state's prohibition on non-speech actions reflected a secular policy, the *Reynolds* view of free exercise permitted no exemptions from that policy for those actions motivated by religion. *Reyn-*

*olds'* belief-action distinction thus reduced the free exercise clause to a primarily rhetorical commitment to protecting religious liberty." Lupu, *Where Rights Begin: The Problem of Burdens on the Free Exercise of Religion*, 102 Harv. L. Rev. 933 (1989).

In some cases in the pre-Warren Court era, however, religious conduct was protected as an exercise of freedom of speech and association. During this early period, the free speech law was richer than the free exercise law. In *West Virginia State Board of Education v. Barnette*, 319 U.S. 624 (1943), Justice Jackson, for the Court, held that the state could not, consistent with the First Amendment, require public school children to salute the flag if it violated their beliefs: "[The government action] invades the sphere of intellect and spirit which it is the purpose of the First Amendment to our Constitution to reserve from all official control." The guarantees of freedom of speech—at least absent grave and immediate danger—extended constitutional protection to religiously inspired conduct at a time during which there was doubt about whether the free exercise clause could provide meaningful protection for such conduct.

Even in the 1940s there were signs of an increasing judicial sensitivity to the potential importance of the burden on religion in reviewing legislative action under the Free Exercise Clause. In *Cantwell v. Connecticut*, 310 U.S. 296 (1940), the Court reversed the conviction of some Jehovah's Witnesses for soliciting religious contributions without a license on both free speech and free exercise grounds.

The Court held for the first time that the Due Process Clause of the Fourteenth Amendment embraced the free exercise guarantee of the First Amendment and was binding on the states. At one point in *Cantwell*, the Court strikes the theme sounded in *Reynolds*—religious belief, which is absolutely protected, is to be distinguished from conduct, which is subject to regulation for the protection of society. However, *Cantwell* concludes by saying that the state's power to regulate conduct must "be so exercised as not, in attaining a permissible end, unduly to infringe the protected freedom [*i.e.*, free exercise]."

## B.  DIRECT OR INDIRECT BURDENS

As discussed earlier, Sunday closing laws pose not only Establishment Clause problems but Free Exercise Clause concerns as well. Just as in *McGowan v. Maryland*, 366 U.S. 420 (1961), the Court upheld a Sunday closing law against Establishment Clause challenge, the Court rejected a free exercise challenge to a Sunday closing law in *Braunfeld v. Brown*, 366 U.S. 599 (1961). Chief Justice Warren's plurality opinion in *Braunfeld* drew a sharp distinction between direct burdens on religious conduct and indirect burdens. A direct burden such as prohibiting conduct mandated by the religion, or requiring conduct prohibited by the religion, posed especially severe free exercise problems. In such cases, Chief Justice Warren declared, "accommodation between the religious action and an exercise of state authority is a particularly delicate task because resolution in favor of the State results in the choice to the individual of either abandoning his religious principle or facing criminal prosecution."

The burden imposed by Sunday closing laws did not make any religious practice unlawful. No one was compelled to be open on Sunday. Instead, the burden was only indirect. It was true that those who observe Saturday as their Sabbath were required because of their faith to close on Saturday and because of the state to close on Sunday. But this was not the doing of the state but of the religious adherent's choice. It was the indirect effect of the Sunday closing law. It might work an economic hardship if the Saturday Sabbath observer chose to close for two days during the seven day week, but this was only an indirect effect of the Sunday closing law. Chief Justice Warren acknowledged that even an indirect burden on free exercise would be constitutionally invalid if the purpose or effect of the law was to impede religion or to discriminate invidiously between religions: "But if the State regulates conduct by enacting a general law within its power, the purpose and effect of which, is to advance the state's secular goals, the statute is valid despite its indirect burden on religious observance unless the State may accomplish its purpose by means which do not impose such a burden."

Chief Justice Warren relied on *Cantwell* for this minimalist limitation on the state's power to enact reasonable legislation designed to achieve secular objectives. *Braunfeld* rejects any argument that the state is constitutionally required to carve out an exemption from a religiously neutral law for the benefit of those whose objections to the law arise from the fact that their Sabbath is a day different than Sunday. On the other hand, Justice Stewart in dissent argued that the state could not constitutionally force a non-Sunday observer to a "cruel choice" between his "religious faith and his economic survival." In a separate dissent, Justice Brennan stressed the "substantial, though indirect" burden on the individual's free exercise of religion. The interest of the state in having everyone rest on the same day, he argued, was inadequate to qualify as a "grave and immediate danger to interests the state may lawfully protect."

The *Braunfeld* Court had merely substituted one conceptualistic distinction for another. It abandoned the simplistic dichotomy between religious belief/opinion and religious conduct that yielded so little free exercise protection for religious conduct. In its place, it substituted a new formalism of direct versus indirect burdens. The state was subject only to marginal limitations flowing from the Free Exercise Clause when it imposed indirect burdens on religious conduct. As long as the state used reasonable means to achieve secular objectives, and there were no alternatives that would achieve the same end as effectively, state regulation was valid regardless of the severity of the indirect burden on religion. The dissents of Justices Brennan and Stewart in *Braunfeld*, however, had suggested a new direction for free exercise adjudication.

## C.   THE REIGN OF COMPELLING INTEREST ANALYSIS

In 1963, the Supreme Court charted a new path in Free Exercise Clause jurisprudence—a path that rejected the formalistic distinction between direct and indirect burdens. In *Sherbert v. Verner*, 374 U.S. 398 (1963), the Court, per Justice Brennan, held that the state could not constitutionally deny unemployment compensation benefits to an otherwise eligible individual, a Seventh–Day Adventist, simply because she refused to work on Saturday, the Sabbath day of her faith. Justice Brennan began from the premise that the fact that the burden was only indirect was "only the beginning not the end" of analysis. Instead, what was critical was the severity of the burden. The complainant was forced to choose between following the precepts of her faith or forfeiting critical unemployment benefits. It did not matter that such benefits are characterized as a privilege rather than a right since the state cannot condition the receipt of government benefits on the surrender of constitutional rights. The critical factor was that the state had imposed an unconstitutional condition. The availability of benefits depended upon the religious believer's "willingness to violate a cardinal principle of her religious faith [which] effectively penalizes the free exercise of her constitutional liberties." In short, the state had imposed a significant burden on the exercise of a fundamental right. On this ground *Braunfeld* was arguably distinguishable since *Braunfeld* did not involve the loss of a government benefit as the price of free exercise. As far as the state was concerned, the religious adherent in *Braunfeld* was free to close on Saturday. But in *Sherbert* the state exacted a penalty—the loss of unemployment compensation—for the exercise of that choice.

Having found that the state statute in *Sherbert* represented a significant burden on a fundamental right, Justice Brennan faced the next question: Could the state justify this burden? He concluded that it could not. The *Sherbert* Court was not satisfied that the law before it reasonably served a secular state interest. Instead, Justice Brennan indicated that the government must demonstrate a "compelling state interest" and that "no alternative forms of regulation" would be sufficient to satisfy that state interest. Even if the state were able to establish its interests in avoiding the filing of fraudulent claims by persons feigning religious objection to Saturday work, there was no showing that alternative forms of regulations were not available to combat such abuses. Today we call this exacting mode of analysis the strict scrutiny standard of review.

Nor did Establishment Clause concerns preclude judicial recognition of a free exercise-based exemption from the state unemployment compensation law. The state was merely equalizing the treatment of Saturday observers with those who observe Sunday as the Sabbath. In this respect, the Court's action "reflects nothing more than the governmental obligation of neutrality in the face of religious difference, and does not represent that involvement of religious with secular institutions which it is the object of the Establishment Clause to forestall." *Sherbert* effectively held that the constitutional guarantee of free exercise requires the state to provide an exemption from a generally applicable law.

*Sherbert* was to provide the controlling precedent for a line of decisions involving government benefits in which the Court invoked the strict scrutiny standard of review. Indiana's denial of unemployment compensation to a Jehovah's Witness who voluntarily quit his job because of his religious belief was set aside in *Thomas v. Review Board of Indiana Employment Sec. Div.*, 450 U.S. 707 (1981). Thomas quit because he was required to work on armaments and he believed his religion forbade participation in such work. The state refused to pay him unemployment benefits and ruled that he quit because of personal philosophical convictions rather than religious belief. Even though many Jehovah's Witnesses did not share his views about working on armaments, the religious sincerity of his belief was accepted by the Supreme Court. Chief Justice Burger, for the Court, acknowledged that Indiana had not compelled any violation of Thomas's religious conviction. But, as in *Sherbert*, the indirect character of the burden only began the inquiry. Even though the law was religiously neutral on its face, it unduly burdened the free exercise of religion: "Where the State conditions receipt of an important benefit upon conduct proscribed by a religious faith, or where it denies such a benefit because of conduct mandated by religious belief, thereby putting substantial pressure on an adherent to modify his behavior and to violate his beliefs, a burden upon religion exists. While the compulsion may be indirect, the infringement upon free exercise is nonetheless substantial."

Just as in *Sherbert*, the state had coerced Thomas in the free exercise of his religion. Having found a substantial burden on free exercise, Chief Justice Burger considered whether an exemption accommodating religion was required. In this instance, the state could not meet the compelling state interest standard. First, there was no evidence in the record indicating that granting an exemption based on religious belief would produce widespread unemployment. Second, no evidence indicated that employers would engage in detailed inquiries into the religious beliefs of job applicants.

Finally, as in *Sherbert*, the *Thomas* Court denied that recognizing an exemption would foster a religious faith in violation of the Establishment Clause. Indeed, any incidental benefit to religion by granting an exemption to the general unemployment compensation law only reflected the tension between the two religion clauses. The state must seek neutrality—neither advancing nor inhibiting religion. Only Justice Rehnquist in dissent in *Thomas* reached for a theme that ultimately—as demonstrated by *Employment Division v. Smith*, 494 U.S. 872 (1990) (*Smith II*)—was going to become dominant. "Where, as here, a State has enacted a general statute the purpose and effect of which is to advance the State's secular goals, the Free Exercise Clause does not require the State to conform that statute to the dictates of religious conscience of any group."

The accommodationist theme of *Sherbert* and *Thomas* which recognized an exemption for religious dissidents from general law, absent compelling justification, was carried forward in *Hobbie v. Unemployment Appeals Comm'n*, 480 U.S. 136 (1987). Denial of unemployment compensation to a Seventh–Day Adventist who was discharged because she refused to work certain scheduled hours on Friday night and Saturday because of a sincerely religious belief was set aside. Further, it did not matter that the claimant had embraced her Seventh–Day Adventist faith after she commenced the employment at issue. The fundamental point was the Seventh–Day Adventist claimant was still confronted with the constitutionally impermissible coercive choice between faith and employment struck down in *Sherbert*.

*Hobbie* reaffirmed the compelling interest analysis standard set forth in *Sherbert* and *Thomas*. The Florida Unemployment Appeals Commission in *Hobbie* had argued for a less demanding "reasonableness" standard articulated a year earlier by Chief Justice Burger for a plurality in *Bowen v. Roy*, 476 U.S. 693 (1986). The state in *Hobbie* failed to meet the requirements of this more exacting standard. See *Frazee v. Illinois Dept. of Emp. Sec.*, 489 U.S. 829 (1989) [holding that a state denial of unemployment benefits to a worker who refused a job because of his belief that, as a Christian, he could not work on Sunday as the job requires, violates the Free Exercise Clause].

The principle that the Free Exercise Clause at times constitutionally requires an exemption from general law was re-affirmed in *Wisconsin v. Yoder*, 406 U.S. 205 (1972). *Yoder* did not arise in the context of state-conferred benefits such as unemployment compensation, but in a challenge to a Wisconsin law mandating compulsory school attendance until age sixteen. The Amish community living in Wisconsin withdrew children from school at the end of the eighth grade. Wisconsin convicted members of the Amish Church of violating its mandatory school attendance law and they were fined $5 each. The Supreme Court, per Chief Justice Burger, overturned these convictions and recognized the First Amendment claim of the Amish that they were entitled to an exemption from the general school attendance law. Unlike previous cases, the burden on the religious practices of the Amish was severe and inescapable. This was the kind of objective danger the Free Exercise Clause was designed to prevent. The Amish must either abandon their beliefs and suffer assimilation or leave Wisconsin. While acknowledging the Establishment Clause danger of creating "an exception from a general obligation of citizenship on religious grounds," the Chief Justice concluded that an exception was required in the present case.

*Yoder* set forth a standard of review which is capable of being interpreted as employing the compelling state interest or strict scrutiny analysis. In fact, however, the *Yoder* decision spoke more obliquely: "[O]nly those interests of the highest order and those not otherwise served can overbalance legitimate claims to the free exercise of religion." The state's asserted interest in developing educated citizens capable of participating in democratic society and in preparing self-reliant and self-sufficient individuals did not justify the burden on the Amish. The Chief Justice stressed the success of the Amish in developing productive and law-abiding members of society. The possibility that Amish children might someday be ill-equipped to enter the larger world as a result of exempting them from the Wisconsin law was deemed to be speculative. Nor was there any evidence that recognizing the primary right of the parents to make decisions regarding the education of their children would jeopardize the health and safety of the children or impose any significant social burden.

The invocation of strict scrutiny does not necessarily mean that an exemption from a general law will always be constitutionally required. At times, the state is able to demonstrate that a compelling justification for denying such an exemption exists. Despite *Yoder*, for example, the Amish have not secured a permanent exemption from general laws. *United States v. Lee*, 455 U.S. 252 (1982) upheld the social security tax against the free exercise-based refusal of an Amish employer to participate in the social security system on behalf of his employees. Chief Justice Burger, for the Court, acknowledged the sincerity of Lee's religious beliefs but observed that not all burdens on religious liberty are unconstitutional: "The State may justify a limitation on religious liberty by showing that it is essential to accomplish an overriding governmental interest." Applying this standard, the Court held that the government had justified its refusal to grant an exemption. Mandatory and continuous participation by all employers in contributing to the social security system was vital to its operation and provided the requisite "overriding governmental interest." Indeed, the social security system would be placed in jeopardy if it were to become studded with exceptions. *Yoder* was distinguished: "[I]t would be difficult to accommodate the comprehensive social security system with myriad exceptions flowing from a wide variety of religious beliefs."

*Lee* is hardly the only case which finds compelling justification for governmental refusal to recognize an exemption even for serious burdens on sincerely held religious beliefs. For example, in *Bob Jones University v. United States*, 461 U.S. 574 (1983), the Court upheld the validity of an I.R.S. ruling which denied tax exemptions to schools with racially discriminatory policies. Bob Jones University, dedicated to the teaching of fundamentalist Christian beliefs, objected to the revocation of its tax exempt status based on its policies prohibiting interracial marriage and dating. The university claimed its policies were based on the Bible and, therefore, governmental interference with them violated its free exercise rights. The Court, however, per Chief

Justice Burger, held that the government had a "fundamental, overriding interest in eradicating racial discrimination in education." That interest substantially outweighed the burden on free exercise and there were "no less restrictive means" available to achieve the government's interest.

Similarly, in *Hernandez v. Commissioner*, 490 U.S. 680 (1989), the Court upheld the refusal by the I.R.S. to allow members of the Church of Scientology to deduct expenditures for training sessions as charitable contributions. The Court questioned whether there really was a substantial religious burden since, unlike the Amish faith which prohibits the payment of social security taxes, nothing in the Scientology faith prohibited the payment of taxes. The only "burden" was that the Church members would have less money available to gain access to the training sessions as a result of the adverse tax ruling. But even if this indirect burden was sufficiently substantial, the burden "would be justified by the 'broad public interest in maintaining a sound tax system,' free of 'myriad exceptions flowing from a wide variety of religious beliefs.' "

The government is especially likely to be successful in meeting the compelling justification standard in tax cases. In part, this is because of the view that payments of taxes is a community-wide burden in which all should share. Also, the heterogeneity of American society with its multiple denominations and their many claims for exemptions from policies their faiths abjure creates an impulse for the courts to reject claims for tax exemption across the board.

Such multiple exemptions arguably would threaten the integrity of the tax system. The fear of fraudulent claims may also play a role.

In summary, what can be said for the workings of the compelling interest analysis inaugurated by *Sherbert*? Basically, compelling interest analysis places a finger on the balancing scale. That finger weighs heavily for the free exercise claim. It creates a presumption in favor of the religious adherent who seeks an exemption from a general religiously neutral law. Invocation of the standard, however, does not mean that the government invariably loses. The showing of a strong interest in subjecting all citizens to the law can be the basis for denying the claimed religious exemption.

## D.   THE REPUDIATION OF JUDICIAL EXEMPTIONS

The compelling interest analysis dominated free exercise discourse until the mid–1980s. But increasingly there were signs of disaffection for this approach both among academic commentators and on the Court itself. Some of the disaffection could be explained as involving free exercise claims in special environments such as the military or prisons where the Court has traditionally been more deferential to government and less protective of fundamental rights. More generally, however, the Court has increasingly characterized laws regulating religious conduct as not involving a significant burden on free exercise of religion. Hence, the laws were not subject to compelling interest analysis.

In 1990, the Court struck an even more devastating blow to those claiming an exemption flowing from religious belief. In *Employment Division v. Smith*, 494 U.S. 872 (1990) (*Smith II*), the Court declared: "We have never held that an individual's religious beliefs excuse him from compliance with an otherwise valid law prohibiting conduct that the State is free to regulate." Citing *Reynolds v. United States*, 98 U.S. 145 (1878), *Smith II* stated that when government adopts a general law which is a "valid and neutral law of general applicability," the fact that such a general law may severely burden a particular religion is insufficient alone to invoke the Free Exercise Clause. If government is asked only to maintain neutrality towards religion, judicially-crafted constitutional exemptions are repudiated and the principle of formal neutrality which once dominated Free Exercise Clause jurisprudence has emerged triumphant.

## 1.   RELIGION IN GOVERNMENT– SPONSORED ENVIRONMENTS

In Chapter XIII, we discussed the highly deferential standard employed by the courts in reviewing freedom of speech claims in government-sponsored environments. That same deferential posture is manifest in judicial treatment of free exercise claims. And, the same rationale that was used to support deference in the free speech cases is employed to explain the judicial deference to government in the free exercise context. For example, laws applicable to government-sponsored environments, challenged under the Free Exercise Clause, are not generally applicable regulations but apply only to a limited sector of the public having a special relationship to the government. Furthermore, at times, the religious claimant has voluntarily entered into the special relationship. Finally, courts often cite the special expertise and capacity of government administrators in balancing competing interests as justifying a judicial hands-off policy. A prime example of judicial deference to government under the Free Exercise Clause is *Goldman v. Weinberger*, 475 U.S. 503 (1986). S. Simcha Goldman, an Air Force officer, an Orthodox Jew and an ordained rabbi, regularly wore his yarmulke in accordance with his religious faith. He challenged an air force regulation prohibiting the wearing of headgear indoors as applied to his religious practice. The Supreme Court, 5–4, upheld the application of the regulation to Goldman.

Justice Rehnquist, writing for the Court, concluded that the air force regulations "reasonably and even-handedly" regulate dress in the interest of uniformity in apparel. No support for applying the dress code provision to Goldman was offered by the government other than the assertions of the military on the need for a standard uniform to promote military preparedness, duty and discipline. In this "specialized society," Rehnquist reasoned, personal preferences had to be subordinated to the government interest in forging a sense of group identity in the military. In fact, the analysis in *Goldman* was little more than rationality review. Military judgment on matters of discipline should not be second-guessed by courts. Instead, Justice Rehnquist cited a litany of precedent establishing that "review of military regulations challenged on First Amendment grounds is far more deferential than constitutional review of similar laws or regulations designed for civilian society."

The free exercise philosophy expressed in the *Goldman* opinion has been analyzed as follows: "First, there is an insensitivity, or perhaps more exactly, a lack of attention to and concern with the burden on the litigant's First Amendment rights. Second, there is a strong deference to the special needs of the military's separate society and an unwillingness to review the military's judgment on the importance of the interest served by the regulation and the need for the restriction to satisfy that interest." Dienes, *When the First Amendment Is not Preferred: The Military and Other Special Contexts*, 56 U. Cin. L. Rev. 779 (1988).

In a concurrence, Justice Stevens, joined by Justices White and Powell, adopted a different approach than that used by Justice Rehnquist in characterizing the government interest justifying denial of the claim for exemption. Rejection of Goldman's claim, in Stevens' view, was required in order to assure uniformity of treatment of religious claimants. If Goldman's claimed exemption for his yarmulke were accepted, how would the military respond to the various claims of the Sikh or the Rastafarian for exemption of their distinctive religious garb? Stevens was concerned that if the military were required to grant exemptions, they would be forced to make inquires into the sincerity of religious claims. An additional problem would be raised by the need to make a subjective calculus of the possible reactions of military personnel as a body to these religious sects. Justice Stevens concluded that the air force regulation making the visibility of the apparel determinative provided "a neutral, completely objective standard."

For the dissenters, Brennan, Marshall, Blackmun and O'Connor, some more demanding standard of interest balancing was required—even in the military context. Justice O'Connor, for example, would require that when fundamental rights such as free exercise are significantly burdened in the military, the government must show "an unusually important" interest and that the interest would be "substantially harmed" by granting the religious exemption. Justice Brennan also questioned the alleged neutrality of the air force regulation since making visibility the determinative factor allowed some service personnel to satisfy their religious obligations while denying that same right to others. Further, it was generally the minority religions with their more distinctive overt religious garb that would be adversely affected by a regulation turning on visibility. He argued that the military should be required to justify bans on particular religious garb under a strict scrutiny standard of review. *Goldman v. Weinberger* provides a classic example of the extremely deferential posture adopted by the courts towards government response to claimed religious exemptions in specialized societies. In evaluating *Goldman's* authority for the future, the special context which shaped it is critical.

*O'Lone v. Shabazz*, 482 U.S. 342 (1987) again applied, 5–4, an extremely deferential "reasonableness" standard—this time in a prison context. Prisoners had made a free exercise-based claim for excusal from the regular work schedule for Friday Islamic religious services. Justice Rehnquist, for the Court in *O'Lone*, reasoned that adherence to routine work details served to simulate societal conditions and hold down the number of guards that would be required to supervise the different activities by different prisoners. Prison officials were also reasonably concerned that accommodating group affinities within the prison would increase security risks in managing exclusive cliques. *O'Lone* also rejected imposing on prison officials the obligation of disproving the availability of alternatives for satisfying the government's legitimate penological interests.

## 2.  THE BURDENS THAT COUNT

Jimmy Swaggart Ministries unsuccessfully sought an exemption from California's sales and use tax for the sale of its religious materials in *Jimmy Swaggart Ministries v. Board of Equalization*, 493 U.S. 378 (1990). The Court distinguished earlier cases invalidating the imposition of a flat license tax on the sale of religious materials. The California sales and use tax was a religiously neutral law which applied to all sales and uses of tangible property in the state. Religious materials were of course affected but the law was not directed at them. Like the Church of Scientology in the *Hernandez* case, the religious precepts of Jimmy Swaggart Ministries did not prohibit the payment of the tax. Further, the burden of the sales and use tax was imposed on the purchaser of the materials; Jimmy Swaggart Ministries was required only to collect and remit the tax. The Ministries complained that they were being required to bear an incrementally larger tax burden. The result, they contended, would be that the Ministries would have less sales and therefore less monies. But such burden as there was arose only because the price of the materials distributed by the Ministries was now marginally higher. This was true, however, with respect to costs and revenues for all distributors of materials subject to the tax. Justice O'Connor, speaking for a unanimous Court, declared: "[T]o the extent that imposition of a generally applicable tax merely decreases the amount of money [Jimmy Swaggart Ministries'] has to spend on its religious activities, any such burden is not constitutionally significant." Since the Free Exercise Clause was not implicated, there was no occasion to use compelling interest analysis.

*Tony and Susan Alamo Foundation v. Secretary of Labor*, 471 U.S. 290 (1985) involved another unsuccessful effort to secure a religious exemption from a generally applicable law. Exemption from the minimum wage provisions of the Fair Labor

Standards Act (FLSA) was sought by the non-profit religious foundation. Most of the Foundation's activities were conducted by associates who received no cash salaries for their labors, but who were given food, shelter, clothing and other benefits. Could the minimum wage and overtime requirements of the FLSA be applied, consistent with the Free Exercise Clause, to the benefits granted these associates by the foundation? The claim for a Free Exercise Clause-based exemption was rejected. Once again there was no significant burden on the free exercise of religion sufficient to trigger *Sherbert*-type compelling interests analysis. The Foundation had claimed that the receipt of "wages" by its associates would violate the associates' religious convictions. Justice White, for the Court in *Alamo*, responded that the FLSA does not require the payment of cash wages so that the associates could continue to be paid in the form of increased benefits which would respect their religious beliefs. Further, if there was some religious objection to the increased benefits, the associates were free to return the "wages" back to the Foundation.

The divisions within the Supreme Court with respect to the question of religious exemption from generally applicable laws was vividly apparent in *Bowen v. Roy*, 476 U.S. 693 (1986). Native Americans challenged provisions of the Aid to Families With Dependent Children (AFDC) program which they contended would violate their religious beliefs. First, Roy, the complainant Native American, objected to a requirement that state agencies use social security numbers in administering AFDC because he believed that the use of a number would harm his daughter's spirit. On this issue, the Court had little difficulty. The Social Security Act did not place any restriction on what Native Americans could believe or do. Nothing in the First Amendment requires the government itself to behave in particular ways that would further the beliefs of particular religious adherents. In short, the federal government's use of a social security number for Roy's daughter "does not itself in any degree impair Roy's 'freedom to believe, express, and exercise' his religion."

Roy's second objection totally fragmented the Court. Roy challenged the AFDC requirement that each applicant or recipient furnish the state agency with his social security number. Chief Justice Burger, joined by Justices Powell and Rehnquist, concluded that no exemption was required by the Free Exercise Clause with respect to this AFDC requirement. In the course of his opinion, Chief Justice Burger challenged the use of compelling interest analysis in free exercise litigation which involved only an indirect burden on religion. While acknowledging that conditioning benefits on acceptance of a social security number confronted AFDC applicants having religious objections with difficult choices, Chief Justice Burger declared for the plurality that this was nonetheless not the kind of burden requiring compelling interest analysis: "We conclude then that government regulation that indirectly and incidentally calls for a choice between securing a governmental benefit and adherence to religious beliefs is wholly different from governmental action or legislation that criminalizes religiously inspired activity or inescapably compels conduct that some find objectionable for religious reasons." Such an indirect burden, Justice Burger contended, is not insulated from judicial review because it is indirect but a different standard of review is applicable: "Absent proof of an intent to discriminate against particular religious beliefs or against religion in general, the Government meets its burden when it demonstrates that a challenged requirement for governmental benefits, neutral and uniform in its application, is a reasonable means of promoting a legitimate public interest." Since requiring a social security number reasonably promoted the legitimate public interest in preventing fraud, the requirement was constitutional.

But what of *Sherbert* and *Thomas* which had employed compelling interest analysis for laws imposing indirect burdens? Chief Justice Burger limited the rule of those cases to the unemployment compensation context where a person was deemed ineligible for benefits if he quit or refused work without good cause. The good cause standard required individualized exemptions. For a state which utilized such an individualized mechanism, the refusal to extend an exemption based on religious hardship "suggests a discriminatory intent." In *Sherbert* and *Thomas*, the state had provided a mechanism for examining good cause. It was discrimination in rejecting the religious claim that required compelling justification. But in *Roy* no such mechanism for individualized determinations was mandated with respect to the neutral assignment of required social security numbers.

Five members of the Court in *Roy*—Blackmun, White, O'Connor, Brennan and Marshall—adhered to *Sherbert* and *Thomas*. Justice O'Connor, joined by Justices Brennan and Marshall, specifically rejected Chief Justice Burger's reasonableness test: "The Court simply cannot, consistent with its precedents, distinguish this case from the wide variety of factual situations in which the Free Exercise Clause indisputably imposes significant constraints upon government." More specifically, Justice O'Connor charged that Chief Justice Burger's reasonableness test rendered the Free Exercise Clause meaningless: "Such a test has no basis in precedent and relegates a serious First Amendment value to the barest level of minimal scrutiny that the equal protection clause already provides."

Nevertheless, it was Justice O'Connor who wrote for the Court in denying a claimed religious exemption in *Lyng v. Northwest Indian Cemetery Protective Ass'n*, 485 U.S. 439 (1988). The United States Forest Service undertook to build a road through government owned lands that three American Indian tribes had traditionally used for religious purposes. Justice O'Connor acknowledged that the construction of the road would "virtually destroy the Indians' ability to practice their religion." But she found no principle in the Constitution that would justify a religiously-based claim to halt the road construction project. While conceding that indirect burdens on the free exercise of religion are subject to First Amendment scrutiny, Justice O'Connor concluded: "This does not and cannot imply that incidental effects of government programs which may make it more difficult to practice certain religions but which have no tendency to coerce individuals into acting contrary to their religious beliefs, require government to bring forward a compelling justification for its otherwise lawful actions." The proposed road building did not put the religious adherents to any choice between sacrificing their religion or sacrificing a critical government benefit. There was no coercion or penalty imposed on the Indians for any religious practice. In short, there was no constitutionally sufficient burden that would require compelling justification. The controlling principle for Justice O'Connor in *Lyng* came from *Bowen v. Roy* and its rejection of the claim that government could not use social security numbers if it offended religious belief. As in *Roy*, there was nothing in the Free Exercise Clause that would require the government to conduct its business in a way consistent with the religious belief of particular citizens. The religious claims of the American Indians "do not divest the Government of its right to use what is, after all, its land."

In dissent, Justice Brennan, joined by Justices Marshall and Blackmun, rejected the proposition that the government's prerogative as landowner should always trump the claims of the religious adherent. The Court had never taken so narrow a view of the range of burdens that count for free exercise purposes as to limit them to outright prohibitions, indirect coercion, or penalties on the free exercise of religion. It is the *effect* and not the *form* of government action on religious practices that should control free exercise analysis.

### 3.   FORMAL NEUTRALITY TRIUMPHANT

In *Reynolds v. United States*, 98 U.S. 145 (1878), the Supreme Court had held that an individual could not be excused from compliance with a generally applicable criminal law which was otherwise religiously neutral. To some extent, the history of Free Exercise Clause law thereafter represents an attempt to modify this holding. Nonetheless, to the astonishment of some and the approval of others, the Supreme Court in 1990 returned to this proposition in *Employment Division v. Smith*, 494 U.S. 872 (1990) (*Smith II*). In *Smith II*, Justice Scalia held for the Court: "[T]he right of free exercise does not relieve an individual of the obligation to comply with a 'valid and neutral law of general applicability on the ground that the law proscribes (or prescribes) conduct that his religion prescribes (or proscribes).' " What is startling to critics of is that the fundamental issue set forth by the Court—whether an individual is subject to a generally applicable criminal law, free exercise claims notwithstanding— was neither briefed nor argued to the Court. The facts of *Smith II* did not even arise in the context of a criminal prosecution.

Two members of the Native American Church, Smith and Black, were fired from their jobs with a private rehabilitation firm because they used peyote for sacramental purposes. Subsequently, they were denied unemployment compensation benefits because they had been discharged for work-related "misconduct." When they complained that denial of benefits violated their free exercise rights, the state responded that denial of benefits was justified since the use of the drug peyote violated Oregon's criminal law. The Oregon state courts upheld the free exercise claims of the Native American Church members on the authority of *Sherbert* and *Thomas*. When the case first came before the Supreme Court in 1987, the Court determined that it was uncertain whether the religious use of peyote would violate the Oregon criminal law. The Court, therefore, vacated the judgment of the Oregon Supreme Court and remanded for resolution of the criminal law issue. *Employment Division v. Smith*, 483 U.S. 1054 (1987) (*Smith I*). On remand, the Oregon Supreme Court determined that the state criminal law made no exception for the religious use of a controlled substance but that application of the criminal law's prohibition on the use of peyote to Smith and Black would violate the Free Exercise Clause. Therefore, the Oregon Supreme Court reaffirmed its holding that the state could not deny unemployment benefits to Smith and Black for having used peyote in religious ceremonies. Once again the case came before the Supreme Court.

In *Smith II*, the Supreme Court, 6–3, reversed the Oregon Supreme Court. A generally applicable criminal law which was religiously indifferent could be enforced despite a free exercise claim for exemption. Because of the general neutrality of the law, the Free Exercise Clause was not even applicable. Since free exercise was not implicated, compelling interest analysis was not implicated either. Justice Scalia began from the premise that the Free Exercise Clause is primarily directed to protecting the right to believe and profess one's religious beliefs. He also acknowledged that a law specifically directed against a particular religious practice would be "prohibiting the free exercise [of religion]." But he denied that the constitutional text must be interpreted as encompassing laws that have only an incidental effect on religious practices: "It is a permissible reading of the text to say that if prohibiting the exercise of religion is not the object of the [law] but merely the incidental effect of a generally applicable and otherwise valid provision, the First Amendment has not been offended."

In a concurrence, Justice O'Connor, joined in part by three dissenting Justices, Brennan, Marshall and Blackmun, rejected Scalia's narrow reading of the text of the Free Exercise Clause: "[A] law that prohibits certain conduct—conduct that happens to be an act of worship for someone—manifestly does prohibit that person's exercise of his religion." Critics of *Smith II* have also argued that the original intent of the Free Exercise Clause accepted religious exemptions from generally applicable laws.

McConnell, *The Origins and Historical Understanding of Free Exercise of Religion*, 103 Harv. L. Rev. 1410 (1990). *Compare* Hamburger, *A Constitutional Right of Religious Exemption: An Historical Perspective*, 60 Geo. Wash. L. Rev. 915 (1992) [original intent did not include a general constitutional right to religious exemption].

Justice Scalia in *Smith II* argued that his categorical rejection of all judicially created Free Exercise Clause-based exemptions was fully consistent with precedent: "We have never held that an individual's religious beliefs excuse him from compliance with an otherwise valid law prohibiting conduct that the State is free to regulate." But for Justice O'Connor and the dissenters, Scalia's interpretation of precedent was inconsistent with "established First Amendment jurisprudence": "[W]e have respected both the First Amendment's express textual mandate and the governmental interest in regulation of conduct by requiring the Government to justify any substantial burden on religiously motivated conduct by a compelling interest and by means narrowly tailored to achieve that interest." Justice Scalia was able to claim that he was adhering to precedent only by distinguishing the prior cases in an unusually limiting way. Authoritative and well-known precedents contrary to his precepts such as *Cantwell v. Connecticut* and *Wisconsin v. Yoder* were distinguished as not really being free exercise cases. Rather, they were hybrid cases involving other constitutional protections such as free speech and press and the constitutional rights of parents. While it might be appropriate to limit *Cantwell* to its free speech moorings, it seems to be an overstatement to say that *Yoder* was not a free exercise case. The principle of *Sherbert*, *Thomas* and their progeny was confined to the unemployment compensation context: "As the plurality pointed out in *Roy*, our decisions in the unemployment cases stand for the position that where the state has in place a system of individual exemptions, it may not refuse to extend that system to cases of 'religious hardship' without compelling reason."

For Justice Scalia and those who joined him in *Smith II*, application of compelling interest analysis to generally applicable laws "contradicts constitutional tradition and common sense." Use of the demanding compelling interest standard to establish a private right to ignore the law would not produce equality of treatment but instead a "constitutional anomaly." Nor did it matter to Scalia how severe a burden the generally applicable law imposed on a particular religious practice. It would be inappropriate, he argued, for Justices to determine the centrality of a religious belief as a precondition for applying compelling interest analysis. Neither "law nor logic" supplied a principle that judges could use to "contradict a believer's assertion that a practice is central to his personal faith." A critic might respond that Justice Scalia's concern for religion was so great that, rather than probe it, he would rather not protect it.

For Justice O'Connor and those who joined her critique, there was no reason to abandon the compelling interest analysis simply because a law is generally applicable and religiously neutral: "There is nothing talismanic about neutral laws of general applicability or general criminal prohibitions, for laws neutral toward religion can coerce a person to violate his religious conscience or intrude upon his religious duties just as effectively as laws aimed at religion." Justice Scalia responded to those who criticized his categorical rejection of judicially-fashioned religious exemptions by referring them to the legislature. He expressed the conviction that the legislature in a society committed to religious freedom would be solicitous of the claims of religious adherents for exemption from generally applicable but religiously burdensome laws. But Justice O'Connor characterized this as nothing more than majoritarianism. Certainly, legislatures would be responsive to religious faiths which either do not offend or express ideas that are widely shared. But where a faith offends or engages in practices that are not widely shared, the First Amendment Free Exercise Clause has a necessary and vital role. Justice Scalia conceded that minority religions would be placed at a "relative disadvantage" in the political process under his approach. Nevertheless, he was not moved: "[T]hat unavoidable consequence of democratic government must be preferred to a system under which each conscience is a law unto itself or in which judges weigh the social importance of all laws against the centrality of all religious beliefs."

For the Court, Oregon's criminal prohibition against the use of controlled substances including peyote was constitutional. It followed, therefore, that the state could deny unemployment compensation benefits to persons using peyote even for sacramental purposes without violating the Free Exercise Clause. Justice O'Connor and the three dissenters agreed that the case should have been governed by compelling interest analysis but they parted company on the proper application of that test. O'Connor, who admitted the question was close, concluded that the uniform application of Oregon's drug laws is "essential to accomplish [the state's] 'overriding interest' in preventing physical harm from the use of controlled substances." For the dissenters, the state's interest was little more than "the symbolic preservation of an unenforced prohibition." The state evidenced its opprobrium for drugs in its statute books but enforcement was hardly vigorous. In such circumstances, the state could not satisfy the compelling interest analysis that a free exercise claim such as this merited.

Commentary on *Smith II* has, on the whole, been unfavorable. Indeed, some who defend the decision and reject judicially-created religious exemptions, nevertheless, are critical of Justice Scalia's analysis: "The *Smith* opinion cannot readily be defended. The decision, as written, is neither persuasive nor well-crafted. It exhibits only a shallow understanding of free exercise jurisprudence and its use of precedent borders on fiction. The opinion is also a paradigmatic example of judicial overreaching."

Marshall, *In Defense of* Smith *and Free Exercise Revisionism*, 58 U. Chi. L. Rev. 308 (1991). Probably, the most frequently expressed criticism of *Smith II* is its majoritarianism. For example, Professor Kathleen Sullivan stresses the opinion's *de facto* discrimination against minority faiths: "Claims for judicial exemption under the free exercise clause emanate almost invariably from members of relatively politically powerless groups toward whom the majority is likely to be selectively indifferent or worse. Minority religionists, like political dissenters, rarely have the political muscle to secure exemptions for themselves on the legislative floor. *Smith* wipes out their alternative recourse." Sullivan, *Religion and Liberal Democracy*, 59 U. Chi. L. Rev. 195 (1992).

As might be expected, Professor Michael McConnell, the principal theorist of accommodationism and of religious exemption hurls a variety of criticisms at *Smith II*. "First and foremost, the *Smith* decision gives social policy, determined by the State, primacy over the rights of religious communities to order their affairs according to their own convictions. [Under] *Smith*, the state is more powerful, the forces of homogenization are more powerful, and the ability of churches to maintain their distinctive ways of life depends on their skill at self-protection in the halls of Congress." McConnell, *Religious Freedom at a Crossroads*, 59 U. Chi. L. Rev. 115 (1992). For Professor Douglas Laycock, *Smith II* represents the triumph of formal neutrality as the mandate of the Free Exercise Clause: "If the Court intends to defer to any formally neutral law restricting religion, then it has created a legal framework for persecution, and persecutions will result." Laycock, *The Remnants of Free Exercise*, 1990 Sup. Ct. Rev. 1. Professor Laycock believes that the balancing approach rejected in *Smith II* is exactly what is necessary to give meaning to the free exercise guarantee: "The cumulative weight of government on religious minorities is sometimes crushing. The impact on government programs of exemptions for religious minorities is often quite minor and almost never crushing. In the exceptional case, government can invoke the compelling interest test." In a critique of *Smith II*, Professor Frederick Gedicks contends that although free exercise is a fundamental right "like privacy, speech, travel and other fundamental rights," the Court now grants it less protection than other fundamental rights. Such rights "should normally be subject to strict scrutiny." Gedicks, *The Normalized Free Exercise Clause: Three Abnormalities*, 75 Ind. L. J. 77 (2000).

What can be said in defense of *Smith II*? One answer might be that the very religious heterogeneity of our society may have prompted a majority on the Court to fear for the integrity of generally applicable law if religious exemptions were to be routinely recognized by the courts. Professor Ira Lupu, while not a defender of *Smith II*, observes that the "Court avowedly fears the 'anarchy' that would result from permitting religion-based exemptions from general laws." Lupu, *Reconstructing the*

*Establishment Clause: The Case Against Discretionary Accommodation of Religion*, 140 U. Pa. L. Rev. 555 (1991). If exemptions in this society are to be recognized, the teaching of *Smith II* is that the responsibility for the creation of such exemptions is a legislative and not a judicial task. Another defense of *Smith II* flows from Establishment Clause concerns: "Special treatment for religion connotes sponsorship and endorsement; providing relative benefits for religion over non-religion may have the impermissible effect of advancing religion." Marshall, *In Defense of* Smith *and Free Exercise Revisionism*, 58 U. Chi. L. Rev. 308 (1991).

In summary, religious exemptions will no longer find a sympathetic hearing in the nation's courts as a result of *Smith II*. Whether the critics or defenders of *Smith II* are right or wrong is for the reader to decide. Whether *Smith II* will endure or whether legislatures or new justices coming to the Supreme Court will produce change is for the future to decide. Congress sought to overturn *Smith II* in the Religious Freedom Restoration Act of 1993 (RFRA) by restoring the compelling interest test used in *Sherbert v. Verner* and *Wisconsin v. Yoder* and requiring its use in all cases where free exercise of religion is substantially burdened. The compelling interest test was to be used in reviewing all laws imposing a substantial burden on religious freedom, even laws of general applicability. But in *City of Boerne v. Flores*, 521 U.S. 507 (1997), RFRA was held unconstitutional as applied to state action. The law was held to exceed Congress' enforcement powers under § 5 of the Fourteenth Amendment. While the Court was unanimous, three justices used the occasion to voice doubts about *Smith II*.

But *Smith II* does not mean that every free exercise claim will be subject to deferential judicial review. In *Church of the Lukumi Babalu Aye, Inc. v. Hialeah*, 508 U.S. 520 (1993), the Court distinguished *Smith II* and, applying strict scrutiny, unanimously invalidated Hialeah city ordinances prohibiting ritualistic animal sacrifice. Unlike *Smith II,* the laws were not neutral since they had the impermissible objective of suppressing religion. Nor were they of general applicability "because the secular ends asserted in defense of the laws were pursued only with respect to conduct motivated by religious beliefs." Justice Kennedy, for the Court, considered whether the laws were neutral. The text and operation of the Hialeah ordinances demonstrated that they were targeted at the Santeria religion, which has animal sacrifice as its central devotional practice. The laws were "gerrymandered" to exempt all secular animal slaughtering from prohibition. Justice Kennedy concluded that the laws were substantially underinclusive since they failed to prohibit nonreligious conduct that involved the same or greater harm to public health and animal protection. In summary, Justice Kennedy declared that a law which targets religious conduct "for destructive treatment or advances legitimate governmental interests only against conduct with a religious motivation will survive strict scrutiny only in rare cases."

The question of whether the law at issue was neutral as to religion was raised once again when the state of Washington established a "Promise Scholarship Program" to aid "academically gifted students" with their college expenses. In compliance with the stringent anti-establishment clause prohibition of the Washington state constitution, these scholarships were not permitted to be used for degrees in devotional theology. A student who had received a "Promise Scholarship" contended that the state restriction precluding him from studying theology was a violation of the Free Exercise Clause of the First Amendment. Relying on *Church of the Lukumi Babalu Aye, Inc. v. Hialeah*, 508 U.S. 520 (1993), the student asserted that the "Promise Scholarship Program" was presumptively unconstitutonal because it was not facially neutral concerning religion. Rejecting the analogy to *Lukumi*, the Court pointed out that there the city sought to target a specific religious practice, the animal sacrifice rituals of the Santeria religion. But the Washington state law placed no burden, civil or criminal, on the student's free exercise rights. The state had simply declined to fund a particular type of educational study. The Court declared that "there is room for play in the joints" between the Establishment Clause and the Free Exercise Clause: "[S]ome state actions are permitted by the Establishment Clause but not required by the Free Exercise Clause." *Locke v. Davey*, 540 U.S. 712 (2004).

The "play in the joints" concept was relied on in *Cutter v. Wilkinson*, 544 U.S. 709 (2005) where the

Court rejected an Establishment Clause based challenge to a provision of a federal statute, the Religious Land Use and Institutionalized Persons Act, which stated that no government should impose a "substantial burden on the religious exercise" of institutionalized persons unless justified by a compelling governmental interest. Inmates of Ohio prisons stated that they were adherents of non-mainstream religions and that Ohio prison authorities had failed to meet their religious needs as required by the statute. Prison officials defended by saying that the statute, by advancing religion, violated the Establishment Clause. Rejecting their Establishment Clause challenge, the Court held, as it had in *Locke v. Davey,* that there was "some space for legislative action neither compelled by the Free Exercise Clause nor prohibited by the Establishment Clause."

In *Gonzales v. O Centro Espirita Beneficente Uniao do Vegetal*, 546 U.S. 418 (2006), the play-in the joints idea asserted itself again. In that case, the federal government sought to ban the importation by a Brazil-based Christian Spiritist group, known as UDV, of a hallucinogenic drug used in its religious services. The drug was banned by the federal Controlled Substances Act. The Court, per Chief Justice Roberts, ruled unanimously that the federal government had failed to demonstrate the compelling interest required by RFRA. *Boerne* was not controlling. *Boerne,* based as it was on § 5 of the Fourteenth Amendment, was directed to the states and localities and not to the federal government.

RFRA was enforceable with respect to the federal government. The Court concluded that the UDV had "effectively demonstrated" that the federal government's action had "substantially burdened" UDV's "sincere exercise of religion." RFRA placed the burden of proof, the Court concluded, on the government and not on UDV. However, the government claimed that pre-*Smith II* cases had asserted the desirability of taking a uniform approach in rejecting claims for religious exemptions. But the Court pointed out that in *Cutter v. Wilkinson* it had re-affirmed the "feasibility of case-by case consideration of religious exemptions to generally applicable rules."

# INDEX

---

---

**BELIEF, FREEDOM OF**—Cont'd
Religious belief
        Generally, 502 et seq.
    See also Religious Rights, this index
Shopping center pamphleteering, 292
Standard of review, 278, 291
Student fees, 291
Theories of protection, 275

**BLACKMAIL**
Absolutist interpretations, 3

**BLUE LAWS**
Establishment Clause cases, 492
Free Exercise Clause cases, 507

**BOYCOTTS**
Association, freedom of, 276

**BREACH OF THE PEACE STATUTES**
    Generally, 83
Fighting words doctrine, 83

**BROADCASTING REGULATION**
    Generally, 405 et seq.
Access to media, 405 et seq.
Cable television regulation, 131
Equal time rules, 417
Fairness doctrine, 406
Indecent speech, 131, 406
Must carry, 41, 411
Right of reply laws, 417

**CAMPAIGN PRACTICE LAWS**
    Generally, 300
Association and belief freedoms, 282, 300

**CAMPUS MILITARY RECRUITMENT**
Association and belief freedoms, 299
Expressive conduct protections, 254

**CANVASSING**
    Generally, 244
See also Solicitations, this index

**CATEGORIZATION**
    Generally, 19 et seq., 242
Balancing compared, 22

**MILITARY**—Cont'd
Campus recruitment—Cont'd
   Expressive conduct protections, 254
Free exercise claims, 519, 521
Government sponsored environments, 306 et seq.
Religious activities, 307

**MINORS**
   See also Child Pornography, this index
Communications Decency Act, 136
Obscenity, distribution restrictions, 104

**MUST CARRY RULES**
Generally, 41

**NATIONAL SECURITY**
Prior restraint justification, 61

**NATIVITY SCENES**
See Holiday Decorations

**NOISE REGULATION**
Public forums, 230

**NUDE DANCING**
Generally, 266 et seq.

**O'BRIEN TEST**
Expressive conduct protection, 254, 261

**OBSCENITY**
   Generally, 101 et seq.
Absolutist interpretations, 3
Advertising prescriptions, 104
Child harming, 103
Child Online Protection Act (COPA), 110
Child Pornography, this index
Commercial exploitation prescriptions, 104
Contemporary community standards, 106, 109
Definitional difficulties, 102, 106
Excerpts vs work as a whole, 101
Expressive conduct protection of nude dancing, 266 et seq.
Feminist views, 105
Indecent Speech, this index
Marketplace of ideas standard, 21
Minors, restrictions on distribution to, 104
Nonobscene erotic materials, 123
Nude dancing, 266 et seq.

**OVERBREADTH**—Cont'd
Narrowing constructions, 52
Obscenity laws, 108
Permit fee schedules, 48
Public housing policies, 51
Saving constructions, 52
Selective enforcement, 46
Specificity of legislation, 53
Substantial overbreadth doctrine, 46, 115
Vagueness distinguished, 53

**PAMPHLETEERING**
See Leafletting, Handbilling, and Pamphleteering, this index

**PANDERING**
See Obscenity, this index

**PARADE PERMITS**
Association and belief freedoms, 298

**PARK, SLEEPING IN**
Expressive conduct protection, 257

**PARODY**
Mental distress claims, 165

**PERJURY**
Absolutist interpretations, 3

**PERMITS AND LICENSES**
Fee schedules, overbreadth, 48
Liquor license regulation
    Church areas, 495
    Nude dancing, 266
Parade permits, 298
Prior restraint challenges, 63, 140

**PERSUASION PRINCIPLE**
Scope of First Amendment, 13

**PEYOTE**
Free Exercise Clause rights, 532

**PICKETING**
Abortion picketing of private property, 242
Embassy picketing regulation as content based or content neutral, 30
Expressive conduct distinguished, 250

## PRESS FREEDOM
Generally, 364 et seq.
Access to electronic media, 405 et seq.
Broadcasting Regulation, this index
Checks and balances analysis, 364
Content neutral regulation of publishers, 366
Courtroom access restrictions, 394 et seq.
Criminal defense rights conflicts, 384, 403
Defamation tort restraints, 367, 383
Electronic media, access to, 405 et seq.
Equal time rules, 417
Fairness doctrine, 406
Fourth branch of government analysis, 364
Gag orders, 384
Grand jury proceedings
    Secrecy, 403
    Subpoenas, 369, 375
Historical context, 365
Injunctions suppressing publication, 57
Internet publishers as protected press, 365
Litigants and attorneys, restraints of, 389
Mental distress tort claims, 383
Negligent publication tort claims, 382
Newsgathering and publishing activities distinguished, 367
Newsracks ordinances, 184
Pamphlets as protected press, 365
Pentagon Papers litigation, 1
Presumptive invalidity of gag orders, 387
Prior restraint, 4, 56 et seq., 384
Privacy invasion tort liabilities, 367, 380
Privilege, Journalist's, this index
Publishing and newsgathering activities distinguished, 367
Right of reply laws, 417
Speech freedom distinctions, 364
Underground newspapers as protected press, 365
Watergate scandal, 368

## PRIOR RESTRAINT
Generally, 56 et seq.
Abortion protest injunctions, 65
Cease and desist orders, 60
Clear and present danger test, 388, 390
Courtroom access restrictions, 394 et seq.
Due process principles, 139
Gag orders, 384

†